Lecture Notes in Computer Science 3551

Commenced Publication in 1973
Founding and Former Series Editors:
Gerhard Goos, Juris Hartmanis, and Jan van Leeuwen

Theo Härder   Wolfgang Lehner (Eds.)

Data Management in a Connected World

Essays Dedicated to Hartmut Wedekind on the Occasion of His 70th Birthday

Springer

Volume Editors

Theo Härder
Kaiserslautern University of Technology
Department of Computer Science, AG DBIS
P.O. Box 3049, 67653 Kaiserslautern, Germany
E-mail: haerder@informatik.uni-kl.de

Wolfgang Lehner
Dresden University of Technology
Database Technology Group
Dürerstr. 26, 01307 Dresden, Germany
E-mail: lehner@inf.tu-dresden.de

Library of Congress Control Number: 2005927609

CR Subject Classification (1998): H.2, D.4.4, H.3

ISSN 0302-9743
ISBN-10 3-540-26295-4 Springer Berlin Heidelberg New York
ISBN-13 978-3-540-26295-4 Springer Berlin Heidelberg New York

Springer is a part of Springer Science+Business Media

springeronline.com

Printed in Germany

Typesetting: Camera-ready by author, data conversion by Boller Mediendesign
Printed on acid-free paper SPIN: 11499923 06/3142 5 4 3 2 1 0

Hartmut Wedekind

Preface

Data management systems play the most crucial role in building large application systems. Since modern applications are no longer single monolithic software blocks but highly flexible and configurable collections of cooperative services, the data management layer also has to adapt to these new requirements. Therefore, within recent years, data management systems have faced a tremendous shift from the central management of individual records in a transactional way to a platform for data integration, federation, search services, and data analysis. This book addresses these new issues in the area of data management from multiple perspectives, in the form of individual contributions, and it outlines future challenges in the context of data management. These contributions are dedicated to *Prof. em. Dr. Dr.-Ing. E. h. Hartmut Wedekind* on the occasion of his 70th birthday, and were (co-)authored by some of his academic descendants.

Prof. Wedekind is one of the most prominent figures of the database management community in Germany, and he enjoys an excellent international reputation as well. Over the last 35 years he greatly contributed to making relational database technology a success. As far back as the early 1970s, he covered—as the first author in Germany—the state of the art concerning the relational model and related issues in two widely used textbooks "Datenbanksysteme I" and "Datenbanksysteme II". Without him, the idea of modeling complex-structured real-world scenarios in a relational way would be far less developed by now. Among Prof. Wedekind's academic achievements is the development of an alternative way for schema design based on the adaptation of the structure of natural languages in combination with the concept of abstraction. With the relational background in mind, he may be called the father of the language-based schema design approach, which is still feasible in tackling complicated schema design issues. He has covered this broad body of knowledge in eight textbooks so far, many of which have appeared in several editions and reprints.

The impact of Prof. Wedekind's work, however, reaches beyond pushing the relational idea (better: fighting an almost religious war at a time when data management systems were dogmatically based on hierarchical or network data models). As a founding member of the Gesellschaft für Informatik e.V. (German Association for Computer Science) in 1969, he greatly contributed to the overall development of computer science as a science in Germany. Even more impressive, and not directly visible through publications, official posts, etc., is the person of Prof. Wedekind. His sharp and brilliant mind in combination with a generally open-minded character is simply fascinating. As a special guest at a database conference in 1998 in Capri, he was introduced with the words "Mr. Wedekind is always concerned about the WHY behind the HOW"—a very appropriate description.

Following one of his citations, "Etwas verstehen heißt verstehen, wie es geworden ist" (Prof. Schnädelbach: "Something to understand means to understand how it has evolved"), it is advisable to say a few words about Hartmut Wedekind's vita.
Prof. Wedekind was born in 1935 in Bochum, Germany. In 1955, he began his studies in industrial engineering ('Wirtschaftsingenieurwesen') with a strong emphasis on mechanical engineering ('Fachrichtung Maschinenbau') at the Darmstadt University of Technology. After finishing his diploma in Darmstadt, he ventured out (1961/62) and earned his Master of Science in Engineering, emphasis on Operations Research, at the University of Berkeley, advised by George B. Dantzig. Back in Darmstadt, he finished his PhD thesis (Dr. rer. pol.) in 1963. Thereafter, Dr. Wedekind joined IBM in Sindelfingen and Frankfurt, where he was involved in application design and programming based on the IBM 1401/1440. Out of IBM, he earned the Venia Legendi through his habilitation, advised by Prof. Bussmann and Prof. Hinhold, 1967. One year later, he accepted a position as professor (for Business Studies) at the TU Darmstadt, where he initiated the now renowned Computer Science Department and became its first dean. During a stay at the IBM Research Lab in San Jose as a visiting scientist in 1972, he worked with Edgar F. Codd. The first ideas of the relational data model were discussed at that time. As he himself points out, it dawned on him that the relational idea was of fundamental importance and implied a revolution in storing and querying data sets—this was a terrific time! ... years before the notion of transaction was born.

In 1979, Prof. Wedekind changed his affiliation and moved to the University of Erlangen-Nuremberg, where he established a new data management group. His successful work is documented in numerous publications. Moreover, he managed a special research program (Sonderforschungsbereich) funded by the German Research Council for 12 years from 1987–1998. He officially stepped down from leading the database group in Erlangen in 2002. In recent years, he has spent even more time in elaborating the foundations of computer science from a philosophy-of-science point of view, and has presented important topics like abstraction, objects and metalanguage, or schemas and instances in academic lectures. He has advocated that these topics are essential for the field, although they are in general not treated in classical computer science courses and in lectures in other sciences that depend upon computer science. Furthermore, he is devoted to computer science education in schools, laying the foundations for the next-generation computer scientists. Nevertheless, he is currently still teaching at three different universities (Friedrich Alexander University of Erlangen-Nuremberg, Darmstadt University of Technology, and Friedrich Schiller University of Jena) and publishing papers in national as well as international journals and periodicals.

In more than 30 academic years, he has "produced" a large number of PhDs (see the pedigree of academic descendants below and in the appendix). As can be seen, his family is already in its fourth generation and the spirit of Prof. Wedekind—take nothing for granted, think around the corner, and always look behind the scenes—is propagated to all his academic descendants.

To honor Prof. Wedekind's work in general and his 70th birthday specifically, we organized an international symposium held from June 30th to July 2nd, 2005 at the International Conference and Research Center for Computer Science, Schloss Dagstuhl. All contributions covered by the book were presented by their authors.

Structure of the Book

This book is logically divided into four parts, which are introduced briefly along with their associated articles.

Part I: Motivation and Modeling Issues

The first part of the book discusses the general perspective of the central role of databases in a modern information society. The contribution

Databases: The Integrative Force in Cyberspace,

authored by *Andreas Reuter*, demonstrates the shift of database technology from a central repository to a platform for transparent integration and efficient analysis of different heterogeneous data sources. Different classes of data are introduced, technological trends are explained, and a shape of future database systems is outlined. The general introduction is followed by an article written by *Bernhard Mitschang*—one of the first grandchildren of Prof. Wedekind—and his group. This discussion,

Federating Location-Based Data Services,

outlines the impact of location awareness on data management services in ubiquitous computing environments. Using the Nexus platform as an example, they point out the different requirements and characteristics for creating a federated data service. Different architectural approaches like LAV and GAV are analyzed in this context. The third piece in this part,

An Agent-Based Approach to Correctness in Databases,

was contributed by *Herbert Stoyan* and his group and discusses the approach of using agent technology to detect semantic inconsistencies, as an illustrative example referring to a database with genealogical data on historic persons belonging to European nobility.

Part II: Infrastructural Services

The second part of this Festschrift volume covers contributions with a focus on infrastructural services. The introductory essay reviews the history of server technology over the last 30 years. The article

Thirty Years of Server Technology—From Transaction Processing to Web Services,

penned by *Klaus Meyer-Wegener*, outlines how (application) server technology developed in recent decades and argues about current trends and future requirements. This overview is followed by a discussion of the various forms of caching in the Internet. Caching—in the sense of weak database replication—is a necessity for distributed applications within a totally connected world.

Caching over the Entire User-to-Data Path in the Internet,

authored by *Theo Härder*, underlines the need for caching Web objects in different proxy caches in the client-to-server path and explains how database caching based on cache constraints enables declarative query processing close to application servers, thereby speeding up the server-to-database path. This contribution is followed by two reports addressing the concept of messaging and notification services. The first of these two,

Reweaving the Tapestry: Integrating Database and Messaging Systems in the Wake of New Middleware Technologies,

contributed by the working group of *Berthold Reinwald* at the IBM Almaden Research Center in San Jose, outlines the issue of adding messaging services to the query-based interaction model of classical database systems. This evolutionary approach is complemented by an almost revolutionary approach of building notification systems by exploiting existing database technology, as described in

Data Management Support for Notification Services,

by *Wolfgang Lehner*. The infrastructural part closes with a discussion on extending search capabilities in database systems to better support applications like full text search, Web page indexing, etc. The final piece,

Search Support in Data Management Systems,

by *Andreas Henrich*, outlines the requirements and presents the current state of the art concerning search methods.

Part III: Application Design

The third part of this book focuses on multiple facets of designing large applications. Application design from the proposed perspective falls into the category of "Programming in the Large," which was always a main focus of Hartmut Wedekind's academic work. The first article, entitled

Toward Automated Large-Scale Information Integration and Discovery,

and authored once again by the group of *Berthold Reinwald*, considers the problem of information integration as a single step towards a more global enterprise application integration. A more conceptual discussion on how to build large applications for a specific class of information systems is described in

Component-Based Application Architecture for Enterprise Information Systems,

by *Erich Ortner*. In a first step, this analysis explores the characteristics of the general component concept, followed in a second step by a discussion of tools and appropriate design methodologies to build enterprise-scale applications. The third contribution reviews the notion of workflows from a general perspective. In

Processes, Workflows, Web Service Flows: A Reconstruction,

Stefan Jablonski discusses the history and future developments of the area of workflow management systems and introduces a general model to specify business processes. The same area is addressed in the discussion of distributed execution of workflows in

Pros and Cons of Distributed Workflow Execution Algorithms,

penned by *Hans Schuster*. His paper states the problem and compares state-of-the-art techniques in this context. He also pinpoints major drawbacks and proposes adequate solutions. The section on application design is rounded out by

Business-to-Business Integration Technology,

written by *Christoph Bussler*, where he sketches the major issues in this area and discusses database extensions in order to fulfil the requirement of being an integrative platform even for cross-organizational, i.e., business-to-business processes.

Part IV: Application Scenarios

The final part of this book is dedicated to application scenarios with a strong emphasis on data management issues. The first two contributions exhibit a financial background. In

Information Dissemination in Modern Banking Applications,

authored by Peter Peinl and Uta Störl, an FX Trading application is used as an example to demonstrate real requirements with respect to state-of-the-art data management platforms. While this article focuses on the structural perspective, the following contribution,

An Intermediate Information System Forms Mutual Trust,

written by *Dieter Steinbauer*, outlines the process including the underlying information system necessary to decide on granting a credit to a customer within the SCHUFA environment. The next article, entitled

Data Refinement in a Market Research Applications' Data Production Process,

illustrates the data production process within the data-warehouse environment of GfK Marketing Services. The most distinctive feature of the application is that data are treated like industrial goods, i.e., highly customized data products are designed for individual customers; *Thomas Ruf* and *Thomas Kirsche* have written this illustrative report. The third application context covered within this series of application-oriented articles is devoted to health care. In

Information Management in Distributed Healthcare Networks,

Richard Lenz discusses the specific requirements of information management in such contexts and outlines major challenges and some solutions. The last but definitely not least contribution comes from *Hans-Peter Steiert* and has the title

Data Management for Engineering Applications.

In his analysis, the integration of data and processes in the engineering application area is discussed at different levels. Furthermore, soft factors of the integration problem, such as dependability management and data flow integration using patterns, are included in his considerations.

To summarize, this book provides a comprehensive overview of the state of the art and future trends in technology and applications centered around data management issues.

Kaiserslautern/Dresden
May 2005

Theo Härder and Wolfgang Lehner

Pedigree of Academic Descendents

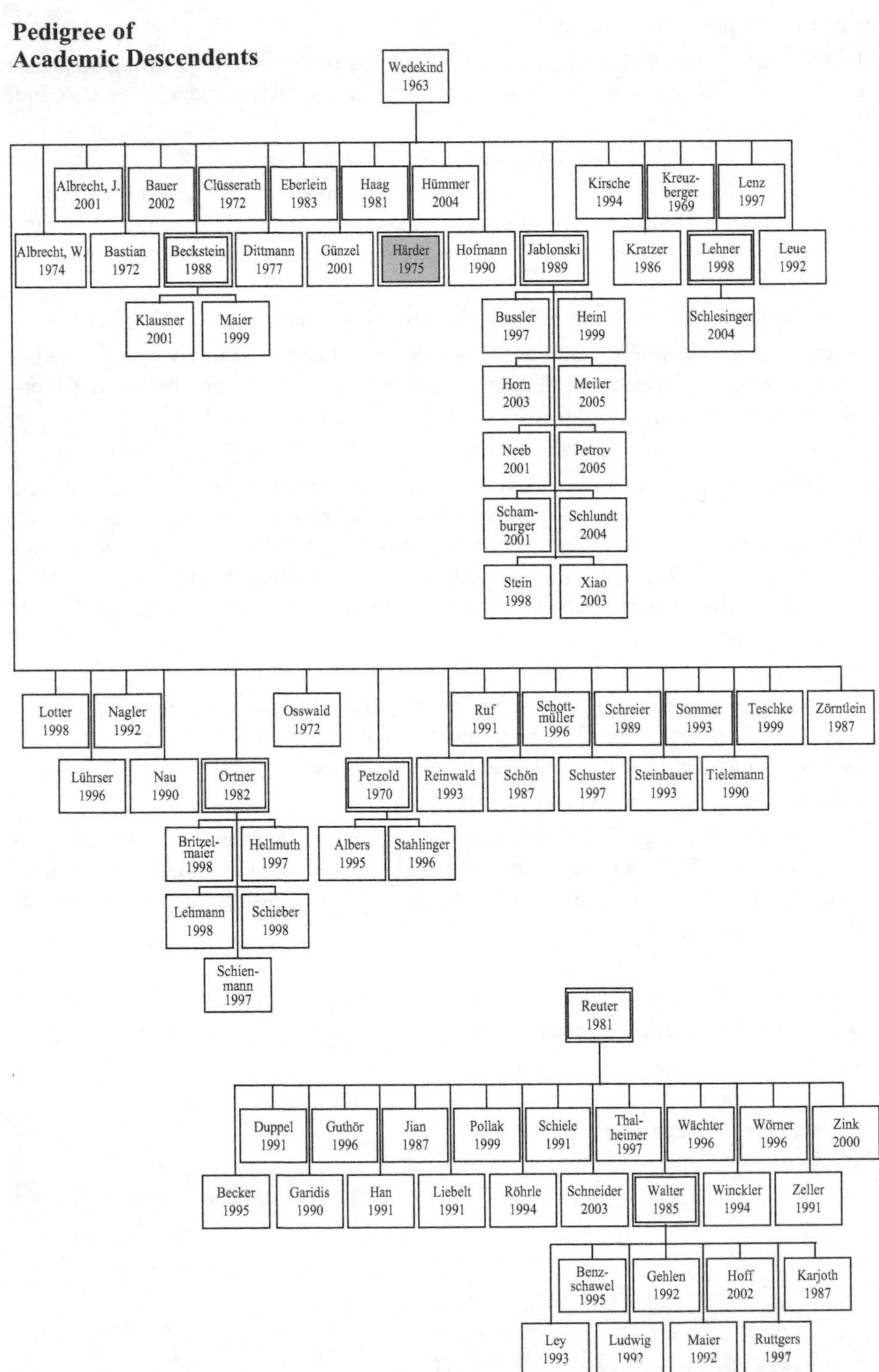

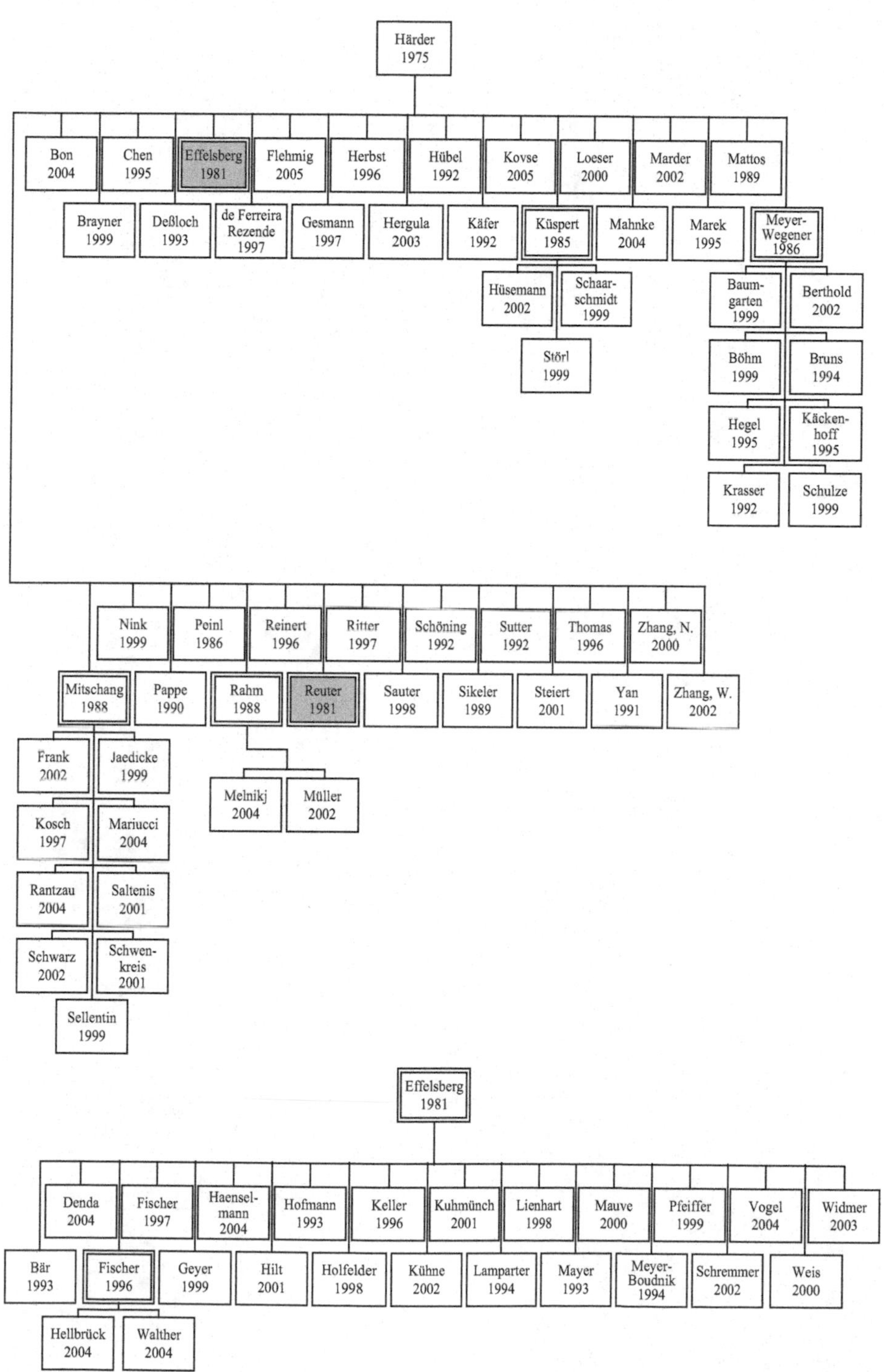
Härder 1975
Bon 2004
Chen 1995
Effelsberg 1981
Flehmig 2005
Herbst 1996
Hübel 1992
Kovse 2005
Loeser 2000
Marder 2002
Mattos 1989
Brayner 1999
Deßloch 1993
de Ferreira Rezende 1997
Gesmann 1997
Hergula 2003
Käfer 1992
Küspert 1985
Mahnke 2004
Marek 1995
Meyer-Wegener 1986
Hüsemann 2002
Schaar-schmidt 1999
Störl 1999
Baum-garten 1999
Berthold 2002
Böhm 1999
Bruns 1994
Hegel 1995
Käcken-hoff 1995
Krasser 1992
Schulze 1999
Nink 1999
Peinl 1986
Reinert 1996
Ritter 1997
Schöning 1992
Sutter 1992
Thomas 1996
Zhang, N. 2000
Mitschang 1988
Pappe 1990
Rahm 1988
Reuter 1981
Sauter 1998
Sikeler 1989
Steiert 2001
Yan 1991
Zhang, W. 2002
Frank 2002
Jaedicke 1999
Kosch 1997
Mariucci 2004
Rantzau 2004
Saltenis 2001
Schwarz 2002
Schwen-kreis 2001
Sellentin 1999
Melnikj 2004
Müller 2002
Effelsberg 1981
Denda 2004
Fischer 1997
Haensel-mann 2004
Hofmann 1993
Keller 1996
Kuhmünch 2001
Lienhart 1998
Mauve 2000
Pfeiffer 1999
Vogel 2004
Widmer 2003
Bär 1993
Fischer 1996
Geyer 1999
Hilt 2001
Holfelder 1998
Kühne 2002
Lamparter 1994
Mayer 1993
Meyer-Boudnik 1994
Schremmer 2002
Weis 2000
Hellbrück 2004
Walther 2004

Table of Content

PART I MOTIVATION AND MODELING ISSUES

PART II INFRASTRUCTURAL SERVICES

PART IV APPLICATION SCENARIOS

Part I Motivation and Modeling Issues

Databases:

The Integrative Force in Cyberspace

Andreas Reuter

EML Research gGmbH, Heidelberg
Andreas.Reuter@eml-d.villa-bosch.de

Abstract. Database technology has come a long way. Starting from systems that were just a little more flexible than low-level file systems, they have evolved into powerful programming and execution environments by embracing the ideas of data independence, non-procedural query languages, extensible type systems, automatic query optimization (including parallel execution and load balancing), automatic control of parallelism, automatic recovery and storage management, transparent distributed execution—to just name a few. Even though database systems are (today) the only systems that allow normal application programmers to write programs that will be executed correctly and safely in a massively parallel environment on shared data, database technology is still viewed by many people as something specialized to large commercial online applications, with a rather static design, something substantially different from the "other" IT components. More to the point: Even though database technology is to the management of persistent data what communication systems are to message-based systems, one can still find many application developers who pride themselves in not using databases, but something else. This is astounding, given the fact that, because of the dramatic decrease in storage prices, the amount of data that needs to be stored reliably (and retrieved, eventually) is growing exponentially—it's Moore's law, after all. And what is more: Things that were thought to be genuinely volatile until recently, such as processes, turn into persistent objects when it comes to workflow management, for example.

The paper argues that the technological evolution of database technology makes database systems the ideal candidate for integrating all types of objects that need persistence one way or the other, supporting all the different types of execution that are characteristic of the various application classes. If database systems are to fulfill this integrative role, they will have to adapt to new roles vis-a`-vis the other system components, such as the operating system, the communication system, the language runtime environment, etc. but those developments are under way as well.

T. Härder and W. Lehner (Eds.): Data Management (Wedekind Festschrift), LNCS 3551, pp. 3-16, 2005.

1 Introduction

Databases have a tenacious habit of just not going away. This is true for the real databases, disks, tapes, software, etc. that are run by big applications; those databases, through the sheer mass of data accumulated have an inertia that reliably protects them from being "moved", technologically, platform-wise or in any other sense. And the same observation holds (albeit for different reasons) for the scientific discipline of database technology. Starting in the mid-80s, database researchers have been organizing workshops and/or panel discussions once every three to five years, fully devoted to the question of whether there is anything interesting left in the database arena. Mike Stonebraker in particular loved to contemplate database-related questions such as "Are we polishing a round ball?" [12]. The motivation for this is quite clear: After having solved all the issues that once were considered interesting and hard (or so it seemed), is the field going to lie fallow—which should trigger everybody to move on to something more fertile, more promising.

The answers suggested in those workshops were mixed—as you would expect. But even those people who still found interesting problems to work on had to admit, that most of those problems were highly specialized compared to the early problems in access paths, synchronization, and all the rest. So based on the discussions in those workshops one would have expected database technology to reach a saturation level quite soon with only marginal improvements in some niches.

Therefore, it is exciting to see that database technology has undergone a transformation during the last couple of years, which few people have predicted to happen this way—even though it is embarrassingly obvious in hindsight. Not only have databases been extended by a plethora of new data types and functions (this was what everybody expected), they rather have mutated from a big but separate system platform for passively storing data into a compute engine supporting a wide range of applications and programming styles. The once-hot debate about object-oriented databases has been settled completely by relational databases absorbing objects, complete with a powerful and efficient extensibility platform, and by database objects becoming first-class citizens in object-oriented languages through a common runtime system [4]. This has largely solved another "old" database problem, the so-called impedance mismatch between relational databases with their SQL-style, declarative programming model and the inherently procedural nature of many programming languages.

But not only have database systems adopted features from other system components; at the same time they have offered their own specific features such as set-oriented programming, parallel programming, content-addressability, etc. as components to a generic programming environment of modern systems.

All this still sounds very technical; one might say that the most annoying, longstanding difficulties have been resolved, that the database people finally got it right. But so what? Why would this justify the claim expressed in the title? The article will argue that databases, as a result of the evolution sketched above, will—in future systems—play a role that is very different from their traditional low-level, obscure role somewhere deep down in the system.

2 New Data Sources, New Usage Patterns

Modern database technology has its roots in business data processing. In his textbook on "Data Organization" [14], which was published in the early 70s and describes databases as an emerging technology, Hartmut Wedekind characterizes databases as the core of management information systems, designed to accommodate different structural and operational schemes of a company—and to provide a query interface. Application areas such as banking, inventory control, order processing, etc. were the driving forces behind database products in the 60s and 70s—and to a certain degree they still are. But all the time databases were considered some kind of passive, low-level infrastructure (something close to the operating system) the only purpose of which was to enable new types of applications, integrated management of data for both online and batch processing, and a whole range of functions for archiving, recovery, etc. Databases were systems for application developers, not for end-users. Even the query interfaces based on different types of "user friendly" metaphors required a fairly educated user—they had to understand the schema (their particular view of it), for example. This is the reason why Paul Larson, senior researcher at Microsoft is quoted saying "Database systems are as interesting as the household plumbing to most people. But if they don't work right, that's when you notice them." This is the view we have come to accept: Databases are definitely necessary, but not particularly attractive—let alone exciting. Jim Gray [6] likes to say that "databases are the bricks of cyberspace". This again emphasizes the importance and the substance of the subject, but bricks are not very attractive either. One could find many other such statements, but why worry about this in the first place?

Let us explain the reason by considering a very instructive analogy: In the early 1980s, one would have ascribed the same properties as quoted above to messaging and distributed systems—necessary yet unappealing. But then something happened that made Butler Lampson say that the greatest failure of the systems research community over the past ten years was that "we did not invent the Web" [10]. And if you think about it: The technology enabling the WWW is exactly what was developed by the "systems research community", but in contrast to what distributed systems were before, the Web is attractive, and it made distributed computing technology available to everybody, not just to technical people. So in order to understand / anticipate what database technology might—or rather: should evolve to, it is essential to understand what caused the transformation of distributed systems from something nerdy and boring into the hottest thing in the IT arena—and beyond.

Obviously, the key point was that the Web offered the possibility of reaching beyond the confines of just one system, of unlimited connectivity on a global scale. True, the underlying Internet had been around for quite a while when the Web came up, but the TCP/IP-stack is not something many people can or want to develop applications on. HTML was not a nice interface either, but it worked on a metaphor people are easily familiar with, i.e., documents, rather than something arcane like a communication protocol. And it offered a totally new quality, the possibility of sharing contents without any restrictions, and without the need to worry about the internal workings. So if a new solution significantly increases the users' power (be it in terms of functionality, or reach, or speed), the quality of the interface initially does not matter too much. Many experts predicted that the Web would never succeed because of the awkwardness of HTML; the same predictions were made for SMS. The experts were wrong on both counts. On the other hand, nice interfaces do not translate into ready success if they do not sufficiently empower the user. The quality of simple, unrestricted access to HTML documents quickly created new usage patterns and new applications. Sharing of text was augmented by function sharing, simple access grew into more sophisticated processing patterns, organizational layers such as portals were introduced, overlay networks came into use, etc. Again, none of these things represented a genuinely new technology, but the way the existing technology was used and employed made all the difference.

Now the reader might ask: Where is the analogy to databases? Clearly, modern database systems have much more powerful and high-level programming interfaces than the TCP/IP protocol stack, there are databases embedded into end-user-oriented application generators, database systems can handle distributed processing in a transparent manner—so what can be learned from the comparison with the Web?

The answer can best be illustrated through an anecdote: At a workshop on future research issues in databases that was held in 1992, about 40 researchers presented their views on great new ways of improving database technology. Towards the end one of the organizers asked a question: "You all have to manage a lot of data, contact addresses, email, project-related data, references and the like. How many of you are using a database system for that purpose?" Two hands went up, while the others eagerly explained how database systems were too complicated to set up and to maintain, how the data types were not adequate, how the integration with other tools was insufficient, and many other such things. This was more than 10 years ago, but had the survey been conducted today, the outcome would certainly not have been much different, because the reasons have not changed. We store, manipulate and query data in many contexts, for a large variety of purposes. Some data is strictly private; other data is shared to some degree. Some data is transient, other data is (semi-) permanent. Each type of data, however, is used and supported by a specific tool: The email end everything pertaining to that lives in the mail system; the appointment data lives in the calender system; project-related data lives in the planning tool; data that requires some calculation may live in a spreadsheet; shared data lives in a company-wide database; and finally, one might have one's own database application (using, for example, Access) for keeping track of the CDs, records, and books. But all those systems are separate as far as data management is concerned. Clearly, for any given project, data related to that project will be found in the mail system, in the calender, in the planning tool, and in some spreadsheets. But there is no way of dynamically creating a "view" on the project that encompasses data from all these sources. Or put it another way: Even if the mail system were built on top of an SQL database (which most mail systems still aren't), there would still be no way of querying that database together with the company database, even if the data types were overlapping. That explains why we are still using a specific tool for every relevant purpose rather than managing all our data in one consolidated store—even if those tools force us into storing the same data redundantly, into representing the same kind of information in different formats, and into manually synchronizing the different versions of the same information—if we ever bother to do so.

Tab. 1 Overview of Categories of Personal Data and the Types of (Technical) Management Support

Category	Tool/ Platform	Properties of data store	Data model	Ref. to other categories
Mail	Email system	Closed file system or database	Folder hierarchy; weakly structured text strings	Many: structural; value-based; concept-based
Addresses	Mail system or directory	Closed or open file system (LDAP)	Quasi-relational; various „standards“	Many: structural; value-based
Appointments	Calender system	Closed file system	Hierarchy of time intervals; unstructured text strings	Many: structural; value-based; concept-based
Scheduling	Planning tool	Closed file system or database	Dependency graph; weakly structured text strings	Many: structural; value-based
Budgeting	Spreadsheet	Closed file system or database	Array; arithmetic expressions; unstructured strings	Various: value-based
Personal inventory	4GL tool	Open database	Relational	Various: value-based
Personal finance (account mgmt.)	Web frontend to bank application	Closed database	Forms-oriented	Many: value-based
Personal finance (invoices, receipts)	Shoebox, paper folder	n/a	n/a	Many

This situation, which characterizes the “state of the art” in managing a person’s private data, is summarized in Table 1.

The above table is far from complete; our personal data "ether" comprises many more categories: Messages from mobile phones and PDAs, insurance contracts and related claims, medical data, tickets, photos, and many more. Thanks to the advances in (mobile) communication technology, ever more powerful data sources are entering the personal domain. But the table suffices to clarify one important fact—a fact so trivial that it is mostly overlooked, or regarded as irrelevant: When it comes to our personal data, we have to deal with many different systems and technologies, ranging all the way from advanced Web services down to paper in boxes. The electronic tools are strictly categorized, using different platforms, different data models, and different engines. As a consequence, integrating related data from different categories is not supported by any of the participating tools and has to be done either by the owner of the data or—more likely—is not done at all. This means both a significant loss of information, as is suggested by the shaded column, and a high level of redundancy.

Table 1 also shows that most of the tools involved do employ database technology somewhere deep down in the system. But even if a tool uses a full-fledged SQL system, it restricts its functionality to its own needs, which means the database's capabilities of selecting, aggregating and joining data cannot be used for integrating the tool's data with those from other sources. It is ironic that many tool developers use this observation as some kind of reverse argument, saying that they build their tool on top of a normal file system instead of database system, because "we don't need all these features". But obviously, considering Table 1, the lack of those features, especially those helping with data integration, is causing a major problem for almost everybody. And the other argument that is very popular with developers, "our customers never asked for that", does not count; hardly anybody asked for the Web before it became available.

So the private domain is a large application (i.e., there are many users) where data of different types have to be managed, some of them in collaboration with other parties. If we view data integration as one of the key reasons for using a database, then here is a big task for database systems, a task they do not fulfil today—even though all the technology needed is there. But this observation holds for other areas (outside the household) as well; let us briefly review some of the more demanding new database applications and usage patterns, again without any claim of completeness.

2.1 Science

In many fields of science, such as astronomy, biology, particle physics, etc. measurement devices ranging from satellites to sequencers and particle colliders produce huge amounts of raw data, which have to be stored, curated, analyzed and aggregated in order to become useful for scientific purposes [7]. The raw data is only partially structured, with some parts that conform to the relational model, but with other parts as well, such as images of many different types, time series of measurements, event logs, and text fields that either contain natural language or some kind of application-specific vernacular [13]. The key properties of those data collections (irrespective of the many differences) are:

- The raw data is written once and never changed again. As a matter of fact, some scientific organizations require for all projects they support that any data that influence the published results of the project be kept available for an extended period of time, typically around 15 years.
- Raw data come in as streams with high throughput (hundreds of MB/s), depending on the sensor devices. They have to be recorded as they come in, because in most cases there is no way of repeating the measurement.
- For the majority of applications, the raw data is not interesting. What the users need are aggregates, derived values, or—in case of text fields—some kind of abstract of "what the text says".
- In many cases, the schema has hundreds or thousands of attribute types, whereas each instance only has tens of attribute values.
- The schema of the structured part of the database is not fixed in many cases. As the discipline progresses, new phenomena are discovered, new types of measurements are made, units and dimension are changed, and once in a while whole new concepts are introduced and/or older concepts are redefined. All those schema changes have to be accommodated dynamically.

Digital libraries belong into this category, too. Traditionally, libraries were treated as something different, both organizationally and technically, but in the meantime it no longer makes sense to separate them from the core business of storing and managing scientific data, because whatever ends up in a scientific library—article, book, or report—is to some degree based on scientific data, which thus should be directly linked with the publications they support [6].

2.2 Data Streams

There is a growing number of applications where databases are used to create a near-real-time image of some critical section of the environment. For example,

- RFIDs support tracking physical parts from the supplier, through the production process, into the final product—until they need to be replaced for some reason;
- the activities of cell phones can be tracked both with respect to their physical location and the calls they place and receive;
- credit card readers allow tracking the use of credit cards and their physical locations;
- sensors allow monitoring processes of all kinds: in power plants, in chemical reactors, in traffic control systems, in intensive care units, etc.

The main purpose of such databases is to provide flexible query functionality, aggregation and extrapolation of the respective processes that can't properly be achieved on the physical objects. Based on those complex evaluations, one can support process optimization, fraud detection, early-warning functions, and much more.

For that purpose, the database must be able to absorb the data at the rates of their arrival. But the situation is different from gathering scientific data, where the streams typically run at a fairly constant speed. For monitoring applications, the system must be able to accommodate significant fluctuations in the data rate, including sharp bursts. And in addition, the data must not simply be recorded. Rather, the incoming data has to be related to the existing data in complex ways in order to compute the type of derived information that is needed for, say, early warning applications. This gives rise to the notion of continuous queries [1], the implementation of which requires mechanisms quite different from classical database algorithms—and different data structures as well.

An important application of this type of processing is the publish-subscribe scenario. Users can subscribe to certain patterns in the incoming data stream and/or to certain events related to them, which are expressed as complex (continuous) queries on the database. Depending on the application, there can be millions of subscribers using thousands of different queries. Subscribers need to be notified of relevant changes in the incoming data in real time, so in case of many subscribers there is a correspondingly huge stream of outgoing data, i.e., notification messages.

Another characteristic property of monitoring applications is the fact that they often track properties of certain objects in space and time. Space is not necessarily the normal 3D space in which we move about, but at any rate, both space and time need to be first-class citizens of the data model rather than just another set of attributes. References to value histories must be supported at the same level as references to the current value, which is what databases normally do.

And finally, the applications require the database to handle (and to trigger) events.

2.3 Workflow Management

Automatic management of complex, long-lived workflows has been a goal for at least three decades [11]. The problem has been tackled from different angles, but so far only partial solutions for special cases have been implemented. There is consensus, though, that database technology has to be at the core of any general-purpose solution. Each workflow instance is a persistent, recoverable object, and from that perspective is similar to "traditional" database objects. On the other hand, workflows have many additional features that go beyond what databases normally support.

A workflow has a very complex internal structure that is either completely described in the workflow schema, or that can change/evolve over time. The latter is particularly true for workflows with a very long duration, because it is impossible to fully structure them in the beginning. Workflows are active objects, as opposed to the passive view that databases normally hold of their objects; workflows react to events, to interrupts, they wait for pre-conditions to become true, they trigger events, etc. Workflows have a huge amount of state (which is why databases are needed), partially ordered (as defined by the schema) by activation conditions, by the temporal dimension, and many other criteria. Workflow variables need to maintain their instantiation history, because references to an earlier execution state are required both for normal execution as well as for recovery purposes.

Another aspect of workflows that can be supported by database technology is synchronization of concurrent activities. Because workflows are long-lived, there will be a large number of them executing in parallel, accessing shared data, competing for resources, creating events that may be conflicting in various ways. Some of those conflicts may not be resolvable immediately, so the conflicting state together with the resources involved has to be stored in a recoverable manner such that automatic or application-dependent conflict resolution can be initiated at the proper time.

We could discuss more areas with novel requirements in terms of data management, but the ones mentioned above suffice in order to make the key point: We see an increasing need for consolidating the management of all kinds of data for all kinds of processing patterns on a single, homogeneous platform—whatever the name of the platform may be. People want to manage all their personal data in a consistent way, creating much more than just a "digital shoebox"—the realm of personal data may well extend into the professional domain, depending on the way people organize their lives [2]. In the scientific domain, we see a convergence of storing scientific data (experimental measurements), the outcome of all types of analyses, and the final publications, including patents and the like. And in the business domain, there is a clear movement towards integrating the management of business data and the management of applications working on those data.

Traditionally, all these fields were treated separately, with different underlying concepts and theories, different techniques, and different technical and scientific communities. Databases were viewed as representatives of the world of structured data (and still are, to a certain degree), whereas collections of text were the subject of "information retrieval systems". The notion of "semi-structured" systems [5] tried to bridge this gap, but still convergence has not been achieved. In the same vein, temporal databases, active databases, real-time databases, etc. have been viewed as different communities, focused more on solving their particular problems rather than trying to come up with a framework for integration. This definitely made good sense because solving the integration problem definitely is a tall order.

Right now it is ironic to see that many people believe in a very simple recipe for integration: XML. As Gray observes in [8], the set of people believing in this approach and those not buying it is stratified by age—yet he continues to say "... but it is hard at this point to say how this movie will end."

3 Technological Trends

When sketching technological trends that will be useful in solving the problems outlined above, we have to consider the database field as well as adjacent areas—whatever measure of "nearness" one may choose to apply. This could result in a fairly lengthy list of new ideas and techniques, which would be beyond the limitations of this paper. Therefore, we will only name some of the key technologies expected to be instrumental in extending the scope of databases such that they can support the novel applications and usage patterns that already have emerged—and that will keep emerging in the future. Since we cannot discuss any of the technological trends in detail, we will only use them to support our core argument that all the ingredients are there (or at least a sufficient number is) to unleash the integrative power of database technology.

3.1 Trends in Database Technology

It is hard to judge which technological change is more important than another one, but clearly one of the most consequential developments in database technology in recent history has been the integration of the relational model (one should rather say: the SQL-model) with object technology. The model-specific problems aside, this required an extension of the database systems' runtime engine in order to accommodate the dynamic nature of object-orientation—as opposed to the static characteristic of a relational schema. In the end, this led to an integration of the databases' runtime engine with the runtime systems of classical programming languages, which greatly enhanced the capabilities of both worlds: The traditional "impedance mismatch" between the database operators and the programming languages they are embedded in largely disappeared. One can run code in (almost) any language inside the database, and / or one can include database objects into class definitions of an object-oriented programming language. Given the powerful declarative programming model of SQL, one can use a database as an execution environment for procedural, object-oriented, declarative, and rule-based programming, whatever fits the problem structure best—all within one coherent framework. This in itself is an extremely useful basis for integrating different data models and execution patterns, as is illustrated by the current work on integrating text into classical databases—two domains that have traditionally been quite separate.

The other important development has to do with the proliferation of methods and techniques for indexing, combining and aggregating data in any conceivable manner. Databases in the meantime efficiently support cubes of very high dimensionality with a vast number of aggregation operators. They also include machine-learning techniques for detecting clusters, extracting rules, "guessing" missing data, and the like. Novel indexing techniques help in supporting a variety of spatial and temporal data models—or rather: embeddings of the underlying data models. All this is accompanied by advanced query optimizers that exploit the potential of those access paths and dynamically adapt to changing runtime conditions. Again, those changes are essential for the task of integrating everything in cyberspace.

Integrating the ever-growing volume of data requires, among many other things, a database system that is highly scalable and can be tuned to the specific performance needs of a wide range of applications. Modern database systems respond to these needs by supporting new internal storage structures such as transposed files (aka column stores), by exploiting the potential of very large main memories, by using materialized views and others types of replication, by applying a rich set of algorithms for computing complex queries, etc.

3.2 Trends in Adjacent Fields

The new developments in database technology have either been provoked by or complemented by new approaches in related fields. Whether it was the competitive or the symbiotic scenario does not matter, it is the result that counts.

A key development in the field of programming languages and systems is the notion of a common language runtime environment [2], which allows for a seamless integration of database functionality and programming languages. It also enables database systems to schedule and execute application programs autonomously, i.e., without the need for a separate component like a TP monitor. This also means that database systems can provide Web services without the necessity of a classical application execution environment.

The consequences of distributed computing, rapidly increasing storage capacities, demands for non-stop operation (to name just a few) have caused operating systems and other low-level system components to adopt database techniques. For example, most operating systems now support ACID transactions in some form, and they offer recovery functionality for their file systems similar to what database systems provide.

Devices other than general-purpose computers increasingly employ database systems. There are two main reasons for that: The first one is to have the device expose a powerful standard interface (SQL) instead of an idiosyncratic, device-specific interface. The other reason is that the device has to keep large amounts of data, which are most easily managed by a standard database system. An example of the latter category is a home-entertainment device that can store hundreds of CDs and provide the user with sophisticated search functions.

The implementation of workflow engines requires an even closer collaboration between database systems and operating systems. The reason is obvious: A workflow is a long-lived recoverable execution of a single thread or of parallel/interleaved computations, so everything that is volatile information for normal OS processes now has to be turned into persistent objects, just like the static objects that are normally stored in databases. Examples for this are recoverable queues, sequences of variable instantiations for keeping track of execution histories, etc. Many database systems support queues as first-class objects, so in a sense the database is the real execution environment of workflows, with operating systems acting only on its behalf by providing expendable objects such as processes and address spaces.

A last important trend is the adoption of schema-based execution in many areas. Databases have had schemas (albeit rather static ones) all along, and so had operating systems. Markup languages made messages and documents schema-based, a development that led to Web services, among other things. Similar ideas can be found in many application systems, where the generic functionality is adapted to the needs of a specific user by populating various "schema" tables with the appropriate values. This process is often referred to as customization, and—just like that classical notion of a schema—it is an example of the old adage that "any problem can be solved by introducing just another level of indirection." And, of course, ontologies as a means of extracting concepts from plain text can be viewed as yet another incarnation of the same idea.

4 The Shape of Future Database Systems

This section will not give a description of what the title refers to—that would be way too ambitious. We will rather summarize the observations from the previous chapter and, based on this, identify a number of aspects that will determine the shape of future database systems.

But first let us re-state the assumption that this paper is built on: Due to the availability of virtually unlimited storage at low cost[1], data from a large variety of sources will be gathered, stored, and evaluated in unforeseen ways. In many application areas, those data collections will establish ever more precise images of the respective part of reality, and those images will be more and more up-to-date. So for many purposes, decisions will not be based on input from the "real world", but on query results from the digital images. Examples of this have been mentioned above.

Since this scenario talks about managing large amounts of data, we will consider it a database problem, even though there is no guarantee that the technology finally supporting such applications will not be given some other name—probably because "database" does not sound cool enough. Anyhow, database systems capable of integrating data of all types and supporting all kinds of processing patterns will have to be extremely adaptive, both in terms of representing the data and in terms of interacting with the environment—which can be anything from sensor devices to applications programs and users. They must not enforce structure upon the data, if there is no structure, or if any structure that can be identified is likely to change. In those cases, schema modifications (together with schema versioning) must be supported as well as (dynamic) schema transformation [3]. In other cases, ontology-based representations might be a better option—XML will certainly be the lowest level of self-descriptive data. Classical applications will still use their more or less static schema descriptions, and in an integrated system, all those techniques must be available at the same time, allowing queries to span different models. For some data it must be possible to have it encapsulated by an object, but make it accessible for certain types of queries as "raw data" as well. Many standard tools and applications organize their data in a hierarchical fashion (e.g. folders), so this kind of mapping must be supported—whether or not the data structure is inherently hierarchical.

Future database systems will, because of the integrative role they have to assume, have to deal with high levels of parallelism and with requests ranging from milliseconds to months or more. This requires new synchronization primitives and new notions of consistency—beyond those implied by the classical ACID transaction model. Most likely, such extensions will be developed in collaboration with researchers from the fields of programming languages, dependable systems, and maybe even hardware architects [9].

Another consequence of the integrative role is the necessity of keeping the system up at any time, under all circumstances. Any tuning, reorganization, repair, recovery or

1. This development is expected to be complemented by the availability of a high-bandwidth mobile communication infrastructure.

whatever has to be performed automatically, in parallel to normal execution. This demand for a self-organizing, self-healing, self-you-name-it database is a subject of ongoing research, and its feasibility will be determined by technical as well as economical constraints.

As was mentioned above, it is not clear if the resulting solution will be perceived as a database system (however "future" it may be), or if it will be dressed up in a different fashion. One possible solution is to move a database system with (ideally) all the extensions mentioned into the operating system and build a next-generation file system on top of that. Such a file system would offer the conventional file types as well as XML-stores, semi-structured repositories, stores for huge data streams, object repositories, queues, etc. But they would all be implemented on top of an underlying database system, which would still be able to talk SQL and provide all the mechanisms for consistency, synchronization, recovery, optimization, and schema translation. But again: This is just a possibility, and by no means the only one.

5 Conclusions

The key message of this article is plain and simple: There are many different applications and usage modes out there, some rather old, some emerging, which hold the potential for integration at the level of the data they are dealing with. Everybody, home user as well as professional, would benefit immensely from a technology that enables them to transparently access and manipulate data in such an integrated view. Database technology, together with a host of "neighboring" technologies, has all the components required to do that. All it needs is an innovation comparable to the creation of the Web on top of the Internet. Referring back to Lampson's statement quoted in the beginning, we should ask ourselves (as members of the technical database community): Will we create this future, global, unified repository? If so, what will it look like? If not, why not?

References

[1] Babu, S., Widom, J.: Continuous Queries over Data Streams. in: SIGMOD Record 30:3, Sept. 2001, pp. 109-120.

[2] Bell, G.: MyLifeBits: A Lifetime Personal Store. in: Proc. of Accelerating Change 2004 Conference, Palo Alto, Ca., Nov. 2004.

[3] Bernstein, P.A., Generic Model Management—A Database Infrastructure for Schema Manipulation. in: Lecture Notes on Computer Science, No. 2172, Springer-Verlag.

[4] Common Language Runtime. in: Microsoft .NET Framework Developer's Guide, http://msdn.microsoft.com/library/default.asp?url=/library/en-us/cpguide/html/cpconthecommonlanguageruntime.asp

[5] Goldman, R., McHugh, J. and Widom, J.: From Semistructured Data to XML: Migrating the Lore Data Model and Query Language. in: Proc. of the 2nd Int. Workshop on the Web and Databases (WebDB '99), Philadelphia, Pennsylvania, June 1999, pp. 25-30.

[6] Gray, J.: The Laws of Cyberspace. Presentation at the International University in Germany, October 1998, http://research.microsoft.com/%7Egray/talks/1998_laws.ppt

[7] Gray, J., Szalay, A.S. et al.: Online Scientific Data Curation, Publication, and Archiving. in: Proc. of SPIE Astronomy, Telescopes and Instruments, Waikoloa, 2002, pp. 103-107.

[8] Gray, J.: The Revolution in Database Architecture. Technical Report, MSR-TR-2004-31, March 2004.

[9] Jones, C., et al.: The Atomic Manifesto: a Story in Four Quarks. in: Dagstuhl Seminar Proceedings 04181, http://drops.dagstuhl.de/opus/volltexte/2004/9.

[10] Lampson, B.: Computer systems research: Past and future. Invited talk, in: Proc. of SOSP'99.

[11] Leymann, F., Roller, D.: Production Workflow—Concepts and Techniques. Prentice Hall, 1999.

[12] Proceedings ICDE Conference on Data Engineering. Vienna, 1993

[13] Ratsch, E., et al.: Developing a Protein-Interactions Ontology. in: Comparative and Functional Genomics, Vol. 4, No. 1, 2003, pp. 85-89.

[14] Wedekind, H.: Datenorganisation. Walter de Gruyter, Berlin New York, 1975.

Federating Location-Based Data Services

Bernhard Mitschang, Daniela Nicklas, Matthias Grossmann, Thomas Schwarz, Nicola Hönle

University of Stuttgart, Germany
{mitschang, nicklas, grossmann, schwarts, hoenle}@informatik.uni-stuttgart.de

Abstract. With the emerging availability of small and portable devices which are able to determine their position and to communicate wirelessly, mobile and spatially-aware applications become feasible. These applications rely on information that is bound to locations and managed by so-called location-based data services. Large-scale location-based systems have to cope efficiently with different types of data (mostly spatial or conventional). Each type poses its own requirements to the data server that is responsible for management and provisioning of the data. In addition to efficiency, it is overly important to provide for a combined and integrated usage of that data by the applications.

In this paper we discuss various basic technologies to achieve a flexible, extensible, and scalable management of the context model and its data organized and managed by the different data servers. Based on a classification of location-based data services we introduce a service-oriented architecture that is built on a federation approach to efficiently support location-based applications. Furthermore, we report on the Nexus platform that realizes a viable implementation of that approach.

1 Introduction

Pervasive computing has drawn increasing attention in the past years. The vision is that smart everyday objects communicate and cooperate to provide services and information to users. Meanwhile, a multitude of applications has been developed. These applications cover different domains, such as tourist guides [9, 1], indoor information systems [11, 10] and smart environments [24], to name a few.

A variety of supporting infrastructures has been proposed, which facilitate the development of applications. However, these infrastructures mostly address a distinct application domain, such as context processing based on sensors [38] or providing application-specific context [9, 40]. Also, when new services, hardware, or environmental information such as maps become available to an application, other existing applications can not automatically use them. Interaction between different applications based

T. Härder and W. Lehner (Eds.): Data Management (Wedekind Festschrift), LNCS 3551, pp. 17-35, 2005.

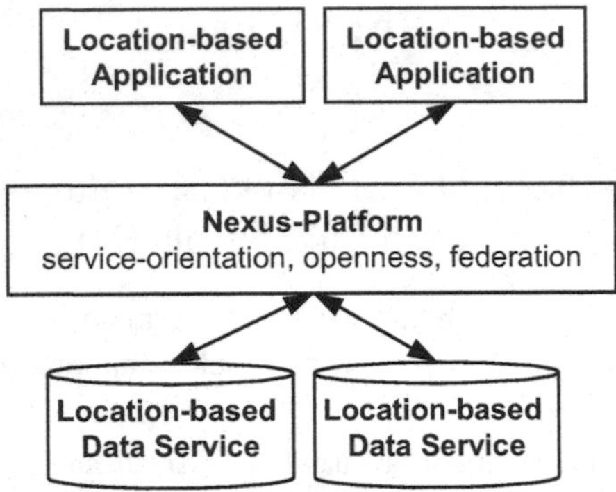

Fig. 1 Architectural Overview

on their context, e.g., identity, location, or state, is not possible if they do not rely on a common representation of this context.

Context-aware systems have attracted researchers in the past years starting from location-aware computing. Early work [39] considered context to be related to the location of users, the people nearby, and resources which can be accessed based on the spatial proximity. Depending on the focus of research projects, further definitions of context have been proposed. Context-aware applications use context information in order to adapt their behavior. The different context sources and characteristics of context information, e.g., type and representation, has led to a number of different approaches to supply applications with context information. Besides specialized approaches, e.g., the context toolkit [38] for sensor integration or the location stack for positioning systems [20], a generic approach based on a database-style management of context information has evolved that typically offers interfaces to query context information or to receive notifications on context changes.

For many context-aware applications, the spatial environment of the user is most relevant. So-called location-based applications, or location-based services (LBS), define a specific class of context-aware systems that adapt their behavior to the spatial context of the user, e.g., by providing local maps and navigational information. In this application area, there are already commercial solutions available, e.g., location-based information systems for mobile phones or car navigation services. They rely on spatial data that has previously been gathered and preprocessed to fit their needs. This data is expensive, because in many cases it has to be manually collected, edited and updated. Typically, spatial data is fused with traditional information from databases or web pages, augmented with a spatial reference, to form what is called the context model.

In the context of the Nexus project [31], we design and implement an open platform to manage such a context model. Based on an extensible set of so-called location-based data services, we introduce a service-oriented architecture that is built on a federation approach to flexibly and efficiently support location-based applications. All this is reflected by the coarse-grained architecture that is depicted in Fig. 1.

In this paper, we detail on that architecture approach and on how the Nexus project realizes that approach. In doing so, in the next section the characteristics of location-based data are discussed and described in the context of a spatial ontology. A definition of as well as a classification of location-based data services is given in section 3, and the federation of the data services to provide for a global spatial context model is discussed in section 4. Finally, section 5 focuses on the Nexus platform, its system architecture as well as on syntactic and semantic data integration issues. section 6 closes the paper with a short conclusion.

2 On Location-Based Data

In this section, we go into the details on the characteristics of location-based data: the difference between virtual and real-world objects and a categorization of spatial ontologies which is helpful to understand what and how location-based data is modelled.

2.1 Virtual and Real-World Objects

We can distinguish two major categories: information that is relevant at a certain location (and can be seen as *virtual objects* residing at this location) and models of *real-world objects* like buildings, persons or sensors. Examples for virtual objects are web pages, time tables or the menu of a restaurant. To make this data location-based, a reference to the real world is needed. It can be either a relation to a real-world object (e.g., the menu as an attribute of a restaurant), or the virtual object is simply bound to a geographic coordinate. In the following, we focus on such location-based virtual objects.

To access and interact with these virtual objects, new user interaction paradigms are needed: virtual objects can be displayed on maps. With augmented reality, virtual objects can be displayed along the natural sight of the user. There are also metaphors of the real world like Virtual Information Towers [26]—equipped with web pages as posters or Stick-E notes [35]—leaving digital notes like Post-ITs which can be found by other users.

It is possible to build simple location-based services by just modeling virtual objects, e.g., Google Local Search [17] or state-of-the-art restaurant and hotel finders. However, for more sophisticated applications like smart environments (e.g., [24] or [4]), capture applications (e.g., [36]) or location-based games [34], more knowledge about the surrounding of the user is needed. Therefore, a model of the real world is needed.

Real-world objects can be used to build up maps (with buildings, streets, sightseeing locations etc.), to navigate (using navigation connections and topological information) or for spatial queries (friend finder using the positions of familiar mobile users). They all have some spatial attributes like position or extent and, for dynamic models, a temporal aspect like valid time. The spatial attributes follow an underlying spatial model which is either topological or geometric. Topological models often use hierarchical addresses like `de/stuttgart/university/building38` and can be queried using a spatial calculus [37]. A geometric or geographical model is most flexible: with spatial predicates and queries, objects can be precisely related to each other (inside, overlap, nearest neighbor), and symbolic or topological information can easily be embedded into the model. A location is described using coordinates, which always have a coordinate system (CS) associated with them. Indoor applications often use a local CS whose origin is a point within the room or building. Outdoors, the position can be obtained from a Global Positioning System (GPS) sensor in WGS84 [44] format. Spatial databases, geographical information systems or map data use even more CSs, e.g., one of the 2824 different CSs contained in the EPSG database [14].

2.2 Spatial Ontologies

Virtual and real-world objects form together the context model. The *context model* is an ontology containing the relevant location-based data that the applications need in order to perform well. Obviously, various kinds of information on different abstraction levels are conceivable. This aspect has been well addressed by the five tiers of spatial ontologies proposed by A. U. Frank (see Tab. 1):

Tab. 1 The five Tiers of Spatial Ontology according to [15]

Ontology Tier 0: Physical Reality
`reality :: world -> property -> spacePoint -> timePoint -> value`
Ontology Tier 1: Observable Reality
`observation :: world -> observationType -> location -> value`
Ontology Tier 2: Object World
`observation :: id -> time -> observationType -> value`
Ontology Tier 3: Social Reality
`getname :: object -> name` `findObject :: name -> environment -> object`
Ontology Tier 4: Cognitive Agents
`rules used or deduction`

Tier 0 is the ontology of physical reality. It contains the assumption that there is exactly one real world; hence, for every property in the world and for a given point in time-space there is a single value.

Tier 1 includes observations of reality. This is the first tier that can be accessed in computational systems. Here, a value can be obtained at a location with a given observation type. The type determines the measurement scale of the value (e.g., nominal or rational) and the measurement unit (e.g., meters or seconds). For spatial values, also a coordinate system must be given. In general, values have a limited accuracy due to observation errors.

In tier 2, single observations are grouped together to individual objects that are defined by uniform properties. Now, the value of an observation is the state of a whole object, given by an id. Andrew U. Frank only considers physical objects in this tier, i.e., "things which exist in the physical world and can be observed by observation methods". They have a geometric boundary in the world but can change over time (e.g., dunes or fluids).

Until now, the ontology tiers cover data that can be seen as agreeable reality—you can send out a team of geographers or students to model physical objects and they will come to an agreement about their observations. In tier 3, the socially constructed reality is represented. Social reality includes all the objects and relations that are created by social interactions. These are properties that are classified and named within the context of administrative, legal or institutional rules. Object names belong to this tier since they are assigned by culture; for many important things (but not all) there are functions to determine the name and to find the object by name in a certain environment.

Finally, in tier 4 the rules are modeled that are used by cognitive agents (both human and software) for deduction. This tier is normally built into database query languages, applications or inference engines of knowledge-based systems.

So, what is the use of these five tiers? They help in understanding what kind of data you have and what level of interpretation they offer. The real-world objects from section 2.1 are typically located in tier 2, unless they represent administrative or business related objects (e.g., city boundaries), which makes them belong to tier 3. Virtual objects are tier 3 since they are socially constructed as links to the digital world.

The higher the tier, the more difficult it is to integrate and share data from different models, because higher tiers incorporate more interpretation. Up to tier 3, scalable and semi-automatic matching is possible. Tier 4 information is highly application-dependent. Either it is part of the applications (and therefore hard to reuse) or it is explicitly given as rules on facts in a fully-fledged ontology. Then, reuse is possible on rather small models, but due to complexity issues, these solutions are not very scalable [6].

3 Classification of Data Services

Large-scale location-based systems (LBS) have to cope with large amounts of different types of data. Each type poses its own requirements to the server that is responsible for management and provisioning of the data. In some cases, it is even impossible to pro-

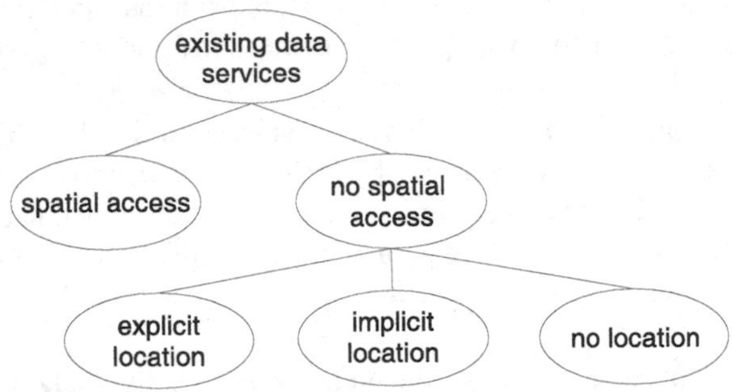

Fig. 2 Classification of Existing Data Services

vide the data via a specialized server, instead existing information systems, e.g., the World Wide Web, have to be integrated with the LBS. This section provides an overview on different kinds of servers.

3.1 Integrating Existing Data Services

The most fundamental functionality of a LBS can be characterized by two functions: f_1:*ID→locations* (given the ID of an object, return its location) and f_2:*locations*→2^{ID} (given a location, return the IDs of all objects belonging to this location). In consequence, to integrate an existing information system (let's call it here: base system) with a LBS, two problems have to be addressed: A wrapping functionality has to be provided, which maps the data model and query language of the base system to the ones of the LBS, and f_1 and f_2 have to be provided, in case they are not already part of the base system's functionality. In some cases, it is also necessary to map different location models: LBS typically represent location as latitude and longitude, while the base system may use a symbolic form, e.g., postal addresses. Mapping symbolic location names to coordinates is known as geocoding.

Fig. 2 shows a classification of base systems. It can be assumed that every system offering f_2 also offers f_1. The *spatial access* class contains systems, which provide f_1 and f_2, e.g., GIS. The other branch contains systems, for which f_2 has to be provided externally, based on more or less complete implementations of f_1. This is usually done by scanning the data of the base system, building a representation for f_2 and storing it in a dedicated access component.

Some base systems provide an explicit, direct machine-understandable implementation of f_1 without providing f_2 (*explicit location* in Fig. 2). An example for this are web pages which contain the `DC.Coverage.Spatial` meta-data element [13]. Given the ID (URL) of such a web page, its location can be easily determined. f_2 can be constructed by a web robot, which searches pages for the `DC.Coverage.Spatial` meta-data element and stores its results in a dedicated access component as mentioned above.

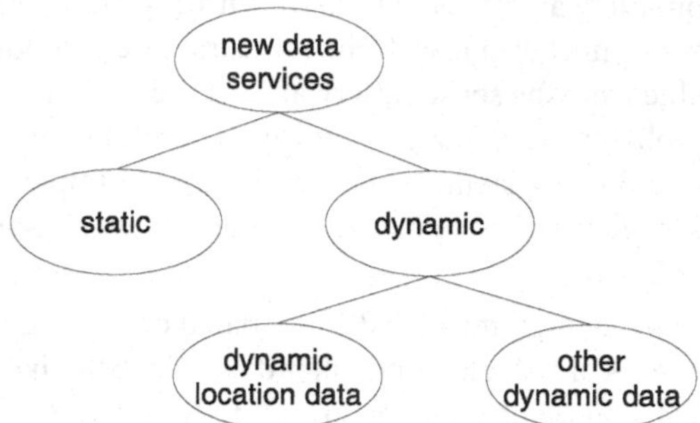

Fig. 3 Classification of new Data Services

The `DC.Coverage.Spatial` meta-data element is actually rarely used. Much more web pages contain implicit location information in human-readable formats, typically by mentioning addresses or location names somewhere in their body (*implicit location* in Fig. 2). Processing those pages is similar to the procedure described above, however, computing f_1 is more complex. Usually, some kind of text analysis has to be applied [22, 23]. Precision and recall is typically much lower than for explicit location information. Base systems may also contain data relevant to certain locations without containing this location information itself, or rather contain the location information in such a way that large amounts of domain knowledge would be necessary to derive it (*no location* in Fig. 2). In this case, f_1 and f_2 have to be built manually.

3.2 Considerations for New Data Services

For data services specifically designed for integration in a LBS, it can be assumed that a matching interface as well as f_1 and f_2 are present. Implementing new data services however opens the chance to optimize the service for special classes of data. Fig. 3 gives an overview of the different types of data.

Representations for objects like buildings, roads or rooms occupy large amounts of data. This kind of data is typically needed for drawing maps, for navigation aides or tourist guides. It can be called *static data*, because it is rarely or never changed. Sets of static data, e.g., all building outlines of a city or the complete facility management of an office building can be very large. Often, this kind of data is hard to collect, resp. expensive to buy, so protection against loss of the data is necessary. Static data can easily be cached. Because of the infrequent updates, the probability that a cached data item gets invalid is very low, so efficient, optimistic approaches usually need not to take special care to prevent from invalid cache data. Standard database systems with geographic extensions are adequate to store static data. For smaller data sets, main memory databases may also be used.

Another type of data often managed by LBSs is what can be called *dynamic data*. In contrast to static data, dynamic data is updated frequently. While static data is typically collected by hand or in a semi-automatic way, dynamic data is mostly fed into the system in a fully automatic way by some kind of sensor. Consequently, dynamic data need not to be protected against data loss. If the infrastructure component crashes, it can retrieve the current value from the sensor afterwards. If the value had been saved before the crash, it would probably be outdated anyway. Therefore, dynamic data may be stored in a pure main memory system. It is even possible to implement servers on extremely small devices, which make the measurement of a few sensors connected to the device available to the LBS.

For location-based services, it must be differentiated between dynamic location data, like positions of persons or vehicles, and other dynamic data, like the temperature of a room. Being the most important selection criterion, frequent updates of the position cause frequent changes to – depending on the actual implementation of the service – index structures or data distribution. This is exactly the case for the location of mobile objects managed, e.g., in a moving objects database [42].

4 Federation Issues

As we have seen in the previous section, location-based data may be stored in many different ways, and may be distributed across several servers and providers. Utilizing all this data in a combined fashion provides major benefits – higher data quality (increased coverage, more detail, more information) and higher availability (not depending on a single provider) – but incurs also additional processing effort and system design considerations, which we discuss in this section. We first collect the requirements to a federating middleware component that performs the combination task. Then, we discuss system architecture, syntactic integration, and semantic data integration issues.

In the following, we discuss these major federation issues. Whenever useful, we report on how the Nexus platform copes with these issues. Then, in section 5, we introduce the Nexus platform in detail.

4.1 Requirements

A federating middleware for location-based services has to meet several requirements: transparency for the application, dynamic data provider configurations, semantic data integration, efficiency, and, in most cases, applications running on mobile devices.

The most important requirement is to make it as easy as possible for an application to access the combined data of many providers. For this, a federating middleware may provide several kinds of transparency characteristics: schema, heterogeneity, location and name, and distribution transparency [8].

Schema transparency lets an application use a single global schema to access all data. If a provider stores its data in a different schema, the federating middleware transforms it to the global schema. In the Nexus platform we require all data providers to perform the transformation step themselves, as they know best how to map their data to the global schema.

Heterogeneity transparency lets an application access all data using a single type of API, like textual SQL queries, JDBC function calls, or SOAP messages. The federating middleware has to offer one or more of those APIs and it has to access each data provider using its own API. In Nexus we have defined the query language AWQL and the data exchange format AWML [33] which are used throughout the platform.

Location and Name Transparency lets an application specify declaratively in which data it is interested in without needing to know where the data is actually located. The federating middleware needs to utilize some kind of directory, naming, or look-up service to determine the location of the desired data. In the Nexus platform we use the Area Service Register for this task.

Distribution transparency hides from the application that the data may be originally coming from different providers, even the data constituting a single object. The federating middleware needs to piece together data fragments originating from different providers but belonging to the same object. In the Nexus platform we use some semantic data integration techniques to merge multiple representations of an object, see below.

The second requirement, dynamic data provider configurations relieves the providers from any obligations. New providers may join the system, old providers may become temporarily (network partitioning) or permanently (bankruptcy) inaccessible, while the overall system should continue to work with what is available right now [31]. This requirement can also be fulfilled using a look-up service (like the Nexus Area Service Register), where new providers can register themselves during run time of the overall system.

The semantic data integration requirement addresses inconsistencies in the data of two providers even after the schemas have been adapted. Different providers may offer data concerning the same physical world entity. Four cases are conceivable here: First, the providers have complementary information on the same object (opening hours vs. special exhibition). Secondly, the data on the same object is overlapping, even conflicting (house is red vs. house is green). Thirdly, one object is an aggregation of several other objects (mall vs. single shops). Fourthly, each provider models a complex real world context using a bunch of objects (large road crossing). In order to hide these inconsistencies (originating from the data's distribution) from the application, the federating middleware needs to apply domain-specific semantic integration algorithms [41] as done in Nexus.

The fourth requirement, efficiency, demands to limit the overhead partially involved by meeting the above three requirements. Therefore, latency times have to be kept at a minimum to not overstrain the users' patience. At the same time the system has to support many concurrent users. These requirements call for integrating load balancing and caching features into the federating middleware [30].

Finally, as location-based applications often run on mobile devices, we have to consider their characteristics. While the federating middleware is always on, has high computational power, and is connected to a wired network with a high bandwidth, the opposite is the case for the mobile device: it is only sometimes on (to save battery), has limited computing resources, and is typically connected to a wireless network with a low bandwidth that is also shared with other devices. This influences especially the interaction patterns between applications and caches on the mobile device on one side and the federating middleware on the other side. Also, as the user's position is an important context information, a moving user also generates a lot of position updates [21].

4.2 System Architecture: Federation Vs. Integration

To combine the data of several providers two different approaches are conceivable: the federation approach and the integration approach.

The federation approach leaves all data at its original storage location and forwards incoming requests on the fly to the data providers, collects all responses, and integrates the responses on the fly to a final response that is returned to the application. Schema and API heterogeneities are dealt with by so-called wrappers. Data inconsistencies are dealt with when integrating the data from the different responses.

The integration approach copies all data to a centralized data warehouse, which is then used as the sole source to get any data from. Schema and API heterogeneities as well as data inconsistencies can be solved when loading the data into the warehouse.

We do not consider approaches that require to alter the original data sources in any way, e.g., change the schema or the data storage software.

The integration approach's advantage is that no complex data transformations need to be performed at run time, leading to fast and predictable response times. However, such a warehouse can easily get very large, as especially spatial data sets tend to be voluminous. Data providers need to give away their data and can no longer impose any access restrictions. Also, the integration of new providers and the removal of quitting ones may require extensive alterations to the warehouse. All updates, e.g., originating from sensor measurements, need to be sent to the single warehouse, which easily becomes a bottleneck.

The federation approach's advantages are the integration approach's disadvantages. The data stays at the providers, new providers can be easily added to the system, and updates can be performed locally at each provider. However, the data needs to be integrated at runtime possibly involving complex semantic data integration algorithms. Also, the overall response time suffers from forwarding the queries to the data providers. And, if a data provider becomes inaccessible, no backup copy of its data is available, as it would be in the data warehouse.

The Nexus platform uses the federation approach due to the requirement to allow for dynamically changing provider configurations, to give the data providers more flexibility, to give them more control over their data, and to enable the decentralized processing of updates.

4.3 Federation Techniques: LAV Vs. GAV

The relationship between a data provider's source schema and the federating middleware's global schema can be described in several ways of which the most important ones are global-as-view (GAV) [16] and local-as-view (LAV) [28].

In the GAV approach a construct in the global schema is defined as a view over one or many constructs in all participating providers' source schemas. While this enables to process queries efficiently, the global schema's definition needs to be adapted when providers enter or leave the system.

The LAV approach is the other way round. A construct in a provider's source schema is defined as a view over one or many constructs in the global schema. While this allows to add and remove providers without altering the global schema, query processing leads to the "answering queries using views" problem, which is known to be NP-hard [19].

In the Nexus platform we use a simplified LAV approach to allow for dynamic provider configurations. In our approach we require the data providers to offer their data in the format of the global schema. The providers have to deal with any data and schema transformations themselves. Now, a local schema construct (an object class) is defined using only one construct of the global schema (the same object class). Additionally, restrictions on the value ranges of all attributes may be defined. So, a provider may, e.g., define to offer hotels in Stuttgart, which connects the local hotel construct to the global hotel construct and restricts the location attribute to a certain area. We store this information in the Area Service Register (ASR). This simplification allows us to process queries without NP-complete query reformulation. The ASR determines the relevant data providers in at most O(*number of registered providers*). Typically this can be done a lot faster if fewer than all providers qualify for a query. All relevant providers can be accessed in parallel as no query sent to a provider depends on the result of another one.

4.4 Semantic Data Integration: Schema Matching and Instance Matching

Integrating the data from many different providers into a single global schema with the goal to eliminate any inconsistencies and duplicates is a two-step process. In the first step the provider's schema needs to be matched to the global schema and mapping rules need to be defined. While the schema matching problem is still an active research area [7], there are already semi-automatic tools available that address this problem [29]. In the Nexus platform we delegate this problem to the data providers and require them to transform their data to our global schema themselves. A provider can either precompute this transformation or process it on the fly in a wrapper component.

Matching the schema does not solve all problems. Different providers may model the same physical world entity in different ways, e.g., if they use different sensors or have different perspectives. Thus, in a second step the instances of different providers have to be matched after they have been transformed into the global schema format. For this, domain-specific algorithms have to be applied (e.g., [43, 12, 45]):

- adapting the level of detail by aggregating a group of objects into a single one or by generalizing an object to strip off unnecessary details,
- by comparing location and other attributes to detect matching objects and then merging them by unionizing their attributes,
- or by merging groups of objects representing parts of a road network, to name just a few.

In the Nexus project we are on the way to implement all of the mentioned algorithms to achieve the tightest possible integration of data providers.

5 Nexus — A Service-Oriented Architecture

The goal of the Nexus platform is to support all kinds of context-aware applications with a shared, global world model. To achieve this, the platform federates (section 4) local models from data services (section 3).

We see the Nexus platform architecture as a service-oriented architecture. In the following subsection we present the characteristics of a service-oriented architecture. After this we introduce the Nexus platform as a service-oriented architecture and point out its major characteristics.

5.1 Characteristics of a Service-Oriented Architecture

In general, a service oriented architecture (SOA) is a collection of services which can communicate with each other. In the following, we will concentrate on SOA definitions which are mainly used in the context of Web Services and can be found in [2].

The overall goal of a SOA is to enable reuse of functionality already provided by existing systems: Why should we do something ourselves if someone else is an expert?

In a SOA, the interacting software agents can be service providers or service consumers. A service is defined as a unit of work, which is offered by a service provider. Service consumers want to use a specific service exploiting the result delivered by that service invocation. Note, that one software agent can be both, a service provider and a service consumer. Basic characteristics of SOAs are:

- SOAs consist of a small set of simple interfaces. The interfaces are available for all providers and consumers. Providers and consumers interact by exchanging messages using the interfaces.
- The interfaces are generic, i.e., application specific semantics have to be expressed in the messages.
- The messages are descriptive rather than instructive, because the service provider itself is responsible for solving the problem.
- Vocabulary and structure of the messages are limited for efficient communication.

- Extensibility of the message schema is vitally important and allows introducing new services.
- A mechanism to discover service providers by service consumers is required.

For scalability reasons, most services are stateless, i.e., each message must contain all necessary information for the provider to process it. Nevertheless, stateful services are existing, too, e.g., for efficient communication or customized services.

5.2 The Nexus Platform

The goal of the Nexus platform is to offer generic support to context-aware applications. The basic approach is to provide a global context model as a federation of local context models (Fig. 4). Typically those local context models provide different types of context information: representations of real world and virtual objects as described in section 2.1.

Our main application area are location-based services, i.e., the most important context in the Nexus platform is spatial information like positions and extents of objects. The Nexus platform offers generic support for different kinds of location-based applications, e.g., multi-modal navigation applications, the Smart Factory [4], the Nexus Rallye [32], and mobile tourist guides [9, 1].

Local context models can be provided by location-based data services (section 3). Existing digital information spaces like the WWW can be integrated as described in section 3.1. Sensors keep local models up to date (e.g., the position of a person).

Now, we will give a short overview over the architecture of the Nexus platform as shown in Fig. 5. For more details see [31].

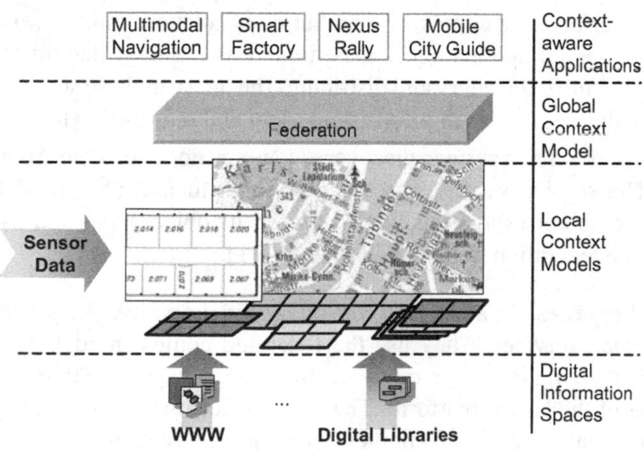

Fig. 4 Nexus Vision

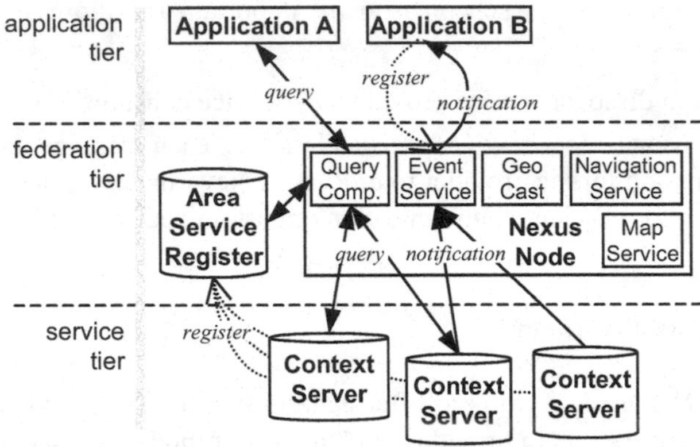

Fig. 5 Nexus Architecture

Context Server. A context server is a location-based data service as described in section 3 and stores a local context model. To be a context server, the location-based data service has to fulfil two requirements: it has to implement a certain interface (simple spatial queries and result representations given in a specified XML language) and it is registered with its service area and object types to the Area Service Register (comparable to a spatially enhanced DNS).

There can be many different implementations of a context server [18]. For providing large scale geographical models, we used a spatially enhanced database. We cope with the high update rates of the positions of mobile users using a distributed main memory system [27]. For the Aware Home we adopted a lightweight spatial server as Context Server [25]. Even small-scale sensor platforms like the ContextCube [3] can be used as a context server.

Federation. A federation node mediates between applications and context servers. It has the same interface as a context server, but does not store models (except caching). Instead, it analyses an application request issued as a query, determines the context servers that could fulfil the query and distributes the query to these servers. Then it combines the incoming result sets to a consistent view and returns this to the application.

For query distribution and service discovery, a Nexus node uses the Area Service Register (ASR). This service is a directory to the available local context models and it stores the address of each corresponding context server, its object types and its extent. More details about the federation tier can be found in [31].

Additional Services. In addition to the query functionality, every Nexus node supports value-added services. They use the federated context model to implement advanced services having their own interface. In Fig. 5, you can see three different value-added services of the Nexus platform: The map service renders maps based on a selected area. The navigation service computes multi-modal navigation routes across the borders of local context models. With GeoCast, you can port a message to a geographically addressed area to be sent to every mobile application that is currently in this region.

Information Access. A context-aware application can use the Nexus platform in three different ways:

- *Pull Mode*. An application can send queries to the federation to get all kind of information about its surrounding including infrastructure, points of interest (POIs), mobile objects (friend finder) and so on.
- *Push Mode*. An application can register to the Event Service [5] to get a notification when a certain state in the world models occurs, e.g., the user has entered a building, the temperature in a room exceeds a certain value, or two persons meet.
- *Value Added Services*. An application can use value added services like the map service or the navigation service to shift basic functions into the infrastructure of the platform.

5.3 The Nexus Platform as a SOA

The Nexus platform contains service consumers and service providers. The federation and value added services can use data providers as service providers, while they are used as service providers by the clients and client applications.

The components of our platform offer a small set of interfaces. Service providers like the federation and the data providers offer the AWQL query language and the AWML data exchange format. In addition, interface definitions for event registration and notification, and for value-added services exist.

The message schema of AWQL and AWML is extensible in such a way, that the underlying global schema is extensible by every data provider, i.e., the message vocabulary of AWQL and AWML can be extended. For some types of value added services (like navigation services or map services) message definitions are predefined. New types of value added services have to define new message formats.

We designed the Nexus platform as a SOA to exploit the benefits a SOA provides. A SOA offers flexible distribution of functionality to different components and easiness of migrating functionality from clients or applications to federation and service tier, e.g., the introduction of new value-added services. Furthermore, the SOA design supports scalability.

6 Conclusion

Location-based systems, same as location-based services, are the special case of context-aware systems that have been implemented in commercial systems and are thus already broadly available. Such systems adapt their behavior to the spatial context of the user, e.g., by providing local maps or navigational information. They rely on spatial data that has previously been gathered and preprocessed to fit their needs. Typically, spatial data is fused with traditional information from databases or web pages, augmented with a spatial reference, to form what is called the context model.

Large-scale location-based systems have to cope efficiently with different types of data (mostly spatial or conventional). Each type poses its own requirements to the data server that is responsible for management and provisioning of the data. In addition to efficiency, it is overly important to provide for a combined and integrated usage of that data by the applications. Since, for example, interactive or personalized maps and other navigational information is computed from that kind of data, it is the most valuable and largest part of the context model for location-based systems.

In this paper we discussed various basic technologies to achieve a flexible, extensible, and scalable management of the context model and its data organized and managed by the different data servers. In the context of the Nexus project, we developed an open platform as a federation of location-based data servers organized in a service-oriented architecture.

Currently, extensibility is the concept in our focus:

- We have already implemented a set of different location-based data servers to adapt to the special needs of different types of data [18]. Also we have integrated existing data sources through wrappers [25] or crawling [22]. This shows the extensibility of our approach regarding the integration of legacy data sources.
- Although we impose a global schema, our approach allows for extensions to this schema in order to accommodate for local extensions of the context model that link to existing concepts through inheritance. For increased interoperability several providers could agree on the extension. Still, existing applications not knowing the extension can make use of the new data, because the Nexus platform provides semantic translations using generalizations.
- We support the dynamic configuration of data servers through a local-as-view-based integration approach in the federation component with the help of the Area Service Register. This way, data sources may enter and leave the system during run time without requiring changes in existing applications.
- Value-added services extend the basic query functions of the platform. They allow to run application-specific functionality in the infrastructure. The two main benefits of this approach are to utilize a very efficient access to the global context model for the value-added services and to disburden the mobile devices from complex computations.

Such extensibility features are key for the success of large-scale context-aware systems. They allow this system to be an open global platform like the web. Both applications and service providers may benefit from this approach: new applications may use existing data, and new providers may offer their data to existing applications.

7 Acknowledgments

The Nexus project was funded 1999-2002 by the German Research Association (DFG) under grant 200989 and is now continued as Center of Excellence (SFB) 627.

References

[1] Abowd, G.; Atkeson, C.; Hong, J.; Long, S.; Kooper, R.; Pinkerton, M.: A mobile context-aware tour guide. Wireless Networks 3 (5), pp. 421-433, 1997.

[2] Barry, Douglas K.: Web Services and Service-Oriented Architectures. Morgan Kaufmann Publishers, 2003.

[3] Bauer, M., Becker, C., Hähner, J., and Schiele, G.: ContextCube—providing context information ubiquitously. Proceedings of the 23rd International Conference on Distributed Computing Systems Workshops (ICDCS 2003), 2003.

[4] Bauer, M.; Jendoubi, L.; Siemoneit, O.: Smart Factory—Mobile Computing in Production Environments. Proceedings of the MobiSys 2004, Workshop on Applications of Mobile Embedded Systems, 2004.

[5] Bauer, M., Rothermel, K.: How to Observe Real-World Events through a Distributed World Model. Proceedings of the 10th International Conference on Parallel and Distributed Systems (ICPADS 2004), Newport Beach, California, 2004.

[6] Becker, Christian; Nicklas, Daniela: Where do spatial context-models end and where do ontologies start? A proposal of a combined approach. Indulska, Jadwiga; De Roure, David (Eds.): Proceedings of the First International Workshop on Advanced Context Modelling, Reasoning and Management. In conjunction with UbiComp 2004.

[7] Bilke, A.; Naumann, F.: Schema Matching using Duplicates. Proceedings of the 21st International Conference on Data Engineering (ICDE 2005), Tokyo, Japan, April 5-8, 2005.

[8] Busse, S.; Kutsche, R.-D.; Leser, U.; Weber, H.: Federated Information Systems: Concepts, Terminology and Architectures. Forschungsberichte des Fachbereichs Informatik Nr. 99-9, TU Berlin, April 1999.

[9] Cheverst, K.; Davies, N.; Mitchell, K.; Friday, A.; Efstratiou, C.: Developing a Context-aware Electronic Tourist Guide: Some Issues and Experiences. Proceedings of the Conference on Human Factors in Computing Systems CHI 2000, Netherlands, 2000.

[10] Conner, W. S.; Krishnamurthy, L.; Want, R.: Making Everyday Life Easier Using Dense Sensor Networks. Proceedings of UBICOMP 2001, Atlanta, USA, 2001.

[11] Cooltown, http://www.cooltown.com/cooltownhome/index.asp

[12] Devogele, T.: A New Merging Process for Data Integration Based on the Discrete Fréchet Distance. Proceedings of the Joint International Symposium on Geospatial Theory, Processing and Applications, Ottawa, Canada, 2002.

[13] Dublin Core Metadata Initiative: DCMI Metadata Terms. http://dublincore.org/documents/dcmi-terms/

[14] European Petroleum Survey Group (EPSG) Geodesy Parameters V 6.3. http://www.epsg.org/

[15] Frank, A. U.: Ontology for Spatio-Temporal Databases. M. Koubarakis et al. (Eds.): Spatio-Temporal Databases—The CHOROCHRONOS Approach. Lecture Notes in Computer Science, Springer 2003.

[16] Garcia-Molina, H.; Papakonstantinou, Y.; Quass, D.; Rajaraman, A.; Sagiv, Y.; Ullman, J.D.; Vassalos, V.; Widom, J.: The TSIMMIS Approach to Mediation: Data Models and Languages. Journal of Intelligent Information Systems 8(2), pp. 117-132, 1997.

[17] Google Local Search, http://local.google.com

[18] Grossmann, M., Bauer, M., Hönle, N., Käppeler, U., Nicklas, D., Schwarz, T.: Efficiently Managing Context Information for Large-scale Scenarios. Proceedings of the Third IEEE International Conference on Pervasive Computing and Communications PerCom, 2005. (to appear)

[19] Halevy, A.Y.: Answering queries using views: A survey. VLDB Journal 10(4), pp. 270-294, 2001.

[20] Hightower, J.; Brumitt, B.; Borriello, G.: The Location Stack: A Layered Model for Location in Ubiquitous Computing. IEEE Workshop on Mobile Computing Systems and Applications, 2002.

[21] Imielinski, T.; Badrinath, B. R.: Mobile wireless computing: Challenges in data management, Communications of the ACM, Vol. 37, No. 10, October 1994.

[22] Jakob, M., Grossmann, M., Hönle, N., Nicklas, D.: DCbot: Exploring the Web as Value-added Service for Location-based Applications. Proceedings of the 21st International Conference on Data Engineering, ICDE 2005, Tokyo, Japan, April 5-8, 2005. (to appear)

[23] Jakob, M., Grossmann, M., Nicklas, D., Mitschang, B.: DCbot: Finding Spatial Information on the Web. Proceedings of the 10th International Conference on Database Systems for Advanced Applications DASFAA, Beijing, China, 2005. (to appear)

[24] Kidd, C., Orr, R., Abowd, G., Atkeson, C., Essa, I., MacIntyre,B., Mynatt, E.,Starner, T., Newstetter, W.: The Aware Home: A Living Laboratory for Ubiquitous Computing Research. Proceedings of 2nd International Workshop on Cooperative Buildings—CoBuild, 1999.

[25] Lehmann, O.; Bauer, M.; Becker, C.; Nicklas, D.: From Home to World—Supporting Context-aware Applications through World Models. Proceedings of the Second IEEE International Conference on Pervasive Computing and Communications PerCom, 2004.

[26] Leonhardi, A., Kubach, U., Rothermel, K.: Virtual Information Towers—A metaphor for intuitive, location-aware information access in a mobile environment. Proceedings of Third International Symposium on Wearable Computers, 1999.

[27] Leonhardi, A., Rothermel, K.: Architecture of a Large scale Location Service. Proceedings of the 22nd International Conference on Distributed Computing Systems (ICDCS 2002), Vienna, Austria, pp. 465-466, 2002.

[28] Levy, A.Y.; Rajaraman, A.; Ordille, J.J.: Querying Heterogeneous Information Sources Using Source Descriptions. Proceedings of 22th International Conference on Very Large Data Bases, VLDB'96, September 3-6, 1996.

[29] Miller, R.J.; Hernández, M.A.; Haas, L.M.; Yan, L.; Ho, C.T.H.; Fagin, R.; Pope, L.: The Clio Project: Managing Heterogeneity. SIGMOD Rec. Vol. 30 Nr. 1, ACM Press, 2001.

[30] Nicklas, Daniela et al: Final Report of Design Workshop. Universität Stuttgart: Center of Excellence 627 (Nexus: Umgebungsmodelle für mobile kontextbezogene Systeme), Fakultätsbericht Nr. 2000/08, 2000.

[31] Nicklas, D., Grossmann, M., Schwarz, T., Volz, S., and Mitschang, B.: A model-based, open architecture for mobile, spatially aware applications. Proceedings of the 7th International Symposium on Spatial and Temporal Databases, SSTD 2001.

[32] Nicklas, D., Hönle, N., Moltenbrey, M., Mitschang, B.: Design and Implementation Issues for Explorative Location-based Applications: the NexusRallye. Cirano Iochpe, Gilberto Camara (Eds.): Proceedings for the VI Brazilian Symposium on GeoInformatics: GeoInfo 2004; November 22-24, 2004.

[33] Nicklas, D.; Mitschang, B.: On building location aware applications using an open platform based on the NEXUS Augmented World Model. In: Software and Systems Modeling, 2004.

[34] Nicklas, D.; Pfisterer, C.; Mitschang, B.: Towards Location-based Games. Loo Wai Sing, Alfred; Wan Hak Man; Wong Wai; Tse Ning, Cyril (Eds.): Proceedings of the International Conference on Applications and Development of Computer Games in the 21st Century: ADCOG 21; Hongkong Special Administrative Region, China, November 22-23, 2001.

[35] Pascoe, J.: The Stick-e Note Architecture: Extending the Interface Beyond the User. Proceedings of the International Conference on Intelligent User Interfaces. Moore, J., Edmonds, E., and Puerta, A. (Eds.), pp. 261-264, 1997.

[36] Patel, S., and Abowd, G.: The ContextCam: Automated Point of Capture Video Annotation. Nigel Davies, Elizabeth Mynatt, and Itiro Siio (Eds.), Proceedings of the 6th International Conference on Ubiquitous Computing (UbiComp), Lecture Notes in Computer Science, Springer, 2004.

[37] Randell, D. A.; Cohn, A. G.: Modelling Topological and Metrical Properties in Physical Processes. Proceedings of the First International Conference on the Principles of Knowledge Representation and Reasoning Processes, 1989.

[38] Salber, D.; Dey, A.; Abowd, G.: The Context Toolkit: Aiding the Development of Context-Enabled Applications. Proceedings of the Conference on Human Factors in Computing Systems CHI, 1999.

[39] Schilit, B.N.; Adams, N.; Want, R.: Context-Aware Computing Applications. IEEE Workshop on Mobile Computing Systems and Applications, 1994.

[40] Schmidt, A.; Takaluoma, A.; Mäntyjärvi, J.: Context-aware telephony over WAP. Personal Technologies 4 (4), pp. 225-229, 2000.

[41] Schwarz, T.; Hönle, N.; Grossmann, M.; Nicklas, D.; Mitschang, B.: Efficient Domain-Specific Information Integration in Nexus. Workshop on Information Integration on the Web, at VLDB 2004. http://cips.eas.asu.edu/iiweb-proceedings.html

[42] Trajcevski, G., Wolfson, O., Zhang, F., Chamberlain, S.: The Geometry of Uncertainty in Moving Objects Databases. Proceedings of the 8th International Conference on Extending Database Technology (EDBT), 2002.

[43] Volz, S., Bofinger, J. M.: Integration of Spatial Data within a Generic Platform for Location-Based Applications. Proceedings of the Joint International Symposium on Geospatial Theory, Processing and Applications, Ottawa, Canada, 2002.

[44] World Geodetic System 1984, http://www.wgs84.com/

[45] Xiong, D.; Sperling, J.: Semiautomated matching for network database integration. ISPRS Journal of Photogrammetry and Remote Sensing 59(1-2), Special Issue on Advanced Techniques for Analysis of Geo-spatial Data, pp. 35-46, August 2004.

An Agent-Based Approach to Correctness in Databases

Herbert Stoyan, Stefan Mandl, Sebastian Schmidt, Mario Vogel

Friedrich-Alexander-Universität Erlangen-Nürnberg, Germany
{hstoyan, stefan.mandl, sebastian.schmidt, mario.vogel}@informatik.uni-erlangen.de

Abstract. When defining the schema of a relational database, integrity constraints are included to describe simple syntactic constraints of correctness that can easily be tested in a centralized way when tuples are inserted, deleted or updated. Complex dependencies may exist between different tuples of a relation. The description of them can be difficult with current formalisms. An example for such an inconsistency is the problem of duplicates, the existence of different tuples describing the same real world entity. Duplicates can occur when one makes typographic or other errors while transferring the representation of a real-world entity to the database. In this paper, we describe a new method to detect dependencies of that kind using continuously active agents that check consistency of a database and propose steps to improve the content of the database.

1 Introduction

Consistency plays an important role in the database literature [2], e.g., it is discussed how to ensure that transactions realize the transition from a consistent database state to another. If a transaction fails, obeying the principle of ACID at least guarantees a roll-back to the last known consistent state. There is consensus to centrally organize control of consistency in the DBMS.

Integrity constraints are classified into static and dynamic constraints. The latter restrict permitted updates (the dead cannot become alive again), the former restrict sets of tuples by constraining singular tuples by relations between some attributes or by claiming relationships between the database relations.

The question is then how to achieve on the basis of integrity constraints the goals of consistency (free of contradictions), data uniqueness, completeness and semantic correctness—under central control. One may move it to the database administrator (or schema designer): He has to formulate the right integrity constrains. At present, typical integrity constraints give restrictions of value sets or enumerate permitted values. A schema designer often can not formulate the right constraints at design time, because usually the complex ones evolve when the database fills.

T. Härder and W. Lehner (Eds.): Data Management (Wedekind Festschrift), LNCS 3551, pp. 37-47, 2005.

Using this, input will be denied if it violates these constraints. This might be a good principle for a database with qualified input personal.

2 The Problem, Preliminaries

Let us define the content of a tuple to be a statement about the existence of an entity with some properties or a statement about relationships between some entities. If so, a database is a set of representations of such statements. The schema of a database specifies the formal structure of the representation of those statements of existence and of relationship. The statements, i.e. the tuples, are constrained by the definition of the database schema. They must be of a certain structure to be acceptable by a relation. Entities of the real world—similar to the statements—cannot be stored, but only represented. Those representations are made up of numbers, enumerations, strings and references. Computers can operate on various ways on numbers and have a contentful comparison facility.

Strings are less flexible: The only comparisons are equality or difference, an operation is the concatenation—both are weakly related to the representation function of the strings. For references the comparison of identity is sufficient. References relate to other statements of existence which can be regarded of being representations of the entity of which the existence is stated.

Generally, databases should contain only (representations of) statements of existence and relationship that are true, although it might be possible to store only false statements for special applications. At a meta-level, false statements are also true: the statement x has been made, but is false. If a database contains only representations of true statements, we call it "absolute correctness".

Because databases usually contain thousands or even millions of such representations (records) striving for absolute correctness is very hard.

Errors have two causes: The representation of a statement relates to a false or a pointless statement. If the original statement was pointless or false already or if the representation failed is unimportant. For our scenario of a community collecting a data set, the latter could be interesting: If several members of the community want to add the same statement the result may be a set of representations: several correct, some false, and some pointless.

Dates of events are typical content of databases. If only exact data are stored, there could be a global consistency check for a date.

Pointless statements like the "X was born 30th February" could be detected this way. But if date approximations or incomplete dates matter the only alternative may be a string representation. If historical dates are to be represented, aberrations from the current Gregorian calendar might obscure the data correctness. So, date descriptions of the "6.Trecember" or "190a|1908" (as an alternative of years) may occur. To exclude such strings from being stored in the date field is much more difficult. The integrity constraints have to enable the definition of a date syntax grammar, which is beyond the current possibilities.

Simple cases of pointless statements due to syntactic errors can be easily detected. More complex ones need extended means of description.

Simply false statements are a hard problem. Imagine the erroneous permutation of two digits in a date leading to the statement that Germany capitulated Word War II on 5/8/1954. In our scenario of the user community it might be found because different users key in the very same event for different dates. By checking for duplicates such aberrations may be detected. If groups of events can be constructed the false date might lead to representations of WWII which last till 1954 and exhibit the error. In other words, if data remains singular and unrelated a wrong tuple might never be detected. If many operations include it and operate on it, it will not survive for long.

Referential integrity can be checked without any knowledge of the domain. In this case, the string comparison might be completely sufficient. If one wants to create a new record but does not know the value of an attribute that must be filled, it makes a difference if this attribute is part of the primary key. Let us assume we want to create a new employee record and we do not know the date of birth that is mandatory for calculating his income. Is it really necessary for the database system to reject this record? One could and probably will work around this problem by specifying a dummy value for that data—no one can hinder users to do so. In such cases a regular completeness test would be a good thing: Reminding the database administrator of problems to be solved. If the name of the employee is not the primary key alone because of common names like Hans Müller, the primary key may consist of name and birth date. Now the dummy value will conflict with the uniqueness constraint of primary keys.

Beside the local correctness of an attribute value (which has impact on the statement's semantics) there are also dependencies between several attributes of a tuple. An employee living in the state of Bavaria cannot have a zip code starting with 0 or 1. There are relations between attributes of a tuple starting with simple functional dependencies (date of birth determines the age of a person—if still alive) to complex constraints. Complex constraints often cannot be described by sets of valid values or pure syntactic constraints. For those complex constraints current database systems hardly offer any solutions.

There are even problems not triggered by a single tuple but by the existence of several interrelated tuples. Imagine a bill of materials which represents products and their parts. All parts which are reachable by chains of part-of relations starting with some module are part of this module. It is an error if a part has a weight which is larger than the weight of the module.

Regarding a relation a database, it has to obey the principle of uniqueness: all stored tuples must be distinct. Checking for uniqueness is easy if the attributes are numbers or of enumeration type. If strings come into account, and considering typing and similar errors, it is obvious that this is a hard and common problem: the duplicate problem. Some easy instances of this problem may be dealt with by strategies that rely on syntactic properties only (as described in [3]). Apart from semantic issues, duplicate entries even affect the database technically: if references between (primary key and foreign key) records are made and distinct tuples exist that should have the same key, the reference must fail. This fact is due to the integrity constraints of primary keys: each primary key must be distinct.

Database research realized this problem early and developed possible solutions. The first one was to define data types and attribute domains in the schema before intra-relational and inter-relational dependencies were addressed. Integrity constrains are permitted to be very complex and include even access to the database itself. These means are not good enough for complex string syntax: syntactic specification of correct attributes is necessary.

If the database is instrumented by flexible formalisms to describe incorrect string attributes, the approach of rejecting incorrect statements is another obstacle. There are many applications, where the quality of the database can be stepwise enhanced if the tuples are existing.

A next important issue is time: A user inserting a new statement does not want to compare all candidates for duplicates. He wants to accomplish his input job as fast as possible. Often, the correctness of tuples cannot be checked in isolation but after a group of inputs has been made. A simple rejection scheme would fail. Afterwards the user will concentrate on correctness issues. Related to our community of input personal it is the database administrator who accepts their input first and later presents the correctness problems. Of course, this strategy can be dangerous: people with the intention to fill the database with messy data could destroy the whole system.

3 The WW-Person Database

WW-Person is a database of historic persons belonging to higher European nobility [4]. It was designed at the chair of Artificial Intelligence to have a testbed for knowledge acquisition and text mining. The database consists of two relations: a Person relation describing people by name, life dates and locations, titles; a Family relation describing families by parents, children and marriage data.

Sources of the database are historic documents (charters, deeds, instruments). These documents often contradict each other. Tuples in the database therefore are not representations of statements about the real age or descent of a person but statements about the content of sources.

Therefore, each person tuple contains a list of used sources. These are easily verifiable by checking the original sources. Failed representation may occur due to typographic errors or mistakes during interpretation, some of the former can be handled by standard means of modern database systems. On the other hand, the sources post statements about historic persons that might be true or false. In this respect, the sources which are lists of such statements can be understood as a kind of database—as far as our discussion of correctness is concerned.

Only a small part of them is really absolutely correct.A good part of the errors can be detected because of the simplicity of the application domain: unknown locations, wrong dates, wrong association of children to parents if all life dates are known. If an error is detected in a source, actualization of the database is not strictly necessary—because of the possible correct mapping between the source and the database. Such a detection may trigger the search for a better source. While syntactic errors in dates are detectable, errors in names of people and places are hard to find. A list of town and village names could be used for the latter problem—the places must have existed and named in some way. Names of people are much harder.

First names for example are differently managed in various European countries. Italian and French first names are fully standardized, while German first names are more freestyle—any spelling might be correct.

Striving for correctness in WW-Person therefore comprises two subtasks: finding errors in the representation of sources and finding errors in the content of sources. Because the sources are in average reliable we use the following heuristics: the sources are assumed to be correct statements about the historic world. All possible errors are assigned to the database. Only in special cases the sources are responsible.

A difficulty makes it impossible to use enumeration types and special types for dates: In many cases the sources report assumptions or guesses, especially for dates. Therefore, the date description language has to cover vague and incomplete dates: dates with unknown parts (days, month or years), alternatives and/or intervals.

3.1 Incorrect Attribute Values

Errors of this kind are local erroneous within a tuple. These errors can be further broken down:

1. An attribute value can be syntactic erroneous.
2. An attribute value is not blatantly syntactic erroneous, but extremely unusual
3. An attribute value is neither syntactic erroneous nor unusual, but nevertheless wrong (often errors of this kind can never be corrected).

Example:

Class	synt. erroneous	unusual	erroneous concerning content
Date:	Munich	30.2.1897 or 12.12.2006	1.4.1900 (instead of 1.5.1900)
First Name	FvP	Müller	Hans (instead of Heinrich)
Name:	Scordi>	Sqrzt	Meier (instead of Müller)
Ort:	2.3.1950	plane crash	Munich (instead of Stuttgart)
Relationship	@Fga1aa		@Fga1aa@ statt @Fga1ab@

3.2 Intra-relational Incorrectness

Errors of this kind are inconsistent combinations of attribute values within a tuple. There may be dependencies between attribute values of a tuple that can result in errors, e.g., the date of birth of a person must always be before the date of death (1.1.1900 as birthday and 31.12.1800 as date of death).

3.3 Inter-relational Incorrectness

The third kind of errors may occur when considering different tuples of one or more relations. These can be further broken down into:

1. Inconsistent redundancy: The date of marriage can differ when it is stored for both persons (e.g., if multiple documents describe the same marriage differently).
2. Inheritance of properties: The date of birth of children must be before the date of death of their mother (and before arbitrary ancestors but the father).
3. Cyclic relationships: Descendants of an individual are also its ancestors. Finding errors in such cycles is hard, because the error must not necessarily be found in the record that rises the cycle. Any record which is part of the cycle can be erroneous.
4. Duplicates: Duplicates are records of the database that describe the same individual of the real world. Typically they occur when names are differently written in sources about the same person. Of course, there must only be one record for each person. Each duplicate has its own net of ancestors and descendants. Only when merging the different nets, the correct relationships arise. An example of a duplicate is:

Name:	Clementia de Montfaucon	Clementia v.Montfaucon
Gender:	f	f
Death:	after 1160	
Marriage:		before 1162

5. Problems of context: Because of the context of an individual (its relationships) some pieces of data seem questionable. In a succession of titles of nobility one can conclude the title of descendants by analyzing the titles of ancestors (by also considering marriages). If those deducted titles are absent, an error is probable.

4 Means of Databases: Constraints and Triggers

Current databases offer two facilities to work for correctness: constraints and triggers. Whereas the first is directly introduced for this purpose, the latter is a general facility which can be used for our purpose [1].

4.1 Constraints

The database schema containing definitions of tables and their relationships defines valid states of the data base. Attributes are constrained by their data types. Because data types do not constrain attribute values enough, the SQL standard defines further restrictions.

These restrictions scope columns, rows and relations. They are restrictions which tuples have to fulfill to be admissible tuples of a relation.

Constraints on tables are defined when creating the table. Providing a boolean expression as integrity constraint (CHECK clause) ensures that only tuples will be inserted or updated that evaluate this expression to true. Adding constraints to a table after table creation is possible only when all records of that table are compliant with the constraint.

The dynamic constraints are not very interesting for WW-Person. There are no fixed rules for updating. Let us consider an example with tables Person (persid, firstname, ..., birthdate, deathdate, parents, family) and Family (famid, father, mother, child). The attributes parents and family are foreign keys for the primary key famid and refer to the parent and the own family, respectively. If we assume that the Person relation contains 4-digit integers for years, a constraint for the birthdate–deathdate relationship could be:

```
birthdate numeric(4) check (birthdate < (
    select deathdate
    from Family f, Person p
    where Person.parents = f.famid
        and f.mother = p.persid)).
```

4.2 Triggers

Triggers are functions which react on events and execute some action sequence. Databases implementing triggers are called Active Databases [6]. The definition of a trigger consist of three parts:

The first part defines the event the trigger will be activated (before insert, after update, ...), the second part defines the condition that must be met for the trigger to execute the action described by the third part. For WW-Person, only AFTER-INSERT triggers are interesting. This would enable the output of warnings, if some conspicuous data are input. French first names, for example, could be compared with entries in a pre-compiled list of common names (Frenchnames). If an unknown name is detected, a warning is issued.

```
create trigger namecheck
after insert on Person
for each row
when firstname is not null and not exists
    (select * from Frenchnames
     where entry = firstname)
begin atomic
    MailNotaCommonName(firstname);
end
```

4.3 Problems with Constraints and Triggers

Main problem of both means from the viewpoint of WW-Person is the weak condition syntax of SQL. Strings can be equal or different. This is fine for standardized first names but very cumbersome for checking rules of a grammar (for vague dates).

Constraints will hinder a new tuple to be inserted if it does not satisfy the rules. BEFORE-INSERT triggers could be used to implement the same behavior. AFTER-INSERT triggers are more acceptable if the new tuple has some information content. Dismissal of tuples that do not conform with the highest quality scheme is not always the best strategy.

Triggers and constraints are activated on pre-defined events. If such an event does not occur, the trigger does not become active. If warnings for conspicuous tuples are issued remedy may be forgotten. A regularly activated tuple scanner would be an important additional feature. This is something which is similar to our agents.

5 An Agent-Based Approach

When concerned with correctness of databases, we suggest to use software agents acting in concert with standard database mechanisms.

Our main idea is to *gradually improve* possibly incorrect data in the database by long-running processes as it is unlikely that general correctness problems in databases can be solved by simple and short-running procedures.

The previous section mentions the fact that expert domain knowledge is inevitable for handling complex correctness problems. This kind of knowledge may not be accessible when developing the schema of a database and the expert knowledge may not be easy to formalize in unambiguous simple rules. Even when candidates for possibly incorrect records are identified by a program, the ultimate decision has often to be made by a human.

Section 3.3 presented the problem of duplicates that, while it is easy to describe, is impossible to solve without a large amount of domain knowledge.

To bring that domain knowledge into the system, we use software agents. According to [7], *software agents* have the following properties:

- *reactivity*: agents sense their environment and the changes in the environment and react according to their goals. In the *Person* database there are three different kinds of change: 1) new records are added to the database, 2) new agents with new services are added or outdated agents are removed, and 3) the user interacts with the system.
- *pro-activeness*: agents have goals and act in order to realize them without being called by others. In our example, agents only have a few goals and most agents wait for task assignments from other agents. When the complexity of our application rises, the property of pro-activeness will gain more importance for us.
- *social ability*: agents communicate with agents and users.

When approaching problems of correctness in WW-Person, agents offer all the possibilities of triggers and constraints. But agents are even more powerful:

- Agents query and use services of other agents explicitly, while triggers can only interact implicitly.
- Agents may be added to or removed from the running system at any time. As long as a certain critical service is offered by at least one agent, the system remains working. Even if such a crucial service is not available for some time, as soon as it is brought back (for example after a short debugging session), the whole system continues to operate. This property is crucial for the design goal of a gradually improving system.
- Agents do not have to be passive. When an important data entry is found, it does not have to wait until asked for its contribution. Instead, it may very well present its important result without being queried explicitly.
- For very large data corpuses with tangled interdependencies, it is better to have agents that work in the background and do not interfere with the user too much. How and why agents interact with the user is easy to customize.
- There may be decisions that can only be made when having specific data. When this data is not accessible in the present environment, mobile agents may migrate to the place of the data that they need to make their decision.

Additionally, we claim that agents should not be too powerful. When a new kind of specification for uncertainty in dates has been observed, it should be possible to make it available to the system by starting a new agent. When agents are too large and powerful, we would need a specialized protocol to update those. Therefore, we suggest that an agent should be expert for only one task.

In contrast to classic function calls, tasks in multi-agent systems are assigned dynamically. For this purpose, there exists a number of established protocols (see [5]). Our approach uses a slightly modified version of the *Contract Net Protocol*. Whenever an agent has produced some result, it expects to receive an evaluation of that result. When that agent was using the results of other agents to do so and the evaluation was positive, then the agent's trust into its collaborators is increasing, otherwise it is decreasing. With this sort of "learning by selection", the system provides a certain robustness against misbehaving agents, which—again—contributes to the goal of gradual improvement.

The actual source of improved agents is not predefined. The expert user is free to extend the system to his needs. Alternatively, agents may provide powerful configuration possibilities or a visual programming language could be used. Employing data mining technology or evolutionary algorithms to create new agents is an interesting option. We developed an agent to translate date specifications with uncertainties into a more accessible form. If the agent encounters a date specification that is not covered by its internal transformation rules, it asks the user to enter a regular expression for that date.

6 Prototypical Implementation

The current implementation of the ideas outlined above is developed using the JADE Agent Platform which in turn is implemented in Java.

According to JADE's pragmatics, we use the provided means of services and facilitators. Each agent registers itself for the services it provides. When an agent needs a service, it queries the facilitator for the agents providing this service. This generalization of standard procedure call allows the presence of multiple (different) implementations of a service at the same time. We want those service implementations that provide better results for their users (which by transitivity is also the human user) to dominate other implementations.

Service implementations that are of no use to others will silently fade away when the system is running for a long time.

- ***UserAgent:*** This agent provides the user interface. It presents candidate duplicates to the user and feeds back the user's response (identical/not identical/don't know) to the agents that delivered the candidate.
- ***TupleProvider:*** Abstract agent providing the common functionality of all agents implementing the tuple-provider service. Some of these agents cluster the person records according to different strategies like name equality or nation equality. Upon request, they provide pairs of person records. Each component record of such a pair is from the same cluster. The use of TupleProvider agents allows for the easy integration of different data pre-processing strategies at the same time. Additionally, new TupleProvider agents with different strategies can be started at any time while the system is running.
- ***NameCompare***: Abstract agent for comparing person names (name-compare service). There exist several specializations that use specific comparison strategies; each of them is offering the name-compare service.
- ***DateCompare***: Abstract agent for comparing dates (date of birth and death, marriage). There exists different implementations each using a different strategy. There even is an interactive implementation that asks the user to provide a regular expression that maps parts of an unclassified date string to the day, month, and year of a date structure.
- ***LocationCompare***: An abstract agent that provides the common functionality for all agents implementing the place-compare service. This agents currently do only string comparison. In the future, we would like to see PlaceCompare-agents that use large tables of known places. There is assumed to be a strong intra-relationship to the date fields of a given person record, as places might have changed their names in the course of time.
- ***PersonCompare:*** This agent and its specializations use the services provided by other agents to decide if two person records represent the same person. They use different values to weight the results provided by the more specific compare agents. Also, based on the feedback they receive for the result they produce, they propagate feed-

back to the agents they used to create the result. Additionally, they build up a trust-table that shows the percentage of correct predictions of used agents.

- ***DuplicateFinder:*** Agents of this kind manage the quest for finding duplicate records. They ruse the services of TupleProvider and PersonCompare agents and communicate their results to UserAgent instances.

7 Conclusion

We described the problem of correctness of tuples in databases. Correctness is not a concept that can be achieved by pure syntactic constraints. Whether or not tuples are correct can only be decided by domain experts. The knowledge they use is often not expressible by deterministic rules, e.g., the problem of finding duplicates in the database of historical persons. There are indications for a tuple to be a duplicate, whether or not those indications hold can only be decided by an expert. Standard means of databases do not offer any possibility to express such requirements. Therefore, we propose software agents to be a centralized knowledge store that can pro-actively interact with a domain expert to gradually improve the content of the database. They are considered as a disciplined way to bring even more application logic right into databases.

References

[1] Ceri, S., Cochrane, R., Widom, J.: *Practical Applications of Triggers and Constraints: Successes and Lingering Issues*. Proceedings of the 26th VLDB Conference, Egypt, 254-262, 2000

[2] Grefen, P.W.P.J., Apers, P.M.G.: *Integrity control in relational database system: an overview.* Data and Knowledge Engineering 10(2):187-223, 1993

[3] Monge, A., Elkan, C.: *An Efficient Domain-Independent Algorithm for Detecting Approximately Duplicate Database Records*, Proc. of the Workshop on Research Issues on Data Mining and Knowledge Discovery, Tucson, Arizona, 1997

[4] Stoyan, H.: *Das Projekt WW-Person*. Archiv für Familiengeschichtsforschung, Vol.1, No.1, 1997

[5] Weiss, G. (Hrsg): *Multiagent Systems*. The MIT Press, 1999

[6] Widom, J.: *The Starburst Active Database Rule System*. IEEE Transactions on Knowledge and Data Engineering 8(4):583-595, 1996

[7] Wooldridge, M., Jennings, N.R.: *Intelligent agents: Theory and practice*. The Knowledge Engineering Review 10(2):115-152, 1995

Part II Infrastructural Services

Thirty Years of Server Technology — From Transaction Processing to Web Services

Klaus Meyer-Wegener

Friedrich-Alexander-University of Erlangen-Nuremberg, Germany
kmw@informatik.uni-erlangen.de

Abstract. Server technology started with transaction-processing systems in the sixties. Database Management Systems (DBMS) soon adopted mechanism like multi-process and multi-threading. In distributed systems, the remote procedure call also needed process structures at the server side. The same is true for file servers, object servers (CORBA), Web servers, application servers, EJB containers, and Web Services. All these systems support a request-response behavior, sometimes enhanced with a session concept. They are facing thousands of requests per second and must manage thousands of session contexts at the same time. While programming the applications that run on the servers and actually process the requests should be as simple as possible, efficiency must still be very high. So a general programming environment should be defined that is easy to use and, on the other hand, allows for the efficient execution of thousands of program instances in parallel. This contribution will identify mechanisms that have been developed in the context of transaction processing and database management. It will then generalize them to server processing of any kind. This includes program structures, context management, multi-tasking and multi-threading, process structures, program management, naming, and transactions. The driving force behind the discussion is to avoid the re-invention of the wheel that far too often occurs in computer science, mostly in ignorance of older and presumably outdated systems.

1 Introduction

Servers are ubiquitous today, and they can be quite small. The services they offer span from remote procedure calls, HTTP requests, and application invocations to Web services. New kinds of server software are being developed, often without knowing that the history goes back into the sixties, when transaction-processing systems were created for the first time. Who among the server implementers of today has ever heard of CICS, CINCOM, DATACOM/DC, UTM, and all the other systems from that time? Most of

T. Härder and W. Lehner (Eds.): Data Management (Wedekind Festschrift), LNCS 3551, pp. 51-65, 2005.

them have not, and the consequence is a repeated re-invention of the wheel. CICS is still in operation today, but it has long been restricted to the domain of IBM mainframe computers. These computers are not very well known among the developers of today. In fact, some of them even refuse to learn about these systems. For them, the world of computing is limited to Windows and Linux.

The purpose of this contribution is to identify the common techniques of all these systems and to describe them in a neutral terminology. This should enable developers of server software to pick from a well-established set of techniques. It also means to identify the "invariants" needed in any kind of server—irrespective of the plethora of names. It has been very hard to find names that are not occupied yet by any of the various servers, and it has not always been successful. In these cases, however, the different meaning is stated explicitly.

2 Kinds of Servers

Transaction-processing systems, also called *online transaction-processing* ("OLTP") systems, are the oldest class of server systems, going back into the sixties. Typically, they were airline reservation systems like the TWA reservation system [12] or banking systems [5]. The first system to mention here is Sabre. The Brainy Encyclopedia describes it as follows: "Sabre (Semi-Automated Booking and Reservation Environment) was the world's first online airline reservations system. Developed through the joint efforts of IBM and American Airlines, it first went online in the fall of 1962, running on an IBM 7090 computer. After going through a series of system upgrades, including a relocation from Westchester County, NY to Tulsa, OK, the system remains operational today (2003) and was the prototype for virtually every mainframe-based online system that followed. Sabre was based on real-time computing advances made by the US Air Force in the development of their SAGE radar-coordination and target tracking system."[1]

The notion of "transaction" here is not used in the sense of databases yet, but simply names a processing step. While in the first approach systems were limited to single-step transactions, they very soon progressed to multi-step transactions. Single-step transactions are much easier—not surprisingly, Web servers also started with them before cookies and other mechanisms were introduced. No context needs to be managed. If information from the last transaction was needed in the next, it had to be re-entered by the user—the trick of including it invisibly in the next input message has been used very early in these systems and is by no means an invention of Web-site developers.

The middleware that has been introduced for this is called a *transaction-processing monitor*, or TP monitor for short [3, 8, 9]. These systems have rarely been investigated in the scientific community, but they have—and still are—used extensively in commer-

1. http://www.brainyencyclopedia.com/encyclopedia/s/sa/sabre_airline_reservations_system.html

cial applications. The market leader is IBM's Customer Information Control System (CICS) [10, 16], but many others have been built.

In the development of operating systems or, more specifically, distributed systems, *file servers* made an important contribution. Here, a file system on one network node can be made accessible to other network nodes, so that they can "mount" it and afterwards use is as if it were a local file system. Hence, the file server has to handle all the file operations, i.e., open, close, read, write, etc. It also has to synchronize accesses to the files, since now not only local processes compete for the files, but also other nodes. The most prominent software for file servers is Sun Microsystem's Network File System (NFS) [6]. In fact, it is rather a collection of protocols to be used by a client system when accessing files on a server. There are many different implementations on a variety of platforms. File structures and operations are much like UNIX. Up to version 3, NFS has been stateless, so the server did not maintain any state for its clients. This has been changed in version 4 to ease synchronization and fault tolerance. Another example is the Andrew File System [7] and its descendant Coda [20]. The project's Web page states very concisely: "Coda is an advanced networked file system. It has been developed at CMU since 1987 by the systems group of M. Satyanarayanan in the SCS department."[2] The main difference from NFS is that very large numbers of workstations may also be included with their files, and high availability is an explicit goal leading to caching schemes that allow for disconnected operations.

RPC servers are even more elementary than file servers (in fact, NFS uses RPC in its definition). A remote procedure call (RPC) serves the purpose to execute any kind of subroutine (procedure) on a different network node. Instead of sending a message and receiving a response, this is bundled in one operation which looks exactly like a local procedure call. So for the client it is transparent whether the procedure is locally available or on another machine. This significantly eases program development and also allows for later optimizations, e.g., by migrating local procedures that turned out to be a bottleneck to a stronger machine. The RPC is the prime mechanism of the so-called "client-server operation." It is stateless, i.e., once a procedure has been executed, the server forgets about the client—which does not mean that the effects of the procedure (e.g., entries in a database) are also forgotten, but these are out of the scope of the RPC mechanism.

Database servers may also be viewed as RPC servers, with the processing of a query as the procedure. However, the specific nature of database processing has led to more specific protocols and different server implementations. The notion of client-server databases has been introduced for sending operations of the data manipulation language (DML) to a remote server. The most important DML today is SQL. Sybase was the first manufacturer of a database management system who consequently defined the architecture based on client-server operation. The transaction defines the context of the DML calls issued by the clients, so the server cannot be stateless. The high performance requirements have led to an early use of multi-process configurations and multi-tasking in database servers.

---

2. http://www.coda.cs.cmu.edu/index.html

Another packaging of RPC servers has been introduced by *Object servers*. Here the remote operations are grouped into interfaces of remote objects. This follows the trend towards object-oriented programming and offers the same paradigm in the distributed setting. The dominant frameworks in this domain are CORBA and DCOM [19]. The operations—which now might be called methods—are still stateless. The server implementation is much like that of an RPC server.

The explosive dissemination of the World-wide Web (WWW) created a completely new type of server with outstanding importance: the *Web server* [23]. It communicates with its clients via the Hypertext Transfer Protocol (HTTP),which is based on TCP, and which has only a few operations (or message types). The most important is the GET operation that fetches a document from the server. Documents were initially coded in the Hypertext Markup Language (HTML), an application of SGML. By now, they can include much more, even executable code. At the server side, documents used to be just files, but now can be much more, too. Often, they are generated dynamically from various sources, including databases. In general, any application can be executed on the server, and the output can then be wrapped with HTML to form a document. HTTP has been designed as a stateless protocol. This has made it simple, but soon became a problem, because more and more applications were moved to the WWW, many of which needed a sequence of requests and responses. Cookies and other mechanisms have been introduced to cope with this problem. Server implementation has undergone many changes. The first approach to call applications, the Common Gateway Interface (CGI), was rather primitive and created a new process for each request. As this became a bottleneck very soon, many other mechanisms have been introduced, e.g., FastCGI and Servlets. Performance is more critical here because there may be billions of users. So there is an ongoing pressure to increase throughput.

When using Web servers with calls to applications in the back, HTTP turned out to be not very suitable. As an alternative, the Web server can be used only to locate the application. Once it is identified, it establishes its own connection with the client, which is then much faster and more appropriate. The server that hosts the applications next to a Web server has been named *Application server*. It has much in common with the older OLTP servers, but many developers did not know about the latter. It can also be an RPC server or Object server.

One of the concepts for application servers received particular attention, namely Enterprise JavaBeans (EJB) [17]. The reason may be twofold: First, the programming language Java is very popular, and second, a concept for component software has been introduced with it. The strong connection with Java is also one of the problems of this approach, because the systems built are language-dependent (which is not the case with the major competitor, Microsoft's .NET). As the Java counterpart to the RPC, Remote Method Invocation (RMI) is used. The server is visible to the application developer in form of the EJB container. Its implementation is still under careful investigation. One of the current dominant systems here is JBoss. The challenge is again to handle a large number of requests simultaneously, even to the same operation of a single Java class. Some implementations, e.g., IBM's Web Sphere, internally used the well-established techniques of their TP monitor, CICS.

The most recent development for server access is named *Web Services* [1, 24]. It uses the ubiquitous infrastructure of the WWW to link applications, namely as a framework for component software. To achieve this, a set of conventions and interfaces is defined so that any application can offer services—potentially to anybody in the WWW. To call the service, SOAP (originally called Simple Object Access Protocol, but now just used as a name, no longer an acronym) is used, which is essentially an RPC packaged in XML. The Web Services Description Language (WSDL) allows to describe the interfaces that must be used to access the services in a uniform way. Directory services like UDDI help to find the proper service for a given task. Again, a server is needed to handle the calls to a Web service—with many administrative tasks around it, and with a potentially very large number of clients. This means a substantial difficulty with respect to authentification and, based on it, authorization. Further standards are needed here, e.g. the RosettaNet Implementation Framework (RNIF) [1]. Encryption must be available. It is covered by WS-Security, an extension to SOAP, and again by RNIF. WS-Security defines a SOAP header block (called "Security") which can carry a signature. It also indicates how the Security block must be processed. The goal is to offer end-to-end security where only parts of the SOAP messages are encrypted. And finally transactions (in the more specific meaning used with databases; see Sect. 5.5 below) are a challenge because of the heterogeneity of the participants. Since processes that use Web Services may take much longer time than usual database applications, the well-known ACID principle [15] is no longer suitable for them. The WS-Transaction protocols [1] can be used here. They are defined on top of WS-Coordination, a set of protocols to control sequences of service invocations in a particular order. WS-Transaction includes protocols that enable all participating Web services to determine if any of them has failed. Long-running activities are treated as Sagas, a well-known concept. Each Web service is then executed as an ACID transaction, and if the whole activity fails, compensation is executed. That means that for each participating Web service, a compensation service must be defined. The long-running sagas are called "business activities," while the standard ACID transactions—which are also available in WS-Transaction—are called "atomic transactions." Implementations of servers employ the available techniques and base systems, e.g., TP monitors. Because this concepts is the youngest, the optimization of servers is just beginning.

And certainly there are more servers with other tasks. It is not intended here to be complete. The list is just to give an idea of how important a really elaborate server design and implementation is today.

3 A General Server Concept

The basic construct for any kind of server is the triplet of Request—Processing (Computation)—Response (Result). As we have seen in the last section, many different protocols can be used for that: RPC, HTTP, RMI, and others. The communication between client and server can be connection-oriented (e.g., TCP) or connection-less (UDP). This makes a difference for fault tolerance, but not for the elementary processing of requests by the server.

There is one important additional concept: that of a “session.” It is used when subsequent requests from the same client have some dependencies. The server then must maintain and use a so-called context. Processing a request terminates in either of two different modes: The session also terminates, or the session continues with the next request, and hence an explicitly named context must be preserved. This concepts is requested by many applications, but not all of the servers mentioned support it. However, a general server concept must include it as well.

4 The Task

Given the general server concept including sessions, the task is now to identify the techniques that make such a server efficient. It should be streamlined to handle thousands of requests per second [2, 11], in the WWW environment maybe even millions. This can lead to the management of thousands of contexts for the sessions.

The main decision is on the number of operating-system processes to be engaged by the server. At one end, the whole server can run as just a single process. At the other, a new process could be created for each incoming request (e.g., CGI). Both has actually been used in early implementations, but neither of the two is optimal, as it soon turned out. To find the right number and also the right task for each of the processes, one has to know quite well the overhead involved in the management of processes and in the process switch that occurs when one process enters a wait state.

On the other hand, programming the applications should be as simple as possible. Obviously, there is a trade-off: The need for efficiency tends to make programming more complex by adding constructs that have nothing to do with the application itself, but just increase the efficiency (e.g., partitioning the application so it can run in separate processes). But this slows down the development of the software and thus creates large costs in a different setting.

Fortunately, a rather early idea allows to avoid this conflict here—as in so many other areas of computer science: separate and generalize mechanisms that are only invented for performance reasons. A proper interface is defined for application developers, and they just call some subroutines to care for efficiency. Today, the term “middleware” is used for such libraries of subroutines. Examples are

- transaction-processing monitors (TPM’s),
- EJB Containers,
- dispatchers,
- …

Using them, the programmer is allowed to concentrate on the prime task of the application, that is,

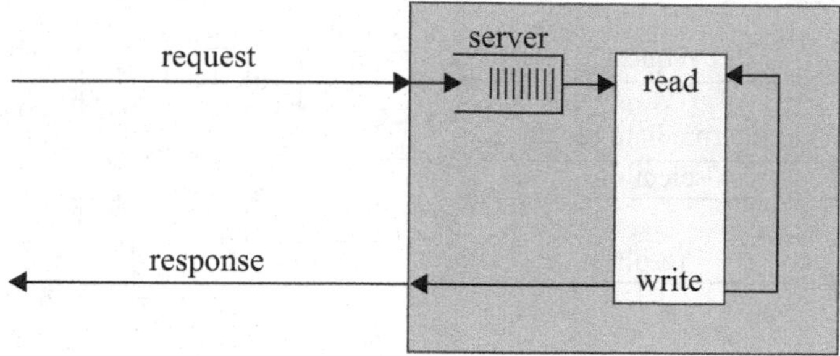

Fig. 1 Elementary Server Operation

- accept a request,
- process it, and
- send back a response containing the result.

Features and properties needed for efficiency but distracting from that prime task can be some of the following:

- The context is treated different from other variables.
- Several cooperating programs must be written to perform a single processing step.
- The multiple parallel execution of the program must be considered and controlled (e.g., by creating and managing "threads").
- Access to shared files must explicitly be synchronized.

The goal, however, must be to free the programmer from all that. This is possible, if the middleware is capable of handling it. Proper interfaces need to be developed.

5 Server Implementation

This section shows the creation of such a middleware step by step. How are programs executed by the server? The simplest solution is shown in Fig. 1. Here, the server maintains the input queue of incoming requests. Each request identifies the program needed to process it. This is done by a function name also called the "transaction code," or TAC for short. The server maps these names to programs. Program management is discussed in more detail in a subsequent section. Here it is important to note that the programmer is liberated from all the issues of processing many requests at the same time. Each program processes exactly one request and simply terminates when this is done. In some systems, the program must include a main loop that goes back to the beginning and then waits for the next input. This is indicated by the arrow to the right of the program in Fig. 1. Such an approach is not optimal, however, because the program then blocks resources while waiting for the next request. It is more efficient to actually terminate the program and restart it only when the next request arrives. The difference is that the server

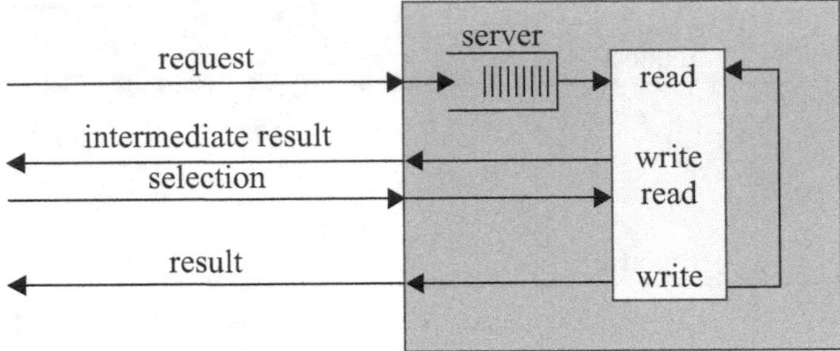

Fig. 2 Server Operation with Session

now controls the resources. For instance, the program may remain in memory if enough space is available, so restart will be quick. But no resources are blocked in case that no request of this kind is present in the input queue and other programs must be executed.

When interaction with a user and thus a context are needed, the situation becomes slightly more complex as shown in Fig. 2. A new operation is used here, namely "write-read" (in some systems called "tandem-I/O"), which presents the intermediate result and continues only when the user-based selection is received. This reflects the typical situation that some input from the user is required before processing can go on.

The standard example where a session and consequently also a context are needed is a request for a seat in a theatre or in an airplane. The intermediate result is then the list of seats that are still available (maybe even a graphical display of them). The user selects one or more seats, and the reservation can be completed.

This is certainly the simplest form of programming. The program processes one request at a time, and the context is maintained in the program itself in terms of local variables. Unfortunately, this turns out to be very inefficient. Waiting times are not used, and they are significant. A specific critical one involves the user, because "the human is in the loop": Once the intermediate result is displayed, seconds or even minutes may pass until the selection is finally received.

Furthermore, other waiting times are hidden in the processing that takes place between "read" and "write." When an input/output operation is executed by the program or more general, when any kind of other server is called, the program again waits. This might not be as long as in the case of user interaction, but still goes in the order of milliseconds. The operating system certainly switches to another process, but the server is deactivated.

The first improvement here leads to the separation of context from the other variables used by the program and to splitting the program into two sections. It is done to reduce the utilization of resources while waiting for the user's response. As shown in Fig. 3, the program now terminates together with sending the intermediate result. This requires a new operation that might be called "write-exit" (to avoid a reference to any particular system). The operation also identifies the program (part) to be executed when the selection arrives. This second program is written to perform the second step of the

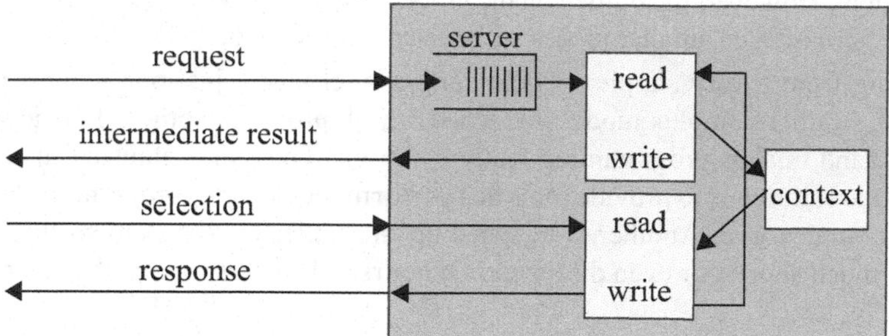

Fig. 3 Separation of Program Parts and Session

session and thus accepts the context from the server software before reading the selection message.

Obviously, programming becomes more complex now. Instead of writing a single program that has everything right at hand in its code, the programmer now has to write two programs with some dependencies. They must perform a common task, and they must agree on the structure of the context. If the session has more than two steps, even more programs must be coordinated.

The second improvement addresses the internal waiting times that arise from input/output or other server calls made by the programs. Here, *multi-tasking* is enabled to proceed with other sessions while one session is waiting. Fig. 4 sketches how the server operates in this case. It must be informed of the fact that one program enters a waiting state, which could again be done via the "write-exit" operation. The server would then pick the next request from its input queue, identify the program to be executed for that and start it. Assuming that this second program later also enters a waiting state and the response for the first program has arrived in the meantime, the server would return to the first session and would start the program that has been identified to it in the previous "write-exit." Because all waiting times are now exploited to proceed with the processing of other requests, this approach is highly efficient and promises significant increase

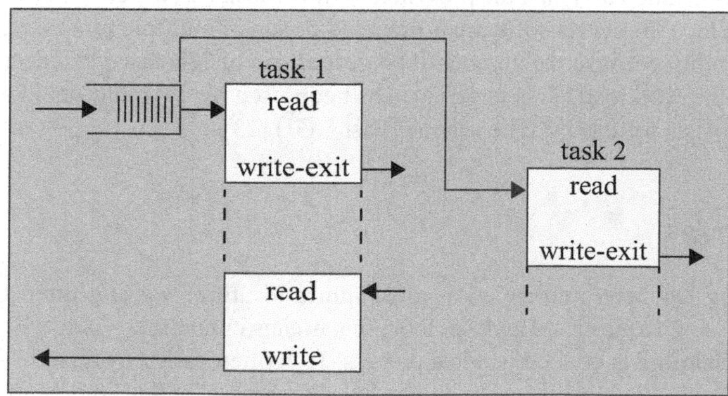

Fig. 4 Separation of Program Parts and Session

in throughput. However, the burden on the programmer is heavy, because again the programs are split in even smaller pieces with many interdependencies.

Starting from a very simple programming model where just one request must be processed, a rather complex model is reached which promises some efficiency but, on the other hand, makes programming really complex. This is not unusual in computer science. One solution is to provide tools that perform the mapping from the simple model to the complex one. Another is to speed up the underlying system so that waiting times are much shorter or even disappear. Of course, the users involved cannot be "accelerated."

5.1 Process Structures

In all the figures used so far, the server has been depicted as a single rectangle. This suggests that it runs as a *single process* of the operating systems, which can in fact be the case. Such an approach makes the development of the server software easier, because it runs as a single program. On the other hand, the structure of this program becomes very complex, because it handles the multi-tasking internally, manages all the contexts, identifies and starts the application programs, etc. Also, this server must run with a very high priority—if it is preempted by the operating system for any reason (page fault, end of time slice), the whole server processing stops.

For these reasons, concepts of using more than one process for the server appeared very soon. As an extreme, a new process could be created for each request, which would make the server software surrounding an application program very small. CGI is an example of this. However, the overhead created by the large number of processes and the dynamics of creating and destroying them is prohibitive. The compromise lies in using a few processes that share the work, in the order of tens to hundreds. This allows to run only one application program in each process, because their waiting times can be used to switch to other processes of the same server. Hence, the server software in such a process remains simple. However, some complexity must be added to transfer contexts among these processes, because the next step of the session can be executed by another process. This is much less than the provision of multi-tasking (which could still be used internally). Once the server software is prepared to run in multiple processes, it has inherent scalability because the number of processes can be increased and decreased depending on the workload. This technique has been used by TP monitors like IMS/DC and UTM [14] as well as by Web servers (Fast CGI) [23].

5.2 Threads

Multi-tasking has been introduced as a technique to utilize waiting times that occur while processing requests. At a closer look, this means in fact that a new unit of execution and scheduling is created inside a process. It is often called a "thread." Other notions are "second-level process" or "light-weight process." Here, the name "task" is used (as in multi-tasking), because it is shorter and also allows to use "thread" for something else—see next subsection.

The concept of a task within a process only makes sense, if its management is much simpler than that of a process. While a process switch usually requires the execution of some 10,000 machine instructions, a task switch must be in the order of a few hundreds. Also, the creation and destruction of tasks typically is much easier and thus much faster than the creation and destruction of processes. As in the case of processes, one could create a pool of tasks to be reused, but, on the other hand, dynamic creation and destruction adapts much better to the actual workload.

In either case, a second-level, or secondary, scheduling takes place in the server process. It can be organized by the server software, but in some cases a similar service is also offered by the operating system itself (MVS [22], Unix, Windows [21]). However, TP monitors are often doing it themselves, because they are to run under many operating systems and thus cannot assume that the service is available. The same is true for many database management systems. In these cases, I/O and external server calls can be intercepted and used to stay in control with other tasks. Page fault and end of time slice, however, deactivate the whole process and cannot be handled. If the operating system offers multi-tasking, it might switch to another task even in the case of a page fault. End of time slice stops the process in either case.

Employing several processes creates the need for inter-process communication, e.g., for the exchange of contexts. Messages are too slow or too expensive for this, so shared memory should be used. The scheduling at two levels that has just been described can also be used to organize the access synchronization to this memory. In some systems, other kinds of data are also placed in the shared memory. As a consequence, more complex ways of synchronization must be provided.

5.3 Program Management

At the beginning of this section, we have pointed out that a programmer only has to deal with the processing of a single request. All servers, however, must cope with a large number of requests being issued at the same time. So many of the tasks and processes involved in the request processing can be forced to execute the same program. The straightforward solution is to give each task its own copy of the program. This would work, but it can lead to an enormous consumption of memory. Even if virtual memory was large enough to handle it in principle, page swapping managed by the operating system would be a significant performance threat.

The most attractive solution seems to be using a single copy of each program. Then each task executing this program creates a "thread" through the code (here the notion fits better). This "multi-threading" is not the same as multi-tasking: If each task receives its own copy of the code, then there is no multi-threading.

Multi-threading, however, has some important prerequisites: Not any kind of code can be used for it. All local variables must be moved to the context which is managed for each task separately. Otherwise, the tasks would interfere in an unpredictable way.

Many compilers support this by creating separate data and code segments from a source. Hence, the code becomes read-only and thus "reentrant." This should be the standard today; it was a different situation in the earlier times of server implementation.

5.4 Naming

Once server structures in terms of processes and tasks have been defined and created in a system, they must be made accessible for potential users. This creates a need for the naming of servers. In general, a many-to-many relationship among servers and network nodes can be assumed. On each node, several servers can be running which must be distinguished by names. Vice versa, a server (from the user's point of view) can be running on more than one node. This introduces the concept of *server class*, which appears to be a single server from the client's point of view, but in fact consist of several servers on different nodes. The meaning here is that these nodes are interchangeable; either of them can be used to process a request. A distribution or load balancing mechanism is needed to assign a particular server to an incoming request. A URL is a common means to address nodes and servers in the age of the Web, but it cannot cope with server classes. Here, a URI would be more appropriate.

Each server offers many services (or operations). Each request identifies exactly one of these and provides it with a set of parameters. It does not make sense to have the identical service on several servers, so a one-to-many relationship is assumed between servers and operations.

Programs should be completely invisible for the users, but the programmers have to design them for the handling of requests. As has been shown in the preceding subsections, there are good reasons to allow the cooperation of more than one programs in the handling of an individual request. It is definitely a burden for the programmer to be forced to create many small fragments of a program. This can at least partially be turned into a virtue, if some of these fragments can be re-used in the processing of other requests. This is not very unlikely. Assuming that in the booking of a theatre seat the user says that he or she is not yet registered. Then the registration process—usually a separate operation—is invoked as part of the booking process.

Many naming services and systems are available today. As examples, take X.500, LDAP, Jini, UDDI, etc.

5.5 Transactions

All these systems have to cope with many kinds of errors and failures. Here, it is important to hide as much as possible from the clients and to always be in an identifiable state. The processing of a request may involve many internal steps and even other subsystems. For the client, however, it appears to be an atomic step. It should be protected from any details of processing (so they can be modified if necessary). When an error occurs, the client can understand only two states: Either the error is reported as the response, and nothing has happened in the server—rather, what has happened has been undone, so that it looks as if nothing had happened. Or the server repairs the error, takes some measures to continue processing with other means and finally reaches a positive result that it can send back as the result. Anything in between is neither comprehensible nor acceptable for the client.

The transaction concept known from database systems [4, 13, 15] can handle this very well. But a database will in many cases be just one of the systems involved in processing a request. So it could be the case that the database has successfully completed its transaction, while other systems involved (e.g., the file system) have not been able to do so. Because the client is not aware of the set of systems cooperating to process its request, it cannot understand the state the system is in then. Consequently, the server administrator must fix this before processing can continue. By manual repair he or she must set the server into a state that is acceptable for the client. In most situations, however, this takes far too long.

The better solution for this problem is the provision of transaction management separated from database management systems in order to make it available for all participating systems. This has been done by defining communications protocols among these systems, e.g., XTP [18].

As a result, transactions are now a service of the server as a whole or rather, the middleware. It guarantees the all-or-nothing property for the overall processing of a request, irrespective of the number and heterogeneity of the subsystems involved. Incomplete operations are rolled back to their beginning, so that it appears as if nothing has happened. The error reported to the client should allow it to distinguish whether a repetition of the request makes sense or not. If the error has been raised by a transient situation in the server, e.g., a deadlock, the repetition is possible. If a program error like a division by zero is encountered, the repetition would only reproduce the error.

On the other hand, complete operations should not be compromised by failures that occur later. Once the result has been reported to the client, it should remain valid even in the presence of all (expected) failures. The message with the result might be lost, but when the client asks for it later, it must be reproduced. Data in the server might be affected by disk errors or other crashes. It must be possible to recreate them. All these guarantees are the responsibility of the middleware and should not be left to the application programmer.

6 Discussion of Server Architecture

In all the development of the concepts listed above, the goal has always been to keep programming simple, while at the same time utilizing the system optimization potential to increase efficiency. This is achieved for multi-tasking, multi-threading, transaction management, and other techniques neglected here for space reasons. It has not been reached in all the cases, because the separation of programs and the management of the context cannot be hidden from the programmer. However, the programs are restricted to the processing of a single request and are not bothered with the coordination of parallel processing. Production of reentrant code is the task of the compiler, not the programmer. And if all local variables are treated as the context, its management can even be left to the run-time system.

The task of the middleware is then to allow for the continuous optimization of internal strategies without affecting the application programs. Scheduling, program management, and transaction management can be completely the field of responsibility of the middleware and hence are not at all visible in the program. The idea of "aspect-oriented programming" looks very interesting in that respect. However, many details remain to be clarified.

7 Summary and Conclusion

The idea behind this presentation is to identify and develop general structures and mechanisms that can be re-used in any kind of server, namely in all the kinds of servers listed in section 2. The techniques presented above can be used in any of these. Partially, this is already the case. However, some have re-invented the wheel, and some are still at a stage that others have left behind for long.

The desire to increase performance, however, is still there. As always, application programming will be influenced by this. Programmers will tweak their programs to make them faster. As a consequence, application logic is mixed with come code only inserted to increase performance.

The ongoing task therefore is to work on the separation of application logic and infrastructure. It must be clear before tools can be designed. Interfaces are needed. J2EE is an approach to this. However, the idea of EntityBeans does not match the set-oriented query processing of relational databases. So there is room for improvement.

The separation of application logic from presentation (layout, rendering) is pretty good already. XML helps significantly, because it offers a platform-independent coding of contents. Layout is added separately.

References

[1] Alonso, G., Casati, F., Kuno, H., Machiraju, V.: Web Services - Concepts, Architectures and Applications. Springer, 2004

[2] Anon. et al.: A Measure of Transaction Processing Power, in: Datamation, Feb. 1985, pp. 112–118

[3] Bennett, M., Percy, T.: A TP Monitor Interface for Data Base Management Systems, in: On-Line Data Bases, Infotech State of the Art Report, Part I: Analysis and Bibliography, Part II: Invited Papers, Maidenhead 1977, Part II, pp. 15–26

[4] Bernstein, P.A., Newcomer, E.: Principles of Transaction Processing. Morgan Kaufmann, San Francisco (1997)

[5] Burman, M.: Aspects of a High-Volume Production Online Banking System, in: Proc. IEEE Spring Compcon 1985, pp. 244–248

[6] Callaghan, B.: NFS Illustrated. Addison-Wesley, 2000

[7] Campbell, R.: Managing AFS: The Andrew File System. Prentice Hall PTR, 1998, ISBN 0138027293

[8] Clarke, R.: Teleprocessing Monitors and Program Structure, in: The Australian Computer Journal, Vol. 14, No. 4, Nov. 1982, S. 143-149

[9] Davenport, R.A.: A Guide to the Selection of a Teleprocessing Monitor. Real-Time Software, Infotech State of the Art Report, Maidenhead (1976) 609-621

[10] Deitch, M.: Analytic queuing model for CICS capacity planning, in: IBM Systems Journal, Vol. 21, No. 4, 1982, S. 454-469

[11] Gray, J., Good, B., Gawlick, D., Homan, P., Sammer, H.: One Thousand Transactions per Second, in: Proc. IEEE Spring Compcon, San Francisco, Feb. 1985, pp. 96–101

[12] Gifford, D., Spector, A.: The TWA Reservation System (Case Study), in: Comm. ACM, July 1984, Vol. 27, No. 7, S. 650-665

[13] Gray, J., Reuter, A.: Transaction Processing : Concepts and Techniques. Morgan Kaufmann Publishers, 1993, ISBN 1-55860-190-2

[14] Häussermann, F.: Recovery Problems in Transaction Processing Systems, in: Proc. 5th Conf. on Computer Communication, Atlanta 1980, pp. 465–469

[15] Härder, T., Reuter, A.: Principles of Transaction-Oriented Database Recovery, in: ACM Computing Surveys, Vol. 15, No. 4, Dec. 1983, pp. 287-317

[16] IBM: Customer Information Control System / Virtual Storage (CICS/VS), General Information, 1982, Order No. GC33-0155-1

[17] Monson-Haefel, R.: Enterprise JavaBeans. Sebastopol : O'Reilly, 1999, ISBN 1-56592-605-6

[18] The Open Group: Distributed TP: The XA Specification. Catalog number C193, ISBN 1-87263-024-3, Feb 1992

[19] Orfali, R., Harkey, D., Edwards, J.: The Essential Distributed Objects Survival Guide. John Wiley, 1996

[20] Satyanarayanan, M., Kistler, J.J., Kumar, P., Okasaki, M.E., Siegel, E.H., Steere, D.C.: Coda: A Highly Available File System for a Distributed Workstation Environment, in: IEEE Transactions on Computers, Vol. 39, No. 4, 1990, S. 447-459

[21] Tanenbaum, A.S.: Modern Operating Systems. 2nd edition. Prentice-Hall, 2001

[22] Witt, B.I.: The functional structure of the OS/360, Part II: Job and task management, in: IBM Systems Journal, Vol. 5, No. 1, 1966, pp. 12-29

[23] Yeager, N., McGrath, R.E.: Web Server Technology. Morgan Kaufmann, San Francisco 1996. ISBN 155860376X

[24] Zimmermann, O., Tomlinson, M., Peuser, S.: Perspectives on Web Services. Springer, 2003, ISBN 3-540-00914-0

Caching over the Entire User-to-Data Path in the Internet

Theo Härder

University of Kaiserslautern, Germany
haerder@informatik.uni-kl.de

Abstract. A Web client request traverses four types of Web caches, before the Web server as the origin of the requested document is reached. This client-to-server path is continued to the backend DB server if timely and transaction-consistent data is needed to generate the document. Web caching typically supports access to single Web objects kept ready somewhere in caches up to the server, whereas database caching, applied in the remaining path to the DB data, allows declarative query processing in the cache. Optimization issues in Web caches concern management of documents decomposed into templates and fragments to support dynamic Web documents with reduced network bandwidth usage and server interaction. When fragment-enabled caching of fine-grained objects can be performed in proxy caches close to the client, user-perceived delays may become minimal. On the other hand, database caching uses a full-fledged DBMS as cache manager to adaptively maintain sets of records from a remote database and to evaluate queries on them. Using so-called cache groups, we introduce the new concept of constraint-based database caching. These cache groups are constructed from parameterized cache constraints, and their use is based on the key concepts of value completeness and predicate completeness. We show how cache constraints affect the correctness of query evaluations in the cache and which optimizations they allow. Cache groups supporting practical applications must exhibit controllable load behavior for which we identify necessary conditions. Finally, we comment on future research problems.

1 Motivation

Internet-based information systems and e*-applications are growing with increasing pace and their users are placing tremendous workloads with critical response-time restrictions on the Internet and the Web servers. For these reasons, scalability, performance—in particular, minimization of user-perceived delays—, and availability are prime objectives for their system development. Most of all, various forms of caching in the Web have proven to be a valuable technique[1] towards these design goals. Three as-

T. Härder and W. Lehner (Eds.): Data Management (Wedekind Festschrift), LNCS 3551, pp. 67-89, 2005.

pects make caching attractive in the Web environment, because it effectively reduces network bandwidth usage, user-perceived latency, and workload on the origin server.

To improve response time and scalability of the applications as well as to minimize communication delays in wide-area networks, a broad spectrum of techniques has emerged in recent years to keep static Web objects (like HTML pages, XML fragments, or images) in caches in the client-to-server path. These techniques, often summarized as *Web caching*, typically support access by object identifiers and aim at locating and possibly assembling user-requested Web objects in caches near the Web client to unburden the Web traffic and to achieve minimal response times. In particular for static Web objects, it can provide various kinds of performance improvements for e*-applications [26]—a reason which amplified the setup of Web caches and the optimization of their usage by tailored replacement strategies [23] in recent years. Nowadays, however, more and more dynamically generated content is needed and offered making Web applications even more attractive and enabling new forms of business: contents' personalization, goal-oriented advertisement, interactive e-commerce, one-to-one marketing, and so on. Obviously, the way caching is performed has to respond to these new requirements. To effectively serve this trend, caches have to be aware of the internal structure of documents (Web pages) to enable selective reuse of static fragments (objects) and exchange of dynamic parts in order to assemble them to the actual document to be delivered in the most cost-effective way. Fragment-enabled caching techniques have to be developed which can distinguish and manage templates and fragments of Web documents separately.

2 The Client-to-Server Path

Conceptually, a Web request is processed as follows: A Web client (client throughout the paper) sends a query containing a URL via HTTP and the Internet to a Web server (origin server or server, for short) identified by the URL. The server processes the request, generates the answer (typically an HTML or XML document), and sends it back to the client. To solve the performance and availability problems sketched above, we add, again conceptually, a Web proxy server somewhere in the client-to-server path. Such a proxy can be used in a number of ways, including

- caching documents and parts thereof
- converting data to HTML/XML format so it is readable by a client browser
- providing Internet access for companies using private networks
- selectively controlling access to the Internet based on the submitted URL
- permitting and restricting client access to the Internet based on the client IP address

In this contribution, we concentrate on the caching functionality of proxies and discuss the client-to-server path how it evolved during the recent past. Caches, in general, store

1. "The three most important parts of any Internet application are caching, caching, and, of course, caching ..."—Larry Ellison, Oracle Chairman & CEO.

frequently accessed content and locally answer successive requests for the same content thereby eliminating repetitive transmission of identical content over network links. Thus, the complete caching solution comprises a networking component and a cache component which work together to localize traffic patterns: A user requests a Web page from a browser. The network analyzes the request and, based on certain parameters, transparently redirects it to a local cache in the network. If the cache does not contain the Web page, it will make its own request to the origin server, which then delivers the content to the cache, which, in turn, delivers the content to the client while saving the content in its local storage, that is, caching the content. Subsequent requests for the same Web page are analyzed by the network and, based on certain parameters, transparently redirected to the local cache.

This process may substantially reduce network traffic and latency time for the client. Based on their use and behavior, we can distinguish four types of caches:

- *Browser cache*: For all user requests, this cache dedicated to the browser is first searched. If the specific content is located in the cache, it is checked to make sure that it is "fresh". Such a private cache is particularly useful if a user scrolls back in his request history or clicks a link to a page previously looked at.
- *Proxy cache*
  While working on the same principle, but at a much larger scale, such a cache is shared, performs demand-driven *pull caching*, and serves hundreds or thousands of users in the same way. It can be set up on the firewall or as a stand-alone device. Unless other search paths are specified, a cache miss sends the request to the next proxy cache in the client-to-server path.
- *Reverse proxy cache*
  This kind of cache is an intermediary also known as "edge cache", "surrogate cache", or "gateway cache". While not demand-driven, such caches reverse their role as compared to proxy caches, because they are supplied by origin servers with their most recent offerings—a kind of *push caching*. Furthermore, they are not deployed by network administrators to save bandwidth and to reduce user-perceived delays which are characteristic for proxy caches, but they are typically deployed by Web masters themselves, to unburden the origin servers and to make their Web sites more scalable, reliable, and better performing.
- *Server cache*
  It keeps generated content and enables reuse without interaction of the origin server. Intermediate results and deliverable Web documents help to reduce the server load and improve server scalability.

With these definitions, we are able to explain how a Web request is processed in detail, as illustrated in Fig. 1. Note, we pursue a functional view and focus on the client-request paths of a single ISP (Internet service provider) to servers connected to the Internet via another ISP.

Each of the ISPs is able to connect a set of clients and servers to a *wide-area network*. C_i and S_j represent clients and origin servers, respectively[2]. BC_i refers to the browser cache of C_i, whereas P_{TL} (top-level), P_n, P_{nm}, ... identify proxy caches typically

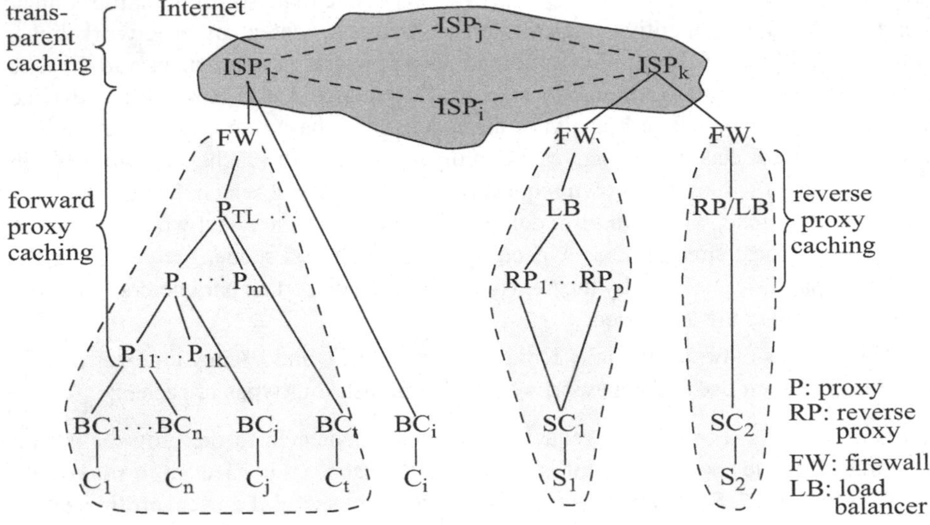

Fig. 1 The Client-to-Server Path through the Internet

allocated in *local-area networks* (LANs) and organized as a multi-level hierarchy in the domain of an enterprise (Intranet). Usually, a stand-alone firewall device (FW) separates the Intranet from its ISP and the Internet; for private clients, the firewall is often combined with the browser cache. An ISP plays two roles: it provides access to the Internet for its clients and usually manages the top-most proxy cache for them. On the other hand, it is a transit provider for routing requests through the Internet. If an ISP offers caching services for routing requests, it is sometimes denoted as transparent caching[3] which is much less effective, because routing may use multiple communication links to the origin server (from ISP_1 to ISP_k in Fig. 1) and select a different path on each re-request. Hence, client-side proxy caching is most effective in the invocation paths from BC up to the corresponding ISP (also denoted as *forward proxy caching*).

In contrast, the caching mechanisms at the server side are primarily directed towards server scalability and overload protection. Requests can be routed to reverse proxies by a number of methods; two of them are indicated in Fig. 1, where some form of load balancing (LB) is involved. This mechanism makes the reverse proxy caching look like the origin server to clients. The incoming requests are either distributed via LB to the reverse proxies (RP_i) or directly to an RP with built-in LB which, on an RP cache miss, forward them to the server cache (SC_j) or a specific server processor, when the server itself is embodied by a processor complex.

2. Using port 80, it is always possible to choose a direct communication link from C to S if the IP address of the origin server is known.

3. While usually the use of a proxy server must be explicitly disclosed to its clients, that of a transparent proxy must not. Hence, caching of such a proxy server remains transparent to the clients.

Another form of reverse proxy caches or edge caches is used in so-called content delivery networks (CDNs) where such caches are distributed throughout the Internet or a part of it. Dynamic content is supplied, if possible, in edge servers. Otherwise, when data is missing or when stale content does not comply with the clients' consistency requirements, the requests are forwarded to the Web server. These edge servers are considered as an extension of the trusted Web server environment, because they are either within the server's administrative domain or within a CDN contracting with the content provider. Enterprise software and CDN solutions like EdgeSuite (Akamai) and WebSphere Edge Server (IBM) are offloading to edge servers certain applications components (such as servlets, JSPs, Enterprise Beans, and page assembly) which usually run at the Web server. For example, Akamai's CDN currently contains up to 15.000 edge servers [1]. A CDN provider sells caching as a service to interested Web sites and guarantees availability of contents on all important Internet nodes for their customers. In this way, customers such as Amazon or MSNBC reach high availability even under extreme load situations without scaling their own Web servers.

3 Web Caching

An important practical consideration concerns the validity of Web objects, particularly in client-side caches. For this reason, the so-called time-to-live algorithm (TTL) is used to determine whether or not a Web object present in a cache can be used to satisfy a client request. Hence, only valid objects can be delivered to the client and are, therefore, kept in the cache. If it runs out of space anyway, some algorithm has to be used to make room for the objects of the current client requests.

3.1 Replacement Strategies

As compared to DB buffer management, which typically provides fixed-length frames and applies LRU- or LRD-based replacement algorithms, Web caching is much more complex. Web objects need variable-length frames and are characterized by more factors that critically influence the replacement decision. To indicate their spectrum, we include the list of important factors from [18]:

- time of the last reference to the object (recency)
- number of requests to an object while in the cache (frequency)
- size of the Web object (size)
- cost to fetch an object from its origin server (cost)
- time of last modification, time when an objects gets stale (expiration time).

The influence or interdependencies of these factors cannot be discussed in detail. We can only summarize the resulting cache replacement strategies which typically exploit the first four factors above. A suitable classification of them was given in [16] and surveyed in [23]:

- *Recency-based strategies* incorporate recency (and size and/or cost) into the replacement process.
- *Frequency-based strategies* exploit frequency information (and size and/or cost) in the replacement decision.
- *Recency/frequency-based strategies* consider both recency and frequency under fixed or variable cost/size assumptions.

3.2 Validity of Cached Objects

A Web cache must be able to locally determine the validity or freshness of its objects. For this reason, the cache is equipped with some checking rules and each object carries a number of parameters in its HTTP header. Some simple ground rules together with object-related parameters allow rapid checking of the object's validity.

The *Expires* HTTP header is the basic means of controlling caches. It tells the cache how long the object is fresh for; after that time, the cache will always check back with the origin server to see if a document is changed. Most Web servers provide a number of ways to set *Expires* response headers. Commonly, they will allow setting an absolute time to expire (e.g., Expires: Mon, 4 April 2005 13:49:31 GMT), a time based on the last time that the client saw the object (e.g., Last-Accessed: Fri, 8 April 2005 23:07:18 GMT), or a time based on the last time the document changed on your server (e.g., Last-Modified: 8 April 2005 21:27:28 GMT). If no *Expires* value as the definite time limit is set (for so-called ZeroTTL objects), the cache may estimate the freshness via *Last-Accessed* or *Last-Modified.* If these values are also undefined, caching of this object is usually not possible.

Although the *Expire* mechanism is useful, it is still somewhat limited. In quite a number of cases, content is cacheable, but the protocol lacks methods to tell the caches how to handle such objects. Some experimental studies have shown that a considerable portion of uncacheable HTTP content is actually cacheable [28]. To improve this situation, HTTP 1.1 introduces enhanced and more flexible object control via the *Cache-Control* response headers which allow Web masters to define how pages should be handled by caches. They include directives to specify what is cacheable, what may be stored, how to modify the expiration mechanism, as well as how to revalidate or reload objects. Useful *Cache-Control* response headers include:

- *max-age=[seconds]*—specifies the maximum amount of time that an object will be considered fresh. Similar to Expires, this directive allows more flexibility.
- *public*—marks the response as cacheable, even if it would normally be uncacheable, e.g., if the object is authenticated, the public directive makes it cacheable.
- *no-cache*—forces caches (both proxy and browser) every time to submit the request to the origin server for validation before releasing a cached copy. This is useful to assure that authentication is respected (together with public), or to maintain rigid object freshness, without sacrificing all of the benefits of caching.

- *must-revalidate*—tells the cache that it must obey any freshness information for the object. This header forces the cache to strictly follow the given rules.

In addition, the checking times of caches, that is, when they control their objects' validities, can be configured, e.g., once per session or time unit. Hence, simple cache-related rules together with object-related parameters determine the freshness semantics of cached objects and guarantee rapid local checking of an object's validity.

3.3 Dynamic Content

So far, our discussion primarily considered static Web objects, typically Web pages containing static HTML/XML data, whose source code is stored at the Web server. In such cases, a page miss in all proxy caches causes the delivery of a fresh page from the Web server.

In the current Internet, however, interactive pages of online shops, member logins of community pages, etc. play a performance-critical role. All of them contain static fragments which have long validity periods and may be shared by many clients accessing essentially the same page in some personalized appearance. On the other hand, some of their fragments are highly dynamic, can only be shared by a few clients or not at all, and must be re-generated almost upon each reference. There are some reasons not discussed here, why proxy caches are of limited use today when dynamic content is frequently needed. However, there are already useful caching mechanisms available at the server side which help to satisfy the requirements and optimize the run-time behavior of the "client-server" loop. In principle, these mechanisms can be refined such that they are also applicable at the client side in the near future.

In cases where a few and small content fragments exhibit high update frequencies, the concept of edge-side includes (ESI) is particularly helpful. Dynamic Web pages are not handled as units anymore, instead fragment-enabled caching allows the management of such pages at a finer level of granularity. Dynamic pages (documents) are decomposed into a template and several fragments for which separate TTL values and URLs can be specified. The template describes the layout of the Web page and specifies the location of each content fragment belonging to it.

For this purpose, the ESI concept—proposed by W3C in summer 2001 and currently the de facto standard for templates in fragment-based documents [27]—offers XML-based language constructs which enable the composition of dynamic Web pages and a fragmentation of their content. Actually, the markup format specifies content fragments for inclusion and assembly in a base template. ESI also includes a complete framework for conditional fetching of fragments, cookie support, and error control. As a consequence, separation of content generation and content provision becomes possible which greatly increases Web server scalability.

As illustrated in Fig. 2, such a fragmentation assigns separate TTL values to the fragments of template-based page, all of them identified by separate URIs. Hence, these fragments can be selectively exchanged (if expired) or flexibly composed to new pages (shared use). If a cache is equipped with the assembly and exchange logic of such tem-

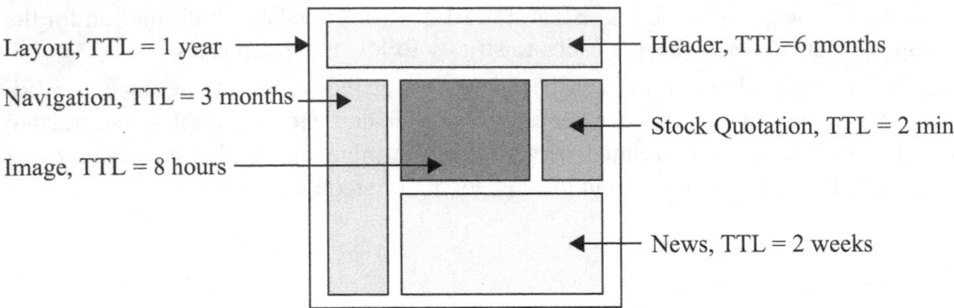

Fig. 2 Fragmentation of a Dynamic Web Document using ESI

plate- and fragment-based pages, much of the extra burden of dynamic page management can be assigned to the caches in the client-to-server path.

Today, ESI is primarily used at the server side, in particular by the edge caches of CDNs. In addition to Web server scalability, its use will gain more and more benefits also at the client side when it conquers the proxy caches or even the browser caches thereby reducing user-perceived delays and network bandwidth usage.

3.4 Future Fragment-Enabled Caching

As sketched above, ESI concepts help to distinguish and manage templates and fragments of Web documents separately. The resulting fragment-enabled caching techniques have to be refined to maximize flexibility of dynamic document assembly and minimize its underlying overhead. Therefore, fine-grained fragment identification is desirable independently of their location on the template, which makes various kinds of fragment behavior possible, for example, fragment movement in a newly assembled document.

Fragment-based documents need efficient and fine-granular update methods, even if the fragment locations change or if some fragments serve personalization purposes. Fragment movements frequently occur, as illustrated in Fig. 3a and b, when in a Web document containing news, actual stories added on the top are pushing the older ones down in the document. A similar situation occurs if personalized pages use the same template, but differ in a few fragments which carry, for example, the salutatory address or some items preferred by the client. Technically, each esi:include tag references a specific URI with a TTL, which is stored in the template file. Hence, all the information related to the template and its fragments is actually present in the template itself. Fragment movement in the current ESI concept can be performed as follows: One option is to update all fragments where the object moved to where it moved from, which seems expensive. Alternatively, the template can be updated such that it contains the URLs of the new locations pointing to the correct fragments [25].

There is no effective and efficient way to solve these problems in the current ESI infrastructure. Neither invalidation of many objects that are actually valid nor invalida-

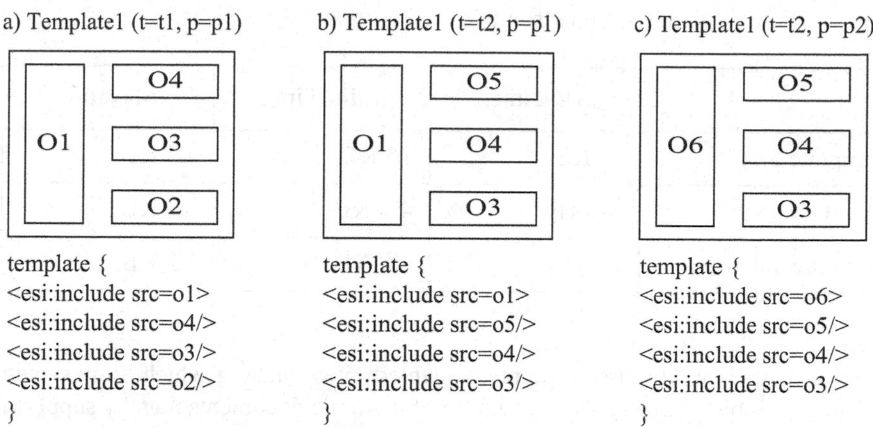

Fig. 3 Personalization and Movement of Fragments

tion of the template which typically needs very little data modification seem appropriate. A new solution is proposed by the DyCA (dynamic content adaptor) approach described in [7]. The essential idea is to extract the objects from the original content thereby achieving the needed separation between template, objects, and object location. DyCA uses a *mapping table* which introduces some kind of reference indirection and, in turn, does not require the template and the objects to be invalidated for spatial changes. Even personalization seems possible with dedicated mapping tables by reusing the original template and all common fragments (Fig. 3c).

The cache holds the mapping table together with the template. When a dynamic document is assembled in the cache, the identifiers of its fragments are looked up in the mapping table. If a fragment is located in the cache and satisfies the TTL or other validity constraints, it is directly integrated into the document; otherwise, a fresh version is fetched from the appropriate URL. Hence, object movement only requires an update of the small-sized mapping table and personalization of documents can be handled by using dedicated mapping tables.

In a recent empirical exploration [7], the update costs of dynamic documents were evaluated in detail. Tab. 1 copies some indicative numbers gained from this experiment referring to large existing Web sites. The update problem caused by object movement (e.g., by a news ticker) was quantified by simulating four different approaches:

- no fragment caching
- static template, fragment updates due to data and spatial changes
- template updates, static objects (fragment updates only to due data changes)
- use of a mapping table.

The evaluation provides interesting empirical data for the "total data transfer between server and cache" and "user-perceived latency". In general, both "template updates, static objects" and "mapping table" clearly outperform the other approaches.

Tab. 1 Comparison of Template and Object Sizes

	NY Times	India Times	Slashdot
Template Size	17 KB	15 KB	1.7 KB
Avg. Object Size	3.6 KB	4.8 KB	0.6 KB
Mapping Table Size	1.0 KB	0.8 KB	2.2 KB

So far, we have discussed fragment-enabled Web caching which allows spatial movement of objects in and personalization of dynamic documents thereby supporting all caching objectives sketched in the introductory section. If the content is delivered as textual sources by information providers, for example, via news tickers, it is edited and formatted as XML or HTML fragments by the origin server and distributed to the clients (either by pull or push mechanisms). If, however, the dynamic content has to be queried and fetched by the Web server from continuously changing data in a possibly remote database, transactional programs (application logic) have to be provided to the server to evaluate the DB queries and to deliver transaction-consistent query results. This kind of content provision and its consistency requirements may introduce another bottleneck into the now prolongated client-to-server path which leads to the point where DB caching comes into play.

4 The User-to-Data Path

As transactional Web applications (TWAs) must deliver more and more dynamic content and often updated information, Web caching should be complemented by techniques that are aware of the consistency and completeness requirements of cached data (whose source is dynamically changed in backend databases) and that, at the same time, adaptively respond to changing workloads. Because the provision of transaction-consistent and timely data is now a major concern, optimization of Web applications has to consider the entire user-to-data path. Because the essential caching issues in the path up to the Web server are already addressed in sufficient detail, we target at specific problems on the remaining path towards DB-managed data.

Several different solutions, summarized as *database caching,* have been proposed in recent years [2, 3, 5]. Fig. 4 focuses on the realm of DB caching and complements the Big Picture of Web caching shown in Fig. 1. For this relatively new problem, currently many DB vendors are developing prototype systems or are just extending their current products [e.g., 14, 15, 19] to respond to the recently uncovered bottleneck for Web information systems or e*-applications.

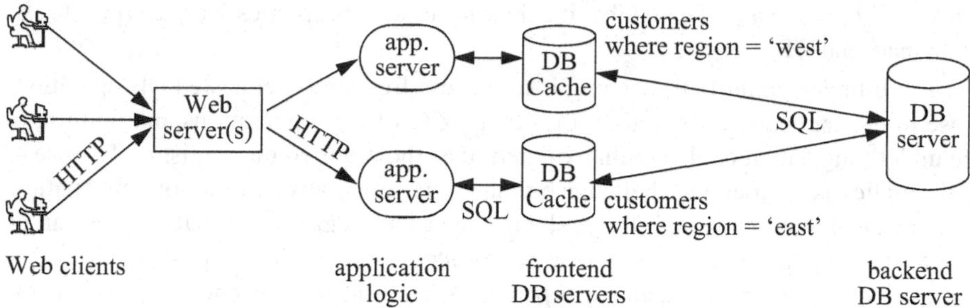

Fig. 4 DB Caching for Web Applications

4.1 Challenges of the Data Bottleneck

What is the technical challenge of all these approaches? When user requests require responses to be assembled from static and dynamic contents somewhere in a Web cache, the dynamic portion is often generated by a remote application server, which in turn asks the backend DB server (backend DB) for up-to-date information, thus causing substantial latency. An obvious reaction to this performance problem is the migration of application servers to data centers closer to the users: Fig. 4 illustrates that clients select one of the replicated Web servers "close" to them in order to minimize communication time. This optimization is amplified if the associated application servers can instantly provide the expected data—frequently indicated by geographical contexts. But the displacement of application servers to the edge of the Web alone is not sufficient; conversely it would dramatically degrade the efficiency of DB support because of the frequent round trips to the then remote backend DB, e.g., by open/next/close loops of cursor-based processing via SQL application programming interfaces (APIs). As a consequence, frequently used data should be kept close to the application servers in so-called DB caches. Note, the backend DB cannot be moved to the edge of the Web as well, because it has to serve several application servers distributed in wide-area networks. On the other hand, replication of the entire database at each application server is too expensive, because DB updates can be performed via each of them. A flexible solution should not only support DB caching at mid-tier nodes of central enterprise infrastructures [6], but also at edge servers of content delivery networks or remote data centers.

Another important aspect of practical solutions is to achieve full *cache transparency* for applications, that is, modifications of the API are not tolerated. This application transparency, which also is a prime aspect to distinguish caching from replication, is a key requirement of DB caching. It gives the cache manager the choice at run time to process a query locally or to send it to the backend DB to comply with strict consistency requirements, for instance. Cache transparency requires that each DB object is represented only once in a cache and that it exhibits the same properties (name, type, etc.) as in the backend DB.

The ultimate goal of DB caching is to process frequently requested DB operations close to the application. Therefore, the complexity of these operations and, in turn, of the underlying data model essentially determines the required mechanisms. The use of SQL implies a considerable challenge because of its declarative and set-oriented nature. This means that, to be useful, the cache manager has to guarantee that queries can be processed in the DB cache, that is, the sets of records (of various types) satisfying the corresponding predicates—denoted as *predicate extensions*—must be completely in the cache. This completeness condition, the so-called *predicate completeness*, ensures that the query evaluation semantics is equivalent to the one provided by the backend.

4.2 Technical Solutions for the Cache Manager

A *full-fledged DB server* used as cache manager offers great advantages. A substantial portion of the query processing logic (parsing, optimization, and execution) has to be made available anyway. By providing the full functionality, additional DB objects such as triggers, constraints, stored procedures, or access paths can be exploited in the cache thereby simulating DB semantics locally and enhancing application performance due to increased locality. Furthermore, transactional updates seem to be conceivable in the cache (some time in the future) and, as a consequence, continued service for TWAs when backend databases become unavailable.

Note, a cache usually contains only subsets of records pertaining to a small fraction of backend tables. Its primary task is to support query processing for TWAs, which typically contain up to 3 or 4 joins [2]. Often the number of cache tables—featuring a high degree of reference locality—is in the order of 10 or less, even if the backend DB consists of hundreds of tables.

A federated query facility as offered in [14, 20] allows cooperative predicate evaluation by multiple DB servers. This property is very important for cache use, because local evaluation of some (partial) predicate can be complemented by the work of the backend DB on other (partial) predicates whose extensions are not in the cache. Hence, in the following we refer to predicates meaning their portions to be evaluated in the cache.

4.3 Database Caching — Conventional Solutions

Static approaches to DB caching where the cache contents have to be prespecified and possibly loaded in advance are of little interest in Internet applications. Such approaches are sometimes called *declarative caching* and do not comply with challenging demands such as self-administration and adaptivity. Hence, what are the characteristics of a promising solution when the backend DB is (frequently) updated and cache contents must be adjusted dynamically?

The conceptually simplest approach—full-table caching, which replicates the entire content of selected backend tables—attracted various DB cache products [22]. It seems infeasible, however, for large tables even under moderate update dynamics, because replication and maintenance costs may outweigh the potential savings on query processing.

So far, most approaches to DB caching were primarily based on materialized views and their variants [4, 5, 8, 9, 17, 21]. A materialized view consists of a single table whose columns correspond to the set $O_V = \{O_1, ..., O_n\}$ of output attributes and whose contents are the query result V of the related view-defining query Q_V with predicate P. Materialized views can be loaded into the DB cache in advance or can be made available on demand, for example, when a given query is processed the nth time ($n \geq 1$). In this way, some kind of built-in locality and adaptivity (together with a replacement scheme) can be achieved. When materialized views are used for DB caching, essentially independent tables, each representing a query result V_i of Q_{V_i}, are separately cached in the frontend DB. In general, query processing for an actual query Q_A is limited to a single cache table. The result of Q_A is contained in V_i, if P_A is logically implied by P_i (subsumption) and if O_A is contained in O_{V_i} (i.e., the output of the new query is restricted by the attributes contained in a query result that is used). Only in special cases a union of cached query results, e.g., $V_1 \cup V_2 \cup ... \cup V_n$, can be exploited. DBProxy [3] has proposed some optimizations at the storage level. To reduce the number of cache tables, a common-schema storage-table policy is used, which tries to store query results V_i with strongly overlapping output attributes in common tables. On the one hand, a superset of the attributes Q_{V_i} may potentially enhance caching benefits of V_i, but, on the other hand, it may increase storage and maintenance costs.

A new class of caching techniques [2, 24] follows the idea that the desired cache contents are specified by so-called *parameterized cache constraints*. As soon as a reference to a parameter causes a cache miss, all records satisfying the specified cache constraint for this parameter value are loaded into the cache. As a consequence, the completeness condition is accomplished for query predicates that match the satisfied cache constraints or are subsumed by them. Hence, cache maintenance guarantees that the corresponding predicate extensions can correctly be exploited for future queries.

5 Constraint-Based Database Caching

Constraint-based DB caching promises a new quality for the placement of data close to their application. The key idea is to accomplish for some given types of query predicates P the so-called predicate completeness in the cache such that all queries eligible for P can be evaluated correctly [11]. All records (of various types) in the backend DB that are needed to evaluate predicate P are called the predicate extension of P. Because predicates form an intrinsic part of a data model, the various kinds of eligible predicate extensions are data-model dependent, that is, they always support only specific operations of a data model under consideration. Cache constraints enable cache

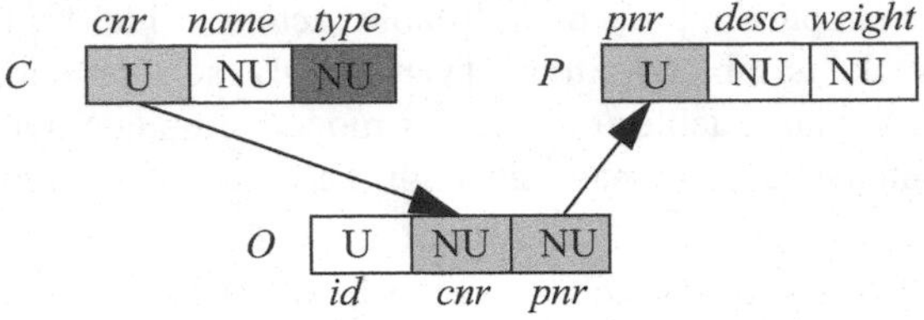

Fig. 5 Cache Table Collection *COP*

loading in a constructive way and guarantee the presence of their predicate extensions in the cache.

The technique does not rely on static predicates: Parameterized constraints make the specification adaptive; it is completed when the parameters are instantiated by specific values: An "instantiated constraint" then corresponds to a predicate and, when the constraint is satisfied (i.e., all related records have been loaded) it delivers correct answers to eligible queries. Note, the set of all existing predicate extensions flexibly allows evaluation of their predicates, e.g., $P_1 \cup P_2 \cup \ldots \cup P_n$ or $P_1 \cap P_2 \cap \ldots \cap P_n$ or subsets/combinations thereof, in the cache.

A cache contains a collection of cache tables that can be isolated or related to each other in some way. For simplicity, let the names of tables and columns be identical in the cache and in the backend DB: Considering a cache table *S*, we denote by S_B its corresponding backend table, by *S.c* a column *c* of *S*.

Assume cache tables *C, O,* and *P* where *C.cnr*, *O.cnr,* and *P.pnr* are unique (U) columns and the remaining columns are non-unique (NU), as illustrated in Fig. 5. In a common real-world situation, *C*, *O*, and *P* could correspond to backend DB tables Customer, Order, and Product. Hence, both arrows would typically characterize PK/FK relationships that can be used for join processing in the cache.

Because all columns of the corresponding backend tables are kept in the cache, all *project* operations possible in the backend DB can also be performed. Other operations like *selection* and *join* depend on specific completeness conditions enforced by cache constraints. Given suitable cache constraints, there are no or only simple decidability problems whether predicates can be evaluated. Only a simple probe query is required at run time to determine the availability of eligible predicate extensions. An important goal for cache processing is to support local evaluation of queries that typically contain simple projection (P) and selection (S) operations and equi-joins (J).

Assume for the moment, the cache enables PSJ queries, for example, with predicate Q_1 = (*C.type* = *'gold'* and *C.cnr* = *O.cnr* and *O.pnr* = *P.pnr*) on *COP*. Then, all evaluable predicates can be refined by "and-ing" additional selection terms (referring to cache table columns) to it; e.g., (and *C.name* like 'Smi%' and *O.pnr* > 17 and ...). Because full DB functionality is available, the results of these queries can further be refined by selection predicates such as Exists, Null, etc. as well as processing options like Distinct, Group-by, Having (restricted to predicates evaluable on the predicate extension), or Order-by.

5.1 Equality Predicates

Let us begin with single cache tables. If we want to be able to evaluate a given predicate in the cache, we must keep a collection of records in the cache tables such that the completeness condition for the predicate is satisfied. For simple equality predicates like *S.c* = *v*, this completeness condition takes the shape of *value completeness:* A value v is said to be value complete (or complete for short) in a column *S.c* if and only if all records of $\sigma_{c=v}S_B$ are in *S*. If we know that a value *v* is complete in a column *S.c*, we can correctly evaluate *S.c* = *v*, because all rows from table S_B carrying that value are in the cache. But how do we know that *v* is complete? A straightforward way is to provide the cache manager with a list of *candidate values* of those columns we want to use in equality predicate queries. Possible candidate values for a column S.c belong to the domain of S_B.c. A list of candidate values can be specified as a complete list (all domain values), an enumeration, a range, or other predicates; candidate values can be expressed positively (recommendations) or negatively (stop-words).

Whenever a candidate value *x* occurs in an equality predicate of a query, the cache manager probes the respective cache table to see whether this value is present: A successful probe query (the value is found) implies that the predicate extension for the given equality query is in the cache and that this query can be evaluated locally. Otherwise, the query is sent to the backend for further processing.

How do records get into a cache table? As a consequence of a cache miss attributed to *x*, the cache manager satisfies the value completeness for *x* by fetching all required records from the backend and loading them into the respective cache table. Hence, the cache is ready to answer the corresponding equality query locally from then on.

Apparently, a reference to a candidate value *x* serves as a kind of indicator that, in the immediate future, locality of reference is expected on the predicate extension determined by *x*. Candidate values therefore carry information about the future workload and sensitively influence caching performance. As a consequence, they must carefully be selected. In an advanced scheme, the cache manager takes care that only those candidate values with high re-reference probability are in the cache. By monitoring the query load, the cache manager itself can dynamically optimize the list of candidate values, for which completeness is guaranteed whenever they appear in the cache. In a straightforward case, the database administrator (DBA) specifies this list of values.

Flexible adjustment of the (dynamic) list of candidate values that are present in the cache is key to cache adaptivity. Because a probe query always precedes the actual query evaluation, completeness for a value *v* can be abolished at any time by removing all records with value *v* from the cache table. Again, in the simplest case, there may be no removal at all, and thus a value, once made complete, is left in the cache forever. Alternatively, complex replacement algorithms could be applied to unload all records carrying a complete value if its re-reference probability sinks. Note, besides the factors memory and storage space, there is always a cost trade-off between the savings for query evaluation and the penalties for keeping the records consistent with their state in the backend.

5.2 Equi-join Predicates

How do we obtain the predicate extensions of PSJ queries? The key idea is to use *referential cache constraints* (RCCs) to specify all records needed to satisfy specific equi-join predicates. An RCC is defined between two cache table columns: a source column $S.a$ and a target column $T.b$ where the tables S and T need not be different. RCC $S.a \rightarrow T.b$ is satisfied if and only if all values v in S.a are value complete in T.b. It ensures that, whenever we find a record s in S, all join partners of s with respect to $S.a = T.b$ are in T. Note, the RCC alone does not allow us to correctly perform this join in the cache: Many rows of S_B that have join partners in T_B may be missing from S. But using an equality predicate on a complete value of column $S.c$ as an "anchor", we can restrict this join to records that are present in the cache: The RCC $S.a \rightarrow T.b$ expands the predicate extension of $(S.c = x)$ to the predicate extension of $(S.c = x$ and $S.a = T.b)$. In this way, a complete value can serve as an entry point for a query.

Depending on the types of the source and target columns (unique: U, non-unique: NU) on which an RCC is defined, we classify RCCs as (1:1), (1:n), and (n:m), and denote them as follows:

- $\text{U} \rightarrow \text{U}$ or $\text{U} \rightarrow \text{NU}$: member constraint (MC)
- $\text{NU} \rightarrow \text{U}$: owner constraint (OC)
- $\text{NU} \rightarrow \text{NU}$: cross constraint (XC).

Note, using RCCs we implicitly introduce something like a value-based table model intended to support queries. Despite similarities to the relational model, MCs and OCs are not identical to the PK/FK (primary key/foreign key) relationships contained in the backend tables. A PK/FK relationship can be processed symmetrically, whereas our RCCs can be used for join processing only in the specified direction. Other important differences are that XCs have no counterparts in the backend DB and that a column may be the source of n and the target of m RCCs. In contrast, a column in the role of PK may be the starting point of k, but in the role of FK the ending point of only one (meaningful) PK/FK relationship. Because a very high fraction (probably > 99%) of all SQL join queries refers exclusively to PK/FK relationships (they represent real-world relationships explicitly captured by DB design), almost all RCCs specified between cache tables are expected to be of type MC or OC. As a corollary, XCs and multiple RCCs ending on a specific NU column seem to be very infrequent.

Assume in our *COP* example of Fig. 5 that $C.cnr \rightarrow O.cnr$ and $O.pnr \rightarrow P.pnr$ are RCCs which, as usual, characterize PK/FK relationships that guarantee regular join semantics when processed in the cache. The specification of additional RCCs $O.id \rightarrow C.type$ or even $O.cnr \rightarrow P.weight$ and $P.weight \rightarrow O.cnr$ is conceivable (assume join-compatible domains); such RCCs, however, have no counterparts in the backend DB schema and, when used for a join of O and C or a cross join of O and P or P and O, it completely remains the user's responsibility to assign a meaning.

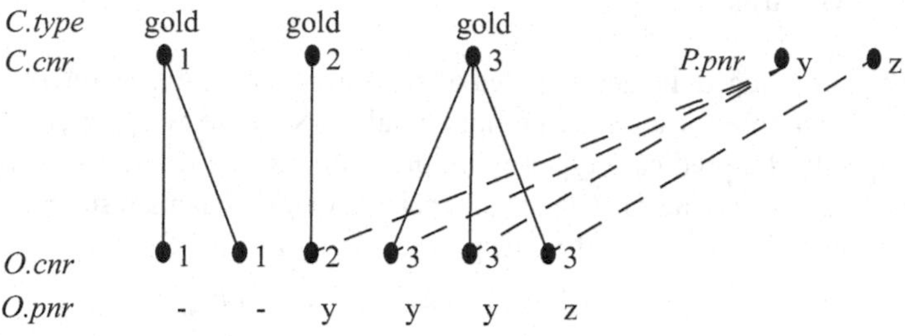

Fig. 6 Construction of a Predicate Extension for *COP*

5.3 Loading of Predicate Extensions

To evaluate predicate *Q* in the cache, the cache manager has to guarantee for *Q* predicate completeness. A collection of tables is said to be predicate complete with respect to *Q* if it contains all records needed to evaluate *Q*, i.e., its predicate extension.

An example of Q_1's predicate extension is illustrated in Fig. 6, where records are represented by bullets and value-based relationships by lines. To establish completeness for value *gold* of column *C.type*, the cache manager loads all records of $\sigma_{type = gold}S_C$ in a first step. For each of these records, RCC $C.cnr \rightarrow O.cnr$ has to be fulfilled (PK/FK relationships, solid lines), that is, all values of source column *C.cnr* (1, 2, 3 in the example) have to be made complete in the target column *O.cnr*. Finally, for all values present in *O.pnr* (y, z), RCC $O.pnr \rightarrow P.pnr$ makes their counterparts complete in *P.pnr* (FK/PK relationships, dashed lines).

In this way, the cache manager can construct predicate extensions using only simple load steps based on equality of values. Accordingly, it can correctly evaluate the corresponding queries locally. To generalize this example, we make the important observation that for the local processing of each PSJ predicate we need an entry point satisfying an equality predicate. Then we can proceed with the processing of equi-joins via reachable RCCs. Hence, each complete value is eligible for deriving a predicate to be evaluated locally.

Note, each cache-resident value of a U column is complete by definition. Furthermore, if only complete values enter a column, all values of this column are complete. This is true for *O.c* in our example. We can generalize this case to *domain completeness* greatly simplifying cache probing: A column *S.c* is said to be domain complete (DC) if and only if all values v in *S.c* are value complete.

Given a domain-complete column *S.c*, if a probe query confirms that value *v* is in *S.c* (a single record suffices), we can be sure that *v* is complete and thus evaluate *S.c* = *v* locally. Unique columns of a cache table (defined by SQL constraints "unique" or "primary key" in the backend DB schema) are DC per se (implicit domain completeness). Non-unique columns in contrast need extra enforcement of DC.

5.4 Cache Groups

So far, we have introduced the general idea of supporting cache-based query evaluation using the *COP* example for a single complete value. Now we will generalize our approach and specify the predicate types to be processed in the cache together with the kind of constraints to load their predicate extensions. Our mechanism supports PSJ queries that are characterized by (valid SQL) predicate types of the form

$$((EP_1 \text{ or} \ldots \text{ or } EP_n) \text{ and } EJ_1 \text{ and} \ldots \text{ and } EJ_m)$$

where EP_i, $1 \leq i \leq n$, is an equality predicate on a specific cache table called root table and the EJ_j, $1 \leq j \leq m$, correspond to RCCs that (transitively) connect the root table with the collection of the remaining cache tables involved.

For equi-join predicates, we have already introduced their specification mechanism: RCC. To establish a parameterized loading mechanism together with an entry option for cache tables, a second type of cache constraint specified on a root table and called filling column is needed: A column *S.k* with an associated list of candidate values is called a filling column. Whenever a candidate value appears in *S.k*, it is kept complete; only candidate values initiate caching when they are referenced by user queries.

Typically, filling columns are assumed simple. A multi-column mechanism different from multiple simple columns is conceivable; then, values are to be composed of simple values belonging to the participating columns. The cache manager guarantees that a candidate value present in the cache is complete. Therefore, these values—provided either manually by the DBA or automatically upon monitoring the cache traffic by the cache manager—can always be used as entry points for predicate evaluation.

Note, candidate values of filling columns play a dual role: They enforce cache loading upon reference and—once in the cache—they represent entry points for querying, because they are complete. The resulting collection of cache tables, filling columns, and RCCs is called *cache group:* the particpating cache tables are linked by a set of RCCs. A distinguished cache table is called the root table R of the cache group and holds i filling columns ($i \geq 1$). The remaining cache tables are called member tables and must be reachable from R via the (paths of) RCCs. For example, our *COP* example constitutes a simple cache group having *C* as its root table, two RCCs (m = 2), *O* and *P* as member tables, and a single equality predicate on *C.type* (n = 1) as its filling column.

Domain-complete filling columns offer a simple way of specification because lists of candidate values are not required, but they do not seem to be generally applicable[4].

Safeness of cache groups. It is unreasonable to accept all conceivable cache group configurations, because cache misses on filling columns may provoke unforeseeable load operations. Although the cache-populating procedure can be performed asynchronously to the transaction observing the cache miss, so that a burden on its own response time

4. In the DBCache project [2], so-called cache keys are used as filling columns defined to be domain complete. Low-selectivity columns or single values in columns with skewed value distributions may cause cache filling actions involving huge sets of records never used later. It is therefore necessary to control the cache loading in a more refined way.

can be avoided, uncontrolled loading is undesirable: Substantial extra work, which can hardly be estimated, may be required by the frontend and backend DB servers, which will influence the transaction throughput in heavy workload situations.

Specific cache groups may even exhibit a recursive loading behavior that jeopardizes their caching performance. Once cache filling is initiated, the enforcement of cache constraints may require multiple phases of record loading. Such behavior always occurs, when two NU-DC columns of a cache table must be maintained, e.g., *C.name* and *C.type* in Fig. 5. A set of values appears in *C.name*, for which *C* is loaded with the corresponding records of C_B to keep column *C.name* domain complete. These records, in turn, populate *C.type* with a set of (new) values which must be made complete, thereby possibly introducing new values into *C.name* and so on.

Cache groups are called *safe* if there is no possibility for recursive load behavior to happen. Upon a miss on a filling column, we want the initiated cache loading to stop after a *single pass* of filling operations through the tables of the cache group. The conditions a safe cache group must meet are explored in [12].

Entry points for query evaluation. A cache table column can be correctly tested and used by an equality predicate *only if the referenced value is complete*. But how do we know that? Of course, candidate values in filling columns are explicitly made complete, and all cache table columns of type U are even domain complete.

Returning to Fig. 5, we find that *C.cnr, O.id,* and *P.pnr* are domain complete. If cache probing is successful for $C.cnr = 1$, $O.id = \alpha$, or $P.pnr = z$, respectively, we can evaluate, in addition to the predicate type *COP* is designed for, the three predicates ($C.cnr = 1$ and $C.cnr = O.cnr$ and $O.pnr = P.pnr$) or ($O.id = \alpha$ and $O.pnr = P.pnr$) or ($P.pnr = z$).

Obviously, cache-supported query evaluation gains much more flexibility and power, if we can correctly decide that other cache columns are domain complete as well. Let us refer again to *COP*. Because $C.cnr \rightarrow O.cnr$ is the only RCC that induces loading of records in *O*, we know that *O.cnr* is domain complete (called *induced domain completeness*).

Note, additional RCCs ending in *O.cnr* would not abolish the DC of *O.cnr*, though any additional RCC ending in a different column would do: Assume an additional RCC ending in *O.id* induces a new value β, which implies the insertion of $\sigma_{id = \beta} O_B$ into *O*—just a single record *o*. Now a new value 7 of *O.cnr*, so far not present in *O.cnr*, may appear, but all other records of $\sigma_{cnr = 7} O_B$ fail to do so.

For this reason, a cache table loaded by RCCs on more than one column cannot have an induced DC column. The same is true for a cache table that carries a filling column and is loaded by an RCC on a different column. Therefore, induced DC is *context dependent,* which leads us to the following definition: A cache table column *S.c* is *induced domain complete,* if it is the only column of *S* that is loaded via one or more RCCs or that is a filling column.

To summarize our discussion of cache groups concerning their population and the domain completeness of their columns: A cache table *T* can be loaded via one or more filling columns or one or more RCCs ending in one or more of its columns. A column of *T* is domain complete if it is a U column or a filling column with a complete list of candidate values or induced domain complete.

5.5 Generalization of Predicates

Cache groups enable specific PSJ queries to be evaluated in the cache. The inherent mechanism is to guarantee value or domain completeness in cache table columns and to maintain via RCCs predicate completeness across a cache group which support selection operations for equality predicates and equi-joins, respectively. Varying the fundamental idea of cache groups, we can apply the probing and completeness conditions needed for local predicate evaluation to other types of SQL predicates. A generalization of constraint specification and probing mechanisms leads us to the key observation [11] that the cache group approach can be extended to

- simple predicates with other comparison conditions $\Theta \in \{<, >, \leq, \neq, \geq\}$
- range predicates or even
- complex predicates composed of them by Boolean operators ($\vee$, $\wedge$, $\neg$).

Furthermore, it is conceivable, however much more complex, to establish predicate completeness for aggregation, recursion, and other SQL predicates (Exists, Subquery, etc.). The usefulness and realization aspects of such extensions have to be explored yet.

6 Seamless Processing of Web Objects

Obviously, all these ideas of constraint-based DB caching are not restricted to the relational model.or to SQL predicates. They may be applied equally well to other data models and the caching needs of their applications, e.g., to XML documents and XQuery operations [27]. This observation delivers another argument for the opportunities and benefits of the upcoming XML database management systems (XDBMS). If they are native, that is, if they provide for the variety of XML language models (such as SAX, DOM, XPath, and XQuery [27]) specific access models to fine-grained storage structures tailored to the processing requirements of XML documents [10], then there is no need anymore to perform frequent, different, and heterogeneous type conversions often complained in RDBMS-based e*-applications. Message data and DB data could be managed and stored in the same way. Hence, queries on DB-based data could be directly evaluated on its native XML storage structures. Their result sets shaped as XML fragments could be forwarded and stored in the various DB and Web caches up to the user thereby only handled by a single and, therefore, homogeneous processing model.

The currently futuristic view of XDBMS dominance was already taken in [13] where innovative DBMS architectures were explored. As a consequence of such a technological change, the myriads of SQL applications would become legacy applications to be emulated on, say, XQuery interfaces—nowadays a rather weird imagination.

7 Open Problems

We have considered the entire user-to-data path in Web applications and have discussed the caching problems occurring under a view which separated the specified problems. Web caching achieved by four different kinds of caches targets at the minimized communication effort and freshness of single Web objects, whereas DB caching attempts to perform as much query evaluation as possible (and cost-effective) in caches close to the edge of the Internet—both to primarily reduce the user-perceived delay of Web requests. In contrast to Web caching where only identifier-based access is supported for Web objects, declarative and set-oriented query processing of database records is in the focus of DB caching.

In the future, fragment-enabled fine-granular caching can essentially improve the effectiveness of all kinds of Web caches. Furthermore, various protocol refinements seem possible to improve caching and content delivery of uncacheable HTTP content [28]. For example, pushing the functionality of uncacheable content generation to the network edge may have a substantial effect. Another promising area is the monitoring and recognizing of access patterns in caches and exploiting their results in prefetching schemes. For DB caching, we seem at the beginning of a promising research area concerning constraint-based and adaptive DB caching. Hence, a number of important issues remains to be solved or explored.

So far, all aspects of cache maintenance [6] were excluded. How difficult is it to cope with the units of loading and unloading? Let us call such a unit cache instance (CI), which is a collection of records satisfying all RCCs of a cache group for a single root record. Depending on their complexity, CIs may exhibit good, bad, or even ugly maintenance properties. The good CIs are disjoint from each other and the RCC relationships between the contained records form trees, for example, a cache group consisting of customer and order only (CO). Then a newly referenced candidate value (NU) of *C.ctype* causes a forest of such trees to be loaded, which, in case of unloading, can be removed without interference with other CIs. The bad CIs form DAGs and weakly overlap with each other. Cache group *COP* in Fig. 6 is an example where several CIs may share records of cache table *P*. Hence when loading a new CI, one must beware of duplicates. Accordingly, shared records must be removed only together with their last sharing CI. To maintain cache groups with cross constraints can be characterized as ugly, because CIs may strongly overlap so that duplicate recognition and management of shared records may dominate the work of the cache manager.

Improvement of adaptivity is another important problem, much more difficult than in Web caches. How can constraint-based approaches evolve with changing locality patterns of the workload? To support frequently requested join operations by additional RCCs or to remove RCCs not exploited anymore needs adaptive RCC specifications! Hence, for each variation of constraint-based caching, quantitative analyses must help to understand which cache configurations are worth the effort. For this purpose, a cache group advisor can be designed to support the DBA in the specification of a cache group when the characteristics of the workload are known. Here, the expected costs for cache maintenance and the savings gained by predicate evaluation in the cache can be determined thereby identifying the trade-off point of cache operation. For example, starting with the cache tables and join paths exhibiting the highest degrees of reference locality, the cache group design can be expanded by additional RCCs and/or tables until the optimum point of operation is reached. On the other hand, such a tool may be useful during cache operation by observing the workload patterns and by proposing or automatically invoking changes in the cache group specification. The kind of self-administration or self-tuning opens a new and complex area of research often referred to as autonomic computing.

Other interesting research problems occur if we apply different update models to DB caching. Instead of processing all (transactional) updates in the backend DB first, one could perform them in the cache (under ACID protection) or even jointly in cache and backend DB under a 2PC protocol. Such update models may lead to futuristic considerations where the conventional hierarchic arrangement of frontend cache and backend DB is dissolved: If each of them can play both roles and if together they can provide consistency for DB data, more effective DB support may be gained for new applications such as grid or P2P computing.

References

[1] Akamai Technologies Inc.: Akamai EdgeSuite. http://www.akamai.com/en/html/services/edgesuite.html

[2] Altinel, M., Bornhövd, C., Krishnamurthy, S., Mohan, C., Pirahesh, H., Reinwald, B.: Cache Tables: Paving the Way for an Adaptive Database Cache. Proc. 29th Int. Conf. on Very Large Data Bases (VLDB'03), Berlin (2003) 718–729

[3] Amiri, K., Park, S., Tewari, R., Padmanabhan, S.: DBProxy: A Dynamic Data Cache for Web Applications. Proc. 19th Int. Conf. on Data Engineering (ICDE'03), Bangalore, India. (2003) 821–831

[4] Anton, J., Jacobs, L., Liu, X., Parker, J., Zeng, Z., Zhong, T.: Web Caching for Database Applications with Oracle Web Cache. Proc. 2002 ACM SIGMOD Int. Conf. on Management of Data, Madison, Wisc. (2002) 594–599

[5] Bello, R. G., Dias, K., Downing, A., Feenan, J. J., Jr., Finnerty, J. L., Norcott, W. D., Sun, H., Witkowski, A., Ziauddin, M.: Materialized Views in Oracle. Proc. 24th Int. Conf. on Very Large Data Bases (VLDB'98), New York (1998) 659–664

[6] Bornhövd, C., Altinel, M., Mohan, C., Pirahesh, H., Reinwald, B.: Adaptive Database Caching with DBCache. Data Engineering Bulletin 27:2, (2004) 11-18

[7] Brodie, D., Gupta, A., Shi, W.: Accelerating Dynamic Web Content Delivery Using Keyword-Based Fragment Detection. Proc. Int. Conf. on Web Engineering, Munich, LNCS 3140, Springer (2004) 359-372

[8] Dar, S., Franklin, M., Jónsson, B., Srivastava, D., Tan, M.: Semantic Data Caching and Replacement. Proc. 22nd Int. Conf. on Very Large Data Bases (VLDB'96), Mumbai (1996) 330–341

[9] Goldstein, J., Larson, P.-A.: Optimizing Queries Using Materialized Views: A Practical, Scalable Solution. Proc. 2001 ACM SIGMOD Int. Conf. on Management of Data, Santa Barbara, CA (2001) 331–342

[10] Haustein, M., Härder, T.: Fine-Grained Management of Natively Stored XML Documents. submitted (2005)

[11] Härder, T., Bühmann, A.: Query Processing in Constraint-Based Database Caches. Data Engineering Bulletin 27:2 (2004) 3-10

[12] Härder, T., Bühmann, A.: Value Complete, Domain Complete, Predicate Complete—Magic Words Driving the Design of Cache Groups, submitted (2005)

[13] Halverson, A., Josifovski, V., Lohman, G., Pirahesh, H., Mörschel, M.: ROX: Relational Over XML. Proc. 30th Int. Conf. on Very Large Data Bases (VLDB'04), Toronto (2004)

[14] IBM DB2 Universal Database (V 8.1). http://www.ibm.com/software/data/db2/

[15] IBM Cloudscape. http://www.ibm.com/software/data/cloudscape/

[16] Jin, S., Bestavros, A.: GreedyDual*: Web Caching Algorithms Exploiting the Two Sources of Temporal Locality in Web Request Streams. Proc. 5th Int. Web Caching and Content Delivery Workshop (2000)

[17] Keller, A., Basu, J.: A Predicate-Based Caching Scheme for Client-Server Database Architectures. VLDB Journal 5:1 (1996) 35–47

[18] Krishnamurthy, B., Rexford, J.: Web Protocols and Practise: HTTP/1.1, Networking Protocols, Caching, and Traffic Measurement, Addison-Wesley, Reading, MA (2001)

[19] Larson, P.-A., Goldstein, J., Zhou, J.: MTCache: Mid-Tier Database Caching in SQL Server. Proc. 20th Int. Conf. on Data Engineering (ICDE'04), Boston, MA (2004) 177-189

[20] Larson, P.-A., Goldstein, J., Guo, H., Zhou, J.: MTCache: Mid-Tier Database Caching for SQL Server. Data Engineering Bulletin 27:2 (2004) 35-40

[21] Levy, A. Y., Mendelzon, A. O., Sagiv, Y., Srivastava, D.: Answering Queries Using Views. Proc. 14th ACM Symposium on Principles of Database Systems (PODS'95), San Jose, CA (1995) 95–104

[22] Oracle Corporation: Internet Application Sever Documentation Library, http://otn.oracle.com/documentation/appserver10g.html

[23] Podlipinig, S., Böszörmenyi, L.: A Survey of Web Cache Replacement Strategies. ACM Computing Surveys 35:4 (2003) 374–398

[24] The TimesTen Team: Mid-tier Caching: The TimesTen Approach. Proc. 2002 ACM SIGMOD Int. Conf. on Management of Data, Madison, Wisconsin (2002) 588–593

[25] Tsimelzon, M., Weihl, B., Jakobs, L.: ESI language specification 1.0 (2001), http://www.esi.org/language_spec_1-0.html

[26] Weikum, G.: Web Caching. In: Web & Datenbanken – Konzepte, Architekturen, Anwendungen. Erhard Rahm/Gottfried Vossen (Hrsg.), dpunkt.verlag (2002) 191-216

[27] W3C Recommendations. http://www.w3c.org (2004)

[28] Zhou, Z., Mao, Y., Shi, W.: Workload Characterization of Uncacheable HTTP Content. Proc. Int. Conf. on Web Engineering, Munich, LNCS 3140, Springer (2004) 391-39

Reweaving the Tapestry: Integrating Database and Messaging Systems in the Wake of New Middleware Technologies

Sangeeta Doraiswamy[1], Mehmet Altinel[1], Lakshmikant Shrinivas[2], Stewart Palmer[3], Francis Parr[3], Berthold Reinwald[1], C. Mohan[1]

1. IBM Almaden Research Center, San Jose, CA
2. University of Wisconsin-Madison, Madison, WI
(while on assignment at IBM Almaden Research Center)
3. IBM T.J. Watson Research Center, Hawthorne, NY

{dorais, maltinel, slp, fnparr, reinwald, mohan}@us.ibm.com, lshrinivas@wisc.edu

Abstract. Modern business applications involve a lot of distributed data processing and inter-site communication, for which they rely on middleware products. These products provide the data access and communication framework for the business applications.

Integrated messaging seeks to integrate messaging operations into the database, so as to provide a single API for data processing and messaging. Client applications will be much easier to write, because all the logic of sending and receiving messages is within the database. System configuration, application deployment, and message warehousing are simplified, because we don't have to manage and fine-tune multiple products.

Integrating messaging into a database also provides features like backup, restore, transactionality & recoverability to messages. In this paper, we'll look at some aspects of messaging systems, and the challenges involved in integrating messaging such as message delivery semantics, transaction management and impact on query processing.

1 Introduction

Over the last decade, we have been witnessing a sea change in computing platforms. Proliferation of Internet technologies, advances in consumer hardware products, and availability of pervasive network bandwidth have fueled the development of a new class of Web-based applications. The foundation of this revolution was laid down by the dramatic advances in middleware technologies and products. New middleware standards such as J2EE [7], and .NET [9], and service-oriented architectures like Web Services [16] have stimulated the development of highly dynamic e-Business infrastructures. Among the many services and components in this new framework, messaging systems

T. Härder and W. Lehner (Eds.): Data Management (Wedekind Festschrift), LNCS 3551, pp. 91-109, 2005.

have emerged as a key component of this enterprise infrastructure. The current trend in middleware architectures indicates that messaging systems will strengthen their role in future middleware infrastructures towards so-called Message-Oriented Middleware (MOM) systems.

Early messaging systems functioned solely as queue managers. In this limited role, they offered queued transaction processing and provided basic services such as security, configuration, performance monitoring, recovery, etc. The common belief was that database systems already covered these features and a full-function messaging system only duplicates them [6]. This viewpoint changed dramatically as messaging systems evolved in the midst of middleware infrastructures. Message queuing systems focus on providing high performance transactional access in cases where there is a high rate of message insertion and deletion to a large number of independent destinations where on average there are few or even zero messages waiting to be received on any individual destination at any point in time. Their new features are sufficiently more complex and sophisticated that providing the same level of functionality in a database system is out of the question. Extended delivery models, highly scalable asynchronous message handling, distributed network protocols and processing, message-specific multiple qualities of service are just a few features of advanced messaging systems. In general, it is not feasible to contain these typical messaging system features inside a database system. In its new role, a messaging system is a core member of an advanced middleware infrastructure. It is the backbone of middleware that glues all other middleware components together. New middleware architectures and standards clearly separate database systems as external data sources. In this model, messaging systems are decoupled from database systems and they utilize a database system only as a (relational) "data source".

Messaging applications have the important characteristic that at any point in time, a significant amount of system and application data is in flight (i.e., stored) in message queues. Hence, messaging systems face two big data management challenges: (1) Coping with increased number of messages and sheer volume of data, (2) Processing the data in message queues to provide a real-time snapshot of the state of a business for critical decision making. Particularly, messaging systems are expected to provide elaborate, scalable data management functions such as powerful message selection (filtering), aggregation, transformation, etc., besides their traditional networking functionality. In other words, messaging systems have been slowly transformed into a new type of database system for transient and distributed data.

On the other side, database system vendors acknowledged the rise of middleware systems and realized the importance of seamless integration into middleware infrastructure. Several major database system vendors made the strategic decision to extend their database engines with core messaging capabilities. This way, they were better connected to a new class of applications, while applying scalable data management techniques (which they excelled in for the last 25 years) to messaging operations. Furthermore, they took advantage of built-in messaging support to develop more effective database services such as data replication or query notification services.

Despite the fact that early messaging systems had a broad range of common characteristics with database systems, the two systems developed and grew independently as stand-alone systems. Messaging systems are characterized by different inherent semantic variances and different levels of support for similar functionalities. Today, independent market segments have been established and different standards have been adopted in each world. As we will discuss in this paper, these inherent differences make the integration of database and messaging systems very challenging.

Modern database and messaging systems share similar functionality, but differ in several aspects. We believe that database and messaging systems can complement each other's technology in many ways. They can come together and mutually benefit from their features in delivering superior services for their applications. In fact, some advanced messaging systems already take advantage of database systems.

In this paper, we explore integration aspects of database and messaging systems from two perspectives. From the messaging system perspective, we identify database features that help messaging systems deliver their functions more effectively. From the database system perspective, we argue that database systems should utilize advanced features of messaging systems instead of trying to re-invent and re-develop them. Our claim is that a loose integration model is more appropriate for database and messaging systems. This integration model not only exploits the synergy of both systems but also allows them to grow more efficiently in their own domains. There are many obstacles and challenges in achieving such a successful database and messaging system integration. We highlight several of them and present our first attempt at introducing a research prototype implementation for an integrated database messaging system.

The rest of the paper is organized as follows. We start by describing state-of-the-art functionality in advanced messaging systems and new technologies built around them. We discuss the challenges in bringing advanced messaging systems and database systems together (section 2 and 3). Next, we provide a snapshot of current integrated database messaging systems (section 4). We then present our research prototype for an integrated database messaging system (section 5). It is a loose, federated integration approach that keeps the two systems separate but seamlessly integrated when necessary. Finally, we conclude the paper by speculating on possible future directions for database and messaging system integration (section 6).

2 Advanced Messaging Systems — The Frontier Beyond Basic Queuing

In this section, we discuss the main features supported in today's advanced messaging systems, point to a commercially available industrial-strength product as a reference implementation, and briefly discuss the evolving role of these systems.

2.1 Features of Advanced Messaging Systems

The salient features of today's advanced messaging systems include:

Standards and JMS: With the advent of J2EE environments, the standard Java Message Service (JMS) Specifications and Messaging API [12] was introduced. Providers of messaging software supported these specifications either with Java implementations or by wrapping their products with Java to support the standard API. Most advanced messaging systems hence play the role of "JMS providers" and support the following JMS features (For detailed information please see [12]):

Point-to-Point Messaging: A producer sends a message onto a "queue"; one or more consumers may compete to receive from the queue, with each message being received and removed from the queue by a single consumer. The "sender" and "receiver" are unaware of each other and the message stays on the queue until it has been consumed.

Publish/Subscribe Messaging: Publish/subscribe allows publishers to publish information such as weather or stock quotes to a "topic" which many different applications may subscribe to. Publishers and subscribers are generally unknown to each other and one published message may be received by any number of subscribers. Subscriptions may be declared "durable"—i.e., a subscribing client may register interest in a topic, disconnect and connect back at a later point in time and be able to retrieve matching messages published in the interim. JMS introduces the concept of an addressable destination which may have either point-to-point or publish/subscribe behavior.

Asynchronous Message Delivery: JMS APIs allow clients to register a 'listener' object with a consumer—when a message arrives at the destination for the consumer, a listener method is invoked by the JMS provider to allow processing of the message.

Persistent and Non-Persistent Messages and Delivery: Persistence properties specified on a destination or by client applications, determine if the message survives failures in the messaging system or network. The messaging system must be capable of doing such things as maintaining a non-persistent copy or storing a persistent copy of the message for later delivery to a third application and also publishing a subset of the message content to an audience of subscribers.

Message Structure: Messages are structured and are comprised of a pre-determined set of header fields, property fields (name, value pairs) and a body (that can be one of five pre-defined Java types in the case of JMS, including a text type that is used for XML messages). This standardization allows new applications to be interwoven transparently into the messaging framework. The JMS API allows a subset of the SQL '92 syntax to be used in selector expressions for filtering messages based on values in the header and properties fields, for purposes such as routing of messages.

MOM offerings support and extend their role of being JMS providers by catering to the J2EE and .NET environments and incorporate support for several sophisticated features including:

Extended Delivery Models: Advanced messaging systems provide a wider variety of delivery modes including:

- *anycast:* a message is sent to a number of potential consumers and is given to exactly one of them
- *unicast:* a message is sent from one producer to exactly one consumer, and
- *multicast:* a message is sent from one producer to a number of consumers.

Multiple Qualities of Service and Transaction Support: A range of qualities of service from best effort up to guaranteed, in-order, exactly once delivery are supported, implying support for both looser transactional models and semantics as well as the strict ACID transactions that database systems traditionally support. Support for timing from low latency, real time notification of events and messages to bulk storage of messages for later retrieval is built into advanced messaging systems.

Message Transformations and Intelligent Routing: Mediation components deployable on destinations allow the application designer to specify messaging transformations and routing on messages in transit (i.e., after they have been produced but before they are consumed). This powerful feature enables:

- Integration of disparate applications with different message formats; transformations are linked to the destination versus requiring that applications be aware of each other's formats and perform conversions at the source or target.
- Augmenting messaging data with reference data retrieved from a database—prior to routing the message elsewhere.
- Building a warehouse of messages for audit, error recovery, data mining, etc.

Interoperability: Advanced messaging must support new emerging standards and practices such as Web Services, firewalls, tunneling, and digital key management. They must also allow for interoperability of different messaging products between different enterprises.

Scalable, Reliable, Distributed Processing: As increasing amounts of corporate data flow through the messaging systems, scalability and reliability factors become critical. These systems must sustain rates of tens of thousands of persistent messages per second. To accommodate such needs, messaging systems maybe deployable in a network configuration—i.e., a "bus" comprised of smaller messaging "nodes" providing multiple points for producing and consuming clients to attach to, as depicted in Fig. 1

Each messaging node supports all requisite messaging functionality. *Location transparency*—i.e., support for a producer/consumer to attach to any node in this bus and send/receive messages to/from a destination without knowledge of which node in the bus persists messages for the destination is an integral feature of this configuration. Nodes communicate with each other via internal distributed protocols, cooperating together to effect a messaging fabric which gets data in flight distributed to all appropriate locations. Support exists for features such as high availability, adaptive routing in the case of link failures, load balancing, integrated administration, etc. Information as to:

- where messages for a particular destination are persisted in the bus,
- how and on which nodes to persist messages that flow through a bus so QoS guarantees can be satisfied,
- how to service remote receive's (i.e., subscriber requests on one node while the messages for the destination reside on another node),
- reconciling messaging state and data after a crash, etc., is built into these systems, freeing administrators from having to administer/manage such complexities and simplifying application program development. Such systems run in a variety of different operating environments from large clusters of SMPs (with support for features such as workload balancing, partitioning of destinations, failover, etc.) to small diskless edge servers where messages are persisted elsewhere in the network.

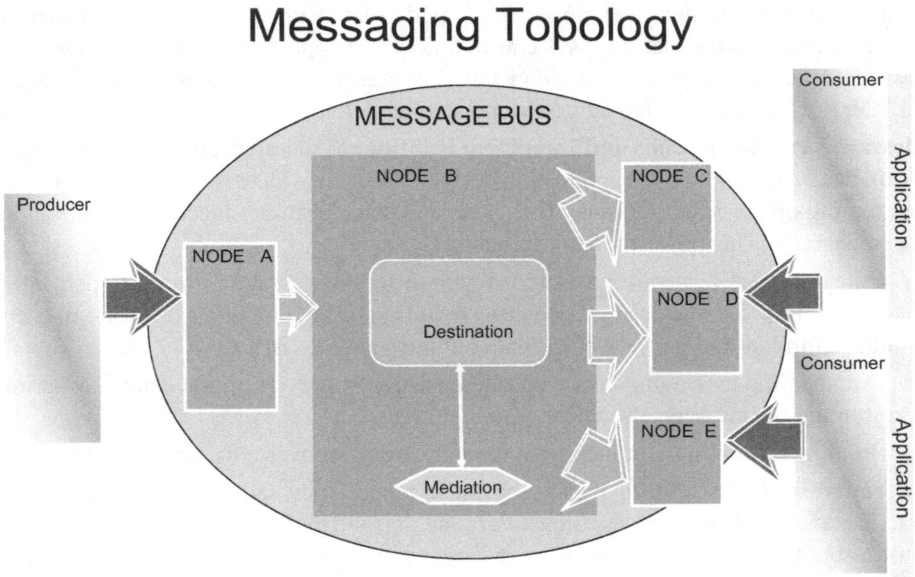

Fig. 1 Messaging Bus, Nodes, Clients, Destination, and Mediation Topology

Optimized and Scalable Matching Engine: While database systems are good at handling a single query against hundreds of thousands of rows, a publish/subscribe system has to solve efficiently the inverse problem—that of evaluating a single published message against hundreds of thousands of subscription criteria, which can be thought of as queries, and delivering the messages with low latency. While it is possible to build such logic into the database system, low latency requirements may not be met if the database system requires data to be persisted for it to perform matching. A highly efficient and optimized matching engine is thus a critical component in any advanced distributed messaging system. The messaging system will do local matching for the local subscribers and will forward the published message to other messaging nodes to do matching for their local subscribers.

Systems Management and Tooling Support: Advanced messaging systems must offer rich, easy-to-use administrative, performance monitoring and tooling support for managing the entire system. Support for tools that ease building of messaging workflows, deployment of mediation components, etc. must be included to enable rapid application development.

2.2 The Enterprise Service Bus

The next step in the evolution of advanced messaging systems is the central role that they play in an Enterprise Service Bus (ESB). For the purposes of this paper, we adopt the Gartner definition of the ESB—i.e., "*a standards-based message-bus capable of linking together standards-based components written to Web standards and other standards*". Advanced messaging systems provide functionality to the ESB and allow applications to integrate with an ESB. ESBs provide the means for building and deploying Service-Oriented Architectures (SOA)—an application architecture within which all functions are defined as independent services with well-defined invokable interfaces which can be called in defined sequences to form business processes.

Advanced Messaging system functionality in the ESB includes standards support (JMS, Web Services, etc.), multiple messaging transport protocols (SOAP/HTTP, Multicast, etc.), event driven (publish/subscribe), demand driven (request/reply) and store-and-forward computing models, intelligent routing and transformation services (mediations). To further quote from [1], Gartner predicts:

"ESB will take messaging to the next level. In addition to simply improving the manageability and throughput of enterprise intersystem information traffic, the new ESB-based platforms will include support for such fundamentals as multiprotocol service-oriented architecture (transcending the current quality of service limitations of Web services), event-driven architecture, coordinated systems management, business activity monitoring and other high-level enterprise-scope expansions to the quality of service of modern IT. More than any other technological advance, the transition of the core ap plication platform infrastructure from RPC-based to ESB-based will enable enterprises to take a major step toward routine real-time-enterprise agility in their information processing.

Gartner predicts that the industry transition to messaging and ESB as the core application platform infrastructure model will mark an inflection point—triggering a new, massive wave of innovation around businesses' use of their information resources, capitalizing on the architecture of events."

3 What Can Databases Do for Advanced Messaging Systems?

Database systems play two diverse, important roles in conjunction with any advanced messaging system. In the first, more limited, role, databases serve as a natural choice for use as persistent "data stores" that messaging systems interface with (via standard mechanisms such as JDBC), to reliably and transactionally store and retrieve messaging data and state information. The messaging system may choose to maintain all of its data and information in its own layer, only using the database for satisfying higher level QoS guarantees that require messaging data to survive across client/system failures.

A more powerful role that database systems can play in conjunction with advanced messaging systems calls for closer synergy between the messaging and database components to more fully exploit the rich functionality that modern databases afford, while providing SQL/XQuery application programmers access to messaging data via programming models they are more familiar with. Apart from enabling a new class of database applications that can now include querying and interacting with messaging data, databases become an important source of information that can connect and interoperate with the ESB.

The next two sub-sections further elaborate upon these two roles.

3.1 Database as the Message Store

In this scenario, the database serves as a backing store. Messaging systems exploit some integral database features (while imposing others that several commercial DBMS vendors now support) including:

Storage Definition, Management, and Underlying Media/Fabric Exploitation: Messaging data maybe stored in one or more database tables—typically messages for one or more similar queues may be stored in a single database table allowing administrators to configure the table characteristics appropriately.

Buffer, Cache, and Spill Management: Messaging data is generally short-lived—a producer publishes (inserts) messages to a destination (table) and a subscribing consumer consumes (deletes) the message very close to the time at which it was inserted; thus, database pages that hold these messages are expected to still be in the database buffer cache affording consumers quick access.

Index Creation, Management, and Reorganization: Messaging data generally have unique IDs; an index on the ID allows for efficient and ordered retrieval of messages. Due to the high intensity of inserts and deletes, indexes may get unbalanced and optimizer statistics may become unreliable, requiring the database system to detect, account for and correct these situations.

Latching and Lock Management: Consumers must not block on publishers (and vice versa) or on each other; hence, row-level locking support is mandated, while lower isolation semantics such as the ability for scans to "skip" over locked messages, read "uncommitted" messages during message retrieval, etc., are highly desirable. Messaging systems at restart may scan database tables to recreate their in-memory state and locks held by in-doubt transactions must not block the restart.

Transaction Management and Coordination: Messaging systems may need to persist messaging data and state information transactionally.

Given the distributed, asynchronous nature of messaging applications, transactions are typically used in messaging operations in the following manner:

1. A "producer" inserts messages to a destination transactionally:
   SEND MESSAGE M1 TO DESTINATION D1
   COMMIT
2. The messaging system may need to persist and propagate this message to another node that is designated as the "owner" of the destination; this propagation happens as part of one or more purely internal transactions that is completely decoupled from the user's original transaction. Advanced messaging systems ensure that local 1PC transactions are used in this step, even if the propagation is to a target destination on a remote machine with its own backing store, using protocols that involve careful orchestration of runtime sequencing actions paired with the appropriate handshake and reconciliation restart steps.

3. A consumer client in a separate transaction consumes this message via:
   RECEIVE MESSAGE M1 FROM DESTINATION D1
   COMMIT

Based on the QoS guarantees, the messaging system may persist the messages and message delivery notices to its backing store either synchronously in a purely local database transaction (but in sync with the user's original transaction), asynchronously (forming batches from messages spanning user transactions and persisting these in a single transaction), or not at all (as in the case of non-persistent messages). Even in the 'synchronous' case, the database transaction is decoupled from the user transaction thus avoiding two phase commit (2PC).

Hence, unless the application specifically dictates use of a 2PC protocol by combining a messaging operation and a non-messaging operation within the same transaction employing an external transaction manager that coordinates this "global" transaction, advanced messaging systems do not use 2PC transactions for any internal work. In situations where an external coordinator is involved, the messaging system (and hence the underlying database) may be enlisted as a participant, in which case the database may need to support the X-Open standard XA Resource Manager APIs as specified in [21].

High Speed, Market Hardened, and Scalable Logging Services: Messaging data may need to be persisted to the database as part of each user transaction, causing log forces at commit time to become a bottleneck. Additionally, "message consumption" (deletes) is a common operation and its runtime performance can be enhanced if database systems minimized logging of the deleted data employing mechanisms like:

- logical deletes—i.e., at runtime the row is marked deleted and sometime after transaction commit, it is physically removed from the data page—so the contents of the row do not need logging.
- non-logged temporary tables—i.e., tables for which data modifications are not logged; these can be used to store non-persistent messaging data.

Messaging systems also benefit from standard database functionality such as restart, media failure, point-in-time, and remote site recovery capabilities, cluster fabric utilization and high-availability/recovery orchestration.

3.2 Improved Database and Messaging Synergy

Database systems can play a double role in solutions that involve messaging interactions. They can serve as the backing store for persistent messages. More importantly, if messaging and database systems co-operated more closely on message schema and typing information, and database systems could access messaging destinations and data, database application developers can rapidly develop solutions that require access to both database and messaging data. Thus, the following features of database systems could be better exploited:

Storage of Message Payloads in Separate Column(s) in the Database Table: If the messaging record format is known, the message body could be stored in a set of SQL columns, to allow querying parts of the message. Storing the payload in a native XML data type column allows for powerful content-based querying of messages, using XPath expressions, for example.

Message Warehousing and Replay Functionality: To allow tracking and analysis of messaging data. The rich set of business intelligence tools that most databases support can be employed against messaging data.

Database system support for extensions such as the ones below would allow database SQL/XQuery programmers to more easily interact with messaging systems:

Enabling the Database for Asynchronous Operations: Message triggers automatically receive arriving messages and drive stored procedures or SQL/XQuery fragments with the arriving message as input parameters.

Use of SQL, XQuery, and XPath Support: APIs that database application programmers are familiar with to allow Search/Update/Join/Aggregation operations, etc. on messaging and non-messaging data in a single query, if so required. Support for syntax such as SELECT FROM DELETE (described in [1]) allow for efficient set-based message consumption.

Publishing to a Messaging Destination: Via database triggers or database replication mechanisms, database change information can be tracked and published to the messaging system allowing database systems to be "producers" of information. This publishing mechanism will need to be highly scalable.

Storing Durable Subscriptions in the Database: Additional support for asynchronous mechanisms that notify the subscriber when a matching message arrives is required.

Consume-with-Wait Support: To allow consumers to wait for a message to become available on a destination (versus continual polling).

4 A Survey of Database and Messaging System Integrations

Several commercial offerings of messaging and database integration solutions have been available for over a decade. In this section, we include a brief description of some of these products, classified by the integration strategy they have chosen to implement.

4.1 Database System's Use of Messaging Systems

Database-Specific Messaging and Queuing: In the nineties, [6] discussed queuing characteristics and made the case that queues are databases. Accordingly, some database systems proceeded to build in extensions to their engines, to provide support for built-in messaging through first class queue objects that reside in and are managed by the database system. Messaging system functionality is incorporated inside the database system, in this style of integration. These solutions have built in engine modifications for efficient "matching" of events to subscriptions, skip-lock isolations so getters can pick up the next "available" message in a queue, Consume-with-wait semantics, etc.

Oracle's AQ product falls in this category, providing proprietary internal APIs (PL/SQL packages) as well as support for JMS APIs for messaging operations such as queuing and de-queuing of messages, DDL support for creating queues in the database, setting up routing rules, etc. Point-to-point and Publish/Subscribe messaging models are supported and more esoteric features such as tracking origins of a message for auditing, etc. are available. A good summary of Oracle AQ's capabilities can be gleaned from [3]. *Microsoft SQL Server's Service Broker* (in the Yukon release) architecture documented in [20], offers SQL extensions (SEND/RECEIVE verbs) for messaging and introduces several additional database objects (contract, service, dialog, etc.) to build its messaging framework, apart from hosting queues in the database; "service programs" (i.e., stored procedures, application programs) encapsulate the application logic. *HP/Tandem's Non-stop SQL-MX* [7] offers messaging support via SQL extensions.

Interface with a Messaging Engine: While [6] made the case for queues in the database, messaging systems requirements have greatly matured since then. More recent work in [5] calls for more sophisticated feature support and refers to issues such as those documented earlier in section 2.1. A less stringent flavor of "light integration" hence chooses to house only the messaging data in the database, integrating with external messaging systems, thus leveraging their highly advanced features versus requiring to build all of this support into the database.

IBM/DB2 [11] uses this approach for exploiting database capabilities while leveraging the messaging capabilities of the market leading WebSphere MQ product. System-provided functions are used to access the MQ interfaces. *Sybase ASE Real-time messaging* [14] follows a similar approach integrating with TIBCO's E4JMS product via built-in functions that encapsulate the messaging interface calls.

Tab. 1 summarizes the messaging integration approaches adopted by these database system vendors.

4.2 Messaging System's Use of the Database System

Message-System-Specific Persistence, Transactions, and Logging: In this approach, the messaging system does not rely on any database system features for supporting messaging functionality—but re-invents several database features for supporting persistence.

IBM's WebSphere MQ (formerly known as MQSeries) [18] family of products offers a comprehensive framework for business integration. The WebSphere MQ product implements a scalable, optimized, file-based persistence mechanism; the only integration points with database systems therefore is via standard XA interfaces (to facilitate global transaction support for messaging and database operations) or via JDBC (for message augmenting support). Messaging solutions offered by providers such as TIBCO [15] and BEA's Weblogic [2] also provide the option of using file stores instead of database systems for persistence.

Tab. 1 Comparison of Integration Approaches

	Messaging Integration	**Messaging API**	**Transactions Supported?**	**Message Model**	**Predicates for message selection**	**Operates on sets of messages?**
Oracle AQ	Native to DB	PL/SQL, C++, Java	Yes	Object type	Arbitrary predicates	No
Microsoft Service Broker	Native to DB	SQL extensions	Yes	Message body column	Very Limited	Yes
Tandem Nonstop SQL/MX	Native to DB	Stream + SQL	Yes	Tuples	Arbitrary SQL predicates	Yes
DB2 MQ Functions	Interface with Messaging Engine	Built-in functions	Uncoordinated	Scalar message body	MQ selectors	Yes (side effects)
Sybase ASE	Interface with Messaging Engine	Built-in functions	Multiple models	Scalar message body	JMS selectors	No

Database as a Persistent Store: In this approach, the messaging system uses a database as a persistent store, to reliably and transactionally save its persistent data.

The default embedded messaging engine in the WebSphere Platform Messaging (WPM) component of IBM WebSphere Application Server V6.0 [17] incorporates the features of advanced messaging systems mentioned in section 2.1 and uses this approach, exploiting the database system's storage, indexing, backup and recovery technologies to maintain and retrieve persistent state and data. The database system can be any JDBC compliant database system supported by WebSphere, including the DB2 family of database products, Oracle, Microsoft and Sybase. Several other middleware offerings, including those from BEA (Weblogic) and Sonic MQ [13], use a similar approach.

4.3 Shortcomings of These Approaches

While incorporating all of the functionality advanced messaging systems must support into the database engine (i.e., the native integration approach) maybe theoretically possible, given the exponential and continuing growth trends of messaging systems and their role in the ESB, market realities are such that database systems that attempt this will always be in the catch-up mode. Also, as previously mentioned, significant investments at the database engine level are needed to support core requirements of messaging listed in section 2.1, including those of low-latency, interoperability, support for looser transaction semantics, to name a few. Enhancing the database system engines to better integrate with the existing systems opens up new opportunities, eases application programming and allows database systems to flow information into the enterprise.

Similarly, advanced messaging systems could exploit features of database systems that have been employed in mission-critical deployments for a few decades now, versus attempting to rebuild all of this technology (i.e., the pure messaging approach). Messaging systems must cooperate more closely with database systems opening up administration APIs, etc. for other applications to integrate more closely and avail of their features.

The next section focuses on describing a prototype of an integration approach that leverages the strengths of each of these systems.

5 An Integrated Database Messaging Prototype

In this section, we present our integrated database messaging research prototype. The aim of the prototype was to explore messaging operations in RDBMSs by integrating with messaging systems. Our main design principle was to provide a convenient and easy way to manipulate message destinations within the SQL language as if they are local tables. In the initial prototype, we decided to support only three basic messaging operations: send, receive and browse.

The prototype has been developed in the context of DB2 UDB by exploiting its existing features and integrating with WebSphere Platform Messaging (WPM) component of the WebSphere Application Server V6.0 product [4, 17]. Message destinations are accessed through information integration features available in DB2 (WebSphere/II [1]). We implemented a messaging wrapper to carry out required mappings between the DB2 engine and WPM. WebSphere/II also provides an infrastructure for transactional integration. In the prototype, users create local table references (i.e., "nicknames" in WebSphere/II terminology) to interact with message destinations. However, due to semantic differences and operations, these references must be separated from other nicknames. We call them "Destinations" in the prototype.

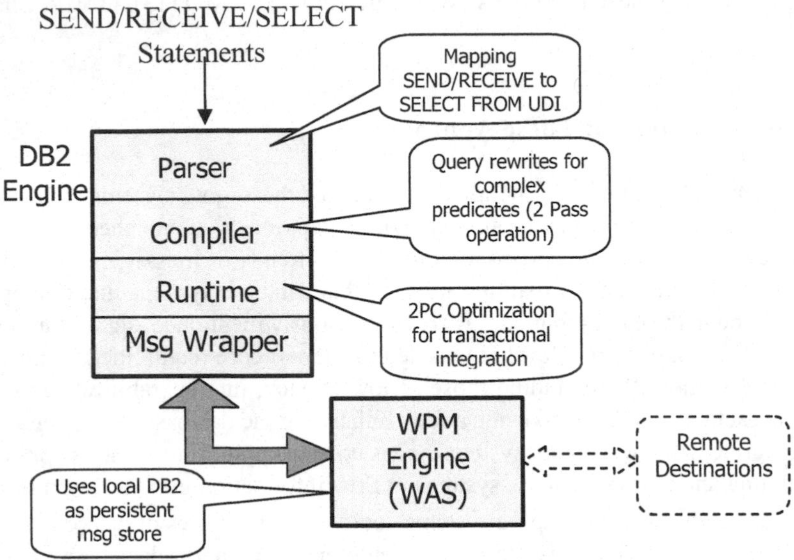

Fig. 2 Modified DB2 UDB Components in our Research Prototype

Note that JMS/WPM message model is essentially non-relational in that every message is a Java object. It follows the JMS specification [12]. Additionally, messaging operations have different semantics, unique parameter types, and most importantly they are not set-oriented. The main job of the message wrapper, hence, becomes the handling of these differences transparently.

There are three sections in a JMS message: Standard headers, application-defined properties and body. Header fields can easily be represented with respective column definitions. However, creating system-supported column structures over the content of application defined properties and message body can be a daunting task. There must be common metadata repository for the definitions of column structures, and agreed methods for composing and decomposing them. This issue was not the immediate focus of the prototype. Hence, application-defined properties and message body appear as a single column in destination definitions.

A high level architecture of our prototype and our modifications within the DB2 engine components are given in Fig. 2. In the rest of this section, we will briefly discuss these changes. We first describe the SQL language extensions in the parser for message operations, and then explain the issues in the compiler and message wrapper implementation. Finally, we present a 2PC optimization that was developed to enhance transactional integration for messaging operations.

5.1 SQL Extensions

In the prototype, we extended SQL with two new statements: Send and Receive. There was no need to create a new statement for browse operation, because a SQL SELECT statement is close enough to provide the desired semantics. The SQL extensions are mostly syntactic sugar on top of SELECT-FROM-UDI [1].

The send statement creates and puts a message into a specific destination. Message contents can be created using table data. In the below example query, a message is sent to the *stockdisplay* destination for each row in the result set of SELECT subquery.

```
SEND TO stockdisplay ($body)
SELECT n.name || '#' || CHAR (q.price)
FROM quotes as q, stocknames n
WHERE q.symbol = n.symbol
```

As a result of the send operation, WPM initializes several important message properties such as message id, timestamp, etc. If the user wants to access this information, the send statement can be embedded into a select statement just like selecting rows from the result of insert operation. For details please see [1].

A Receive operation is basically a destructive read from a destination. Hence, it is internally modeled as an embedded delete operation inside a select statement. Again, the SELECT-FROM-UDI framework provides the necessary infrastructure to accomplish this. It also guarantees the enforcement of required semantics for receive statement throughout the compilation. The following receive statement example gets messages created in the last hour for *stockdisplay* destination.

```
RECEIVE $body
    FROM stockdisplay
    WHERE MINUTEDIFF(CURRENT TIMESTAMP -
                        TIMESTAMP($timestamp)) < 60
```

5.2 SQL Compiler Issues

Send and receive statements cause side effects. Therefore, there were two main issues in the SQL compiler: (1) Guaranteeing ordered execution of query blocks during the optimization when multiple query blocks are given in a single statement, (2) Handling complex predicates on message queues (in each query block). The first problem was not a big issue, because the SELECT-FROM-UDI feature clearly defines query semantics for select statements with side effects. However, we had to work on the second problem as WebSphere/II infrastructure does not have adequate support for statements with side effects.

Obviously, an SQL statement can handle much more sophisticated predicates than those supported by WPM. Therefore, the SQL compiler must decide on the right set of predicate pushdowns when complex predicates are issued against message queues. The key point here is that messaging operations cause side effects on the queues, so push-down analysis must be done carefully. A straightforward solution is to perform receive operation in two steps. In the first step, the query plan can access multiple messages through a non-destructive browse operation on the message queue with push-downable predicates. Then, it can apply the complex predicates on the retrieved message set. In the second step, only the qualifying messages are destructively received from the queue using unique message ids.

Note that the browse operation described above should lock the messages being examined to prevent other consumers from destructively consuming them. This is however not a commonly supported feature, in messaging systems (including WPM) or specifications. Because **all** messages being browsed need to be locked, poorly designed queries can adversely affect consuming applications. Ideally, the database isolation level for the query must be enforced at WPM. But this support is not possible today, so applications must tolerate the unusual behavior that may arise when complex predicates are issued against destinations.

Another issue can arise in transaction semantics. WPM does not return a message on a receive operation if the message was added to the destination by a send operation issued in the same transaction—whereas many database systems allow a transaction to delete or browse a row it previously inserted. As a result, transactions involving message operations exhibit different behavior that must be also tolerated by the applications. When inserting into a destination, the normal and expected case is that the "sender" will not be a receiver and hence is never presented with the view of available messages presented to receivers; similarly receivers are not expected to see the destination as perceived by senders. It is this clear separation of send and receive views of a destination which allows efficient implementation of send and receive operations on remote destinations, and prompts a transactional model different from database table operations where it is a normal case for one application to both read and update rows in a single table under one transaction. Getting a message inserted into a queue by a sender and removed from it by a separate consumer, always takes two transactions in a messaging system; in contrast, reading a database table and then updating or inserting and/or deleting rows from it can be done by one application in a single database transaction.

5.3 Message Wrapper

We implemented a new message wrapper to map messaging operations and to achieve transactional integration between the RDBMS and WPM. The Message wrapper does not only offer support for DML operations. DDL operations to create and manage local references to WPM destinations, and populating local DB2 catalogs are also implemented thanks to the extensible WebSphere/II framework. When a nickname is created for a WPM destination, the wrapper automatically assigns column structures for standard message headers, application defined property and message body. The current prototype creates nicknames only for existing WPM destinations.

While generating the corresponding WPM message operations for input SQL statements, the wrapper also performs data transfers. Send and receive operations are handled within a transaction context. Our modifications in the SQL compiler identify executable portions of input queries by the wrapper. By analyzing the execution environment, the wrapper generates the right parameters including the predicate syntax for message selection in the WPM engine. To provide set-oriented semantics, all the available messages are retrieved (considering an input time-out period) for receive or select statements. Applications can specify limits on the number of messages that they want to retrieve.

5.4 2PC Optimization

As mentioned in section 3.1, pure-messaging solutions do not incur 2PC unless they are application specified and coordinated externally. With integrated database and messaging, database applications on the other hand can commonly choose to update database tables and invoke messaging operations in the scope of the same transaction. For example, when the messaging operation is triggered off by a database change, such as:

```
    INSERT INTO ORDERS VALUES (PART_NUMBER,...)
SEND PART_NUMBER TO SHIP_FROM_WAREHOUSE_Q
COMMIT
```

Based on the integrated database and messaging solution support, the spectrum of options on transactional behavior in this case range from the success of the database and messaging commands being treated as independent of each other, to requiring both operations to succeed for the transaction to commit. In the last, most stringent case that calls for transaction atomicity, a 2PC protocol may be used. However, 2PC is known to be expensive, because it requires multiple synchronous forces of the database transaction log and incurs network communication overheads.

However, for the common case where the database system is the transaction coordinator (i.e., there is no external transaction coordinator) and the backing store for the messaging system and the database impacted by the local updates in the transaction are the same, solutions that allow for database connection sharing between the database and messaging system or other means of transaction sharing, are employed to avoid 2PC. Thus, on Oracle AQ, for example, an API is supported that allows retrieval of the original database connection established for messaging operations, while in WPM the database connection for Container Managed Persistence operations and messaging operations is shared allowing messaging and database updates to share a connection to avoid 2PC.

In our prototype, the local update to the database and WPM's persistent operations are carried out in the scope of two separate database connections; hence, we employ a scheme that is based on the XA join/suspend tightly coupled behavior, that allows two database connections to perform work on behalf of the same transaction; the original transaction context established by the database update is flowed to the messaging system which is flowed back to the database when the messaging system performs its persistent operations. The transaction management functionality recognizes this scenario and forces the transaction log only once for this transaction.

6 Conclusions

Middleware infrastructures and messaging systems have evolved dramatically. Today the functionality gap between database and these systems is much bigger than what it used to be 10 years ago. This trend changes the computing architectures and forces developers to reexamine integration models. In this paper, we focused on database and messaging systems integration on this new computing platform. We described advanced features in modern messaging systems and argued that database systems should exploit those features through federated integration architectures rather than attempting to develop native messaging systems.

We presented a research prototype that we developed to validate and identify potential problems in this approach. We made minor modifications in the DB2 UDB engine and exploited WebSphere Information Integrator features to access an advanced messaging system, namely WebSphere Platform Messaging. The prototype allows users to perform messaging and database operation using the SQL language. We also implemented an optimized 2PC transaction mechanism that helps to achieve closer integration.

There are still many challenges to be tackled. Easy and transparent administration of integrated database messaging is perhaps the most important one. Another key challenge is to provide mechanisms inside database engines for scalable asynchronous message processing. Despite these difficulties, synergy between database and advanced messaging systems can bring many advantages to applications by offering the state-of-the-art features from both systems today and in the future.

Acknowledgments. We would like to thank Stephen Todd, Tim Holloway, Paul Brett, Hamid Pirahesh, Jim Kleewein, Peter Niblett, Tim Vincent, Connie Nelin, Dan Wolfson and Paul McInerney for their help and support. Their insights and invaluable feedback influenced every aspect of our project.

References

[1] Behm, A., Rielau, S., Swagerman, R.: Returning Modified Rows—SELECT Statements with Side Effects, VLDB 2004, Toronto, Canada, September, 2004

[2] BEA Weblogic Platform, http://www.bea.com/

[3] Gawlick, D., Mishra, S.: Information sharing with the Oracle database, H.-A. Jacobsen, editor. 2nd Intl. Workshop on Distributed Event-Based Systems (DEBS'03), San Diego, CA, USA, June 2003. ACM Press.

[4] D.H. Brown Associates, "IBM WebSphere Application Server, Version 6 Delivers Business Flexibility", White Paper, http://www-306.ibm.com/software/webservers/appserv/was/WAS_V6_DH_Brown.pdf, September 2004

[5] Gray, J.: The Next Database Revolution, Proc. of the ACM SIGMOD Int. Conf. on Management of Data, Paris, France, June 13-18, 2004

[6] Gray, J.: THESIS: Queues are Databases, http://research.microsoft.com/research/pubs/view.aspx?pubid=496, January, 1995

[7] Java 2 Platform, Enterprise Edition (J2EE), http://java.sun.com/j2ee/

[8] Hanlon, M., Klein, J., Linden, R. V., Zeller, H.: Publish/Subscribe in NonStop SQL: Transactional Streams in a Relational Context, 20th International Conference on Data Engineering, Boston, Massachusetts, April, 2004

[9] Microsoft .NET, http://www.microsoft.com/net/

[10] Natis, Y. V., Gartner: Predicts 2004: Application Integration and Middleware, http://ww4.gartner.com/resources/119000/119085/119085.pdf, Dec 2003

[11] IBM DB2 UDB Manuals: How to use WebSphere MQ functions within DB2, http://publib.boulder.ibm.com/infocenter/db2help/index.jsp?topic=/com.ibm.db2.ii.doc/ad/ciiwsmqf.htm

[12] J2EE Java Message Service (JMS), http://java.sun.com/products/jms/

[13] Sonic Software, http://www.sonicsoftware.com/products/sonicmq/index.ssp

[14] Sybase Real-Time Data Services, http://www.sybase.com/products/informationmanagement/realtimedataservices

[15] TIBCO Messaging Solutions, http://www.tibco.com/software/enterprise_backbone/messaging.jsp

[16] Web Services Activity, http://www.w3.org/2002/ws/

[17] WebSphere Application server V6.0, http://www-306.ibm.com/software/webservers/appserv/was/

[18] WebSphere Information Integrator, http://www-306.ibm.com/software/data/integration/

[19] WebSphere MQ, http://www-306.ibm.com/software/integration/wmq/

[20] Wolter, R.: A First Look at SQL Server 2005 Service Broker, http://msdn.microsoft.com/library/default.asp?url=/library/en-us/dnsql90/html/sqlsvcbroker.asp, July, 2004

[21] X/Open CAE Specification; Distributed Transaction Processing: The XA Specification, http://www.opengroup.org/onlinepubs/009680699/toc.pdf

Data Management Support for Notification Services

Wolfgang Lehner

Technische Universität Dresden, Germany
lehner@inf.tu-dresden.de

Abstract. Database management systems are highly specialized to efficiently organize and process huge amounts of data in a transactional manner. During the last years, however, database management systems have been evolving as a central hub for the integration of mostly heterogeneous and autonomous data sources to provide homogenized data access. The next step in pushing database technology forward to play the role of an information marketplace is to actively notify registered users about incoming messages or changes in the underlying data set. Therefore, notification services may be seen as a generic term for subscription systems or, more general, data stream systems which both enable processing of standing queries over transient data. This article gives a comprehensive introduction into the context of notification services by outlining their differences to the classical query/response-based communication pattern, it illustrates potential application areas, and it discusses requirements addressing the underlying data management support. In more depth, this article describes the core concepts of the *PubScribe* project thereby choosing three different perspectives. From a first perspective, the subscription process and its mapping onto the primitive publish/subscribe communication pattern is explained. The second part focuses on a hybrid subscription data model by describing the basic constructs from a structural as well as an operational point of view. Finally, the *PubScribe* notification service project is characterized by a storage and processing model based on relational database technology.

To summarize, this contribution introduces the idea of notification services from an application point of view by inverting the database approach and dealing with persistent queries and transient data. Moreover, the article provides an insight into database technology, which must be exploited and adopted to provide a solid base for a scalable notification infrastructure, using the *PubScribe* project as an example.

1 Introduction

The technological development in recent years has created an infrastructure which enables us to gather and store almost everything that can be recorded. However, the stored

T. Härder and W. Lehner (Eds.): Data Management (Wedekind Festschrift), LNCS 3551, pp. 111-136, 2005.

data gets frequently lost in the existing varieties of databases. The main reason is that nobody is willing to browse multiple databases and specifically search these databases for certain entries.

Multiple methods from a database-technological point of view are trying to leverage this very general problem. The context of information integration [26] tries to come up with an either logically (multi-database systems or virtual database systems) or physically integrated data set, often seen in data warehouse environments [16]. From a more application-oriented point of view, methods and techniques coming from the area of knowledge discovery in databases try to generate hypotheses which might be of some interest for the users of the data set. The real benefit of this approach is that a user may specifically focus on these results as a starting point for an interactive analysis [10, 19, 9].

A completely different approach is taken when inverting the current way of interacting with databases by moving from a *system-centric* to a *data-centric* behavior [22, 23]. The query-based approach follows the request/response paradigm, where the user (or client) is posing a query and the (database) system tries to execute the query as fast as possible. The result is delivered via basic interfaces (like ODBC, JDBC, or CLI) to the user's application context. Fig. 1a illustrates this interaction pattern with database management systems on the one side acting as data providers and clients on the other side acting as data consumers. Both parties are in a close relationship with each another, i.e. every client has to know the location and the context of the specific database.

1.1 Publish/Subscribe as the Base for Notification Systems

Inverting the "request/response" idea leads to the communication pattern very well known as "publish/subscribe" [5], which is used in various situations. For example, publish/subscribe is utilized in software engineering as a pattern [12] to connect individual components. In the same vein, publish/subscribe may be used to build a data-centric notification service. Notification services consist of publishers, subscribers, and finally, a (logically single) notification brokering system. Fig. 1b gives a conceptual overview of the scenario. On the one side, publishing systems (or publishers) are acting as data providers, generating information and sending data notifications to the brokering component as soon as the information is available. Notifications are collected, transformed into a pre-defined or pre-registered schema and merged into a global database. Depending on the type of subscriptions (section 3.1), notifications may remain in the database only for the time span required to notify interested subscribers.

On the other side, subscribers—acting as data consumers—are registering "interest" (information template, profile, ...) providing the delivery of certain notifications using specific formats and protocols with a pre-defined frequency. The notion of interest is manifold and will be further discussed in the following section. Furthermore, query specification and result transmission are decoupled from a subscriber's point of view. Once a query is formulated, the user is no longer in contact with the notification system but receives a notification only if new messages of interest have arrived at the database system or if a given time interval has passed. The advantage for the user is tremendous:

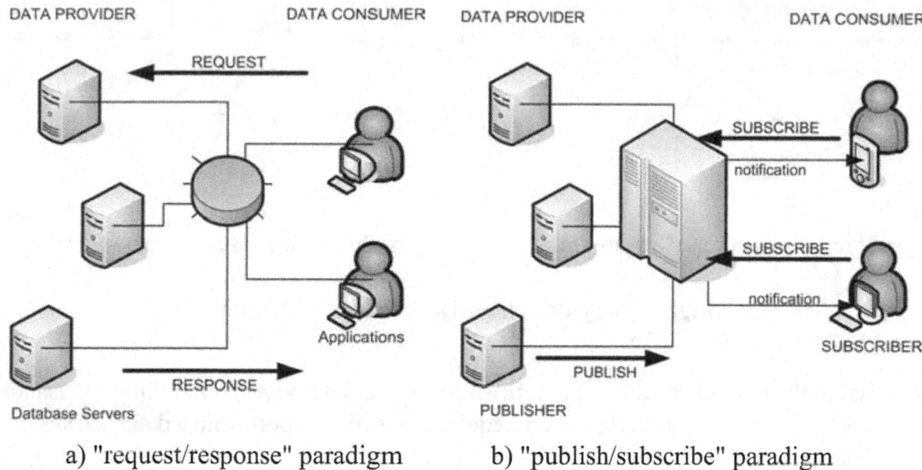

a) "request/response" paradigm b) "publish/subscribe" paradigm

Fig. 1 Comparison of "Request/Response" and "Publish/Subscribe" Paradigm

once a query (in form of a subscription) is specified, the user does not have to wait for the answer of the query, because the result will be delivered automatically according to the pre-defined delivery properties.

Obviously, publisher and subscriber are roles associated with certain applications or (human) users implying that, for example, received notification messages may be forwarded to another notification system. In this scenario, a single component is then acting as subscriber and publisher at the same time. The benefit of notification services from an application point of view consists in the following facts:

- Data providers and data consumers are decoupled and do not know each other—the connection is purely data-driven.
- Profiles articulating a subscriber's interest allow (depending on the current system) a very detailed specification of the requested piece of information.
- Information is delivered only if certain delivery criteria are fulfilled. Therefore, notification systems may be regarded as a core mechanism to tackle the problem of a general information flood.

1.2 Data-Centric Versus System-Centric Data Delivery

From a database point of view, notification services exhibit properties which have a dramatic impact on the way data is treated and queries are executed. Fig. 2 illustrates the basic principle of the different prerequisites compared to the request/response-driven querying model. While database queries are executed within transactions and therefore isolated from each other, the notification evaluation queries are now clustered together and executed simultaneously [27, 20], thus decreasing the overall query run time and

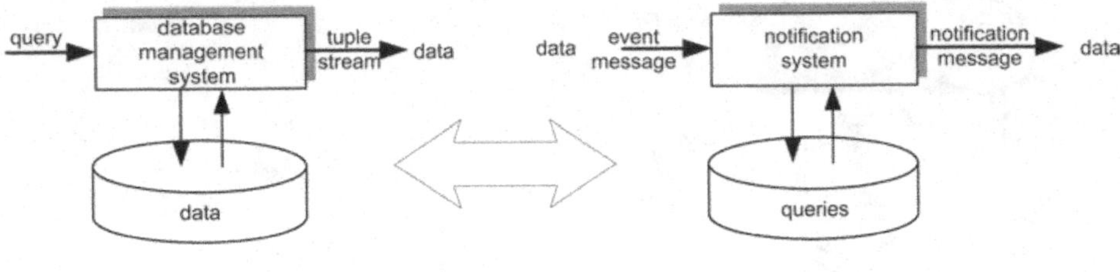

a) "request/response" paradigm b) "publish/subscribe" paradigm

Fig. 2 Query-driven vs. Data-driven Execution

increasing the overall capacity of a notification system. Obviously, handling thousands of subscriptions within a single system requires specific support from a database system [30, 3, 20].

To put it in a nutshell, the main difference from a database point of view consists in the fact that data structures no longer reflect the main object of management. In contrast, queries are now efficiently stored, indexed, and transformed, providing the basis for optimizations with regard to the set of standing queries, which have to be applied to the stream of incoming event messages. Furthermore, a notification system may comprise multiple local (and only partially integrated) schemas according to the registration of the publisher. Because a publisher may come and go, the set of local schemas is highly volatile, implying an integration process either on-the-fly during the registration of a standing query or partially by the user itself.

1.3 Application Scenarios

In most application scenarios, notification systems can be seen as an add-on and not as a full substitute for a regular query-driven database management system. Notification systems are used in applications requiring a pro-active propagation of information to specific consumers. In the following, three very different application scenarios are discussed:

- *News service*
  A very popular and already prospering service implementing a very limited kind of notification technique may be seen in news services, which send e-mails or short messages containing abstracts of various news articles on a regular basis (one of the first was [35] followed by many others like [25]). The functionality of news notification services highly varies from system to system. For instance, notifications could depend only on time stamps or time periods since the last delivery, or they might be based on the evaluation of specified predicates within subscription templates. For example, a notification can be generated if the stock price of IBM reaches a certain value. Simple news services are often synonymous to the "push service" of documents.

- *Business intelligence applications*
  Combining the idea of a notification service and the concept of data warehousing [16] leads to the pro-active support of decision support systems. A data warehouse system provides an integrated, long-term, and logically centralized database to retrieve information necessary for decision support, supply chain management, customer relationship management, etc. Due to the nature of data warehousing, these database applications exhibit specific characteristics with regard to data volume, update characteristics, and aggregation-oriented organization of data. Information stored in a data warehouse are usually exploited by using pre-defined reports printed on a regular basis, by interactive exploration using standard OLAP tools, or by exportation into special statistical software packages . In such a scenario, for example, all sales orders are flowing through a notification system. The system keeps track of the sold products of a certain category within a specific region and can automatically re-order the required products. This application domain highly correlates with the attempt of building active data warehouse systems. Notification systems are a necessary requisite.
- *Production monitoring*
  Notification systems in the small (also called streaming systems) are able to monitor the manufacturing quality of a machine within a long assembly line. The streaming system has to ensure that incoming event notifications are analyzed and evaluated against the set of standing queries within a certain period of time. If tolerances are too high or if a pattern of irregular behavior within the assembly line is discovered, notification messages are sent out to slow or shut down some machines.

It can be seen that notification services, on the one hand, cover a broad spectrum of applications and, on the other hand, exhibit a strong impact on the evaluation strategies for answering multiple standing queries. Moreover, the application areas shown above motivate the classification of notification systems into the following two classes:

- *Subscription systems*
  A subscription system is used to evaluate a huge number of potentially complex-structured standing queries on incoming data. In comparison to the characteristics of a data stream system, each publication reflects an isolated action, i.e. publications of a single publisher are (except for the schema) not related to each other—which especially holds for their time stamps. Typical publications, for example, may consist of large XML documents [32].
- *Data stream systems*
  A data stream system is used to analyze continuous streams of data typically coming from data sensors. Publications usually arrive periodically and comprise single individual values (like temperature values).

In the following, we focus on subscription systems which typically require more advanced functionality from a modeling as well as an architectural point of view as proposed for example in [31]. For further information on application scenarios in the context of data stream technology, we refer our readers to [15, 2, 6, 4]. Notification systems and subscription systems are therefore used synonymously.

1.4 Structure of the Contribution

The remainder of this contribution is focusing on the notification management system *PubScribe*, which aims to build a notification system solely based on the publish/subscribe communication pattern and exploits advanced database technology. Therefore, the following section outlines the basic characteristics of *PubScribe* in the context of a general architecture and communication pattern scheme. Section 3 then discusses the subscription data model used by *PubScribe*, which will be mapped to a processing model in section 4. Section 5 finally summarizes and closes the contribution with an outlook on further work to be done in this context.

2 General Architecture and Characteristics

In this section, we identify and explain a number of different characteristics, which apply to the family of notification systems, and provide a general overview of the components required to build a notification system.

2.1 General Architecture

A notification system basically consists of three major components (back-end, front-end, and brokering component), which can be seen in Fig. 3. In general, a notification system accepts event messages and cleans, transforms, and combines these messages with other data available to the notification system. Finally, individual notification messages are generated and delivered to the consumer, i.e. subscriber. The general structures and their functions are as follows:

- *Event message provider*
  The component of an event message provider accepts incoming event messages and transforms them into a shape which can be processed by the underlying notification engine (similar to wrapper technology as described in [26]). Usually, each message is decomposed into multiple rows spread over multiple relational database tables. In Fig. 3, an event message provider exists for XML documents, for the result of SQL statements (e.g. in the context of the execution of stored procedures), and for a service that periodically crawls specific web sites to retrieve data and propagate them to the notification system. The output of an event message goes into a message table, which is exploited by the subscription system.

- *Notification message delivery component*
  The notification message delivery component extracts the results provided by the notification engine and creates appropriate notification messages, personalized either for a human user or—according to a given message schema—for an application as consumer. Fig. 3 depicts three different delivery handlers to forward notification messages via the HTTP-protocol for web access, the SMTP-protocol for use of electronic mail, and a generic file protocol to store messages in a regular file.

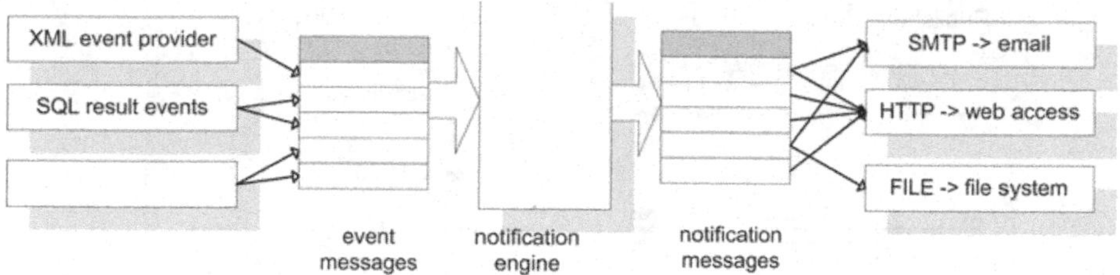

Fig. 3 General Architecture of a Notification System

More sophisticated push-based delivery methods require either an adequate network infrastructure or a cooperating client software. Whenever pushing data to a client is not directly supported by the underlying transport protocols (i.e. TCP, HTTP, ...), push services are implemented in an extended pull style. In this case, a specific piece of software is running in the background on the client side, permanently polling for new information, and thus, pretending a server push to the client. Such strategies are called smart pull or pull++. Another technique for simulating push is server-initiated pull. In this case, the server sends a short notification to the client stating that there is new data ready for delivery. The client then downloads the notification message using a regular pull operation. It is worth mentioning here that a notification service which is logically based on the publish/subscribe paradigm can be implemented using push as well as pull techniques for data delivery.

- *Notification brokering component / notification engine*
  The central piece of a notification system consists of the brokering component which is tightly integrated into an underlying database engine to efficiently answer the registered standing queries for incoming messages. Because the event message provider and the notification message delivery component are of little interest from a database perspective, we focus on the brokering component in the remainder of this contribution.

2.2 General Communication Pattern

Within the *PubScribe* system we pursue a communication pattern on two different levels. From a user (publisher and subscriber) point of view, the notification service consists of five service primitives, as depicted in Fig. 4.

In a very first step, publishers are requested to register their publications at the notification system (REGISTER primitive), which will set off the initiation of the appropriate event message provider and the creation of the appropriate message tables for this specific publishing component. Even more important, each publisher must submit a schema definition of the proposed messages. After registration, publishers use the publish/service primitive to submit event messages for further processing.

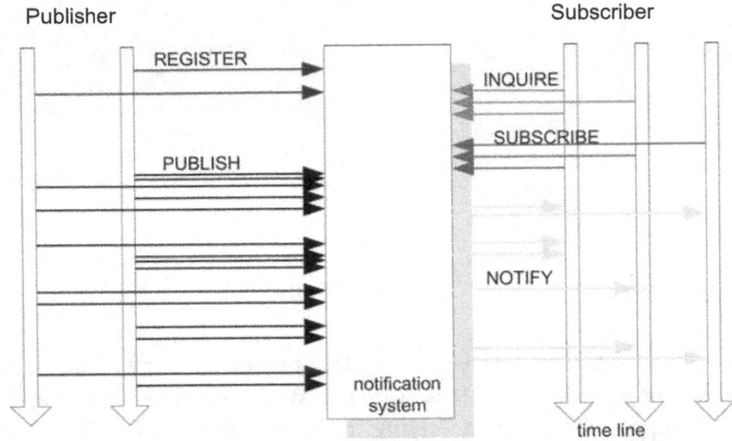

Fig. 4 Communication Pattern in Publish/Subscribe-Notification Systems

On the subscriber side, a potential user may issue an INQUIRE primitive to learn about publishers currently present and their local schemas. The consumer may then decide to place a subscription (standing query) based on their schemas including start, stop, and delivery conditions (section 3.1) using the SUBSCRIBE primitive. Once a notification message is ready, the notification message delivery component is using the NOTIFY primitive on the consumer side to deliver the result.

On a lower (communication) level, describing the interaction mechanisms of different components within a network of notification systems, the *PubScribe* system applies the publish/subscribe paradigm and maps the five service primitives on the application level to the publish/subscribe communication pattern. The REGISTER and INQUIRE primitives are mapped onto a so-called one-shot publish/subscribe pattern, implying that a subscription is only valid as long as a single notification message has not arrived. More interestingly, the PUBLISH and SUBSCRIBE/NOTIFY primitives are also translated into a publish/subscribe pattern. After registering, the *PubScribe* notification system subscribes at the publisher and places a subscription to ask for event messages. The PUBLISH primitive on the application level then corresponds to the PUBLISH primitive on the communication level. Similarly, the SUBSCRIBE primitive of a consumer is mapped to the SUBSCRIBE primitive at the lower level, and the NOTIFY primitive is treated as a PUBLISH primitive issued by the notification delivery component (taking on the role of a publisher with regard to the subscriber).

2.3 Classification of Notification Systems

As a final consideration with regard to the general perspective of notification systems, we provide some properties which might be used to classify the very broad set of notification systems. It is worth mentioning that these properties are not completely orthogonal to each other, i.e. certain combinations may not make that much sense from an application point of view.

Document-Based Versus Data-Stream-Based Notification Systems

The most distinctive feature of a notification system lies in the differentiation between document-based and data-stream-based characteristics. In the context of document-based systems, each message consists of an individual entity and is treated separately from every other message. Especially the "birth" of the message in a document-based environment is not related to the "birth" of other messages of the same publisher. This means that from an application point of view, there is no system-relevant correlation of the publication of individual messages. Typical examples of document-based notification systems are news tickers that report on current developments.

The other extreme is characterized by data streams. In this case, the publication of a message happens periodically in the sense that a message does not reflect an individual entity, but is comprised of on-going data either to complete or to bring the current state up-to-date. In the former case, data is added to the message, while in the latter case, data is overwritten, thus implying that the notification system holds the most current state with regard to some real-life object. An example for streaming systems is the control procedure of an assembly line, where sensors are reporting the current state of a machine on a periodic basis [7, 29].

PubScribe, which serves as an example within this contribution, is a classic representative of a document-based notification system. Streaming systems dealing with an infinite set of tuples are not discussed. The reader is referred to excellent literature like [15, 24, 3, 14] that focuses on this topic from an architectural point of view.

Time-Driven Versus Data-Driven Notifications

The second characteristic with regard to information delivery is the classification of the kind of "event" which has to happen in order for a notification to be sent out to the client. Notifications are either dispatched periodically after a specified amount of time or they are initiated due to a data-driven event. A typical example for the first case is to send out an electronic newsletter every day at 6 p.m. A new letter (or a collection of accumulated single news articles) is simply sent out after another 24 hours have passed. Alternatively, a subscriber may be interested in getting notified by the notification system aperiodically, i.e. only when a certain event occurs, e.g. a certain stock value passes a certain threshold. Data-driven events are usually connected to insert or update operations in the underlying database and result in aperiodic notifications. They are closely related to the trigger concept of active and relational database systems [21]. In practice, the combination of both notification modes is most interesting. For example, a user might want to be informed immediately if the IBM stock falls below a certain value, and additionally, get a weekly summary for its performance throughout the week.

Full Update Versus Incremental Update

For the subscription management system, it is important to know what to do with data which was already received by the client through a previous delivery. In case of a thin client like a simple web browser without any application logic and local storage capacity, the server always has to deliver a full update to the client. However, if the client is only interested in the current value of a business figure, e.g. a certain stock value, or if it is able to combine the values already received with the latest value on its own, the server system should choose an incremental update strategy, i.e. it will only send the delta changes and thus save network bandwidth and perhaps server memory as well. The combination of complex-structured context and the required functionality of delta propagation leads, for example, to the hybrid data model proposed within *PubScribe* (section 3.2).

3 Subscription Message Data Model

In this section, we briefly outline the underlying data model and the operators used to formulate standing queries. These operators are then subject of optimization and mappings to relational database systems, which will be shown in the subsequent section.

3.1 Types and Conditions of Subscriptions

From a theoretical point of view, a subscription may be represented as a mathematical function which is not yet saturated, i.e. the result of this function is still being computed or, in other words, the data which the computation of the function is based on is either not yet complete or changing over time. The bottom line for subscription systems from a database perspective is that a user registers a query once and regularly receives a notification of the query result derived from the actual state of the underlying data set. Therefore, the query may be considered the "body" of a subscription, which is subject to evaluation, if a corresponding delivery condition is met. Furthermore, subscriptions are instantiated, if corresponding opening conditions are satisfied. Analogously, subscriptions are removed from the system, if the present closing conditions evaluate to true.

Different Types of Subscriptions

The set of subscriptions can be classified into *feasible* and *non-* or *not yet feasible subscriptions*. A subscription on "the highest prime number twins" may be an example for a not-yet feasible subscription, because it is (still) unknown whether such numbers exist at all. Obviously, we have to restrict ourselves to feasible subscriptions. Moreover, we are able to classify these types of subscriptions in more detail from a data point of view into the following three categories:

- *Snapshot subscriptions*
  A snapshot [1] subscription may be answered by referring only to the currently valid information, i.e. the answer may be retrieved by processing only the most current message of a publisher. Snapshot subscriptions require "update-in-place" semantics. **Example:** A subscription regarding the *current* weather conditions only refers to the last available information. Old data is no longer of interest.

- *Ex-nunc ('from now on') subscriptions*
  Ex-nunc subscriptions are based on a set of messages. This set of messages is constructed starting from an empty set at the time of the registration of a subscription.
  Example: Computing the value of a three-hour moving average of a stock price starts with a single value for the first hour, the average of two values for the second hour, and the average of three values for all other hours.

- *Ex-tunc ('starting in the past') subscriptions*
  Ex-tunc subscriptions are based on data from the past plus current information.
  Example: A subscription of the cumulative sum of trading information of a specific stock needs an initial overall sum, which can be maintained using new messages.

The *PubScribe* system supports (classic) snapshot-based, ex-nunc and ex-tunc subscriptions. To provide ex-tunc subscriptions, the system has to implement an initial evaluation mechanism, which provides feedback to the user on whether or not this specific subscription with the specified requirements can be instantiated.

Condition Evaluation Semantics

The evaluation of a subscription query (body of a subscription) is controlled by conditions. The *PubScribe* system uses the following three conditions to control the execution and delivery of a result of a subscription:

- *Opening condition*
  A subscription becomes active, i.e. the body and the following two conditions are instantiated as soon as the opening condition is satisfied the first time.

- *Closing condition*
  A subscription is removed from the system as soon as this condition evaluates to true.

- *Delivery condition*
  If and only if the delivery condition evaluates to true, the body of the subscription gets updated, i.e. messages which have arrived since the last delivery are "merged" into the current state of the subscription.

Once the opening condition is satisfied, the delivery and closing conditions are evaluated. If the delivery condition is satisfied, the subscription body is evaluated and the result is delivered to the corresponding subscriber.

If the closing condition evaluates to true, the subscription is removed from the system. It is worth to note here that the system provides "at least once" semantics for the execution of a subscription in the context of an initial evaluation for ex-tunc and one-shot subscriptions: the delivery condition is checked *before* the closing condition is evaluated. Thus, if the delivery condition is satisfied, the subscription body is evaluated and delivered before a satisfied closing condition removes the subscription from the system.

header attributes | body attributes

StockName	StockExchange	Price	ChangeAbs	TradingVolume	TradingInfo
<StockName> Oracle </Stockname>	<StockExchange> FSE </StockExchange>	<Price> 97.50 </Price>	<ChangeAbs> 2.75 </ChangeAbs>	<TradingVolume> 3400 </TradingVolume>	<TradingInfo> <InfoSource> W. Lehner </InfoSource> <Comment> buy or die.... </Comment> </TradingInfo>

Fig. 5 Example for a MSGSET Data Structure

3.2 The *PubScribe* Message Data Structures

The data model of the *PubScribe* system consists of data structures and operators defined on these structures to formulate standing queries. The very interesting point within the hybrid modeling approach consists in the fact that the model reflects the duality of state-based and consumption-based data management by introducing message sequences and message sets.

Messages and Message Attributes

The messages produced by registered publishers must follow a message scheme announced during the registration process of a publisher at the notification management system. The scheme of a message $M = (H, B)$ consists of a header $H = (H_1,...,H_n)$, a (possibly empty) set of header attributes H_i $(1 \leq i \leq n)$, and a message body $B = (B_1,...,B_m)$ with at least one body attribute B_j $(1 \leq j \leq m)$. Header attributes may be seen as an equivalent to primary key attributes in a relational model [8] without the requirement of definiteness and minimality. The instances of attributes are valid XML documents [32, 17] and must follow an XML-schema [33, 34] definition, locally defined by the publisher. Attributes without further structuring are so-called basic or single-level attributes. Moreover, complex-structured attributes are not allowed in the header. Fig. 5 shows a single message regarding stock information. The complex attribute *TRADINGINFO* holds a comment together with the source of the quote.

Message Sets and Message Sequences

Messages of the same type may be collected as sets (unordered with regard to their generation time) or sequences [28]:

- *Message sequence (MSGSEQ)*
  The data structure of a message sequence holds a list of messages ordered by the arrival time of the message in the system. Each message in a sequence is implicitly extended by a header attribute *ValidTime*.
- *Set of sequences (MSGSET)*
  In order to reflect the stable set of information in addition to streaming data, MSG-

SET structures represent descriptive data to annotate incoming messages. From a logical point of view, a set of sequences reflects a consistent and (for that specific moment) complete state at every point in time.

Sample Scenario

Throughout the remainder of this contribution, a consistent example refers to a stock notification system about current trends, news, comments, and so on. A publisher StockInfo periodically delivers information about the current stock price added to a MEGSEQ structure. A second producer publishes comments on a fully incremental basis (section 2.3), i.e. the set of messages always reflects the current opinion of the publisher. Obviously, the messages go into a MSGSET structure. Fig. 5 shows an instance of the StockInfo publisher; Fig. 6 holds an example for a MSGSET regarding comments and rankings.

StockName	Ranking	Comment
<StockName> Oracle </Stockname>	<Ranking> **** </Ranking>	<Comment> Oracle is a member of the NASDAQ since ... </Comment>
<StockName> IBM </Stockname>	<Ranking> ***** </Ranking>	<Comment> IBM has a long tradition and .... </Comment>

Fig. 6 Example for a MSGSET Data Structure

3.3 The *PubScribe* Message Operators

The data structure may be used by operators to specify complex queries. Fig. 7 illustrates the data model and the underlying message operators to formulate a subscription. Within this query, only 5-star-ranked stocks after a join are considered. Based on the trading information, a dynamic window operation of size 3 is defined. Finally the average and the total volumes are computed as a result for the user.

The different operators are only sketched within this context. The reader is referred to [18] and [19] for a detailed description and a more comprehensive example:

- *Filter operator*
  The *FILTER()* operator is defined for header attributes. Hence, the resulting data structure holds only messages with values in the header attributes satisfying a given predicate. A selection criterion is restricted to conjunctive predicates without negation. Each predicate only contains the operators =, < , > and ~= for textual attributes. Example:
  [InterestedStocks] ⇐ FILTER(StockName IN ('Oracle', 'IBM'))[StockInfo]
- *Attribute migration operator*
  The attribute migration (*SHIFT()*-) operator allows the transition of a body attribute to the set of header attributes. The new header attribute must be of an atomic type. A good example for attribute migration is the definition of groups. For example, an

EVAL() operator extracts the month out of a time stamp stored in a body attribute. The *SHIFT()*-operator moves the newly created attribute to the set of header attributes providing a way to identify values on a monthly basis.

- *Internal message computation*
  The *EVAL()*-operator is used to perform computations within a single message. In fact, the model distinguishes three categories of internal message operators:

  The first category includes all regular binary scalar functions like *PLUS()*, *MINUS()*, *MULT()*, *DIV()* and equality operators (*GREATER()*, ...). Additionally, the class comprises a set of calendar functions like *YEAR()*, *MONTH()*, *DAY()*. The following example returns the relative change based on the current price, the price difference, and the turnover.

  [ExtendedStockInfo] ⇐ EVAL(Price, TradingVolume,
  ChangeRel:DIV(ChangeAbs, MINUS(Price, ChangeAbs)),
  Turnover:MULT(Price, TradingVolume))[StockInfo]

  The second category holds aggregation functions like *MIN()*, *MAX()*, *SUM()*, and *COUNT()* which are usually used in combination with the *COLLAPSE()* operator (see below).

  The third category encompasses all operators used to work on the content of complex-structured attributes. *EXTRACT()* is used to extract pieces of complex-structured attribute values. *COMBINE()* does the opposite: it merges two complex-structured attribute values to a new attribute value.

  [ExtractedStockInfo] ⇐
  EVAL(CommentList:EXTRACT(Comment, TradingInfoList),
  InfoSourceList:EXTRACT(InfoSource, TradingInfoList))[StockInfo]

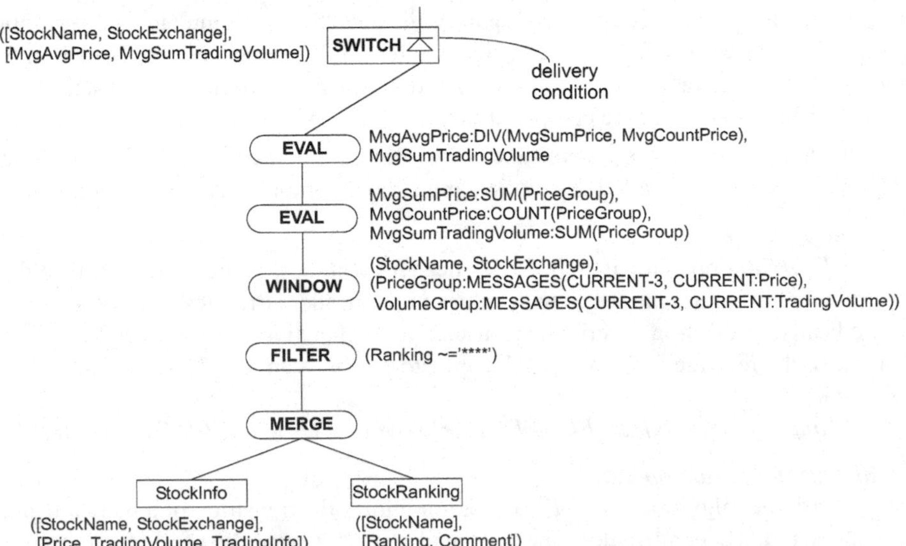

Fig. 7 Example for a Subscription Body

The identity function can be seen as a special form of one of these two operators. The syntax is abbreviated by just listing the attribute names.

- *Generation of static groups*
  The *COLLAPSE()* operator allows the definition of static (or: partitioning) groups with regard to a set of header attributes of a MSGSET or MSGSEQ structure. The following example groups message entries by the name of the stock value:
  GroupedStockInfo ⇐ COLLAPSE((StockName),
  (TradingVolumeGroup:TradingVolume,
  TradingInfoGroup:TradingInfo))[StockInfo]
  The result of a *COLLAPSE()* operator consists of head attributes (first parameter) and set body attributes (second parameter). A succeeding aggregation step has to be done explicitly by calling an *EVAL()* operator. The following expression computes the total sum as well as the number of contributing messages based on the attribute *TradingVolumeGroup*. Other attributes are not affected by this operation.
  SumStockInfo ⇐ EVAL(TradingVolumeSum:SUM(TradingVolumeGroup),
  TradingVolumeCount:COUNT(TradingVolumeGroup),
  TradingInfoGroup)[GroupedStockInfo]
  Furthermore, in contrast to the following dynamic group generation, the static groups are defined without regard to time or any other ordering characteristics.

- *Generation of dynamic groups*
  The main idea of dynamic grouping is that entities (i.e. messages) are grouped by a certain order and not by specific values. This implies that the definition of the *WINDOW()* operator is only based on MSGSEQ structures. The group definition can be performed either according to the number of messages or according to a time interval. The following example illustrates the effect of the operator, by defining an open window ranging from the first to the current entry and a sliding window covering all entries within a symmetrical 90-minutes slot:
  [WindowedStockInfo] ⇐ WINDOW((StockName),
  (TrVolOpenWindow:
  MESSAGES(BEGIN:CURRENT, TradingVolume),
  TrVolClosedWindows:
  TIMESTAMPS(-45.00:+45.00, TradingVolume)))
  [StockInfo]
  Analogously to the principle of static groups, dynamic groups have to be evaluated using an additional *EVAL()* operator, e.g.:
  [MvgSumStockInfo] ⇐ EVAL(TrVolCumSum:SUM(TrVolOpenWindow),
  TrVolMvgSum:SUM(TrVolClosedWindow))
  [WindowedStockInfo]

- *Merge operator*
  A merge operator joins two data structures of potentially different type and forms a new structure. Because this operator is crucial for the creation of more sophisticated results, it is described explicitly below.

- *Switch operator*
  The special switch operator returns NULL as long as the control input (right input in Fig. 10) representing the condition testing is FALSE. Otherwise, the switch operator returns the messages from the data input. The *SWITCH()* operator is used to implement the test of various conditions.

Merging Two Message Data Structures

Within the *PubScribe* data model, a merge approach is applied relying on positions and values. Content-based joins are possible whenever a MSGSET is involved. A positional join is used to merge two MSGSEQ structures with multiple different join semantics. The non-commutative *MERGE()* operator implies four combinations as outlined below:

- *Join of messages in MSGSET structures*
  This case is comparable to a natural join in the relational model. More important, however, is the distinction between symmetric and asymmetric joins. In the first case, both messages exhibit the same set of header attributes. In the second case, one partner holds a superset of header attributes. If $H_1 \not\subset H_2$, $H_2 \not\subset H_1$ with $H_1 \cap H_2 \neq \emptyset$ holds, then the join is not defined; otherwise:
  $SET(H_1, B_1 \cup B_2) \Leftarrow SET_1(H_1, B_1) \bowtie SET_2(H_2, B_2)$
  with the join condition:
  $\forall(h_2 \in H_2)\, \exists(h_1 \in H_1)\; h_1 = h_2$

- *Join of messages in MSGSEQ with messages of MSGSET structures*
  This cross-structural join reflects the most important join in notification systems; incoming messages are enriched with additional information coming from relational sources using outer join semantics. If the set of header attributes in the MSGSET structure H_2 is not a subset of the header attributes of the MSGSEQ structure H_1, the join is not defined; otherwise:
  $SEQ(H_1 \cup \{ValidTime\}, B_1 \cup B_2) \Leftarrow SEQ(H_1 \cup \{ValidTime\}, B_1) ⟖ SET(H_2, B_2)$
  with the join condition independent of the time stamp attribute:
  $\forall(h_2 \in H_2)\, \exists(h_1 \in H_1)\; h_1 = h_2$

- *Join of messages in MSGSET with messages of MSGSET structures*
  Joins between messages from sets enriched with messages from sequences are not defined.

- *Join of messages in MSGSEQ structures*
  In addition to a join between messages of MSGSET structures, a positional join with $H_2 \subseteq H_1$ is defined as follows:
  $SEQ(H_1 \cup \{MAX(ValidTime_1, ValidTime_2)\}, B_1 \cup B_2) \Leftarrow$
  $SEQ(H_1 \cup \{ValidTime_1\}, B_1) ⟖ SEQ(H_2 \cup \{ValidTime_2\}, B_2)$
  The new message has the same valid time as the younger join partner. The join condition may be denoted as
  $\forall(h_2 \in H_2)\, \exists(h_1 \in H_1)\; h_1 = h_2$ and $\Theta(\text{ValidTime}_1, \text{ValidTime}_2)$.

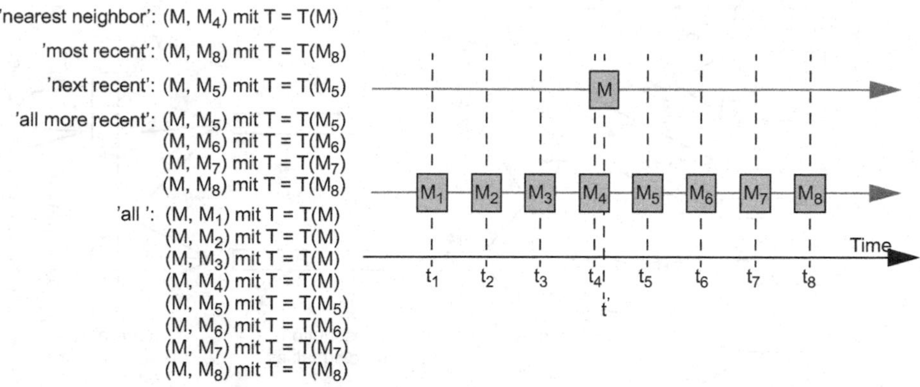

Fig. 8 Different Semantics for SEQ-SEQ Joins

The Θ-operator implies a huge variety of possible bindings. Fig. 8 shows multiple situations to find a join partner for a specific message *M*. A pointwise join features the following variations:

- *nearest neighbor*: candidate with the minimal distance to the message (M_4 in Fig. 8)
- *next recent*: candidate with the minimal timely forward distance (M_5)
- *most recent*: candidate with the highest time stamp values (M_8)

Additionally, interval joins are defined within the *PubScribe* data model to combine a single message with potentially multiple messages coming from the partner sequence:

- *all more recent*: set of messages with a valid time equal to or younger than the one of the reference message. In Fig. 8, message *M* would be combined with messages M_5 to M_8.
- *all*: a resulting message is produced for all members of the candidate sequence.

The following example shows a join between a MSGSEQ and a MSGSET; current stock prices, etc. are complemented by comments and rankings coming from a different source.

RankedStockInfo ⇐ *MERGE()[EVAL(Price, TradingVolume)[StockInfo], EVAL(Ranking)[StockRanking]]*

The set of operators provides a solid base for a user to specify very complex descriptions (see table in the appendix for an overview). The notification system has to accept all feasible subscriptions and perform optimizations based on these structures. The processing model is outlined in the following section.

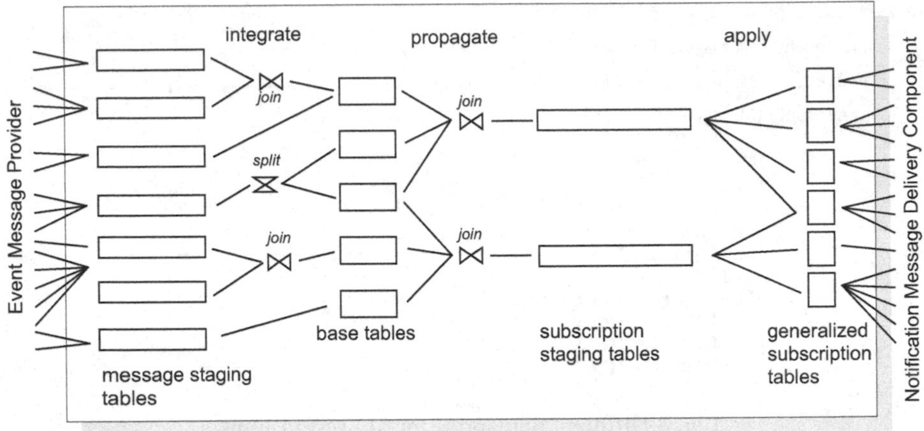

Fig. 9 *PubScribe* Message Processing Model

4 Subscription Processing Model

Using the set of operators and the structure, this section outlines the processing model of the *PubScribe* notification system, subdivided into a structural and an operational part.

4.1 Structural Layout and Processing Phases

The overall goal of the proposed *PubScribe* approach is to clearly decouple incoming messages from the resulting notifications as much as possible, and thus, to enable the notification system to optimize the processing of the subscriptions by operator clustering [27] and materialization [13]. As an underlying storage (!) model, *PubScribe* uses the relational model [8] and maps each message to a single row in a table. The system comprises multiple processing stages, each using different sets of tables as outlined below (Fig. 9):

- *Integration phase*
  Event messages are stored in message staging tables, where they are kept in their original (received) form. In a preliminary step, single messages may be integrated into base tables via join or split. Several options are possible: a message contributes to exactly one single base table; a message needs a join partner to generate an entry for a base table; or a message feeds two or more base tables, i.e. the content of a message is split into multiple entries in the base tables.

The generation of notification messages is subdivided into three phases, which are introduced to share as much work as possible. For the coordination of this huge data pipeline, the system additionally introduces two sets of temporary tables:

- *Subscription staging tables*
  The purpose of staging tables is to keep track of all changes to the base tables, which are not yet completely considered by all dependent subscriptions. It is worth to mention here that a system may have multiple staging tables, and each staging table covers only these subscriptions which do only exhibit a lossless join. Lossy joins are delayed to the propagate or apply phase.
- *Generalized subscription tables*
  A generalized subscription table serves as basis for the computations of the notifications for multiple subscriptions (i) referring to the same set of base tables (at least a portion of them) and (ii) exhibiting similar delivery constraints. Each subscription may either be directly answered from a generalized subscription table, or retrieved from the generalized subscription table with either a join to another generalized subscription table or a back-join to the original base table. It is worth to note here that it must be ensured that the state of the base tables is the same as the state at the propagation time of the currently considered message.

It is important to understand that subscription staging tables are organized from a data perspective, whereas the set of generalized subscription tables is organized according to delivery constraints, thus providing the borderline from incoming to outgoing data.

- *Propagation phase*
  Comparable to the context of incremental maintenance of materialized views [13], the *PubScribe* system exhibits a second phase of propagating the changes from base tables to a temporary staging area. The resulting data is already aligned with the schema of the outgoing message, i.e. the relational peers of message operators (joins, selections, projections, and aggregation operations) have already been applied to the delta information. We have to mention here that the propagation appears immediately after the update of the base table.
- *Apply phase*
  The staging table holds accrued delta information from multiple updates. This sequence of delta information is collapsed, implying that the primary key condition is satisfied again and the resulting data is applied to one or more generalized subscription tables. In this phase, subscriptions exhibiting lossy joins are combined from entries of multiple staging tables or a back-join to the base tables. The result of the apply phase is picked up by the notification message delivery component and propagated to the subscriber.

Subdividing the process of subscription evaluation into multiple independent phases implies that the system has a huge potential for optimization. The basic strategies and the mapping to a relational query language are demonstrated below.

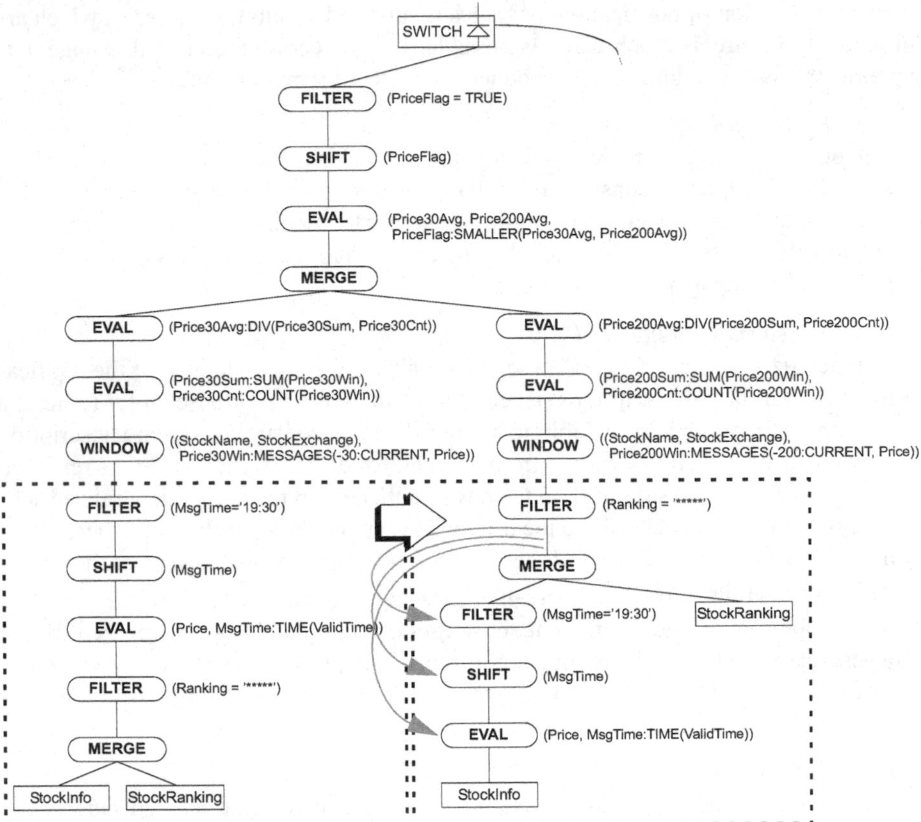

Fig. 10 Local Restructuring of *PubScribe* Subscriptions

4.2 Subscription Optimization and Relational Mapping

The optimization of subscription evaluation during the compilation is again subdivided into two phases. The first phase of local restructurings aims at the generation of a better execution plan using mechanisms restricted to the individual subscription. In this phase, the basic idea of optimizing relational queries is transferred to the subscription data model. A partially more important goal of this phase consists of generating a normal form, which reflects the working platform for the following inter-subscription optimization process. Fig. 10 shows a subscription plan with the same sub-expression before (left branch) and after (right branch) the local restructuring. The local operators *FILTER()*, *EVAL()*, and *SHIFT()* are pushed down to the leaf nodes.

The global subscription restructuring phase (second phase) targets the identification and exploitation of common sub-expressions by merging a newly registered subscription into an existing subscription network (first ideas published as Rete network in [11]). The merging process relies on the concept of building compensations. For exam-

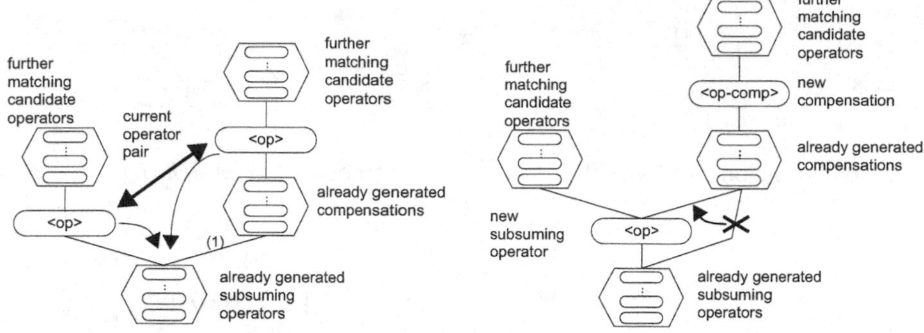

Fig. 11 Propagation of Multiple Operators

ple, if two expressions are of the same type and exhibit similar parameters, it might be worthwhile to compute the most general form of the operator only once and add compensation operators on top of the general form to produce the specific result for each consuming operator. Fig. 11 illustrates the process of using the stacks of operators and merging them step-by-step. As soon as a single pair matches at a specific level, the general form of the new subsuming operator and the two compensation operators for the individual subscription query are created. Additionally, the already generated compensations (with the newly created compensation operator and the operaters still to be matched on top of it) are now provided with data from the newly created subsuming operator. Obviously, if the operator does not produce all messages required by the lowest operator of the compensation, the whole matching procedure for that specific level fails. The overall process starts bottom-up and continues as far as possible (ideally up to the highest operator). The more similar the subscriptions are, the more operators can be shared. To enable pairwise comparison, the general form of the subscription—produced in the local restructuring phase—is extremely important.

The general process at a relational level is illustrated in [36, 20]. From the subscription-specific standpoint, it is worth to consider each operator regarding the matchability characteristic and the necessary compensations. Fig. 12 shows the most important operators and their corresponding compensations. A *FILTER()* operator regarding a predicate P_1 can be replaced by another *FILTER()* operator with a weaker predicate P_2 and a compensation consisting again of a *FILTER()* operator with the original or a reduced predicate to achieve the same result.

For a *SHIFT()* operator, the subsuming operator has to move only a subset of the attributes required by the matching candidate, such that the compensation moves the attributes still missing to the header of the message. The *EVAL()* operator can be easily compensated, if the subsuming operator generates all attributes required for the compensation, which introduces the scalar operations. In the case of a *COLLAPSE()* operator, a match is only successful, if the group-by attributes exhibit a subset relationship, i.e. the subsuming operator generates data at a finer granularity; the final groups can then be generated within the compensation. This first step is accomplished by a *COLLAPSE()* operator; the alignment of the grouping values requires an additional

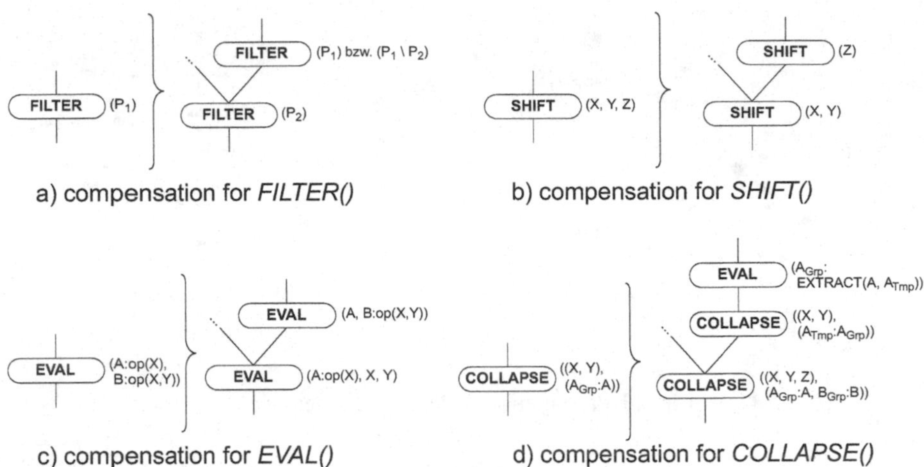

Fig. 12 Rules for Generating Compensations

EVAL::EXTRACT() operator to compensate for the additional nesting within the aggregation attributes.

For dynamic grouping, there is no easy way of building compensations [20]. A match is only successfully recorded, if the two parameter sets are equal, i.e. show the same window size and window characteristics. For *MERGE()* operators, a compensation depends on the similarity of the join predicates and the join type, i.e. the type (MSGSEQ or MSGSET) of the join partners. To weaken these restrictions, the join characteristics in the case of a MSGSEQ/MSGSEQ join can be exploited using the following partial ordering of the join characteristics:

ALL ≺ (NEXT NEIGHBOR |
ALL NEXT RECENT ≺ (MOST RECENT | NEXT RECENT))

For example, a join with NEXT RECENT can be derived from a *MERGE()* operator with join characteristic ALL NEXT RECENT or simply ALL.

After restructuring the subscription query network both locally and globally, the final step consists in generating SQL expressions allowing the efficient mapping of the operator network onto operators of the relational storage model. Fig. 13 also shows this step for the branch next to the StockInfo publisher. In a last and final step, the database objects in a relational system are subject of pre-computation, if the corresponding operator in the subscription network has a potentially high number of consumers.

Fig. 13 illustrates the optimization process of a subscription operator network using our current example of stock trading information. It can be seen that the lowest two blocks (blocks denote relational database objects of either virtual or materialized views) of the operator network are the result of the matching process and reflect the set of subsuming candidates. The two parallel blocks denote compensations built on top of the commonly used query graph.

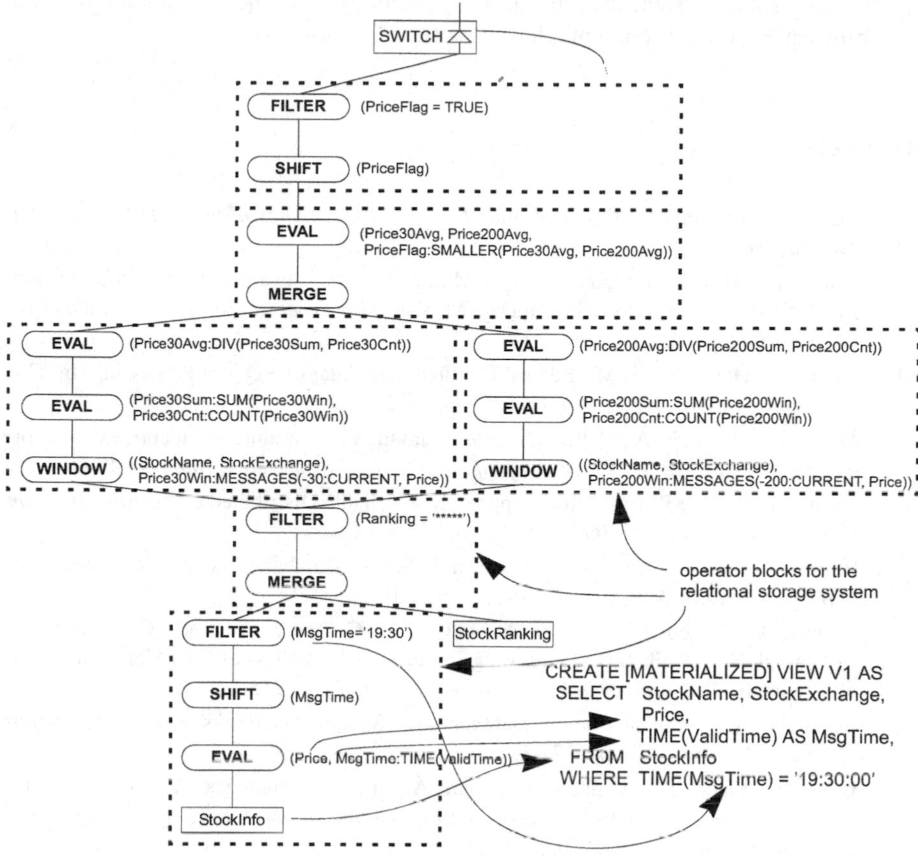

Fig. 13 Generating Subscription Execution Networks

5 Summary and Conclusion

Notification systems reflect a special kind of data management systems working like a huge data pipeline. Data items (documents) are entering the system, posted in form of event messages. Within the system, standing queries (subscriptions) are forming a complex-structured network of specific operators. Messages are routed through the operator network in multiple phases and finally arrive as notification messages at the delivery component responsible for sending out the messages in any supported format using a huge variety of protocols. In order to make these data pipelines work very efficiently and support a huge number of standing queries with similar structure, advanced database technology has to be adopted and exploited to a large extent. From a more global perspective with a database management system as an information provider, it is safe to say that notification systems help the user to efficiently filter the vast amount of available information to focus only on relevant pieces of information.

References

[1] Adiba, M., Lindsay, B.: Database Snapshots. In: *Proceedings of the VLDB Conference, 1980*, pp. 86-91

[2] Arasu, A., Babcock, B., Babu, S., Datar, M., Ito, K., Nishizawa, I., Rosenstein, J., Widom, J.: STREAM: The Stanford Stream Data Manager. In: *Proceedings of the SIGMOD Conference, 2003*, p. 665

[3] Avnur, R., Hellerstein, J.M.: Eddies: Continuously Adaptive Query Processing. In: *Proceedings of the SIGMOD Conference, 2000*, pp. 261-272

[4] Madden, S., Shah, M.A., Hellerstein, J.M., Raman, V.: Continuously adaptive continuous queries over streams. In: *Proceedings of the SIGMOD Conference 2002*, pp. 49-60

[5] Birman, K.P. : The Process Group Approach to Reliable Distributed Computing. In: *Communications of the ACM, 36(12), 1993*, pp. 36-53

[6] Bonnet, P., Gehrke, J., Seshadri, P.: Towards Sensor Database Systems. In: *Proceedings of the Mobile Data Management Conference, 2001*, pp. 3-14

[7] Carney, D, Çetintemel, U., Cherniack, M., Convey, C., Lee, S., Seidman, G., Stonebraker, M., Tatbul, N., Zdonik, S.B.: Monitoring Streams - A New Class of Data Management Applications. In: *Proceedings of VLDB Conference, 2002*, pp. 215-226

[8] Codd, E.F.: A Relational Model of Data for Large Shared Data Banks. In: *Communications of the ACM, 13(6), 1970*, pp. 377-387

[9] Cortes, C., Fisher, K., Pregibon, D., Rogers, A., Smith, F.: Hancock: A Language for Extracting Signatures from Data Streams. In: *Proceedings of the Knowledge Discovery and Data Mining Conference, 2000*, pp. 9-17

[10] Foltz, P.W., Dumais, S.T.: Personalized Information Delivery: An Analysis of Information Filtering Methods. In: *Communications of the ACM, 35(1992)12*, pp. 51-60

[11] Forgy, C.L.: Rete: A Fast Algorithm for the Many Pattern/Many Object Pattern Match Problem. In: *Artifical Intelligence, 19(1982)1*, pp. 17-37

[12] Gamma, E., Helm, R., Johnson, R., Vlissides, J.: *Design Patterns: Elements of Reusable Object-Oriented Software*. Addison-Wesley, 1997

[13] Gupta, A., Mumick, I.: *Materialized Views: Techniques, Implementations and Applications*. MIT Press, 1999

[14] Hellerstein, J.M., Franklin, M.J, Chandrasekaran, S., Deshpande, A., Hildrum, K., Madden, S., Raman, B., Shah, M.A.: Adaptive Query Processing: Technology in Evolution. In: *IEEE Data Engineering Bulletin 23(2), 2000*, pp.7-18

[15] Koudas, K., Srivastava, D.: Data Stream Query Processing: A Tutorial. In: P*roceedings of VLDB Conference, 2003*, p. 1149

[16] Lehner, W.: *Datenbanktechnologie für Data-Warehouse-Systeme* (in German). dpunkt.verlag, 2003

[17] Lehner, W., Schöning, H.: *XQuery: Grundlagen und fortgeschrittene Methoden* (in German). dpunkt.verlag, 2004

[18] Lehner, W.: *Marktplatz omnipräsenter Informationen - Aufbau und Analyse von Subskriptionssystemen* (in German). B.G. Teubner Verlag, 2002

[19] Lehner, W. (Hrsg.): *Advanced Techniques in Personalized Information Delivery*. Technical Report, University of Erlangen-Nuremberg, 34(5), 2001

[20] Lehner, W., Pirahesh, H., Cochrane, R., Zaharioudakis, M.: fAST Refresh using Mass Query Optimization. In: *Proceedings of the ICDE Conference, 2001*, pp. 391-398

[21] McCarthy, D.R., Dayal, U.: The Architecture Of An Active Data Base Management System. In: *Proceedings of the SIGMOD Conference, 1989*, pp. 215-224

[22] Oki, B.M., Pflügl, M., Siegel, A., Skeen, D.: The Information Bus - An Architecture for Extensible Distributed Systems. In: *Proceedings of the SOSP Conference,1993*, pp. 58-68

[23] Powell, D.: Group Communication (Introduction to the Special Section). In: *Communications of the ACM 39(4), 1996*, pp. 50-53

[24] Pu, Y., Liu, L.: Update Monitoring: The CQ Project. In: *Proceedings of the International Conference on Worldwide Computing and Its Applications, 1998*, pp. 396-411

[25] Ramakrishnan, S., Dayal, V.: The PointCast Network. In: *Proceedings of the SIGMOD Conference, 1998*, pp. 520

[26] Roth, M.T., Schwarz, P.M.: Don't Scrap It, Wrap It! A Wrapper Architecture for Legacy Data Sources. In: *Proceedings of the VLDB Conference, 1997*, pp. 266-275

[27] Sellis, T.: Multiple Query Optimization. In: *ACM Transactions on Database Systems, 13(1), 1988*, pp. 23-52

[28] Seshadri, P., Livny, M., Ramakrishnan, R.: Sequence Query Processing. In: *Proceedings of the SIGMOD Conference, 1994*, pp. 430-441

[29] Sullivan, M., Heybey, A.: Tribeca: A system for managing large databases of network traffic. In: *Proceedings of the USENIX Annual Technical Conference, 1998*

[30] Terry, D.B., Goldberg, D., Nichols, D., Oki, B.M.: Continuous Queries over Append-Only Databases. In: *Proceedings of the SIGMOD Conference, 1992*, pp. 321-330

[31] Tian, F., Reinwald, B., Pirahesh, H., Mayr, T., Myllymaki, J: Implementing a Scalable XML Publish/Subscribe System Using a Relational Database System. In: *Proceedings of the SIGMOD Conference, 2004*, pp. 479-490

[32] World Wide Web Consortium: *Extensible Markup Language (XML), Version 1.0, Second Edition*. W3C Recommendation.
Electronically available at: `http://www.w3.org/TR/2000/REC-xml-20001006`

[33] World Wide Web Consortium: *XML Schema Part 1: Structures*.
Electronically available at: `http://www.w3.org/TR/xmlschema-1/`

[34] World Wide Web Consortium: *XML Schema Part 2: Datatypes*.
Electronically available at: `http://www.w3.org/TR/xmlschema-2/`

[35] Yan, T.W., Garcia-Molina, H.: SIFT - a Tool for Wide-Area Information Dissemination. In: *Proceedings of the USENIX Winter Conference, 1995*, pp. 177-186

[36] Zaharioudakis, M., Cochrane, R., Pirahesh, H., Lapis, G., Urata, M.: Answering Complex SQL Queries Using Summary Tables. In: *Proceedings of the SIGMOD Conference, 2000*, pp. 105-116

Appendix

Tab. 1 Listing of all *PubScribe* Operators

Description	Operator Specification
filtering	X' ⇐ FILTER(<attr> [= , ~=, <, >] <val>, <attr> IN (<val$_1$>, ..., <val$_n$>), ...)[X]
attribute migration	X' ⇐ SHIFT(<attr>, ...)[X]
attibute operator - scalar operator - aggregations operator - structural modification operator	X' ⇐ EVAL(<attr>, <attr'>:<scalar-op>(<attr$_1$>[,<attr$_2$>]), <attr'>:<aggr-op>(<attr>) <attr'>:<attr-op>(<attr$_1$>, <attr$_2$>), ...)[X] <scalar-op> ∈ { PLUS, MINUS, MULT, DIV } <scalar-o1opd> ∈ { GREATER, SMALLER, EQUAL } <scaler-op> ∈ { DATE, YEAR, MONTH, DAY } <scaler-op> ∈ { TIME, HOUR, MIN } <aggr-op> ∈ { MIN, MAX, SUM, COUNT } <attr-op> ∈ { EXTRACT, COMBINE }
static group by	X' ⇐ COLLAPSE((<attr$_1$>, ..., <attr$_n$>) (<attrGrp$_1$>:<attr$_1$>), ..., (<attrGrp$_m$>:<attr$_m$>))[X]
dynamic group by	X' ⇐ WINDOW((<attr$_1$>, ..., <attr$_n$>), (<attrWin$_1$>:<win-spec>(<start>:<stop>, <attr$_1$>), ..., <attrWin$_m$>:<win-spec>(<start>:<stop>, <attr$_m$>))[X] <win-spec> ∈ { MESSAGES, TIMESTAMPS } <start> ∈ { BEGIN, CURRENT, <int-val>, <time-val>} <stop> ∈ { END, CURRENT, <int-val>, <time-val>}
join	X' ⇐ MERGE(<join-spec>)[X$_1$, X$_2$] <join-spec> ∈ { NEXT NEIGHBOR, MOST RECENT, NEXT RECENT, ALL RECENT, ALL }

Search Support in Data Management Systems

Andreas Henrich

Otto-Friedrich-Universität Bamberg, Germany
andreas.henrich@wiai.uni-bamberg.de

Abstract. In consequence of the change in the nature of data management systems the requirements for search support have shifted. In the early days of data management systems, efficient access techniques and optimization strategies for exact match queries had been the main focus. Most of the problems in this field are satisfactorily solved today and new types of applications for data management systems have turned the focus of current research to content-based similarity queries and queries on distributed databases. The present contribution addresses these two aspects. In the first part, algorithms and data structures supporting similarity queries are presented together with considerations about their integration in data management systems, whereas search techniques for distributed data management systems and especially for peer-to-peer networks are discussed in the second part. Here, techniques for exact match queries and for similarity queries are addressed.

1 Motivation

For decades one main focus of data management systems had been the efficient processing of *fact queries*. A typical—yet rather simple—example would be the search for all open invoices for a customer with a given reference number. Current database management systems are optimized to process large numbers of such queries on dynamic data sets and most problems related to queries of that type are already solved more or less satisfactorily (see [12], for example).

On the other hand, the growing amount of digital documents and digital multimedia documents shifts the requirements for data management systems. In situations where text documents or multimedia documents have to be maintained, a strong requirement for content-based queries is induced. Here a typical query is given by an example document or a query text describing the requested documents. Given a set of images, a query can for example be defined by an example image and in this case query processing is concerned with finding *similar* images. Content-based retrieval has been considered for a long time in the area of information retrieval (see, e.g., [1]). However, information retrieval (IR) has mainly addressed flat text documents in the past. Today, structured

T. Härder and W. Lehner (Eds.): Data Management (Wedekind Festschrift), LNCS 3551, pp. 137-157, 2005.

documents (for example, XML documents) and also structured multimedia documents have to be maintained. Many commercial database management systems claim to be the most suitable systems to manage XML data and multimedia data. As a consequence, sophisticated content-based retrieval facilities will be an important distinguishing feature of data management systems.

Another important aspect in data management systems is the decentralized character of cutting edge data management systems. One important trend in this respect are peer-to-peer networks (P2P networks) which are made up of autonomous peers contributing to an administration-free overlay network. The efficient processing of similarity queries in these networks is an important field of research and not yet satisfactorily solved.

In the rest of this contribution, we will first discuss techniques and algorithms for the efficient processing of complex similarity queries in a local scenario. Thereafter, we will discuss approaches towards an efficient processing of content-based similarity queries in P2P networks.

2 Processing Complex Similarity Queries

In recent years, structured multimedia data has become one of the most challenging application areas for data management systems, and search support for structured multimedia data is an important research topic in this respect. To emphasize the key problems in this field, let us assume tree-structured multimedia documents, in which the internal nodes represent intermediate components, such as chapters or sections, and where the leaves represent single media objects such as text, image, video, or audio. In order to support the search for such documents—or document fragments—we need search services which address the following requirements [15]:

- *Dealing with Structured Documents:* The fact that documents are complex-structured objects in our scenario, brings up various interesting research issues.
  First, the search support component of a data management system must allow to search for arbitrary granules ranging from whole documents over intermediate chunks to single media objects. Second, with structured documents many properties of an object are not directly attached to the object itself, but to its components. For example, the text of a chapter will usually be stored in separate text objects associated with the chapter object via links or relationships. Third, additional information about an atomic media object can be found in its *vicinity*. Exploiting the structure of a multimedia document, this concept of vicinity can be addressed navigating one link up and then down to the sibling components.
- *Feature Extraction and Segmentation:* With multimedia data the semantics is usually given implicitly in the media objects. For example, an image might represent a certain mood. Therefore, a search support component should allow to extract features from the media objects potentially describing their semantics. Furthermore, it should

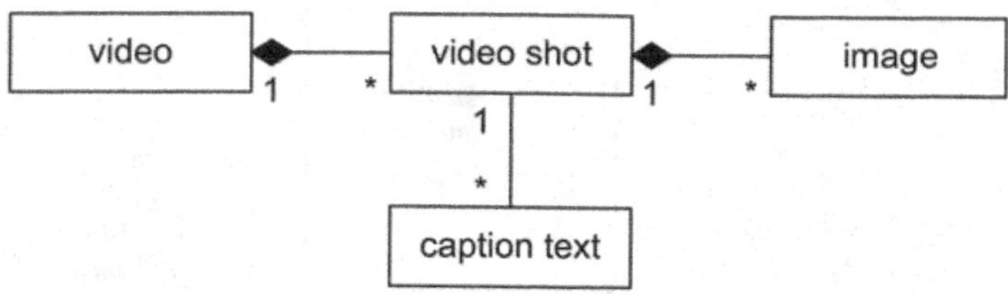

Fig. 1 Small Class Diagram for our Example Query

provide means to subdivide media objects such as images or videos into semantically coherent segments.

- *Similarity Queries:* Because of the vagueness in the interpretation of the media objects and in the formulation of the user's information need, similarity queries should be facilitated. The search support component should provide the definition of ranking criteria for media objects. For example, text objects can be ranked according to their content similarity compared to a given query text. To this end, the well-known vector space model can be applied, for example [1]. Images can be ranked with respect to their color or texture similarity compared to a sample image [34].
- *Combination of Several Similarity Queries:* Images are an example of a media type, for which no single comprehensive similarity criterion exists. Instead, different criteria are applicable addressing, e.g., color, texture, and shape similarity. Hence, algorithms to combine multiple ranking criteria and to derive an overall ranking are needed. To calculate such a combined ranking algorithms such as Nosferatu, Quick-Combine, or *J** have been proposed (cf. section 2.3).
- *Derivation of a Ranking from a Ranking for Related Objects:* With structured documents, ranking criteria are often not defined for the required objects themselves, but for their components or other related objects. An example arises when searching for images where the text in the "vicinity" (e.g. in the same subsection) has to be similar to a given sample text. In such situations, the ranking defined for the related objects has to be transferred to the required result objects. However, neither the semantics nor the implementation of such a "transfer" is self-evident (cf. section 2.4), because there will usually be a *1:n*-relationship or even a *n:m*-relationship between the objects.

2.1 Components Contributing to Similarity Queries

The main components contributing to the processing of a similarity query can be clarified by an example. Assume a query searching for video shots dealing with hydrogen-powered cars and presenting the cars in a nice sunset scenario. Furthermore, assume that this query has to be processed on a database containing complete videos. Fig. 1 depicts the class diagram underlying our example. This diagram reflects the need to break the videos into shots by means of a shot detection algorithm which in fact is a media-type-

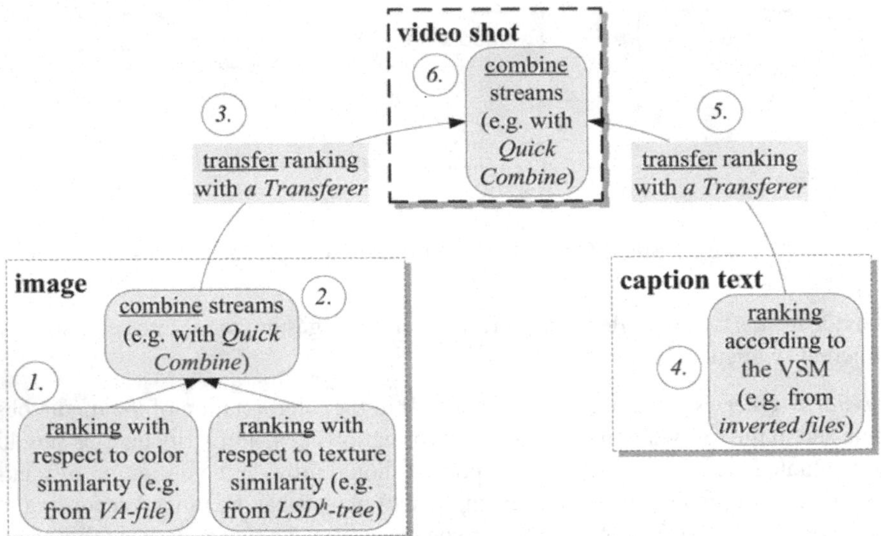

Fig. 2 Steps to Process our Example Query

specific segmentation algorithm. Furthermore, each shot consists of single images, and caption texts are attached to the video shot objects. These caption texts might be created manually or automatically using a speech recognition algorithm. Of course, the segmentation of a video into shots and images as well as the speech recognition could be done at query time; however, it is more reasonable to perform these steps when a video is inserted into the system or by some type of batch process.

When we consider our example query in a little more depth, we note that there are two criteria for a video shot to become a good result of our query:

1. The shot should deal with "hydrogen-powered cars". This criterion can be defined based on the caption text objects associated with the video shot objects and processed using techniques from the field of information retrieval.
2. The shot should present the cars in a "nice sunset scenario". This condition can be tested based on the images constituting the video shots. A video shot containing images similar to an example image representing a sunset might be considered a good result.

It is important to note that both criteria can be interpreted as similarity conditions. With the first criterion, caption texts similar to the query text "hydrogen-powered cars" are required. With the second criterion, images similar to an example image are required. Furthermore, it is important to note that both conditions are not defined for the desired video shot objects directly, but for associated objects.

In the following, we will explain how our example query can be evaluated and which components contribute to the query processing (cf. Fig. 2).

We assume that the segmentation of the videos into shots and images as well as the caption extraction have been performed before query time. Then the query processing consists of the six steps also depicted in Fig. 2:

1. Query processing starts with the "nice sunset scenario" criterion. We assume that access structures for color features and texture features are maintained for the image objects. These access structures (addressed in more detail in section 2.2) both derive a ranking of the image objects according to their similarity to an example image showing a sunset scenario.
2. The first step has yielded two rankings of image objects. Now these two rankings have to be combined into one ranking. In the literature, various algorithms for this purpose have been proposed (cf. section 2.3). The result of this step is a combined ranking of the image objects.
3. Unfortunately, we are not interested in a ranking of image objects, but in a ranking of video shot objects. Therefore, we have to derive a ranking for the related video shot objects from the ranking of the image objects calculated in step 2. To this end, we can exploit that the image objects in the ranking are usually associated with so-called retrieval status values. As a consequence, we can derive a ranking for the video shots associating each video shot with the maximum (or average) retrieval status value of an associated image (cf. section 2.4).
4. Now the second criterion saying that the video shot has to deal with "hydrogen-powered cars" has to be addressed. We start performing a similarity query based on the query text "hydrogen-powered cars" on the caption texts. The usual access structures supporting such text similarity queries are inverted files (cf. section 2.2). This yields a ranking of the caption text objects.
5. Since we are not interested in a ranking of the caption text objects but in a ranking of the video shot objects, we have to transfer this ranking analogously to step 3.
6. Now we have got two rankings for the video shot objects stemming from the "nice sunset scenario" criterion and from the "hydrogen-powered cars" criterion. These two rankings have to be combined into one ranking analogously to step 2.

An important aspect of the process described above is that query processing can be performed in a stream-oriented lazy evaluation approach (client-pull concept). This means that the component computing the final result restricts itself to a small result size in the beginning (maybe the querier is interested in the ten best matches only, with the option for further extensions). Then this component (corresponding to step 6 in Fig. 2) will demand only the minimum amount of input elements from both its input components (corresponding to steps 3 and 5 in Fig. 2) required to calculate the first ten result elements.

In the following we will discuss the single components contributing to the process in more depth. Furthermore, we will discuss query optimization issues in the given context in section 2.5.

2.2 Access Structures for Similarity Queries

Access structures for similarity queries determine a ranking of objects for a set of objects (usually containing all objects of a given type or class), a given query object, and a given similarity measure. Three main categories of access structures can be distinguished: inverted files, trees, and fast sequential scan techniques.

Inverted Files. Inverted files are the most important access structure in information retrieval. Here queries and documents are represented by sparse high dimensional vectors. The dimensionality t of the vectors is given by the number of words occurring in the documents and the vector $(w_{d1}, w_{d2}, \ldots, w_{dt})$ describing a document d has non-zero entries only for the components corresponding to words occurring in d. Furthermore, the vector $(w_{q1}, w_{q2}, \ldots, w_{qt})$ representing a query q has non-zero components only for the components corresponding to words occurring in q. In the literature, many approaches have been presented to calculate the concrete values for the non-zero components [1]. Here it is sufficient to know that the components are usually between zero and one.

In this situation, an inverted file stores a list for each component $k \in \{1, \ldots, t\}$ (i.e., for each dimension of the t-dimensional space). And the list for component k contains elements for all documents d with $w_{dk} > 0$. Because the similarity between a query q and a document d is often defined by the scalar product

$$\sum_{k=1}^{t} w_{qk} \cdot w_{dk},$$

we have to access only the lists for components with $w_{qk} > 0$ when processing a query q. The other dimensions cannot contribute anything to the similarity values.

Inverted files are an extremely efficient access structure in situations where two conditions are met: First, the vectors representing the documents should be sparse in order to avoid a huge amount of long lists. Second, the query should contain only few non-zero components, because in such situations only very few of the t lists have to be accessed in order to process the query. If these conditions are not met, inverted files tend to be rather inefficient.

In the literature, various optimization techniques for the implementation of inverted files have been presented (see [4]). Moreover, the use of inverted files has also been suggested in a modified variant for image retrieval [23].

Trees. In the area of spatial data management, many tree-based access structures have been developed starting around 1980. Later on, algorithms for nearest-neighbor queries have been proposed for these structures [13, 19, 31]. When these algorithms were adapted to high-dimensional feature vectors, it turned out that they can yield a sub-linear performance only for dimensions up to about 10.

Fig. 3 depicts a simple tree-based access structure on the left side. The structure is a k-d-tree also used as the basis behind the LSD^h-tree [14] or the hB-tree [22]. The 2-dimensional data space $[0.0; 1.0] \times [0.0; 1.0]$ is partitioned by the root of the tree in dimension 1 at position 0.5. In the left subtree an additional split is made in dimension 2 at position 0.4. The right subtree contains further splits in an analogous way. The corresponding data space partitioning is presented at the right side of Fig. 3. The crosses

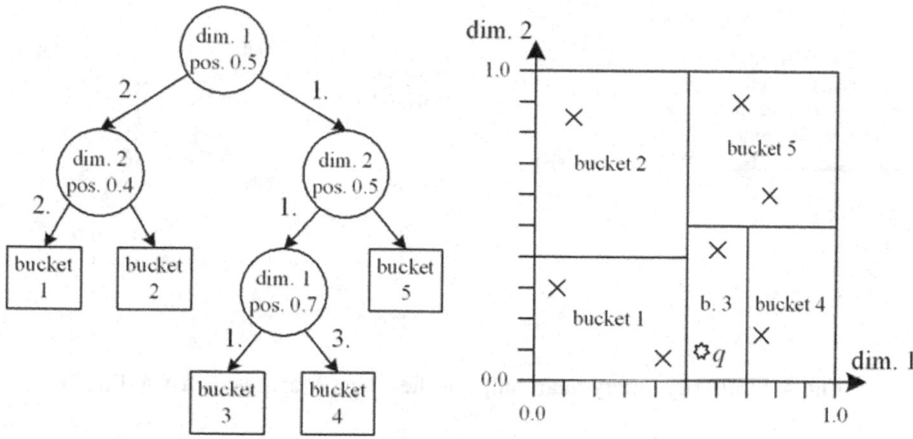

Fig. 3 Example of a Similarity Query on a Tree Structure

represent objects maintained in the access structure. For example, there is an object (0.08;0.3) stored in bucket 1.

If we assume a similarity query with the query vector (0.55; 0.1), represented by a star in Fig. 3, we start processing at the root of the directory and search for the bucket for which the bucket region (i.e., the part of the data space associated with the bucket) contains q. Every time during this search when we follow the left son, we insert the right son into an auxiliary data structure *NPQ* (= node priority queue), where the element with the smallest distance between q and its data region (i.e., the part of the data space associated with the subtree) has highest priority; and every time we follow the right son, we insert the left son into *NPQ*.

Then the objects in the bucket found (bucket 3 in our example) are inserted into another auxiliary data structure *OPQ* (= object priority queue), where the object with the smallest distance to q has highest priority. Thereafter the objects with a distance to q less than or equal to the minimal distance between q and the data region of the first element in *NPQ* are taken from *OPQ*. Unfortunately, there are no objects with such a small distance in *OPQ* in our example, because the bucket region of bucket 1 is closer to q.

Now the directory node or bucket with highest priority is taken from *NPQ*. In our example, this means that we have to follow the path marked with "2." in the tree at the left side of Fig. 3. Bucket 1 determined in this way is processed inserting the objects into *OPQ* and extracting the objects with a distance to q less than or equal to the minimal distance between q and the first element in *NPQ* from *OPQ*. This way we extract the closest object (0.42; 0.07). If further objects are needed in the ranking, we have to continue the process. In our example we would now follow path "3." in the tree.

The sketched algorithm is rather efficient for spatial applications with 2- or 3-dimensional data and it can also outperform sequential scan techniques for dimensions up to about ten dimensions. However, the *curse of dimensionality* makes it impossible for

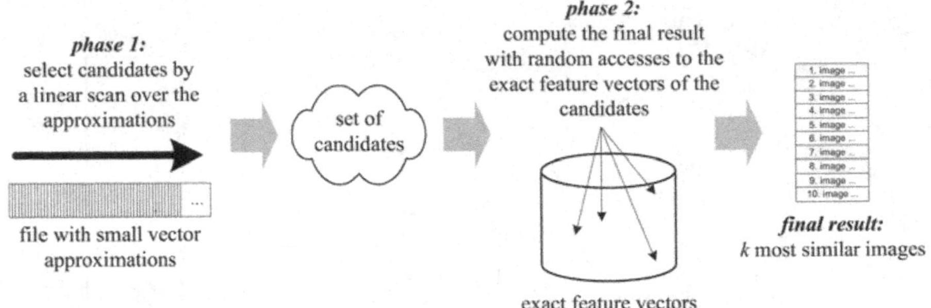

Fig. 4 Similarity Query Searching for the *k* best Matches on a VA-File

tree-based access structures to obtain better than linear complexity for similarity queries in spaces with dimensionality $t > 10$ [38].

Fast Sequential Scan Techniques. The *curse of dimensionality* mentioned above opened the floor for fast sequential scan techniques. As a consequence, the basic idea of the VA-file [38] (*VA* for *vector approximation*) is to accept linear complexity, but to minimize the overhead in order to be faster than tree-based structures. A VA-file stores each feature vector twice. Once in full precision—i.e., with a 32-bit floating point value per component— and once as a rough approximation with about 6 bits per vector component. Of course, the approximations do not suffice to calculate the exact result of a *k*-NN query (searching for the *k* next neighbors or best matches), but a fast linear scan over the approximations can be used to compute a small set of candidates surely including the *k* most similar objects, where *k* can be chosen arbitrarily. Only for the elements in the candidate set the exact feature vectors have to be accessed in order to calculate the *k* most similar objects exactly. Fig. 4 summarizes the phases of such a *k*-NN query.

In the literature, a variety of variants of the VA-file can be found: Balko and Schmidt [3] improve on the VA-file using a different data representation for the approximations and the A-tree proposed by Sakurai et al. [32] improves approximation and query efficiency by creating a tree of approximations. In [26], parallel processing of phase 1 is proposed and, in [25], the IVA-file is proposed as a variant optimized for a specific similarity measure.

None of the three presented types of access structures is superior in all situations. Inverted files are well suited for sparse feature vectors, tree-based structures provide a sublinear performance for low-dimensional feature spaces, and fast sequential scan techniques are well suited for high-dimensional spaces.

2.3 The Data Fusion Problem

In various situations, multiple rankings exist for a set of objects based on different ranking criteria. An example arises when a set of images has to be ranked with respect to the similarity to a given sample image. Here, different similarity criteria addressing color, texture, and also shape are applicable. Hence, components which merge multiple streams representing different rankings over the same base set of objects into a combined ranking are needed.

Because each element of each input stream is associated with some type of similarity value or retrieval status value (RSV), a weighted average over the retrieval status values in the input streams can be used to derive the overall ranking [10]. Other approaches are based on the ranks of the objects with respect to the single criteria—i.e., the position in the stream [15]. To calculate such a combined ranking, efficient algorithms, such as Fagin's algorithm, Nosferatu, Quick-Combine, or J^* have been proposed [9, 29, 11, 27].

The basic idea of the Nosferatu algorithm is to access the input streams in parallel. Let $\alpha_{i,q}$ be the relative importance of input ranking i ($i \in \{1,2\}$ in the case of two input rankings) for query q. Furthermore, let m_i be an upper bound for the $\mathrm{RSV}_{i,d}$ values of the elements not yet read from input ranking i. This upper bound can be initialized to some theoretical maximum value at the beginning, and during the algorithm it corresponds to the $\mathrm{RSV}_{i,d}$ of the last element read from stream i. The algorithm maintains an auxiliary data structure in which the already calculated part of

$$\mathrm{RSV}_{res,d} = \sum_i \alpha_{i,q} \cdot RSV_{i,d}$$

is maintained for each "document" d for which an entry has been read from at least one input stream. If k elements are requested in the result, the algorithm stops as soon as unread entries from the input rankings can no longer affect the top k elements of the output ranking.

In contrast to the Nosferatu algorithm which uses only sequential accesses on the input rankings, the Threshold Algorithm (TA) presented by Fagin is based on sequential and random accesses. This means that as soon as an entry for a document or object d is read from one input stream i, the missing $\mathrm{RSV}_{j,d}$ values are determined via random accesses. This means that the algorithm starts with parallel sequential reads from all input rankings. Then the missing $\mathrm{RSV}_{j,d}$ values are determined via random accesses. If documents, not yet considered on at least one input stream, can still become part of the top k elements in the result, a further step is performed. Otherwise the process is stopped. Note that

$$\mathrm{RSV}_{res,d} \leq \sum_i \alpha_{i,q} \cdot m_{i,d}$$

can be used to calculate the potential retrieval status values of documents not yet considered.

The Quick-Combine algorithm is similar to the Threshold Algorithm. However, it reads only from one list at a time and selects the list for the next sequential read depending on the weights α_i and the current descent in the values of the input rankings. This causes some additional effort for the calculations and potentially fewer accesses on the input rankings if the assumptions concerning the characteristics of the RSV-values are correct.

Experimental results [17] show that under typical assumptions Quick-Combine will be about 10 to 20% faster than the Threshold Algorithm. Nosferatu performs much worse as long as all α_i values are approximately equal. However, for diverse α_i values Nosferatu can outperform the other algorithms.

2.4 Derived Rankings

As mentioned in the motivation, with structured documents ranking criteria are sometimes not defined for the required objects themselves but for their components or other related objects. An example arises when searching for images where the text nearby (for example in the same section) should be similar to a given sample text. The problem can be described as follows: We are concerned with a query which requires a ranking for objects of some desired object type ot_d (*image* for example). However, the ranking is not defined for the objects of type ot_d, but for related objects of type ot_r (*text* for example).

We assume that the relationship between these objects is well-defined and can be traversed in both directions. In object-relational databases, join indexes and index structures for nested tables are used to speed up the traversal of such relationships. For a further improvement additional path index structures can be maintained on top of the OR-DBMS. Furthermore, we assume there is an input stream yielding a ranking for the objects of type ot_r. For example, this stream can be the output of an access structure supporting similarity queries or a combine algorithm as described in the previous section.

To perform the actual transfer of the ranking, we make use of the fact that each object of type ot_r is associated with some type of retrieval status value (RSV_r) determining the ranking of these objects. As a consequence, we can transfer the ranking to the objects of type ot_d based on these retrieval status values. For example, we can associate the maximum retrieval status value of a related object of type ot_r with each object of type ot_d. Another possibility would be to use the average retrieval status value over all associated objects of type ot_r. The retrieval status value calculated for an object of type ot_d according to the chosen semantics will be called RSV_d in the following.

Based on these assumptions, the "transfer algorithm" [16] can proceed as follows: It uses the stream with the ranked objects of type ot_r as input. For the elements from this stream, the concerned object—or objects—of type ot_d are computed traversing the respective relationships. Then the RSV_d values are calculated for these objects of type ot_d according to the chosen semantics and the object of type ot_d under consideration is inserted into an auxiliary data structure maintaining the objects considered so far. In this data structure, each object is annotated with its RSV_d value. Now the next object of type ot_r from the input stream is considered. If the RSV_r value of this new object is smaller than the RSV_d value of the first element in the auxiliary data structure which has not yet been delivered in the output stream, this first element in the auxiliary data structure can be delivered in the output stream of the transfer component.

Analytical and experimental considerations show that the performance of the transfer of a ranking is heavily influenced by the selected semantics [17]. The maximum semantics yields a better performance than the average semantics. Furthermore, it has to be mentioned that for example the *J** algorithm [27] allows for the integration of a transfer step into the combine algorithm.

2.5 Query Optimization for Similarity Queries

Now that we have sketched some algorithms contributing to the processing of complex similarity queries, it remains to be described how these algorithms can be integrated into the query execution processes of relational databases (see [12], for example).

There are some obvious problems in this respect: First, whether an element belongs to the result of a query or not, cannot be decided based only on the object itself and the query. We have to consider the whole set of objects to find out if there are objects more similar to the query. Second, we are no longer dealing with sets or bags, but with rankings or lists. As a consequence, some standard rules for query optimization are no longer applicable when concerned with similarity or ranking queries.

One important research direction in this respect considers the optimization of so-called *top N* queries. For example, Carey and Kossmann [5] explore execution plans for queries defining a ranking criterion in the `ORDER BY`-clause and a limitation of the result size in a `STOP AFTER`-clause. As another example, Chaudhuri and Gravano [6] study the advantages and limitations of processing a *top N* query by translating it into a single range query that traditional relational DBMSs can process efficiently. In both cases, optimistic and pessimistic variants exist. In the case of the optimistic variants, small intermediate results during query processing are achieved with a risk of ending up with fewer than the desired *k* best matches. In these cases, a restart of the query processing with larger intermediate results is needed. In short, the range condition used to filter out bad matches has to be relaxed in this case, whereas the pessimistic variants avoid restarts at the price of larger intermediate results.

Another approach presented by Herstel, Schulz, and Schmitt aims for a specific similarity algebra [18, 33]. For this algebra, the applicability of the optimization rules known from classical relational algebra is considered. It turns out that, e.g., weighted combinations of similarity criteria cause problems with respect to associativity and distributivity.

At present, most approaches towards algorithms or systems for complex similarity queries have to be considered as interesting building blocks for specific applications. A general framework with a maturity similar to the frameworks and architectures for processing classical set-oriented relational queries is still an open issue.

3 Processing Similarity Queries in P2P Networks

In section 2, we have described concepts and algorithms for the processing of complex similarity queries in a centralized scenario. We have not considered issues concerning the distribution of the data. However, distributed data management systems and especially the management of data in P2P networks is an important new field of research and data management in grid infrastructures is strongly related. Therefore, we will address concepts and algorithms for similarity queries in P2P networks in this section. We omitted the adjective *complex* here, because currently even the processing of "simple" similarity queries is not really solved for P2P networks.

Roughly spoken, a P2P network is an overlay network where each peer knows its neighbors, which usually form only a small fraction of the P2P network. If a peer wants to distribute a message—maybe a query—in the network, the peer sends the message to its neighbors which, in turn, forward the message to their neighbors and so forth.

To maintain a P2P network three types of administrative operations are needed: (1) *Initial Introduction*: This operation has to be performed when a peer enters the network for the first time. In this case, the peer has to announce itself to the network. (2) *Leave*: When a peer wants to leave the network temporarily there might be a need to do some local reorganization in the network in order to transfer the tasks of the peer to some of its neighbors. (3) *Join*: This operation is used when a peer is entering the network again after a previous leave operation. Then the peer can take over its responsibilities again.

When a peer is in operation, it can perform its intrinsic tasks. For example, it can search for data or information out there in the P2P network. In the following sections, we will mainly concentrate on this operation and discuss *Initial Introduction*, *Leave*, and *Join* only as far as necessary to understand the search operation.

3.1 Looking Up Documents by Their Identifiers

Early P2P systems mainly performed search operations based on *identifiers* rather than content-based similarity queries. A usual query was to look up an item defined by a unique key in the P2P network.

For example, Freenet [7]—whose goal is efficient, anonymity-preserving publication—uses an innovative symmetric lookup strategy for query processing. Within each node a *routing table* is maintained, which contains a list of neighboring peers along with information about which data they furnished in the past. Queries are forwarded from node to node until the desired object is found by a gradient ascent search algorithm with backtracking. In doing so, the goal of anonymity creates some challenges. To provide anonymity, Freenet avoids associating a document with any predictable server or forming a predictable topology among servers. The search is based on unstructured routing tables dynamically built up using caching. As a consequence, unpopular documents may simply disappear from the system, because no server has the responsibility for maintaining replicas. Another consequence is that a search may often need to visit a large fraction of the Freenet network. Freenet is not able to find out in a guaranteed

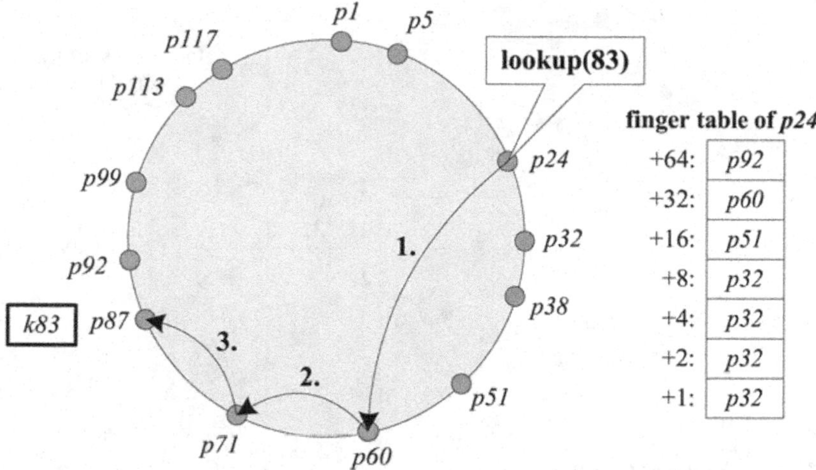

Fig. 5 A Chord Ring and the Course of a Query in the Ring

number of hops, if a given item is present in the P2P network or not. This problem is overcome by distributed hash tables (DHTs) while sacrificing anonymity. In the following, we will consider Chord and CAN as two implementations of a DHT.

Chord — ADHT Organized Like a Skiplist. Chord [36] is an example of a system implementing a DHT (see [2] for an overview with references to various other DHT approaches). With Chord each peer is mapped to a unique ID—usually a 160 bit number. The peers are arranged in a logical ring. Such a ring is given for an ID-length of 7 bit (i.e., IDs from 0 to 127) in Fig. 5. The peers are indicated by small dark grey circles on the ring. On the other hand, objects to be maintained in the P2P network are identified by keys and these keys are also mapped to ID values of the same length. Each object is maintained on the peer with the smallest ID which is equal to or higher than the object's ID. In our example, the object with the ID *k83* is maintained by the peer with ID *p87*.

To speed up the search for an object with a given key, each peer maintains a finger table. This table contains the IP address of a peer halfway around the ring, a quarter around the ring, an eighth around the ring, and so forth. In our example, the finger table for peer *p24* is given. In case of a query, a peer *p* forwards the request to its successor in the ring, except for situations where the ID of the requested object is higher than the ID of a peer in the finger table of *p*. In this case, the request is forwarded to the peer in the finger table with the greatest ID smaller than the ID of the requested object. Fig. 5 depicts the course of a search for the object with ID *k83* issued by peer *p24*. Obviously, the cost of a query (i.e., the number of peers which are involved) grows logarithmically with the number of peers in the network.

To maintain the ring structure in a volatile P2P network, some redundancy has to be introduced [36]. The higher the redundancy, the more reliable the network becomes.

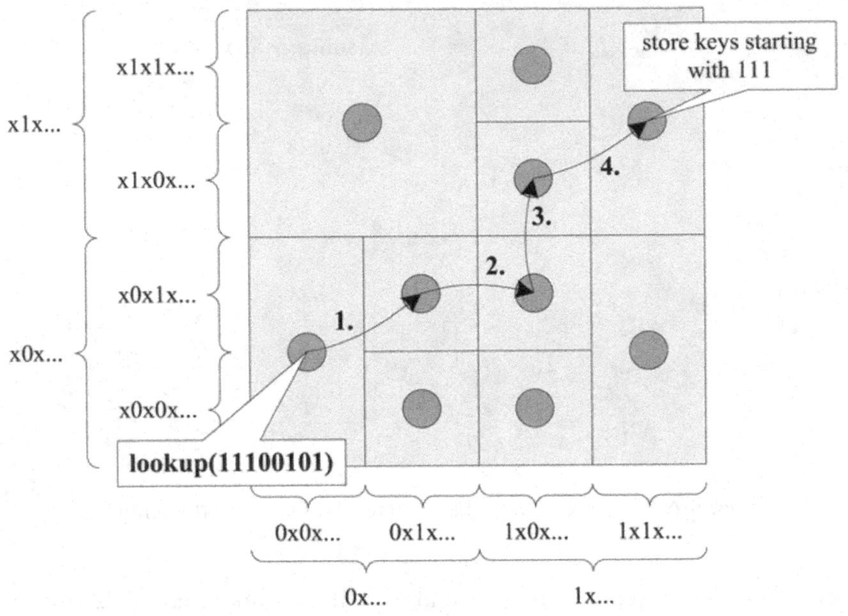

Fig. 6 2-dimensional Coordinate Space of a CAN

Finally, it has to be mentioned that the peer responsible for a given object according to its ID can either maintain the object itself or a reference to the peer physically storing the object.

A Chord-like structure can also be used for simple keyword-based text search operations. Here each object is associated with a small set of keywords. These keywords are mapped to IDs and a reference to an object is maintained on all peers which are responsible for one of its keywords IDs. This can be seen as a first step towards inverted files distributed in a P2P network (cf. section 3.2).

CAN — A *d*-dimensional Implementation of DHTs. Content Addressable Networks (CANs) [30] provide another way to realize a distributed hash table. To this end, a CAN uses a d-dimensional Cartesian coordinate space. The coordinate space is partitioned into hyper-rectangles, called *zones*. Each peer is responsible for a zone. A key is associated with a point in the coordinate space. For example, a key can be mapped to an ID and the ID can be used to generate the coordinate values by interleaving. For $d = 2$, the first, the third, the fifth, … bit form the coordinate value in the first dimension and the second, the forth, the sixth, … bit form the coordinate value in the second dimension. This way each object is maintained at the peer whose zone contains the coordinates derived from the object's key. In order to process queries, each peer maintains a routing table of all its bordering neighbors in the coordinate space (cf. Fig. 6).

If we search for an object with a given key, the query is forwarded along a path that approximates the straight line in the coordinate space from the peer posing the query to the peer maintaining the key. To this end, each peer forwards the query to its neighbor closest in the coordinate space to the peer maintaining the key. The cost of a query processed this way is $O(d \cdot \sqrt[d]{N})$ where N denotes the number of peers in the network. This becomes $O(\sqrt{N})$ for $d = 2$.

At first glance, one might think that a CAN could also be used for similarity queries in a d-dimensional space. For this, we could use d-dimensional feature vectors instead of interleaved IDs in order to position the objects in the d-dimensional coordinate space. Unfortunately, this approach fails because, due to the curse of dimensionality, we would have to access all peers in order to obtain the most similar object in this way for $d > 10$. Furthermore, the administrative data which has to be maintained on each peer would be rather huge for high values of d. Another weak aspect from our point of view is that CANs (as any distributed index structure) require sending a substantial amount of feature vectors (possibly all of them) to other peers when entering the network ([37] takes this approach).

3.2 Performing Similarity Queries in P2P Networks

While most DHTs deal with one-dimensional IDs (CANs, as an exception use low-dimensional vector spaces for routing), there is now more and more research concerning information retrieval queries in P2P networks.

Performing Content-Based Queries on Text Data. Joseph [20] proposes NeuroGrid, which (like some other current P2P approaches) permits keyword-based search for annotated items. NeuroGrid exploits the fact that each item is described by just a few keywords. As in Freenet, routing tables are maintained in each peer to guide the query processing.

FASD [21] uses the same query routing scheme as Freenet, however, it uses *term vectors* of full documents (*i.e.,* the vector of words present/absent in a document) to make the routing decisions. This approach is particularly effective in situations where the queries consist of only a few keywords. On multi-keyword queries, however, this scheme is likely to suffer from the curse of dimensionality.

Cuenca-Acuna and Nguyen [8] provide full-text information retrieval in their PlanetP system. In PlanetP, the content of each peer is summarized using a *bloom filter*. A bloom filter is a bit array that represents a set S with fewer than $|S|$ bits. In this case, the set represented by the bloom filter is the *set of terms* (words) present in a peer. Each peer distributes its bloom filter using a rumor-spreading algorithm. Thus after a short period of time *all peers* contain the descriptors of *all other peers* within the network. Query processing is done by visiting peers starting with the most probable provider of a match.

Similarity Queries for Multimedia Data. Tang et al. [37] present two approaches for text retrieval in P2P systems and suggest that these approaches can be extended to image retrieval. One of them (pVSM, peer vector space model) stores *(term, document_id)* pairs in a DHT, and then retrieves such pairs to perform text retrieval. According to the authors this approach can be handled due to the fact that terms are Zipf distributed, and one can thus limit the index for each document to a few strongly weighted terms. This approach seems to be hard to translate to image data: [35] reports the need for a large number of features when using text information retrieval methods on image data.

The other approach suggested in [37], pLSI, is based on Latent Semantic Indexing: Singular Value Decomposition is used to decrease the dimensionality of the feature vectors, and the reduced feature vectors are stored in a hierarchical version of a CAN (eCAN). For each *document* of the collection, *(feature vector, document id)* pairs are stored in the eCAN. The curse of dimensionality is addressed by partitioning each feature vector into several lower-dimensional feature vectors. Each of these vectors is said to be in a *plane*. The first of these lower-dimensional partial vectors is stored in a CAN_1, the second in CAN_2 and so on through CAN_m. A given query is then split into several queries of lower dimensionality. Together with aggressive pruning, Tang et al. manage to achieve impressive results on text data: few nodes need to be accessed for achieving a high precision. The future will have to show whether or not these results can also be achieved on image data.

Ng and Sia [28] present the Firework Query Model for information retrieval and CBIR in P2P networks. In the Firework Query Model, there are two classes of links, normal *random* links, and privileged *attractive* links. A query starts off as a flooding query forwarded to all neighbors. If a peer deems the query too far away from the peer's local cluster centroid, it will forward the query via a random link, decreasing the time to live (TTL) of the query, which gives a limit for the number of hops a query can make. Otherwise, it will process the query, and forward it via all its attractive links without decreasing the TTL. From these approaches two main research directions can be identified:

- pVSM can be seen as a distributed implementation of an access structure—or, more specifically, of inverted files. Here the single files carrying references to the objects/documents containing a certain word are distributed in the P2P network. For a query consisting only of very few words this might be adequate. However, with queries containing multiple terms the merging of the lists will cause a significant communication overhead.
- Techniques like PlanetP are based on short content descriptions for each peer's content. In PlanetP, each peer stores compact descriptions of *all* other peers in the network. With a given query, it can forward the query only to those peers which seem promising according to their compact description.

A Scalable Approach to Similarity Queries Using Peer Descriptions. To conclude the considerations on similarity queries in P2P networks, we want to sketch the Rumorama approach [24] aiming towards scalable summary-based search in P2P networks. The goal of the Rumorama protocol is to establish a robust hierarchy of PlanetP networks. The leaves within the Rumorama hierarchy are PlanetP networks (called leaf nets). Inner nodes within the Rumorama hierarchy allow accessing the leaf nets.

The situation in a Rumorama net is depicted in Fig. 7 analogously to the situation for a CAN in Fig. 6. As usual, each peer is identified by an ID. The ID of the peer used as the querier in Fig. 7 is 01011000... . This peer is located in a leaf net (indicated by a grey rectangle with a dashed border) and it maintains compact peer descriptions for all 18 peers in that leaf net. With all peers in the leaf net the peer shares the first two bits "01" of its ID. More precisely, each peer maintains a so-called *friends' mask* representing the prefix of the ID which is equal for all peers in the leaf net. In our case, the friends' mask is 01. In order to communicate with peers in other leaf nets, our peer maintains additional information about simple neighbors. In contrast to friends in the leaf net, the peer does not maintain compact peer descriptions for its neighbors. Our example peer has two neighbors for each bit in its friends' mask. It has a neighbor with an ID starting with 0 and it has a neighbor with an ID starting with 1 for the first bit. For the second bit, it has a neighbor with an ID starting with 00 and it has a neighbor with an ID starting with 01.[1]

When a peer wants to issue a query it is important to distribute the query to all leaf nets. For this, the querier forwards the query to its neighbors with an ID starting with 0 and with an ID starting with 1. In addition, the query is augmented with a parameter denoting the length of the prefix already covered in the distribution process (1 for the first step). The two peers, contacted in that way, check whether the length of the prefix *pre* already covered in the distribution process is equal to or greater than the length of their friends' mask. In that case, a leaf net is reached and in this leaf net the query can be processed for all peers with prefix *pre*. Otherwise, the query is forwarded to the neighbors maintained by these peers at the next level.

In Fig. 7, the course of a query is sketched. The indicated querier forwards the query to two neighbors (one with an ID starting with 0 and one with an ID starting with 1). For these two peers, leaf nets are not yet reached and therefore the query is again forwarded to the respective neighbors for prefix length two.

The prefixes are indicated in Fig. 7 in squared brackets. Note that this second step is processed in parallel on the two peers reached in the first step. For the peers reached with the prefixes 11, 10 and 01 leaf nets are now reached. Only the peer reached for the prefix 00 has to forward the query one more time. Now five leaf nets forming a disjoint and exhaustive partitioning of the whole P2P network are reached and the query is processed in each leaf net. If the querier is interested in the *k* best matches, they are calculated for each leaf net separately. Thereafter the results obtained for the leaf nets are merged following the paths on which the query was distributed in reverse order.

Obviously, this schema cannot overcome the curse of dimensionality. But it allows for a scalable implementation of PlanetP-like P2P networks. Peers have to maintain

---

1. Note that it is necessary in the concrete implementation to maintain some redundant neighbors in order to keep the system fit for work in a volatile network. Furthermore, it has to be noted that each peer can decide the length of its friends' mask independently and that this length can be changed during the lifetime of a peer.

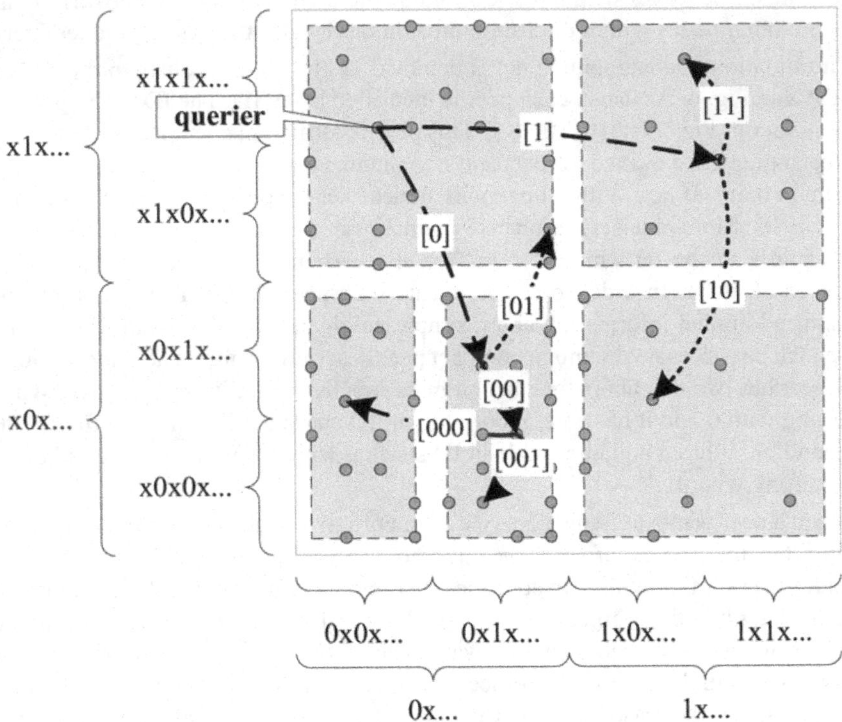

Fig. 7 Distribution Example of a Similarity Query to the Leaf Nets in Rumorama

compact peer descriptions only for a small set of peers with tunable size and the query distribution can be performed in logarithmic time. For the local processing of the queries in the leaf nets, various heuristics trading result quality for processing time are applicable. For example, we could access only a fixed fraction of the peers in each leaf net concentrating on the peers most promising according to their compact representation.

4 Conclusion

In the present contribution, we have discussed the efficient processing of similarity queries in a central scenario and in a P2P scenario. Since algorithms for simple similarity queries have reached a mature level for the central scenario the focus is now turning to complex similarity queries with multiple ranking criteria based on a complex object schemata. For the P2P scenario, scalable algorithms for content-based similarity queries are currently coming up. Here thorough analytical and experimental considerations of the upcoming concepts will be necessary in order to reach a mature and commercially applicable state of the systems.

References

[1] Baeza-Yates, R., Ribeiro-Neto, B.: *Modern Information Retrieval.* ACM press. Pearson Education Limited, Harlow, England, 1999.

[2] Balakrishnan, H., Kasshoek, M. F., Karger, D., Morris, R., Stoica, I.: Looking Up Data in P2P Systems. *Commun. ACM,* 46(2):43–48, Feb. 2003.

[3] Balko. S., Schmitt, I.: Efficient Nearest Neighbor Retrieval by Using a Local Approximation Technique - the Active Vertice Approach. Technical Report 2, Fakultät für Informatik, Universität Magdeburg, 2002.

[4] Buckley, C., Lewit, A.: Optimization of inverted vector searches. In *Proc. 8th International ACM SIGIR Conference on Research and Development in Information Retrieval*, pages 97–105, New York, USA, 1985.

[5] Carey, M. J., Kossmann, D.: On saying "Enough already!" in SQL. In *Proc. 1997 ACM SIGMOD Intl. Conf. on Management of Data*, pages 219–230, Tucson, Arizona, 13–15 June 1997.

[6] Chaudhuri, S., Gravano, L.: Evaluating top-*k* selection queries. In *Proc. 25th Intl. Conf. on Very Large Data Bases, September, 1999, Edinburgh, Scotland, UK*, pages 397–410, 1999.

[7] Clarke, I., Sandberg, O., Wiley, B., Hong, T. W.: Freenet: A distributed anonymous information storage and retrieval system. In H. Federrath, editor, *Designing Privacy Enhancing Technologies*, volume 2009 of *LNCS*, 2000.

[8] Cuenca-Acuna, F. M., Nguyen, T. D.: Text-Based Content Search and Retrieval in ad hoc P2P Communities. Technical Report DCS-TR-483, Department of Computer Science, Rutgers University, 2002.

[9] Fagin, R., Lotem, A., Naor, M.:. Optimal aggregation algorithms for middleware. In *Proc. 10th ACM Symposium on Principles of Database Systems: PODS*, pages 102–113, New York, USA, 2001.

[10] Fagin, R., Wimmers, E. L.: A formula for incorporating weights into scoring rules. *Theoretical Computer Science*, 239(2):309–338, May 2000.

[11] Güntzer, U., Balke, W.-T., Kießling, W.: Optimizing multi-feature queries for image databases. In *VLDB 2000, Proc. 26th Intl. Conf. on Very Large Data Bases*, pages 419–428, Cairo, Egypt, 2000.

[12] Härder, T., Rahm, E.: *Datenbanksysteme: Konzepte und Techniken der Implementierung.* Springer, Heidelberg, 2nd edition, 2001.

[13] Henrich, A.: A distance scan algorithm for spatial access structures. In *Proc. of the 2nd ACM Workshop on Advances in Geographic Information Systems*, pages 136–143, Gaithersburg, Maryland, USA, 1994. ACM Press.

[14] Henrich, A.: The LSD^h-tree: An access structure for feature vectors. In *Proc. 14th Intl. Conf. on Data Engineering, February 23-27, 1998, Orlando, Florida, USA*, pages 362–369. IEEE Computer Society, 1998.

[15] Henrich, A., Robbert, G.: Combining multimedia retrieval and text retrieval to search structured documents in digital libraries. In *Proc. 1st DELOS Workshop on Information Seeking, Searching and Querying in Digital Libraries*, pages 35–40, Zürich, Switzerland, Dec. 2000.

[16] Henrich, A., Robbert, G.: Ein Ansatz zur Übertragung von Rangordnungen bei der Suche auf strukturierten Daten. In *Tagungsband der 10. Konferenz Datenbanksysteme für Business, Technologie und Web (BTW 2003)*, volume 26 of *LNI*, pages 167–186, Leipzig, Deutschland, Feb. 2003. GI.

[17] Henrich, A., Robbert, G.: Comparison and evaluation of fusion algorithms and transfer semantics for structured multimedia data. In C. Danilowicz, editor, *Multimedia and Network Information Systems (Vol. 2) (1st International Workshop on Multimedia Information Systems Technology)*, pages 181–192, Szklarska Poreba, Poland, September 2004. Oficyna Wydawinicza Politechniki Wroclawskiej.

[18] Herstel T., Schmitt, I.: Optimierung von Ausdrücken der Ähnlichkeitsalgebra SA. In *INFORMATIK 2004 - Informatik verbindet - Beiträge der 34. Jahrestagung der Gesellschaft für Informatik e.V. (GI), Band 2*, volume P-51 of *LNI*, pages 49–53, Ulm, Germany, September 2004.

[19] Hjaltason, G. R., Samet, H.: Ranking in spatial databases. In *Advances in Spatial Databases, 4th International Symposium, SSD'95, Portland, Maine, USA, August 6-9, 1995, Proceedings*, volume 951 of *LNCS*, pages 83–95. Springer, 1995.

[20] Joseph, S.: Adaptive routing in distributed decentralized systems: Neurogrid, Gnutella and Freenet. In *Proc. of workshop on Infrastructure for Agents, MAS, and Scalable MAS, at Autonomous Agents*, Montreal, Canada, 2001.

[21] Kronfol, A. Z.: A Fault-tolerant, Adaptive, Scalable, Distributed Search Engine, May 2002. Final Thesis, Princeton.
URL: http://www.searchlore.org/library/kronfol_final_thesis.pdf

[22] Lomet, D. B., Salzberg, B.: The hb-tree: A multiattribute indexing method with good guaranteed performance. *ACM Trans. Database Syst.*, 15(4):625–658, 1990.

[23] Müller, H., Squire, D. M., Müller, W., Pun, T.: Efficient access methods for content-based image retrieval with inverted files. Technical Report 99.02, Computer Vision Group, University of Geneva, July 1999.

[24] Müller, W., Eisenhardt, M., Henrich, A.: Scalable summary-based search in P2P networks. submitted for publication, 2004.

[25] Müller, W., Henrich, A.: Faster exact histogram intersection on large data collections using inverted VA-files. In *Image and Video Retrieval: 3rd Intl. Conf.* CIVR. Proceedings, volume 3115 of LNCS, pages 455-463, Dublin, Ireland, July, 2004. Springer.

[26] Müller, W., Henrich, A.: Reducing I/O cost of similarity queries by processing several at a time. In Proc. MDDE '04, 4th International Workshop on Multimedia Data and Document Engineering, Washington DC, USA, July 2004. IEEE Computer Society.

[27] Natsev, A., Chang, Y.-C., Smith, J. R., Li, C.-S., Vitter, J. S.: Supporting incremental join queries on ranked inputs. In VLDB 2001, Proc. of 27th Intl. Conf. on Very Large Data Bases, pages 281–290, Roma, Italy, 9 2001.

[28] Ng, C. H., Sia, K. C.: Peer clustering and firework query model. In Poster Proc. of The 11th Interational World Wide Web Conf., Honululu, HI, USA, May 2002.

[29] Pfeifer, U., Pennekamp, S.: Incremental Processing of Vague Queries in Interactive Retrieval Systems. In Hypertext - Information Retrieval - Multimedia '97: Theorien, Modelle und Implementierungen integrierter elektronischer Informationssysteme, pages 223–235, Dortmund, 1997. Universitätsverlag Konstanz.

[30] Ratnasamy, S., Francis, P., Handley, M., Karp, R., Schenker, S.: A scalable content-addressable network. In Proc. 2001 Conf. on applications, technologies, architectures, and protocols for computer communications, San Diego, CA, 2001.

[31] Roussopoulos, N., Kelley, S., Vincent, F.: Nearest neighbor queries. In Proc. 1995 ACM SIGMOD Intl. Conf. on Management of Data, San Jose, California, May 22-25, 1995, pages 71–79, 1995.

[32] Sakurai, Y., Yoshikawa, M., Uemura, S., Kojima, H.: The A-tree: An index structure for high-dimensional spaces using relative approximation. In Proc. of the 26th Intl. Conf. on Very Large Data Bases, pages 516–526, Cairo, 2000.

[33] Schmitt, I., Schulz, N.: Similarity relational calculus and its reduction to a similarity algebra. In 3rd Intl. Symposium on Foundations of Information and Knowledge Systems (FoIKS'04), volume 2942 of LNCS, pages 252–272, Austria, 2004. Springer.

[34] Smith, I., Chang, S.-F.: VisualSEEK: A fully automated content-based image query system. In Proc. of the 4th ACM Multimedia Conf., pages 87–98, New York, USA, Nov. 1996.

[35] Squire, D. M., Müller, W., Müller, H., and Raki, J.: Content-based query of image databases, inspirations from text retrieval: inverted files, frequency-based weights and relevance feedback. In 11th Scandinavian Conf. on Image Analysis, Kangerlussuaq, Greenland, 1999.

[36] Stoica, I., Morris, R., Karger, D., Kaashoek, F., Balakrishnan, H.: Chord: A scalable Peer-To-Peer lookup service for Internet applications. In Proc. ACM SIGCOMM Conf., San Di ego, CA, USA, 2001.

[37] Tang C., Xu, Z., Mahalingam, M.: pSearch: Information retrieval in structured overlays. In First Workshop on Hot Topics in Networks (HotNets-I), Princeton, NJ, 2002.

[38] Weber, R., Schek, H.-J., Blott, S.: A quantitative analysis and performance study for similarity-search methods in high-dimensional spaces. In Proc. Intl. Conf. on VLDB, New York, USA, 1998.

Part III Application Design

Toward Automated Large-Scale Information Integration and Discovery

Paul Brown, Peter Haas, Jussi Myllymaki,
Hamid Pirahesh, Berthold Reinwald, Yannis Sismanis

IBM Almaden Research Center
{pbrown1, phaas, jussi, pirahesh, reinwald, syannis}@us.ibm.com

Abstract. The high cost of data consolidation is the key market inhibitor to the adoption of traditional information integration and data warehousing solutions. In this paper, we outline a next-generation integrated database management system that takes traditional information integration, content management, and data warehouse techniques to the next level: the system will be able to integrate a very large number of information sources and automatically construct a global business view in terms of "Universal Business Objects". We describe techniques for discovering, unifying, and aggregating data from a large number of disparate data sources. Enabling technologies for our solution are XML, web services, caching, messaging, and portals for real-time dashboarding and reporting.

1 Introduction

Efficient business management requires a flexible, unified view of all data in the enterprise. Many mid-sized and large companies are now facing the challenging problem of bringing together all of their data in a unified form. Enterprise business data is typically spread across hundreds or thousands of sources: inside applications such as SAP, Siebel, and PeopleSoft, on web sites, as syndicated data feeds, in content-management warehouses and marts, in email archives, in spreadsheets and other office documents, and inside a tremendous variety of custom applications. Data collected over a long period of time is juxtaposed with ready-made data sources that come as part of turnkey systems.

Disparate data sources are brought together through business acquisitions and mergers. The various operational systems within an enterprise are usually isolated, have data that is inconsistent both in format and semantics with other operational systems, and offer different end-user tools for data retrieval and reporting. There is a marked lack of data integrity; for example, a given entity can have different names in different operational systems, distinct entities can have the same name, and an entity may exist in some systems but not in others. Adding to the problem, most traditional databases were

T. Härder and W. Lehner (Eds.): Data Management (Wedekind Festschrift), LNCS 3551, pp. 161-180, 2005.

not designed with future data integration in mind. These databases, which place a premium on data integrity and consistency, are usually encased in a very large body of difficult-to-change procedural code that is inextricably entwined with the schema semantics.

The major costs of an integration project are usually incurred while trying to "understand the data," i.e., trying to figure out the schema of each input data source, the constraint rules that govern the data in each schema, and, perhaps most importantly, the rules that describe the relationships between data from different sources. These assertions are borne out in the traditional setting for data integration, namely data warehousing. Traditional warehouses try to provide a unified view of the data while hiding the diversity of the underlying operational systems. Experience with data-warehousing projects suggests that the capital cost of integration is very high, and an average design time of six months to two years causes many projects to fail. Manual schema integration constitutes the bulk of the expense. At least one vendor [11] estimates that labor costs for large warehousing projects currently comprise 70% of the total costs, and we believe that the relative labor costs for traditional warehousing solutions will only increase in the future. The initial per-document cost of enterprise content management systems is less than that of data warehouses, but the deep document-analytic functionality provided by content management systems is frequently inferior to the BI capabilities of data warehouses.

In this paper, we outline a next-generation integrated database management system (DBMS) that brings together information integration, content management, and data warehousing with business intelligence. The integrated DBMS (1) taps into the data flow between operational systems and captures raw data, (2) automatically constructs a global business view in terms of Universal Business Objects (UBOs), (3) provides warehousing functionality for the UBOs such as cube queries, advanced analytics, and efficient propagation of data changes, and (4) provides rich interfaces for browsing and searching UBOs that hide the details and variety of the underlying operational systems. We take a data-centric integration approach in that we capture raw data only, and do not rely on any schema information. To ensure that the system scales to very large numbers of information sources, we employ asynchronous messaging and crawling techniques similar to those found in web-scale applications such as Google. We apply machine-learning techniques to map information across disparate sources, and develop new algorithms to map information sources into higher-level business artifacts; these artifacts can either be discovered by the system or introduced into the system through enterprise data dictionaries, taxonomies, and ontologies. We introduce a new query paradigm that takes queries over UBOs and converts them into queries over specific information sources based on discovered relationships between their sources. The enabling core technologies for this next-generation integrated DBMS are XML, web services, tools for information dissemination and dashboards, frameworks for unstructured information management (such as IBM's UIMA architecture) and advanced search capabilities.

2 A Next-Generation Integrated Database Management System

In this section, we outline the architecture of a next-generation integrated DBMS, giving a high-level view of the components and the flow of data through the system. We also describe a hypothetical end-to-end application scenario.

2.1 Architecture

Fig. 1 outlines the architecture of the integrated DBMS. The architecture comprises three layers: the operational systems layer, the integrated DBMS layer, and the business applications layer. The operational layer at the bottom of the figure displays some typical data sources that might exist in an enterprise, such as CRM and HR applications with proprietary data formats or database schemas, content management systems, and Office productivity tools. The operational systems in an enterprise interoperate today through synchronous or asynchronous communication such as message queues, email, paper, and so forth, typically in a point-to-point and ad hoc fashion. In the future, web services and the "enterprise service bus" (ESB)—which provides mediation and transformation services—will play an important role in facilitating interoperability. The communication trail for a business transaction can usually be reconstructed based on application-specific information in the exchanged data. For example, we observe that a customer sent an order referencing the customer ID, that the seller sent an invoice referencing the order ID, and so forth. Whereas this kind of information is sufficient for reasoning about point to point operational interactions, approaching an enterprise top-down from the business layer requires an integrated business view to answer high-level queries or automatically produce high-level reports. The goal of our integrated DBMS is to close the gap between the business layer and the operational layer.

The integrated DBMS taps into the operational data flow to capture input data. The system analyzes the input data, assigning the incoming data values to disjoint "data sets" and then computing a synopsis for each data set. The synopsis is then used to compute one or more "signatures" for each data set. The signatures can then be used to derive similarity measures between a pair of data sets. In particular, by identifying similarities between an input data set and a reference data set, the system can identify low-level business artifacts such as "telephone number" or "North American surname." Using methods from graph theory, these low-level identifications can be combined and used to identify higher-level artifacts such as "customer", "order", "account", and so forth. We call these high-level artifacts *Universal Business Objects* (UBOs). The data sets that define a UBO may come from different data sources. Relationships between the UBOs can also be identified. Enterprise data dictionaries, ontologies, and reference data all may be incorporated in the foregoing process. The system permits the UBOs and other discovered metadata to be cached or instantiated in the integrated DBMS for purposes of indexing, querying, etc., just like ordinary warehouse data today. The

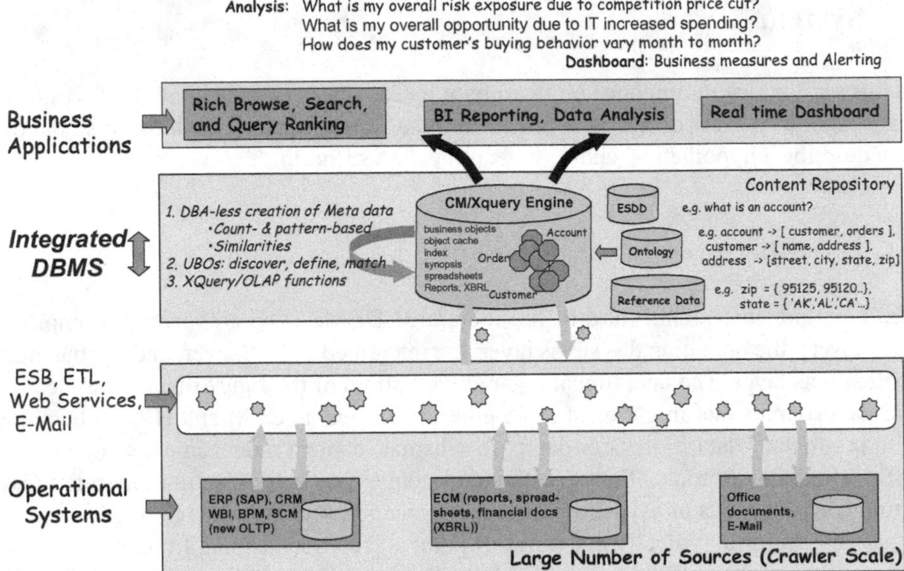

Fig. 1 System Architecture

UBOs are also exposed to the business applications for rich browsing, search, report generation, data analysis, UBO updating, and real-time dashboards.

2.2 Repository Dataflow

In this section, we describe in more detail the dataflow within the integrated DBMS (Fig. 2). The details of the various components in the dataflow are described in subsequent sections.

The integrated DBMS takes in a large collection of XML documents. The documents in the collection are partitioned into mutually disjoint sets, and we say informally that documents in the same partition come from the same *data source*. Heuristically, documents from the same data source are similar to one another in origin, destination, structure, and content. For example, a given data source might comprise the XML messages returned from a specified web service in response to a particular kind of message, or perhaps the source might comprise purchase orders generated by a specified application.

The data values in the XML documents that come from a given data source are assigned to disjoint *data sets*, as follows. Each XML document from a given data source can be viewed as a "tree data structure", with data values stored at the leaf nodes. Each leaf node (as well as each internal node) of the complex structure is uniquely identified by an XPath expression; the set of XPaths (i.e., nodes) for a given data source can be computed simply by submitting every XML document from the data source to a generic SAX parser. There is a data set associated with each leaf node, and for the *i*th leaf node we denote the corresponding data set as $ds_i = \{v_1, v_2, ..., v_n\}$, where v_j is the data value at the ith leaf node in the jth XML document from the specified data source. Observe that ds_i is a multiset, because the same data value can appear in multiple documents. Also observe that each data set can be identified uniquely by data source and XPath expression for the corresponding leaf node. The *domain* associated with a data set *ds* is the set of distinct values obtained from *ds* after removal of duplicates.

As described in subsequent sections, the DBMS computes a synopsis of each data set from a given data source. The synopsis contains statistical information about the data set such as sample values and histogram data. The resulting synopses for the data source are stored in the *DataSet* repository. For each data set, the DBMS uses the synopsis to derive one or more *signatures*; a signature summarizes a specific characteristic of the data set that is pertinent to evaluating the similarity of the data set to other data sets. The signatures are stored with the corresponding data set in the *DataSet* repository. In our initial prototype, the signatures comprise a space-constrained concise Bernoulli sample and a hash-counting data structure. Patterns are, for example, rules for phone numbers, credit card numbers, zip codes, and so forth. The pattern signature is derived from the synopsis using an automaton-based technique that is described in a subsequent section.

Next, the DBMS uses the signatures to compute similarities between data sets. The computed similarities for each related pair of data sets are combined via a *Synthesize* function and stored in the *Similarities* repository. When there are N input data sets, a direct pairwise comparison of all these data sets is an $O(N^2)$ operation. Since N is usually very large, such a computation is typically too expensive. The DBMS therefore first compares each input data set to one or more *reference* data sets, where a reference data set is typically derived from a data dictionary, ontology, or from a previous discovery phase of the DBMS. Such a comparison is typically an $O(NM)$ operation, where M is the number of reference data sets. Because M is typically smaller than N by orders of magnitude, this computation is usually feasible. Then, when comparing input data sets, only data sets that are both similar to a common reference data set need to be compared.

The similarity-identification process now proceeds from low-level data sets to higher-level structures. After computing similarities for leaf-level nodes in the XPath only (e.g. city, zip code, street name), the DBMS invokes the Matcher component to compute similarity metrics between internal nodes, e.g., address, customer. The Matcher algorithms are based on graph theory. In addition to computing similarity metrics, the DBMS also identifies constraints between pairs of data sets such as key-to-foreign-key relationships and functional dependencies; the data sets in a pair may be from the same or different data sources. Finally, given all the similarities between data sets, the similarities between internal nodes, and the discovered constraints, the DBMS applies a recursive splitting algorithm to discover UBOs.

2.3 A Hypothetical Application Scenario

To make the forgoing discussion more concrete, we now describe a hypothetical (small scale) end-to-end application scenario. This scenario encompasses a collection of data

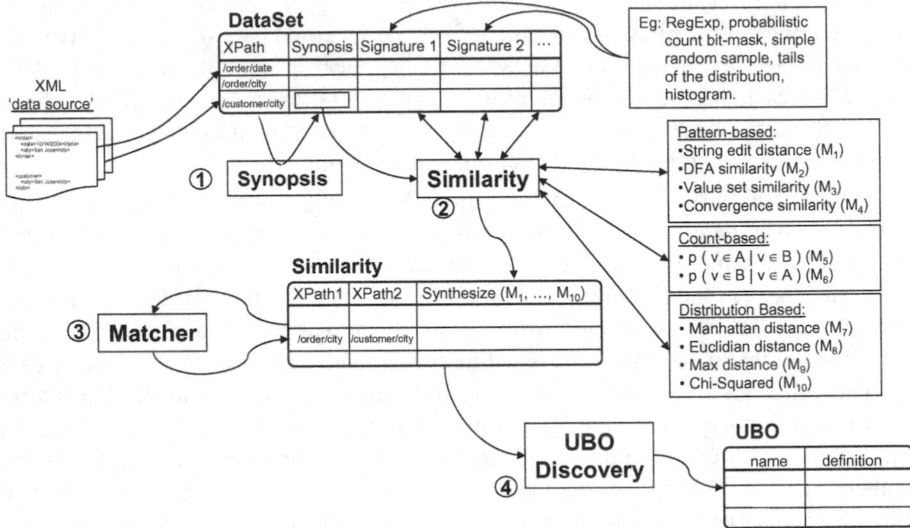

Fig. 2 Repository Dataflow

sources at the lowest level and a client spreadsheet application at the highest level (see Fig. 3). We capture XML documents from four data sources. The system analyzes the data sources, discovers the data sets, and computes both XPath identifiers and synopses. Suppose that three sources of reference data are available: product category information from the United Nations Standard Products and Services (UNSPSC), time information (i.e., a calendar), and location information from the United States Census Bureau. The system creates synopses for the reference data as well.

The system would then analyze the data sources and reference data to compute similarities between data sets and composite nodes. Ultimately the system would identify three new UBOs W', X', and Y' along with their domains, constraints, and relationships both to each other and to the metadata. Semantic analysis of W', X', and Y' might suggest names such as Customer, Product, and Order. Applying some OLAP tools, the system can then generate a spreadsheet containing the quarterly sales figures.

3 Automated Similarity Analysis

In this section, we describe in more detail the various techniques that the DBMS uses to create synopses, compute signatures, derive similarity measures for both data sets and internal XML nodes, and discover constraints.

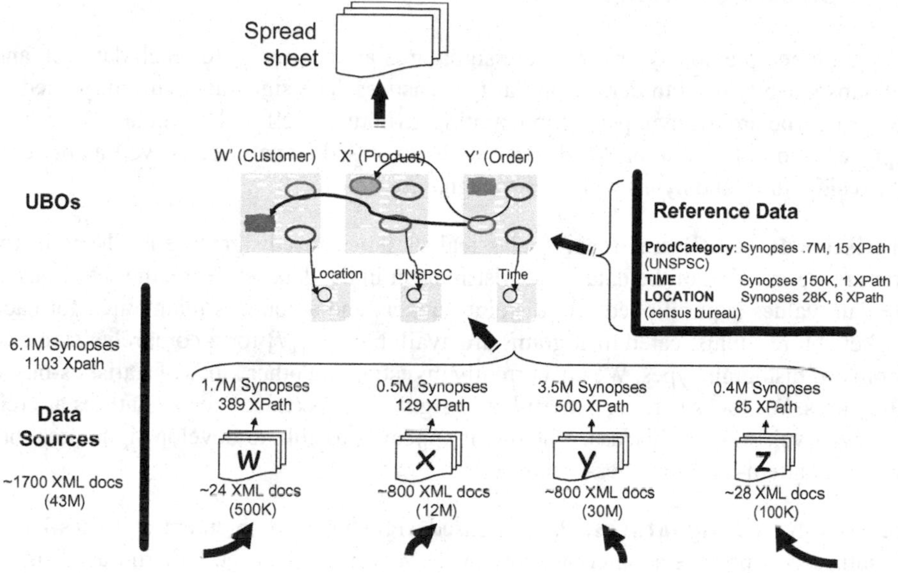

Fig. 3 Example

3.1 Synopsis Creation

The synopsis maintained for a data set in our current prototype comprises several components. The first component is a space-constrained sample from which a uniform random sample can be extracted as needed. If the number of distinct values in the incoming data is small enough, the sample can be stored in a concise form similar to that described in [5].

The second key component of the synopsis is a hash-counting data structure. The idea is that each incoming data element is fed into a "probabilistic counting" algorithm; see, e.g., [2]. Such algorithms estimate the number of distinct values in a data set in a single pass using a fixed amount of memory. The value of the incoming element is hashed, and this hash value is used to update an appropriate data structure. The data structure is then used to estimate the number of distinct values. In the most naïve algorithm, the data structure is simply a bit vector, where each bit corresponds to a hash bucket. For most algorithms, it is the case that two hash-data structures created from two disjoint data sets can be combined into a single structure of the same type and used to estimate the number of distinct values in the union of the data sets.

Other information maintained in the synopsis includes the data set cardinality, the path expression that specifies the data set, and the k highest and k lowest data values encountered, along with corresponding frequency counts.

3.2 Signature Creation

As mentioned previously, one or more signatures are computed for each data set, and are subsequently used to derive similarity measures. The signatures currently used in our prototype are the synopsis hash-counting structure itself and a regular-expression representation of a pattern. We discuss statistics-based signatures, as well as pattern-based signatures and hybrids of the two signature types.

Statistics-Based Signatures. A classical statistics-based signature is a lossy histogram representation of the data value distribution in the data set. Here, the set of possible data values is partitioned into disjoint buckets and a count is maintained for each bucket. More sophisticated histograms are available; see [7] for a comprehensive taxonomy of histogram types. We are currently investigating other kinds of statistics-based signatures. We focus here on pattern-based signatures, because such signatures are relatively novel. Also, as discussed below, it appears possible to develop signatures that are both pattern- and statistics-based.

Pattern-Based Signatures. Pattern-based signatures complement statistics-based signatures and provide an alternate way to characterize a data set. Pattern-based signatures can reveal similarities between data sets that statistics-based signatures will miss. For example, one data set might contain telephone numbers in the 408 area code while another may contain telephone numbers in the 650 area code. A statistics-based synopsis can be computed for each data set, but comparing the two data sets via their statistics-based synopses might reveal no similarity between the data sets because they have no values in common. Yet clearly the two sets are similar because both contain telephone numbers. A similar problem occurs when the values of two data sets are formatted differently. For instance, the data sets might contain the same set of telephone numbers but use different delimiters to separate an area code from the local phone number.

Pattern-based signatures are computed by taking the sample data values stored in the synopsis of a data set and determining a regular expression that is matched by (almost all of) the values in the data set. Pattern discovery is based on the theory of deterministic finite automata and builds on the existing work on induction of regular languages and DFAs [1, 3, 8]. A matching automaton consists of nodes, transitions and symbol ranges and is constructed incrementally for a given input value set. A node matches a symbol (character) or range of symbols appearing in a specific position of an input value. A directed arc between two nodes-source and destination-means that the source symbol immediately precedes the target symbol. Fig. 4 shows a sample automaton that matches postal codes defined by "950xx" where x can be any digit.

Fig. 4 Pattern for Matching Postal Codes 950xx

The pattern-signature computation includes a set of expansion steps on the automaton to make it more general. For instance, if the input value set consists of digits 0-3, 5, and 7-9, we might want to expand the set to cover all digits 0 through 9. We measure expansion as the ratio of the size of the expanded set to the size of the input set, so for this example the expansion ratio would be 10 to 8, or an expansion factor of 1.25. Expansion reduces the accuracy of the pattern, as in this case digits 4 and 6 were not in the input set. A user-defined control parameter sets the upper limit for the maximum allowed expansion factor.

A set of reduction steps are performed to simplify the pattern. Values that have common prefixes share nodes in the automaton, and nodes which match identical or similar symbol sets (after potential expansion) and share predecessor and successor nodes can be combined. Fig. 5 shows how postal codes 950xx and 951xx are combined into a single, compact pattern. Again, loss of accuracy is possible and a control parameter ensures that the pattern is not overly generic.

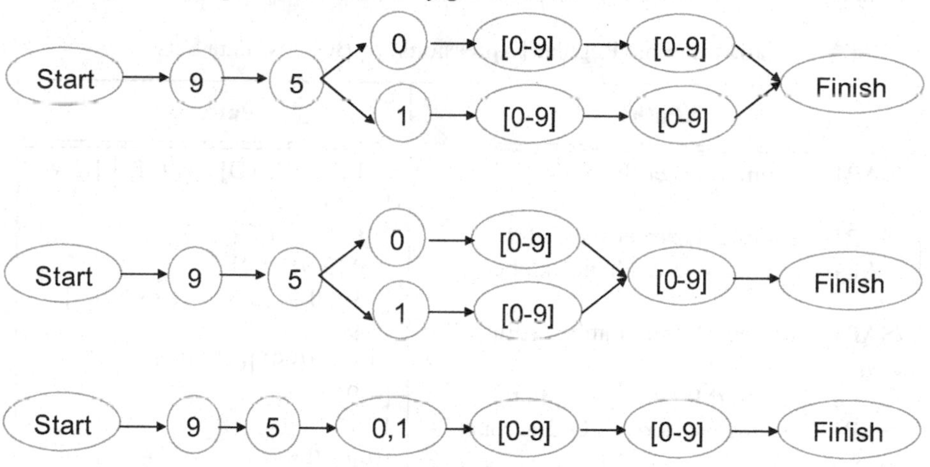

Fig. 5 Merging of Nodes in Pattern

Repeating symbol sequences are identified and the minimum and maximum repetition length is recorded in the automaton. This allows the DBMS to detect patterns such as the one shown in Fig. 6—a sequence of digits of length one or two.

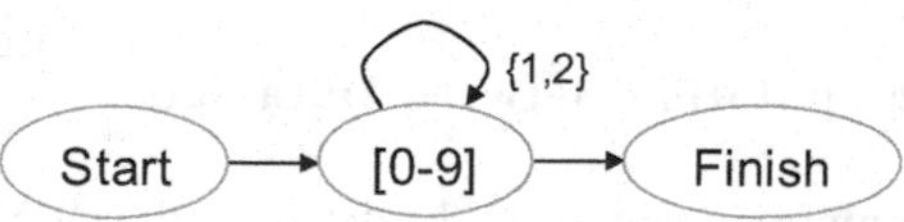

Fig. 6 Repeating Pattern

To facilitate more accurate comparison and matching, patterns may be subjected to further simplification by removing delimiters. A delimiter is defined as a node in the automaton that matches exactly one symbol and is visited by all paths through the automaton. A delimiter may appear anywhere in the pattern and is easily identified and removed from the automaton.

An alternative way to use delimiter information is to break compound values into their constituent parts. For instance, a telephone number can be broken into three parts (area code, exchange number, and local extension) and signatures can be computed for each part. This enables the DBMS to match the area code part of a telephone number with another data set that contains area codes only. Observe that the signatures for the different parts can be statistics-based; in this manner, we can develop signatures that are a hybrid of the statistics-based and pattern-based approaches.

Our current prototype externalizes discovered pattern signatures as regular-expression strings because of their compact form and convenience for storage and display purposes. We also note that XML Schemas and XML parsers have built-in support for regular expressions and regular expression engines are readily available. Table 1 shows several regular expressions discovered for business data sets.

Tab. 1 Sample Regular Expressions for Business data Sets

<table>
<tr><th>XPath</th><th>Pattern</th></tr>
<tr><td>/SAP4_CustomerMaster/State</td><td>A[LR] | C [AO] | [FI] L | [HW]
I | [MV] A |</td></tr>
<tr><td>/SAP4_CustomerMaster/PostalCode1</td><td>N[CV] | OH | TX</td></tr>
<tr><td>/SAP4_CustomerMaster/PhoneNumber1</td><td>950 [0-9] [0-9]
[0-9] [0-9] [0-9] \– [0-9] [0-9]</td></tr>
<tr><td>/SAP4_CustomerMaster/NumberOfEmploy-
ees</td><td>[0-9] \
- [0-9] [0-9] [0-9] [0-9]</td></tr>
<tr><td>/SAP4_CustomerMaster/. . . /OrgEntity1</td><td>[0-9] {2,3}</td></tr>
<tr><td>/SAP4_CustomerMaster/. . . /OrderProbabil-
ity</td><td>US[0-9] [0-9]1?
[0-9] [0-9]</td></tr>
<tr><td>/SAP4_CustomerMaster/. . . /NumDelivery-
Allowed</td><td>[123]
[0-9] {1,4}</td></tr>
<tr><td>/SAP4_Order/OrderId</td><td>950[0-9] [0-9]</td></tr>
<tr><td>/SAP4_Order/. . . /
SAP4_OrderSoldToInfo:PostalCode1</td><td>\– [0-9] | [0-9] {1,2}</td></tr>
<tr><td>/Siebel_BCAccount/RevenueGrowth</td><td></td></tr>
</table>

3.3 Similarity Computation Between Data Sets

After computing one or more signatures for the data sets, the DBMS then computes similarity measures between pairs of data sets; such a measure equals 0 if there is no apparent similarity between a pair of data sets and becomes larger as the degree of similarity becomes greater. Either both data sets are input data sets or one data set is an input data set and the other data set is a reference data set.

We assume that for the ith signature type there exists a similarity metric m_i that measures the similarity between any two signatures of that type. Then, given two data sets ds_1 and ds_2, along with signatures $s_1, s_2, \ldots, s_k$, the most general form of a similarity measure is

$$\text{Similarity}(ds_1,ds_2) = \text{Synthesize}[m_1(s_1(ds_1),s_1(ds_2)), \ldots, m_k(s_k(ds_1),s_k(ds_2))],$$

where the function *Synthesize* combines the multiple similarity measures into a single measure. (Actually the system allows multiple similarity measures to be computed for each signature, as in Fig. 2). We are currently investigating possible *Synthesize* functions.

Recall that the domain of a data set is the set of distinct values that appear in the data set. Often the domain of a reference data set coincides with the reference data set itself, and we call such a reference data set a *domain set*, which we abbreviate simply as a *domain* when there is no risk of confusion, i.e., the reference data set is a true set rather than a multiset. If there is a strong similarity between an input data set and a domain set, we say that we have "discovered the domain" of the input data set. Similarly, if two input data sets are each similar to the same domain set, then we say that the two input data sets "share the same domain." If the system is computing a similarity measure between an input data set and a domain set, then the system measures the similarity between the domain of the input data set and the domain set.

In the rest of this section, we describe similarity measures m_i that can be computed for different kinds of signatures, with an emphasis on the kinds of signatures that the prototype currently computes. These measures can be used separately or combined together.

Similarity for Hash-Count Signatures: As discussed previously, one signature that the DBMS computes is the hash-counting structure created during execution of a probabilistic counting algorithm. This signature is identical for any two data sets having the same domain. Thus a similarity measure on hash-count signatures is ideal for comparing an input data set with a domain set, since the domain of the input data set does not need to be computed explicitly. One such measure is the Jaccard metric, which is a normalized measure of the intersection of the domains of two data sets. The idea is to use the probabilistic counting algorithm associated with the hash count signature to estimate C1 = $Card[Domain(ds_1)]$ and C2 = $Card[Domain(ds_2)]$. Then the two hash-count structures are merged into a combined hash-count structure and the probabilistic counting algorithm is then applied to obtain an estimate of

$$C3 = \text{Card}[\text{Domain}(ds_1) \cup \text{Domain}(ds_2)].$$

Then the size of the intersection of the two domains is computed as C4 = C1 + C2 - C3, and the Jaccard metric is computed as J = C4 / C3.

Similarity for Histogram Signatures. A histogram summarizes the distribution of data values within a data set. Suppose for simplicity that histogram signatures of data sets ds_1 and ds_2 are exact and can be represented as vectors $f_1 = (f_{1,1},\ldots,f_{1,k})$ and $f_2 = (f_{2,1},\ldots,f_{2,k})$, where $f_{i,j}$ is the relative frequency of the jth value in the ith data set. Then the similarity between the two signatures can be computed, for example, as $1/d(f_1,f_2)$, where d is any of the standard vector space metrics, e.g., Euclidean distance $d(f_1,f_2)$ =

$((f_{1,1}-f_{2,1})^2 + ... + (f_{1,k}-f_{2,k})^2)^{1/2}$, L_1 distance $d(f_1,f_2) = |f_{1,1}-f_{2,1}| + ... + |f_{1,k}-f_{2,k}|$, L_∞ distance $d(f_1,f_2) = \max_j |f_{1,j}-f_{2,j}|$ or the symmetric Kullback-Liebler distance $d(f_1,f_2) = (f_{1,1}log(f_{1,1})/log(f_{2,1})) + \ldots + (f_{1,k}log(f_{1,k})/log(f_{2,k})) + (f_{2,1}log(f_{2,1})/log(f_{1,1})) + \ldots + (f_{2,k}log(f_{2,k})/log(f_{1,k}))$. Variants of these metrics are available when the histogram is lossy or the data values are real numbers.

Similarity for Pattern Signatures. We have devised several similarity metrics for pattern signatures. One metric, which is naive but easy to compute and useful, is obtained by simply comparing the regular expression strings of each pattern. For example, we can first compute the Levenshtein string-edit distance [8] between the regular-expression strings, divide it by the length of the longer string, and then convert the normalized distance d to a similarity measure by setting m = 1 - d. For instance, patterns "95xxx" and "96xxx" look very similar even though the underlying domains are different. On the other hand, two patterns may define the same domain in a different way, resulting in an incorrect assessment of their similarity. For instance, patterns "[1-3]" and "1 | 2 | 3" look very different but define the same domain.

A value-based similarity measure is slightly more expensive but more reliable. For this measure, we count the number of elements in one data set that satisfy the pattern for the other data set, and vice versa. Data values may be generated from the pattern or retrieved from the sample that is stored in the synopsis. Consider the following two patterns "200[0-9]" and "20[01][0-9]". The first pattern defines the domain "first decade of 2000" and the second "first two decades of 2000". All ten distinct values generated from the first pattern (2000, 2001, …, 2009) are accepted by the second pattern. Half the numbers generated from the second pattern are accepted by the first pattern. The sum (10 plus 10) is divided by the total vocabulary size (10 plus 20) and we get a similarity score of 2/3. Note that for the patterns of the earlier example ("[1-3]" and "1 | 2 | 3") the similarity score would be a perfect 1.0.

3.4 Similarity Measures Between Complex Structures

We now discuss how the DBMS defines similarity measures between pairs of complex structures. The goal is to identify complex structures that are structurally similar to other complex structures; we often call this process "schema matching". The inputs to this process are structure definitions and leaf-node to leaf-node similarities. Structure definitions, or parent-child relationships, can be extracted from the synopses of each data source.

Fig. 7 illustrates a scenario where SRC A, SRC B and SRC C represent the structures of three data sources that all contain the same information, albeit structured differently. They describe a number of products, sales of those products, and product deliveries consequent to sales. In SRC A, product information contains sales information, which contains delivery information. This arrangement might be common in a product support department where information is organized by product. SRC B might correspond to a shipping department. Information is organized by delivery, with associated

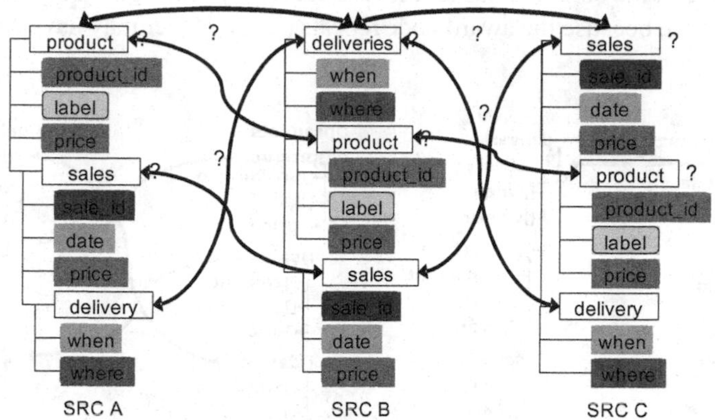

Fig. 7 Example of Schema Matching

product and sales information. SRC C is a sales department and hence sales data includes products and deliveries.

The shading of each leaf node indicates its domain. That is, when two leaf nodes share a shading it means that the system has determined that the two nodes derive their values from the same domain. The problem of matching is ambiguous. For example, considered as a whole, we might say that product in SRC A matches deliveries in SRC B and sales in SRC C, because all three structures contain the same information. On the other hand, it might be equally useful to record that product in SRC A matches deliveries/product in SRC B and sales/product in SRC C, because the information at each of these nodes is the same.

We start by constructing a schema tree for each data source using the parent-child relationship information that is recorded in the DataSet repository. We then construct a *flow network* for each pair of trees. One of the trees is labeled "source tree" and links inside it are oriented from parent to child. The other tree is labeled "sink tree" and its links are oriented from child to parent. These links are assigned an infinite flow capacity. A flow capacity of 1.0 is assigned to all those leaf-node to leaf-node pairs whose similarity exceeds a certain threshold. The Matcher computes the *Max-Flow* of the flow network, which indicates, for each node in the sink tree, the cumulative amount of flow from the source available at that node. Note that the flow at the root of the sink tree always matches the flow at the root of the source (flow preservation principle).

Similarity of two internal nodes n_A and n_B is calculated by the following formula:

$$\frac{MinCut(n_A, n_B)^2}{|Leaves(n_A)| * |Leaves(n_B)|}$$

where $MinCut(n_A, n_B)$ returns the flow from n_A to n_B in the flow network, $Leaves(n_A)$ returns number of leaves under n_A and $Leaves(n_B)$ returns the number of leaves under n_B. The number of leaves under an internal node is calculated in one of two ways, leading to two similarity metrics. In metric M1, all descendants of an internal node are included, while metric M2 includes only descendants that are not repeated. In Fig. 8a, the member node in the sink tree has five leaves according to M1, but only four according to M2 (Fig. 8b), because the award node repeats (i.e., a player may have earned several awards).

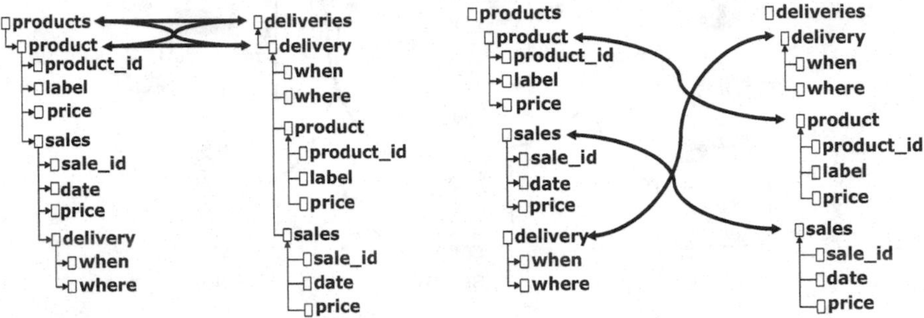

Fig. 8 Similarity of Internal Nodes according to Metric M1 (a) & M2 (b)

3.5 Discovering Constraints

In addition to computing similarity measures between data sets and more complex structures, the DBMS also discovers constraints within and between data sets such as *keys, relative keys, correlations, algebraic constraints*, and *functional dependencies*. As mentioned earlier, the data sets under consideration may come from the same data source or different data sources. The techniques for finding keys, key-to-foreign-key constraints, algebraic constraints, and correlations can be adapted from those in Brown and Haas [3] and Ilyas et al. [6]. In the current setting, the accuracy of some of these methods, which utilize distinct-value counts based on samples, can be improved: estimated counts based on a complete scan of the data can be derived from the hash-count data structure. For example, if the size of the domain of a data set (as estimated from the hash-count data structure) is close to the size of the data set itself (which is computed exactly), then the data set clearly satisfies a key constraint.

4 Identifying UBOs

Business objects are high-level data structures that reflect the business activity of an enterprise. For instance, a company engaged in selling of manufactured goods might care about business objects such as Customer, Order, Product, and Invoice. Inside each business object one may find other objects. For instance, an Order object may contain Product objects—products that a Customer ordered in that Order. We call these "nested objects". Alternatively, an object may contain a foreign key to another object. An Invoice object, for instance, could contain the ID number of the Order object it pertains to.

Business objects are important because they permit analysis and information integration at a higher level of abstraction. As we shall see in the next section, higher-level business objects are also useful when interfacing with the user. The schema (definition) of business objects may be discovered automatically or it may be derived from an enterprise data dictionary. In large corporations it is not uncommon to find efforts to standardize various activities such as purchasing or sales across geographical and other divisions. An enterprise data dictionary is one of the objectives of such standardization efforts.

Universal Business Objects (UBOs) are those objects that are common to many data sources. More precisely, the *structure* of a UBO can be found in multiple sources. Consider the Customer UBO. Many sources contain customer information—order management systems, customer relationship management systems, marketing management systems, and so on. Customer information is used for different purposes but the basic structure is the same. Customer has attributes such as name, address, telephone numbers, and email address. Each source typically has additional attributes for the Customer. The order management system would probably contain the credit card number of the customer, while the CRM system would contain flags indicating the preferred contact method (phone, email, mail) for the customer.

UBOs are identified by computing a *degree of sharing* (DoS) measure for each schema structure and selecting the highest-scoring structures as candidate UBOs. DoS is computed from three inputs: source schemas expressed as leaf-level data elements and tree-like composite structures (as described in the *Dataset* repository), similarity of elementary and composite data structures across and within data sources (as described in the *Similarity* repository), and foreign key relationships across and within data sources. The system uses a number of heuristics to eliminate candidate objects that are unlikely to be UBOs. For instance, a candidate structure is probably not a UBO if only a single instance exists or if the structure is too small (e.g., city name) or too large (entire product catalog).

The UBO discovery process starts by considering each data source to be a single UBO and iteratively breaking large composite objects into smaller ones. A DoS score is computed for each object O as the sum of three components: *structural sharing*, *value relationships*, and *foreign key relationships*.

To compute a *structural sharing* score, the system looks at the links from O to its parent and superclasses—the more parents or superclasses O has, the higher the score. The link from O to its immediate parent(s) has a value of 1.0. Links to the parent's parents have a value of 0.5. Each level of ancestry has a value that is one-half of what the immediately lower level has. For instance, if O is 3 levels down from the root in a tree structure, it has a structural sharing score of 1 + 0.5 + 0.25 = 1.75.

Value relationship considers the similarity of O to other objects and uses the structural sharing value of those other objects to increase the score of O. For instance, if O is similar to object X (similarity value 0.8) and X has a structural sharing value of 1.5, then the overall score of O is incremented by 0.8 * 1.5. This is repeated for every object that O is similar to.

A *foreign key relationship* means that a specific instance of O (its key field) is referenced by another object X (its foreign key field). If the foreign key relationship has strength 0.9 and X has a structural sharing value of 1.75, the system increments the overall score of O by 0.9 * 1.75. This is repeated for every foreign key relationship that points to O (its key).

Objects with a sufficiently high DoS score are marked candidate UBOs. Candidate UBOs are split off from their parent object and a foreign key is inserted into the parent (1:1 relationship) or into the UBO (1:N relationship). If the relationship between the parent and UBO is N:M, a separate relationship object is created. Similar UBOs are merged together, applying the intersection or union semantic.

To illustrate how UBO discovery works, consider the scenario depicted in Fig. 3. The system analyzes data from four sources (W, X, Y, and Z) and produces a synopsis for each of the data sets that they contain. The system also produces a synopsis for the reference data sets (ProdCategory, TIME, LOCATION). Similarities between the data sets in W, X, Y, and Z and the reference sets are computed at leaf node and internal node levels. A similarity is discovered between some pairs of data sources: W and LOCATION, X and ProdCategory, Y and TIME, and Z and LOCATION. A similarity is then calculated between W and Z, because both have some similarity to LOCATION, and it is determined that W is very similar to Z. Further analysis of the data sets reveals that both W and X are referenced from Y through a foreign key relationship. Object W has a high DoS score, because a very similar structure exists in another source (Z), it has some similarity to a reference data set (LOCATION), and it is referenced by another source (Y). Object W is merged with Z because the two have very similar structures, resulting in UBO W' (Customer) which is the intersection of the two objects. Object X is defined as UBO X' (Product) because it is referenced by Y and has similarity to the ProdCategory reference data set. UBO Y' (Order) is produced from Y and has a lower score than the other UBOs, because it only has similarity to one other data set (TIME).

5 Querying

In this section, we describe how a user can perform rich browse and search on our integrated schema and content repository. We first define the search space provided by our system. Then, we describe in detail how basic keyword search works and the nature of the returned results. Finally, we show how sophisticated search and analysis (BI) can be performed on the integrated data in terms of OLAP cubes and real-time dashboards.

5.1 Search Space

Searches in our integrated DBMS are specified in terms of UBOs (and not the underlying base data sets). In general, each UBO encapsulates a set of low-level data from various data sources. Conceptually, the search space is a graph of UBOs, where each node corresponds to either an *entity UBO* or a *relationship UBO*. Relationships represent "facts" in BI terminology. Fig. 9 shows an example of a search space. The example shows a graph with entity UBOs labeled "Product" and "Customer" that are connected through relationship UBOs labeled "Orders" or "Complaints". For illustrative purposes,

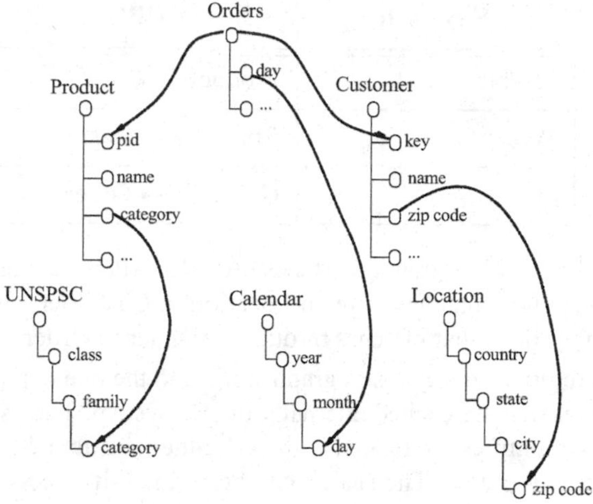

Fig. 9 Search Space Example

we have annotated the graph with UBO fields such as product name, customer key and order date. The percentages on the relationship links correspond to the "strength" of the relationship. In our example, 90% of Products relate to Orders and 40% of Products relate to Complaints. Similarly, 80% of Customers related to Order and 60% to Complaints. Additionally, the search space contains UBOs (*reference UBOs*) that correspond to reference data (like UNSPSC for products, Calendar for time, and Location for addresses).

5.2 Conceptual Keywords: Rich Browse, Search, and Ranking

The most basic form of searching that the system provides is the "conceptual" keyword based search, where keywords do not correspond to actual words in the underlying base data sets (as is the situation in typical text search engines) but to labels of entities or relationships between UBOs in the search space. We also assume that we have a synonyms catalog that contains synonyms for various keywords. For example, a synonym for the keyword "where" is "address", for "time" is "calendar", etc.

In order to explain how the conceptual keyword search works, let's assume that the user specifies the following query:

"product where when"

Using a synonyms catalog, the keywords are mapped to UBOs, as shown in the following table:

Keyword	UBO
Product	Product
Where	Location → Customer
When	Calendar → Order

In our example, keyword "Product" matches directly to Product, keyword "where" has a synonym "street" that matches through Location to Customer, and keyword "when" has a synonym for "day" that matches through Calendar to Order.

The system returns a query result graph similar to the one depicted in Fig. 3, along with some samples that are cached internally by our system. The user has the choice of seeing exactly how entities are related with each other and actual examples of such entities in the underlying data. The search can be refined, if necessary, by further constraining the result graph. For example, the user might not be interested in the UNSPSC categorization and can discard the corresponding part of the graph.

To handle the potentially huge number of subgraphs that match the query, the system can rank the matching subgraphs and display only the highest-ranked results. The ranking uses the similarity metrics that are computed during UBO discovery.

5.3 BI Support and Dashboarding

The metadata returned by the conceptual keyword search can be enhanced and exploited by the user to perform exploratory cube queries in an easy, intuitive way. Typically, the reference data sets contain (or can be easily enhanced with) well-known hierarchies such as time (day, week, month, year) or a standard hierarchical product categorization such as UNSPSC. The results of the basic keyword search are annotated by the system with such hierarchies. The user can designate certain attributes as measures (like the price of product) and certain entities as dimensions (like customer or product) just by clicking on the result graph. Operations like rollup or drilldown can then be easily performed by simply choosing the appropriate aggregation level in case of the hierarchies that are presented in the result graph. Because response time is very important for intensive BI applications, the performance for executing such queries must be optimized using techniques like pre-materializing certain parts of the cube using, for example, the techniques in [9].

Our system can also be used to support real-time dashboarding. Specifically, the user (via the intuitive data cube interface) can specify certain aggregations as "real-time". The system then monitors the specified aggregated values and triggers appropriate actions when user-defined thresholds are crossed. In many cases, maintaining many such complex aggregates in real time requires approximation, and the techniques described in [10] can be applied. The results of BI reporting, data analysis, and real-time dashboards are stored using XML and interfaces to office productivity tools such as spreadsheets.

6 Conclusion

Modern businesses need to integrate thousands of highly heterogeneous information sources. These information sources are typically not tables of records, but rather collections of complex business objects such as purchase orders, invoices, and customer complaints. The traditional data warehouse approach of "manual" schema design and ETL is not feasible anymore, because this methodology does not scale and relies on expensive human resources.

We have outlined an approach to massive automated information integration that addresses these problems. Our framework exploits the enabling technologies of XML, web services, caching, and portals. Our approach also incorporates novel methods for automated similarity analysis that rest on synopsis-construction techniques such as sampling and hashing, pattern matching via automata, graph-analytic techniques for object identification, and automatic discovery of metadata for business objects. Our system provides a powerful querying interface that supports a wide variety of information-retrieval methods, including ad-hoc querying via intuitive keyword-based search, graph querying based on similarities, automatic report generation, graphical and traditional OLAP, spreadsheets and other office productivity tools, data mining algorithms, and dashboards.

Our system is far from complete. Important ongoing research issues include further improvement and empirical evaluation of data set signatures and similarity measures, scalability and deployment studies, more sophisticated methods for business object discovery, exploitation of ontologies, and incorporation of new query processing paradigms. The system must be able to exploit not only open standards such as XML, but also deal with domain-specific standards such as XBRL for financial solutions. In the long run, our system can potentially lead to an enormous enhancement of business productivity by providing users with a rich querying environment over information not only within the enterprise, but in the entire supply chain and beyond.

Acknowledgements

We thank Michalis Petropoulos for implementing the "Matcher" component in our prototype system, and Kai-Oliver Ketzer for implementing the incremental synopsis management.

References

[1] Angluin, D.: On the Complexity of Minimum Inference of Regular Sets, Information and Control, December 1978, 39(3), pp. 337-350

[2] Astrahan, M., Schkolnick, M., Whang, K-Y.: Approximating the Number of Unique Values of an Attribute without Sorting, Information Systems, 12(1), 11-15, 1987

[3] Brown, P. G., Haas, P. J.: BHUNT: Automatic Discovery of Fuzzy Algebraic Constraints in Relational Data. Proc. 29th VLDB, pp. 668-679, 2003

[4] Carrasco, R. C., Oncina, J.: Learning Stochastic Regular Grammars by Means of a State Merging Method, Grammatical Inference and Applications, Second International Colloquium (ICGI), 1994, pp. 139-152

[5] Gibbons, P. B., Matias, Y.: New Sampling-Based Summary Statistics for Improving Approximate Query Answers. Proc. SIGMOD'98, pp. 331-342

[6] Ilyas, I., Markl, V., Haas, P. J., Brown, P. G., Aboulnaga, A.: CORDS: Automatic Discovery of Correlations and Soft Functional Dependencies. Proc. SIGMOD'04, pp. 647-658

[7] Poosala, V., Ioannidis, Y. E., Haas, P. J., Shekita, E. J.: Improved Histograms for Selectivity Estimation of Range Predicates. Proc. SIGMOD'96, pp. 294-305

[8] Pitt, L.: Inductive Inference, DFAs and Computational Complexity. 2nd Int. Workshop on Analogical and Inductive Inference (AII), 1989, pp. 18-44

[9] Sismanis, Y., Roussopoulos, N.: The Polynomial Complexity of Fully Materialized Coalesced Cubes. Proc. VLDB'04, pp. 540-551

[10] Sismanis, Y., Roussoupoulos, N.: Maintaining Implicated Statistics in Constrained Environments. Proc. ICDE'05

[11] Teradata Corporation: Getting it Together. Data Warehousing Report, 5(4), August, 2003. Online at: http://www.teradata.com

Component-Based Application Architecture for Enterprise Information Systems

Erich Ortner

Technische Universität Darmstadt, Germany
ortner@winf.tu-darmstadt.de

Abstract. The paradigm of reuse is a traditional concept of surviving for humanity that manifests itself in human languages. The words (components) will be taken out of a lexicon (repository) and then combined to sentences (applications) according to the rules of a specific syntax (grammar). The paper points out the parallels between the component-based approach of human languages on the one hand and component-based application-system design in the software-engineering discipline on the other hand. We describe some instruments (e.g., repositories, part lists) for managing component-based system design, and introduce a language-critical middleware framework supporting the development and processing of component-oriented e-commerce applications (e.g., an electronic marketplace for trading software components). Furthermore, we present a classification of component types and a component specification framework. The existence of standards and exchange forums (e.g., market places) is — besides a sophisticated component- and configuration theory — a substantial prerequisite for superior component-based application development and system life-cycle management.

1 Introduction

The idea of component-based development of application systems was first introduced into the debate about a construction tenet for database applications in [22]. Before that it was discussed as a possible approach to software engineering from an economic point of view in 1968 by McIlroy [6].

Only when large software vendors such as Microsoft, Sun Microsystems, IBM, SAP, Oracle started to change their products into component-based solutions was component orientation taken seriously in computer and information science. From a theoretical point of view, the term "software component" is not yet considered a technical term in computer and information science, when, for example, compared with the term "machine element" in mechanical engineering.

T. Härder and W. Lehner (Eds.): Data Management (Wedekind Festschrift), LNCS 3551, pp. 181-200, 2005.

The component paradigm in language-based computer and information science [10] can—compared with natural languages used by human beings—in general be described as follows:

> The components (words) are retrieved from a repository (lexicon) and are then put together as applications (sentences) in accordance with a syntax (grammar) to achieve a particular goal, for example, to accomplish a task.

Example 1: Human languages

In order to air a room, one person X says to another person Y:

> "Y, could you please open this window?"

Example 2: Application systems development

For organizing a sales information system, the following (software) components are connected in mutual functional dependence:

> Together, a program for maintaining customer data, one for maintaining orders, and a billing program combined with accounts receivable, accomplish the tasks of a sales information system within an enterprise.

Based on a grammar you can create almost any number of new sentences by reusing words (components), which can thus express new associations of ideas (ways of carrying out tasks). Linguists and paleoanthropologists even think that along with the continued evolution of grammar in human languages (so called "natural languages"), creative power and imagination (creativity) in human beings developed accordingly. The linguist Derek Bickerton expressed this view in an interview [1] as follows: "If, for example, you look at barbs, be it barbs for harpoons or else for darts...—Believe me: there is a great deal of grammar in the development of the barb". And the physicist Albert Einstein (1879-1955) when asked about thinking and language is believed to have said: "A thought occurs to me, and then I have difficulties in expressing it."

Fulfilling the component paradigm in application system development requires a variety of unambiguous definitions. We need to systematically build component catalogs, clearly define the functional scope of (software) components and reconstruct a "rational grammar" [5] in order to connect components with natural language systems, and we need to establish quality standards for components and systems worldwide, to be able to communicate in a digitalized world (interactions via cyberspace). Only when all this has been achieved, we can really speak of a construction tenet for application systems. Looking at it in an integrated way, such a tenet always consists of linguistic components (for example, knowledge and software) and non-linguistic components (physical things and occurrences). It is becoming more and more important (because of ubiquitous computer aid, e.g., [18]), to partly redefine the science of engineering—including its youngest child, computer science—from the point of view of language theory and (constructive) logic [3].

Regardless of the discipline: mechanical engineering, electrical engineering, civil engineering or computer science [23], when construction processes are to be computer-aided, "construction" is always considered a kind of "text modification" (from the specification of requirements to construction plans) based on language theory (e.g., grammar) and constructive logic.

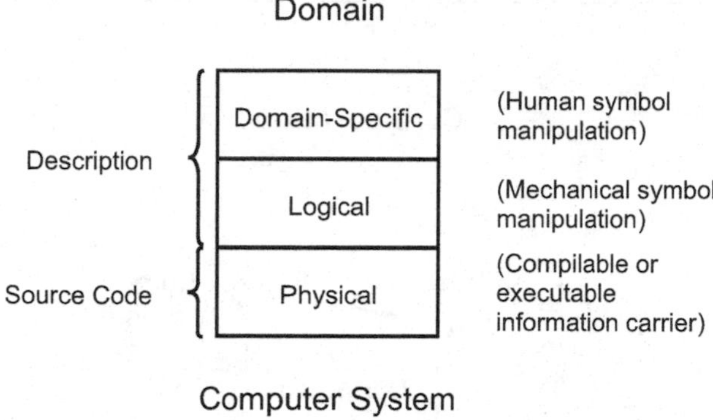

Fig. 1 Source Code and Functional Scope of a Component

2 Components

In computer science, components are more correctly called software components. They are parts of a program (Fig. 1), which provide specialized services from the domains (domain components) or generalized services, for example, services that offer data management (system components) in information processing contexts. They correspond to subject words (nominators and predicators) in the natural languages of their users, which are generally called object languages, as well as in the language used by software developers, often called meta languages. For example, a component "customer maintenance" offers specialized services for use in the business (commercial) application systems such as storing addresses, credit classification, interest profiles, etc.

Looking at software components it is important to distinguish between their physical representation, the source code (Fig. 1), and their description. The description may be intended for implementing and operating the component on a computer, or, for example in the case of interactive applications, for the user to understand the component (human symbol manipulation).

As computer science is almost exclusively concerned with languages and language artefacts [10] in the field of construction, the above-mentioned concept of component orientation in human languages, which has matured over thousands of years, applies almost unchanged. Shaw and Garlan have, for example, presented a component model (Fig. 2) in their works on the architecture of application systems [16] that is based mainly on components and connectors, just as human languages (natural languages) do. In human languages "subject words", (e.g., "customer" or "bill"), are available to describe components, and "particles" or "many-place predicators", (e.g., "is", "on", but also "buy", "send", etc.) to describe connectors.

A component's services are made available to the outside world via an interface (binding in Fig. 2) that ensures its correct invocation, (i.e., the permitted use of the component). This way, the realization of individual services (that is the implementation of

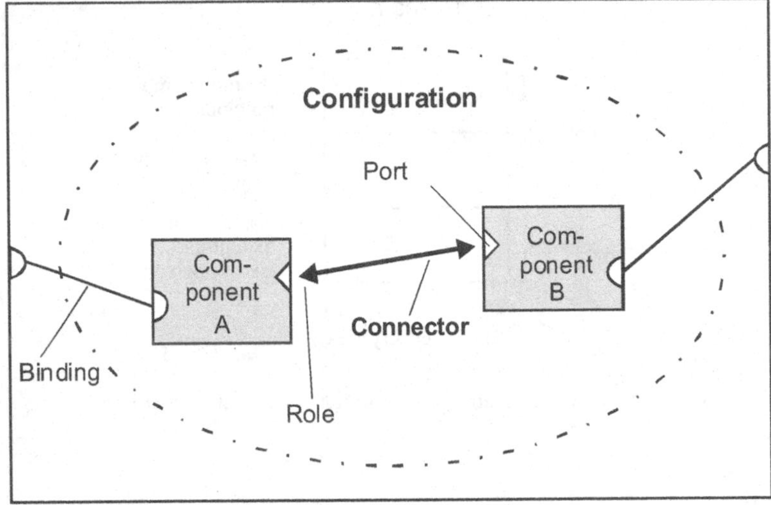

Fig. 2 The Component Model by Shaw and Garlan

the component) can be hidden from the outside world to a large extent (information hiding). This means that the component can be used by solely knowing the interface, that is in accordance with the so-called "black box principle". This makes system maintenance and applying corrections (exchanging a component, adding a new component, removing a component) much easier.

A connector (Fig. 2), which can be a component itself, has on its own side the interface "role" and on the communication and interaction partner's side the interface "port". Because of the reciprocal calling of services, the components take on a different role in the communication each time, which is supported by the "protocol" (for example, as a connector). For example, the component "customer maintenance" plays the role "party making request" towards a (connector) component "order maintenance", while the component "article maintenance" takes on the role "party making offer" towards the (connector) component.

In addition to establishing a clear component model (Fig. 2), various ways of classifying components must be considered. This is important for creating a classification system, for example, to aid searching in catalogs. In some classification models (Fig. 3), the distinction between components and connectors is abandoned and "component" is used as a general term.

Components can firstly [19] be classified into simple (but ready) components and complex components. Simple components are then further classified into system components (which implement generic functions) and domain components (which fulfil application-specific functions) as shown in Fig. 3.

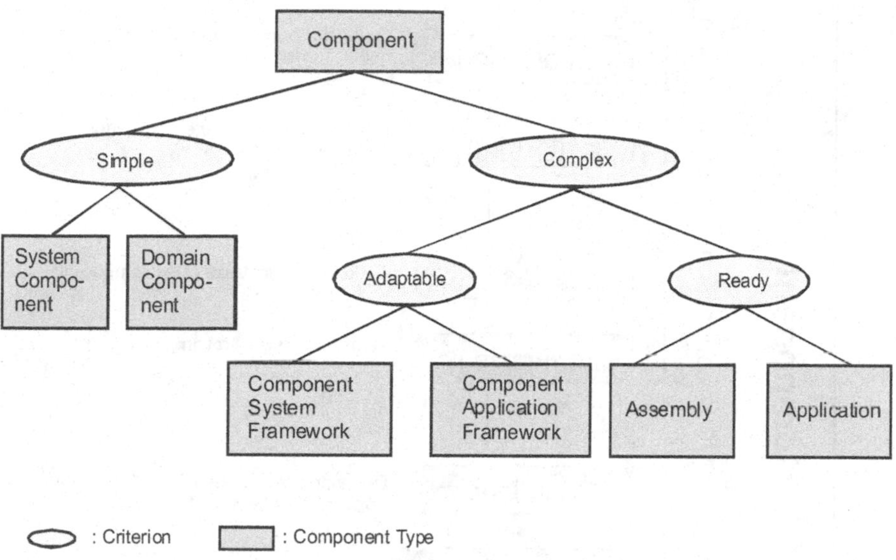

Fig. 3 Component Types

The group of complex components distinguishes between components, which can be "modified" (be adapted or expanded by adding further components), and ready complex components. Adaptable complex components are called "component system frameworks" in the context of implementing generic functions (such as data maintenance, process control or communication support). In the context of implementing application specific functions (such as enterprise resource planning, supply chain management, or customer relationship management), they are called "component application frameworks".

Last but not least, complex system and domain components in Fig. 3 are called "assembly groups". Beside assembly groups, there are applications. They form larger units in this classification, and can be used separately or in combination with other applications or components to form even larger application systems.

For the development of a component market as well as for trade in (software) components, a standardized description of these components is of vital importance. [14] suggests such a specification framework, as shown in Fig. 4 in a simplified way. The specification framework aims at describing a component's exterior view as completely as possible, to be able to evaluate the component's usability in application development merely by reading its description (cf. Fig. 1).

The seven aspects of the specification framework for components can be assigned to the topics "administration" (technical and economic), "conception" (domain-specific) and "specification" (logical) to give them further structure. You can picture the physical representation (e.g., the source code) of a component as appended to its "interface" (Fig. 4).

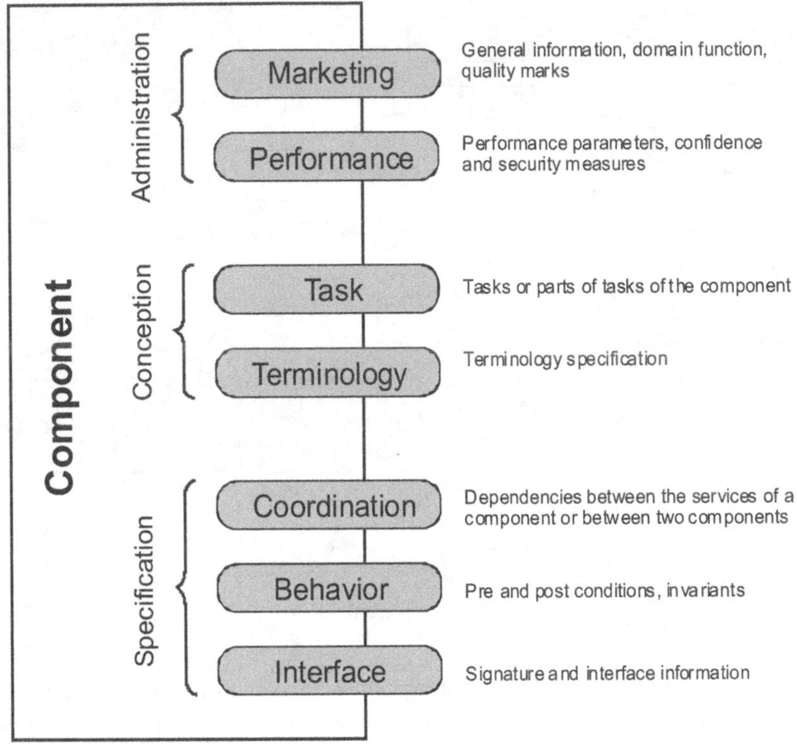

Fig. 4 Specification Framework for Software Components

Measured by the standard directory service UDDI (Universal Description, Discovery and Integration) for Web services and components that is currently being developed, the subject field "administration" can be compared with the so-called "white pages" and "yellow pages" (which contain information about businesses and addresses). The field (logical) "specification" can be associated with the "green pages" (which contain information concerning "mechanical symbol manipulation"). Whereas for the field "conception", which documents the domain semantics (contents, application domain) of a component, the above directory service (UDDI) ought to be extended by, for example, a category "blue pages" (which contain information concerning "human symbol manipulation").

3 Tools

Fig. 5 presents the new distribution approach for software and knowledge companies on the vendor side, user companies and private users on the customer side, as well as consulting firms/companies who support customers in the implementation of individual solutions in the component market on the interaction side.

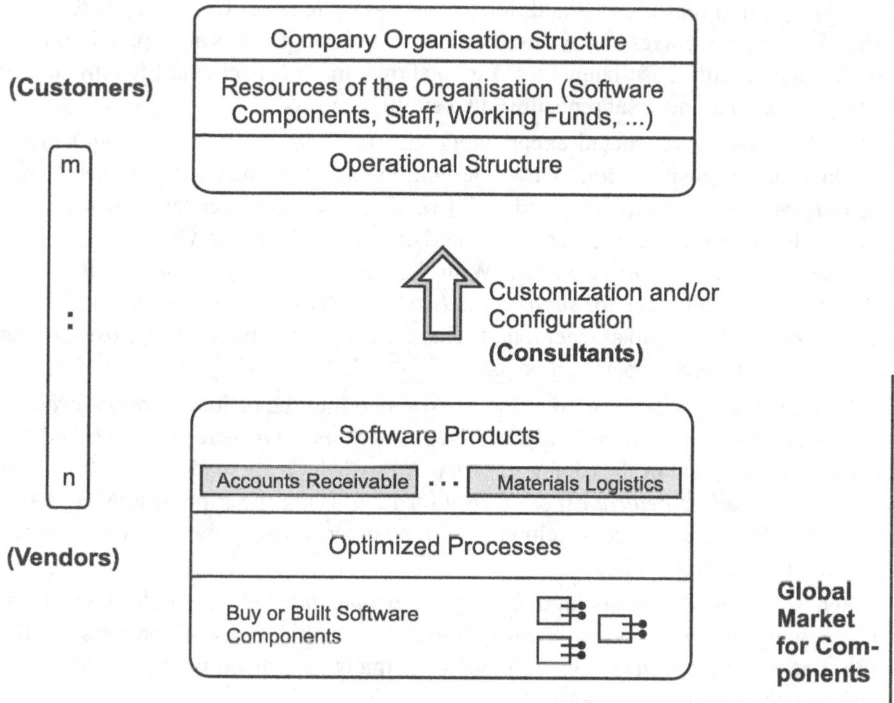

Fig. 5 Marketing of Component-based Application Software

A software vendor offers software products that can be flexibly customized (tailored) to the individual situation of a customer and his goals. This can be done using so-called framework solutions and/or by configuring application systems from components. To be able to do this, the software product, which is imaginary when it is on offer, must consist of components that are available for use in the user's optimized work routines/processes. These components can either be bought on the component market or self-built and must be available in a large number of variants, which are maintained in repositories (catalogs) for easy access. The actual composition (and installation) of the software solution sold is done individually at the customer site after the contract has been signed, possibly with the help of a consultant. Simulation may be used as a means to find the optimum solution.

To handle the paradigm shift in the fields of software and knowledge that is due to component orientation, there are further tools, such as organizing trade in software and knowledge components in electronic market places, or developing comprehensive repository structures for the life-cycle management of component-based application systems on the part of the vendor and at the customer's site.

In the process of building up such repositories, it is important to ensure the constant description of the components through all life-cycle phases, from the specification of requirements, through their design and configuration, through operation to removal or replacement by other systems.

For integration reasons, it is additionally necessary to describe in a repository [13] the development languages that are used as well as the components and application systems developed with these languages. Fig. 6 shows the meta schema (documentation structure) of such a universal repository in a simplified way.

A company's reconstructed expert language (*normative expert language*) that is maintained in a repository consists of the components "(normative) grammar" (*sentence patterns*) and "(normative) lexicon" (*words*). The rules according to which the words can be combined into sentences are laid down in a grammar. One way of formulating these rules is *sentence patterns*. With the help of *structure words* such as "a", "and", "or", etc. and blanks for *subject words* such as "customer", "Smith" or "hire", a *sentence pattern* defines in a general and schematic way the structure *propositions* can have in a reconstructed expert language.

The *subject words*, also called terms, are divided into the disjoint subsets' *predicators* (e.g., generic names, verbs, and adjectives) and *nominators* (proper names and designations). The content of the (domain) *propositions*, which are made during the development phase *method-neutral expert design* for identifying the expert knowledge (domain knowledge) relevant for development is also determined by the *subject words* that are maintained in the lexicon.

Each *proposition*—we distinguish *singular propositions* about single things or individuals and *general propositions*, which express combinations of concepts—fulfils exactly one *sentence pattern*. On the other side, many *propositions* can be built in accordance with the same *sentence pattern*.

In a *catalog* (Fig. 6), *connector components* (e.g., Session Beans) and *object components* (e.g., Entity Beans) are described under the common designation *component*. They can, still documented in the *catalog*, be grouped into assembly groups (*configuration*), according to the component model by Shaw and Garlan.

In the *application system-part* of the repository, *object components*, *connector components* and *configuration components* (assembly groups) form the *components used* from which *applications* are configured.

Using the meta object type *documentation object*, all (domain) *propositions* relevant for an object in the *catalog* or in the *application system-part* of a repository's meta schema, can be assigned easily. This may be relevant for gaining information, securing consistency or for maintenance purposes.

A repository or a catalog is also an important part of an electronic market place for global trade in software components (Fig. 7) on the Internet. CompoNex [9]—Component Exchange—has originally been designed for the B2B (Business-to-Business) field and supports the emergence of a world-wide component market, which analysts expect to grow considerably. CompoNex can be integrated directly into other development environments (e.g., Microsoft Visual Studio .NET) and thus provides better support for the development and life-cycle management processes of component-based application systems in an organisation it is based on.

Software components require a great deal of explanation, as they are not commodities. Therefore, their implementation provides several special services to support mar-

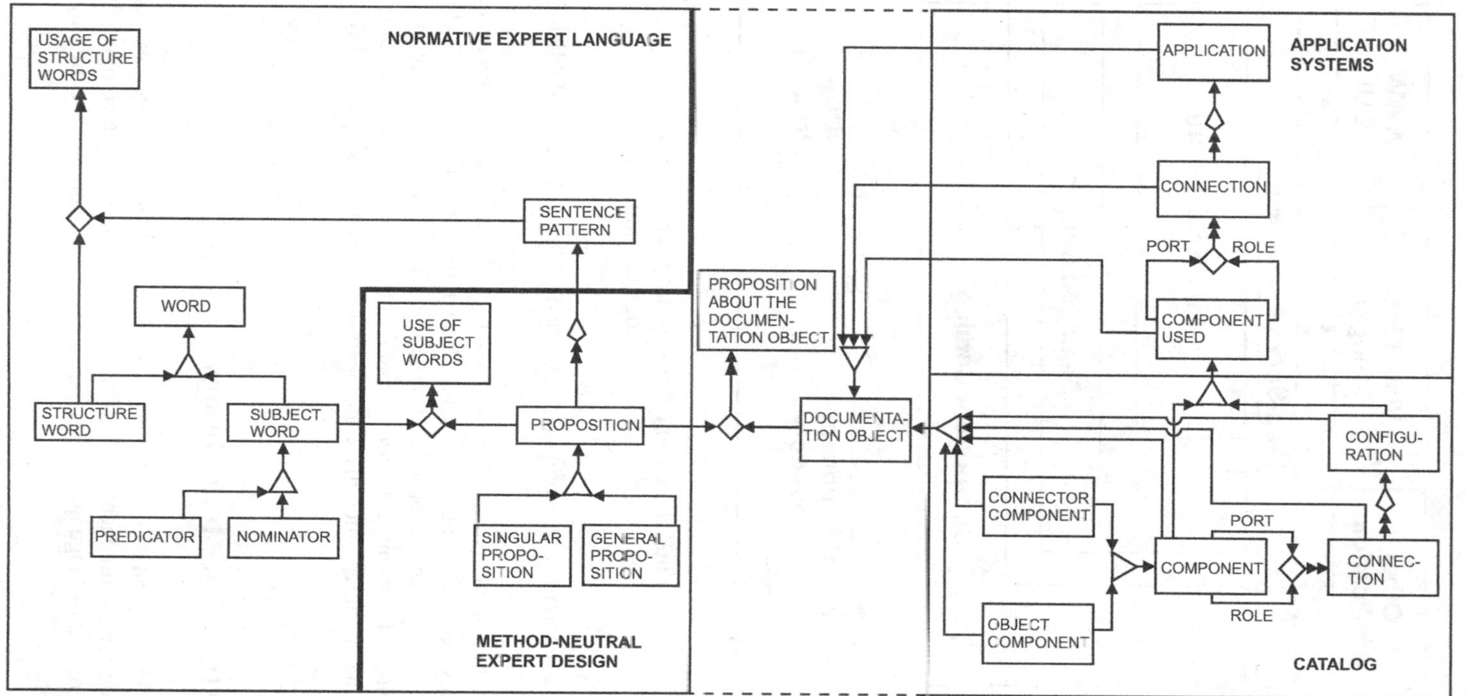

Fig. 6 Meta Schema of a Development Repository for Component-based Application Solutions

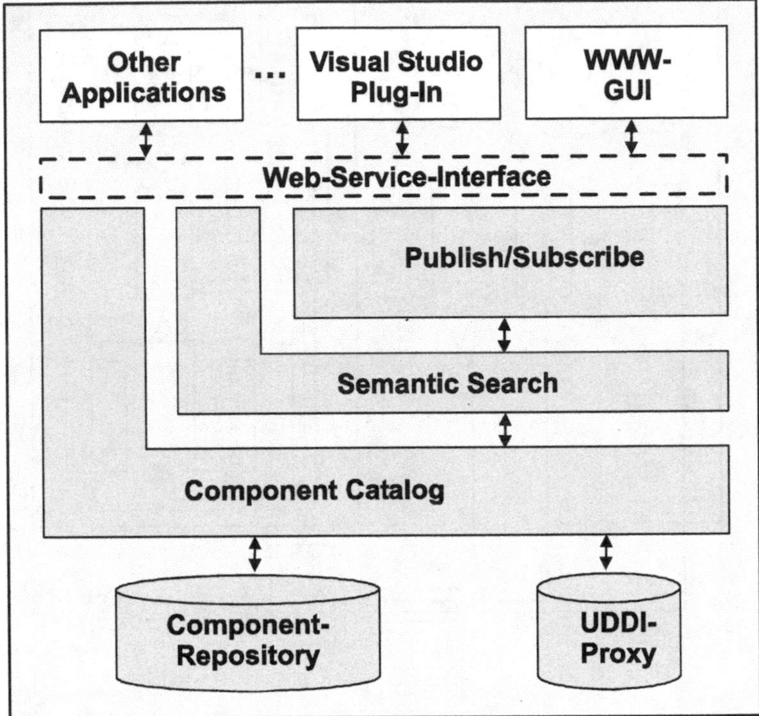

Fig. 7 Electronic Market Place for Trade in Software- and Knowledge Components

keting. These are mainly the components "catalog", "search" and "Publish/Subscribe" (Fig. 7).

At the moment, the market place does not provide an interface for human users [8]; instead it provides a machine-readable interface in the form of an XML Web service. A variety of user interfaces are based on this service, thus making access more convenient for human users. Performing a trade transaction (payment and downloading of a component) has been implemented in a component-oriented way using a workflow management system.

4 Construction Methodology

Considered in a general way, parts lists describe how (physical) goods are composed of parts and complex components [17]. If we apply this to software components [7], that is to pieces of text or language artifacts, then parts lists represent the grammar of a language system.

From a point of view of logic and mathematics, parts lists are an application of mereology (part/whole theory) in the field of composing items of any sort from parts [15]. [20] even describes a symbolism (Tab. 1) based on mereology and an algorithm for resolving general variant parts lists.

In [10] it is attempted to demonstrate that variant parts lists can be used also to configure individual software solutions made of components with a large number of variants, that is as a kind of configuration grammar.

Tab. 1 Node Types for the Representation of a Variant Parts List

Node Type	Meaning	Symbol
Part Node	Represents a part. Parts can be components or components that were put together into a new unit. The number at the connecting line indicates how many times the part is included in the superior structure.	○
Conjunctive Node	Combines all parts into new unit via connecting lines (corresponds to the logical And).	△
Alternative Node	Exactly one of the incoming connecting lines is chosen (corresponds to the logical exclusive Or). The selected part de facto replaces the alternative node.	▽
Empty Node	Is needed to model the optimum selection when using an alternative node.	Ⓐ

Fig. 8 shows how a configuration grammar is used (in the way of a procedure using variant parts lists) for component-based development of a software solution to manage the annual balance sheet of a company.

The software is composed of the components "profit and loss account" and "balance account". Additionally, a diagrammatic representation of the calculated results, e.g., in the form of bar charts, can be included in the solution as another component. Configuration grammar (Fig. 8) provides the empty node to account for the fact that it is an optional configuration decision. The "balance account" can be included in the annual balance sheet in a component-based way either as "trade balance account" (Variant 1), or as "tax balance sheet" (Variant 2).

Using variant parts lists makes administration of a configuration process of software systems from software components flexible (grammar). Before that lies a developer's construction effort that produced nothing less than an expert design [12] of the application solution. To be able to "process" (e.g., combine) software components in variant parts lists, it is necessary to describe components in a suitable way (e.g., in a repository) as shown in Fig. 6. Only then can developers be requested to make the comparative effort necessary in the decision making process. A component model based on mereology (Fig. 2), architectural standards (e.g., Fig. 10, Tab. 2, Fig. 11) and the spec-

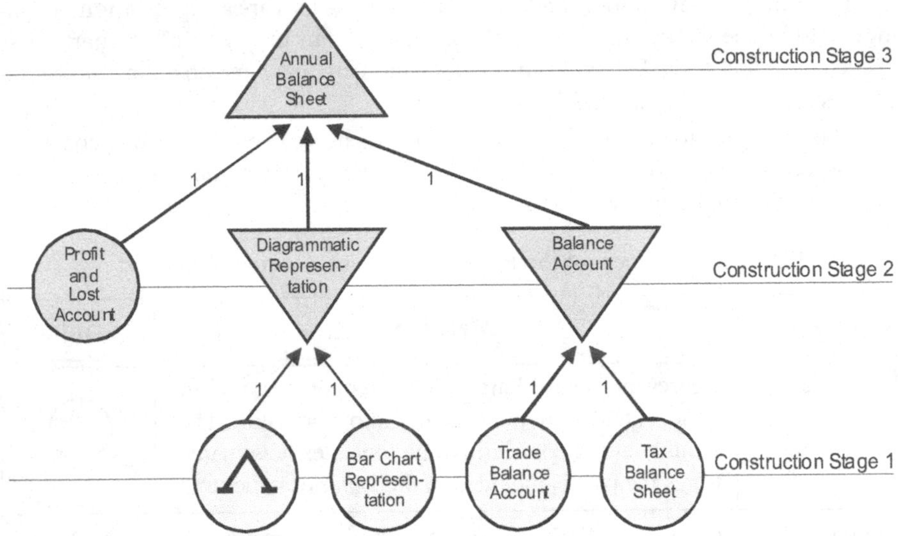

Fig. 8 Variant Parts List for the Annual Balance Sheet of a Company

ification frame (shown in Fig. 4) together form the ideal prerequisites. They open up an entirely new way of using software components, as shown, for example, in Fig. 9.

When developing application systems from components in accordance with the "multipath process model" [12], a main process—the configuration process—and a secondary process—the selection process (Fig. 9)—are distinguished during the configuration phase (part of the process). Here it becomes obvious that developers who do not work in a professional way and like to tinker will be confronted with the so-called "hare and tortoise barrier", with respect to the change between configuration and the choice of components. The cleverer tortoise wins the race against the quicker hare by means of "reuse". Stubborn, prejudiced developers prefer to program each component they need for a software solution themselves, or reprogram somebody else's component according to their own ideas. Systems that were developed in this way can practically not be maintained, are usually badly documented and are understood, if at all, only by the authors themselves.

Every selection process requires a selection effort on the part of the developer (Fig. 9). Not everyone finds that easy. In other fields of engineering, the selection decision is aided by clear calculation results, security grades, etc. of the relevant field, e.g., in civil engineering. In the field of software engineering, such selection aids are still scarce. On the configuration side, after putting the application together, the integration effort must be implemented on a technical, constructive, and linguistic level, for example, with respect to the entire architecture of the application system for an enterprise (compare Fig. 11).

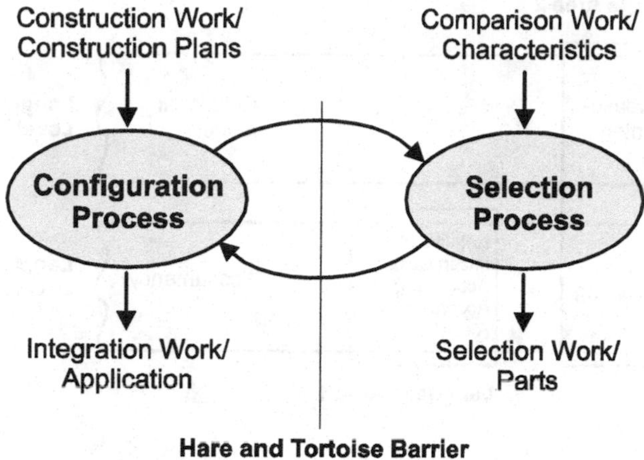

Fig. 9 Part of a Process Model for Developing Application Systems from Components

5 Application Systems Architecture

Architecture of large applications systems today is, beside being component-based, characterized by distinguishing abstraction levels and/or language levels (Fig. 10), and by distinguishing generic and specific functions of the components within the overall system (Tab. 2).

If cyberspace, for example, is considered a world-wide, huge address space, which is being created again and again through a network of stationary and mobile computers (when they start operating), the issue of giving the area a clear structure for its population with software and knowledge is raised. In addition to the concept of abstraction levels (e.g., database systems [2]), a useful instrument to provide such a structure is the distinction between language levels, which comprise a language change in the sense of object/meta language [13], and language areas, which refer to a specific domain (e.g., to an expert language such as that of merchant's accounts).

In this way, applications that have been developed on an object language level for example, can be described on a meta-language level (repositories). Alternatively, single applications of a specific domain (e.g., accountancy [21]) are integrated in the common language area (Fig. 10) they are assigned to.

In the context of computer-based information systems, drawing the distinction between generic and specific leads to a classification of software into basic systems and (basic system) applications. Basic systems implement generic functions such as "(data) management", "reasoning", or "controlling" of processes. In addition, there are (basic system) applications, which must be developed or bought and implemented as a standard application when purchasing a basic system (e.g., a database management system) for specific uses in a company (for example production). Thus, specific application sys-

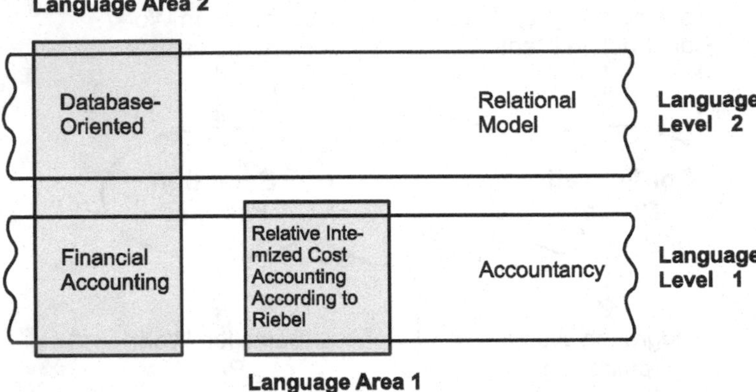

Fig. 10 Language Levels and Language Areas (in Cyberspace)

tem solutions always require the employment of basic systems (database management systems, workflow management systems, repository systems).

This type of software has been combined into a middleware framework in [9], named "E-NOgS" (Electronic New Organon {Server, Service, Servant}). A specific application system solution can be developed based on this framework. It is component-based and can therefore be used flexibly, i.e., component by component, in the development of basic system applications.

The "proof of concepts" for E-NOgS has so far been given with respect to its implementability, especially in the field of e-commerce applications, e.g., the implementation of an electronic market place [9] for world-wide trade in software components.

It is remarkable that E-NOgS made a continuous language-critical foundation not only of applications [11] but also of basic systems possible for the first time. Tab. 2 shows the result of this foundation.

Based on the concept of schema and instances or language action (that bring about the creation of instances on the basis of schemas) respectively, and the concept of creating language levels and language areas, generic language actions (types of language actions) were reconstructed from the concrete use of languages in speech communities or companies. Generic language actions that do not yet have a reference to a specific application, lead to the so-called basic systems (system type in Tab. 2) in language-based computer and information science. In a company, they can only be used after the applications (specific types of language action or language operation types) for it have been developed. The specific computer-based language action "customer maintenance", for example, forms the database application that belongs to the generic computer-based language action "data management" using a database management system.

Tab. 2 shows the fields of application for the various generic functions and makes suggestions for development as to which logic might form the basis for the specification of the relevant solutions (basic systems and applications).

System Type / Characteristic	Database Management Systems	Workflow Management Systems	Decision Support Systems	Communication Management Systems	...	Consideration Management Systems
Prevalent Language Action Typ	utter/ understand	initiate/ control	ask/ answer	agree/ decline		judge/ provide
Level Pair *)	Schema/ Instances	Control/ Execution	Premises/ Conclusions	Transformation/ Interaction		Meta Language Level Object Language Level
Primary Modelling Item	Subject Entities	Occurrences	Reasoning	Understanding		Considerations
Logic as the Basis of System Development	Standard Logic (Relational Calculus)	Modal Logic (Imperative Logic)	Syllogism (Question Logic)	Interaction Logic (Dialogical Logic)		Metatheory (Metalogic, etc.)
⋮						
Fields of Application	Production and Administration	Management and Controlling	Analysis and Decision-Making	Translation and Imparting of Knowledge		Construction and Invention

*) **Note:** The level pair "schema/instances" is orthogonal to the levels "control/execution", "premises/conclusion", "transformation/interaction", and "meta language level/object language level".

Tab. 2 Fundamentals of Language-logically and Language-critically Reconstructed Basic Systems (generic functions)

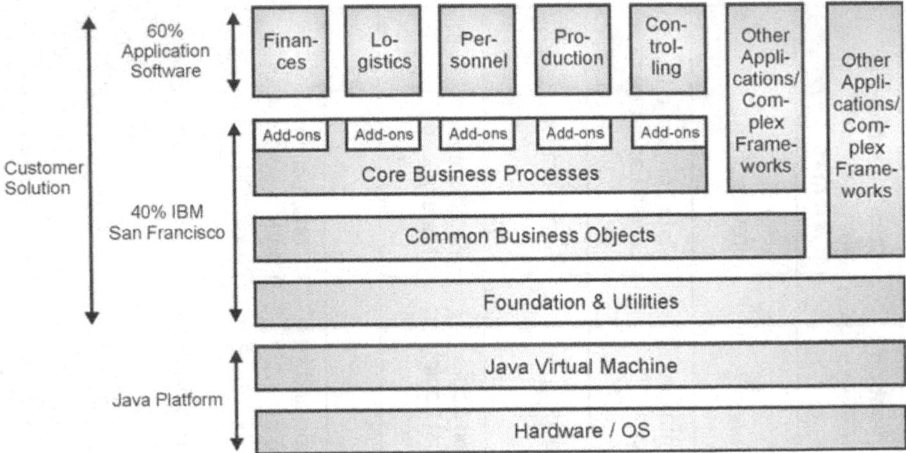

Fig. 11 The San Francisco Framework

Using the above characterized structural means (component orientation, language levels, basic systems and applications, etc.) there are two approaches today with respect to application architectures:

1. Customizing systems using ready architectures
2. Configuring application systems from components by distinguishing language levels as well as generic and specific functions.

ad 1.: "San Francisco" (Fig. 11) is a framework for complex application systems whose development in 1996 first began using C++ and was continued later using Java. It is a proprietary IBM product. However, SAP and ORACLE are two well-known companies among the vendors of such systems.

The framework serves developers as orientation for complying with (generic and specific) standards and, on the other hand, it provides a frame, a preliminary product or "semi-finished product", for the customer-specific installation of applications (add-ons). From a programming point of view, development of San Francisco is based on the EJB (Enterprise Java Beans)-technology—Java 2 Enterprise Edition (J2EE).

With Common Business Objects—they can be basic systems such as database management systems or workflow management systems—San Francisco uses the basic classes of Foundation & Utility-Layer (which can be compared with the CORBA services).

The superior level (Fig. 11) consists of the so-called core business processes, which implement the basic business processes and the necessary modules. Finally, this architecture is completed by the developments of customers themselves or by purchased customizable application software of other vendors.

With this kind of construction of application systems, you buy only the general framework, which you must then tailor. The term "customizing" was introduced to describe this. Customized application systems have the great advantage that large parts of the operations (for data processing) do not have to be programmed anew. Nevertheless, it remains necessary to specify definite descriptions, particularly for data. A special kind of definite description takes place, namely a customizing definite description, e.g., the object that is usually called "member" may be named "associate" in a company.

ad 2.: An entirely different kind of construction of complex application systems is configuring applications from components. Here, the decision is not to adapt, or tailor (customize), semi-finished products or preliminary products, because a sufficiently large number of variants of the individual components is available for the configuration. This means that there is absolutely no danger of customizing individual applications and no cost is incurred for version maintenance of the various implementations at the customer's site. If you compare the configuration of applications systems from components, which are available in large numbers of variants (and thus do not need to be customized) with component orientation in other fields of engineering (e.g., mechanical engineering), it is by far the more professional approach to this task. Only in times of hardship and war are components adapted when reusing components, because the right variant is not available.

Fig. 12 shows a distributed, complex application system, which was developed entirely in accordance with the idea of configuring application systems from components by choosing variants and not by adaptation (versioning). Specification of the basic systems was done using the CORBA (Common Object Request Broker Architecture) middleware architecture.

CORBA is the description of a distributed system for object maintenance, which was specified by the Object Management Group (OMG). It determines how distributed objects (e.g., applications) can communicate with each other via an Object Request Broker (ORB). In addition to ORB, the OMA (Object Management Architecture) includes four more areas (Fig. 12): CORBA Services, CORBA Facilities, Domain Interfaces and Application Objects.

The CORBA Services are a collection of fundamental basic services, which in general can also be provided by a (distributed) operating system. The CORBA Facilities provide even more functionality per component and comprise distributed basic systems such as database management systems, workflow management systems or reasoning management systems. Meta-data maintenance (the repository system) is a special CORBA facility or component. It can be used to describe all components of the architecture (application objects or (single) applications also), to control their life-cycle and to ensure their language integration via the terminology of the company relevant for the application.

Using CORBA, you can now include each application component in merchant's accounts (Fig. 12) or replace the application components by other variants that are compatible with the interface, until an individual solution for the customer is found. The architecture is completed by the component-based operational and organizational structure of the company (customer) and its hardware infrastructure (devices, networks, etc.)

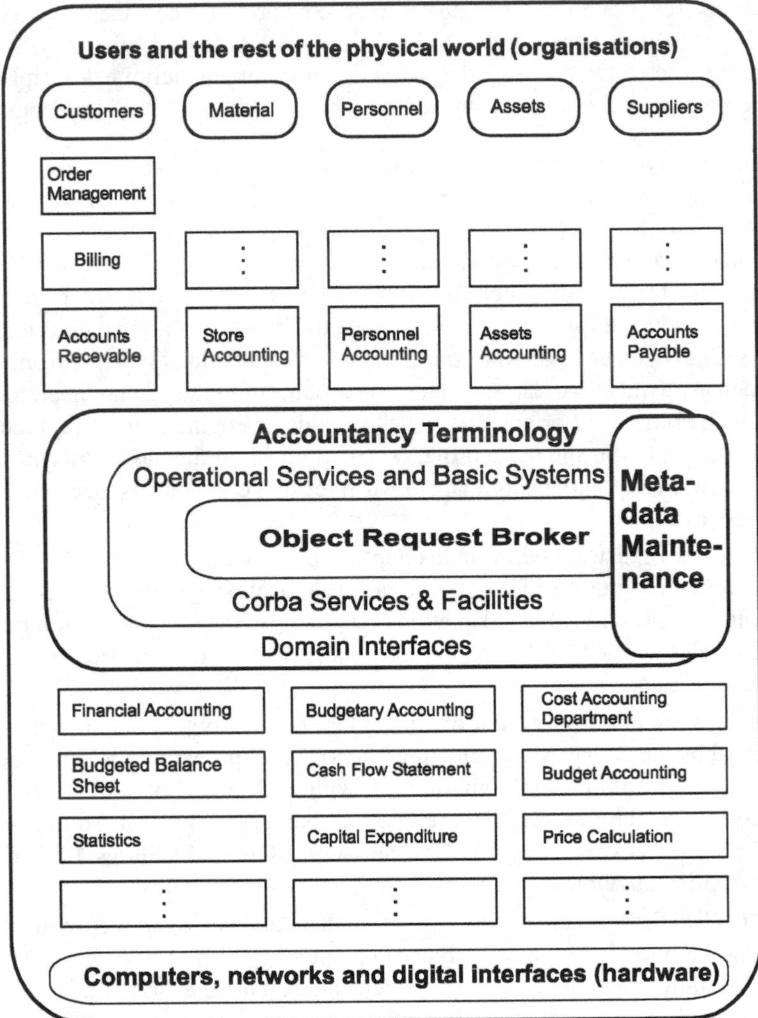

Fig. 12 Component-based Architecture of Merchant's Accounts in a Company

6 Future Perspectives

Fig. 13 summarizes the future strategy for reusing software or the application software vendors' marketing policies.

One of the main differences between software and physical products is that software can be changed so easily (v. Neumann-Rechner). This may sometimes encourage developers to modify the static program code of a software component when they are

	Adaption	Selection
System	Customizing	Standard Software
Component	Version	Variant

Fig. 13 Strategies for Reuse

reusing it and this seems to be a quick way to satisfy a customer's special requirements. Therefore, framework-oriented development of application systems—to which the so-called reference-model-oriented or model-driven development of application systems mainly belongs [4]—will still be on the market for quite some time, in spite of its customizing of individual solutions and time-consuming versioning (Fig. 13).

Considering carefully the advantages and disadvantages, over the medium term the variant-oriented, component-based development of application systems (Fig. 13, right column) seems the more professional choice. This paper shows that in the meantime (compared with the state-of-art in [22]) great progress has been made in the variant-oriented approach also from a theoretical, methodological and conceptional point of view. The marketing and distribution strategists in software companies such as IBM, SAP, ORACLE or Microsoft seem not to be sufficiently aware of this.

References

[1] Bickerton, D.: Was ist "Was"? in: DER SPIEGEL, Nr. 43, 2002, pp. 223-228.

[2] Härder, Th., Rahm, E.: Datenbanksysteme – Konzepte und Techniken der Implementierung, Springer Verlag, Berlin/Heidelberg 1999.

[3] Herrig, D.: Gibt es eine Konstruktionsalgebra? in: Wissenschaftliche Zeitschrift der Pädagogischen Hochschule Dr. T. Neubauer, Erfurt/Mühlhausen 1978, pp. 1-11.

[4] Kühne, Th.: Automatisierte Softwareentwicklung mit Modellcompilern, in: Wörner, J.-D. (Hrsg.), Vom Wort zum Bauelement, thema FORSCHUNG, Heft 1, 2003, Technische Universität Darmstadt, Monsheim 2003, pp. 116-122.

[5] Lorenzen, P.: Lehrbuch der konstruktiven Wissenschaftstheorie, B.I. Wissenschaftsverlag, Mannheim/Wien/Zürich 1987.

[6] McIlroy, M.D.: Mass Produced Software Components, in: Naur, P., Randell, B. (Hrsg.), Software Engineering: Report on a Conference by the NATO Scientific Affairs Division, Brussels 1968, pp. 138-150.

[7] Ortner, E., Lang, K.-P., Kalkmann, J.: Anwendungssystementwicklung mit Komponenten, in: Information Management & Consulting, 14 (1999) 2, pp. 35-45.

[8] Ortner, E., Overhage, S.: CompoNex: Ein elektronischer Marktplatz für den Handel mit Software-Komponenten über das Internet, in: Wörner, J.-D. (Hrsg.), Vom Wort zum Bauelement, thema FORSCHUNG, Heft 1, 2003, Technische Universität Darmstadt, Monsheim 2003, pp. 28-32.

[9] Ortner, E., Overhage, S.: E-NOgS: Ein komponentenorientiertes Middleware-Framework für E-Commerce-Anwendungen, in: Wörner, J.-D. (Hrsg.), Vom Wort zum Bauelement, thema FORSCHUNG, Heft 1, 2003, Technische Universität Darmstadt, Monsheim 2003, p. 22-27.

[10] Ortner, E.: Sprachbasierte Informatik – Wie man mit Wörtern die Cyber-Welt bewegt, Eagle-Verlag, Leipzig 2005.

[11] Ortner, E.: Aspekte einer Konstruktionssprache für den Datenbankentwurf, S. Toeche-Mittler Verlag, Darmstadt 1983.

[12] Ortner, E.: Ein Multipfad-Vorgehensmodell für die Entwicklung von Informationssystemen – dargestellt am Beispiel von Workflow-Management-Anwendungen, in: Wirtschaftsinformatik, 40 (1998) 4, pp. 329-337.

[13] Ortner, E.: Repository Systems, Teil 1: Mehrstufigkeit und Entwicklungsumgebung, Teil 2: Aufbau und Betrieb eines Entwicklungsrepositoriums, in: Informatik-Spektrum, 22 (1999) 4, S. 235-251 u. 22 (1999) 5, pp. 351-363.

[14] Overhage, S.: Die Spezifikation – kritischer Erfolgsfaktor der Komponentenorientierung, in: Turowski, K. (Hrsg.): Tagungsband des 4. Workshops Komponentenorientierte betriebliche Anwendungssysteme, Augsburg 2002, pp. 1-17.

[15] Ridder, L.: Mereologie – Ein Beitrag zur Ontologie und Erkenntnistheorie, Vittorio Klostermann GmbH, Frankfurt am Main 2002.

[16] Shaw, M., Garlan, D.: Software Architecture—Perspectives on an Emerging Discipline, Prentice Hall, Upper Saddle River, New Jersey 1996.

[17] Schneeweiß, C.: Einführung in die Produktionswirtschaft, 7. Auflage, Springer Verlag, Berlin 1999.

[18] Spur, G., Krause, F.-L.: Das virtuelle Produkt, Management der CAD-Technik, Carl Hanser Verlag, München/Wien 1997.

[19] Turowski, K. (Hrsg.): Vereinheitlichte Spezifikation von Fachkom-ponenten, Memorandum des Arbeitskreises 5.10.3, Komponentenorientierte betriebliche Anwendungssysteme, Selbstverlag, Augsburg 2002.

[20] Wedekind, H.: Müller, Th.: Stücklistenorganisation bei einer großen Variantenzahl, in: Angewandte Informatik, 23 (1981) 9, pp. 377-383.

[21] Wedekind, H., Ortner, E.: Aufbau einer Datenbank für die Kostenrechnung, in: Die Betriebswirtschaft, 37 (1977) 5, pp. 533-542.

[22] Wedekind, H., Ortner, E.: Systematisches Konstruieren von Datenbankanwendungen – Zur Methodologie der Angewandten Informatik, Carl Hanser Verlag, München/Wien 1980.

[23] Wörner, J.-D. (Hrsg.): Vom Wort zum Bauelement, Komponententechnologien in den Ingenieurwissenschaften, thema FORSCHUNG, Heft 1, 2003, Technische Universität Darmstadt, Monsheim 2003.

Processes, Workflows, Web Service Flows: A Reconstruction

Stefan Jablonski

Friedrich-Alexander-University of Erlangen-Nuremberg, Germany
stefan.jablonski@informatik.uni-erlangen.de

Abstract. The last decade was heavily focusing on process-oriented approaches for application integration. It started with the advent of workflow management technology at the beginning of the nineties. This development has been continued with the definition of flow concepts for Web services. In this article, we discuss the purpose and advantages of process-oriented concepts for application integration. Therefore, workflow technology and Web service flows are briefly introduced. Then we assess both technologies with respect to their role in application integration. Especially, we will reconstruct the fundamental differences between workflows and Web services.

1 Application Integration

Today's business is infinitely more complex than it was a long time ago. Each company has running a large number of major applications that implement the business functions. At separate points in time, various people used different technologies to write those applications for distinct purposes. This has resulted in application diversity which was initially not much of a problem, because applications were meant to automate self-sufficient, independent functions.

Meanwhile, applications are so dominant that most of the crucial business functions are implemented by them; their integration has now become a vital issue for an enterprise. Integration is especially of concern to large organizations which need to improve efficiency and collaboration across disparate organizational functions. There are many different approaches to integration Sect. 12: technology integration, data integration, and application integration. In our considerations, we focus on the latter, the most comprehensive and challenging form of integration, namely (enterprise) application integration. Enterprise application integration (EAI) is a whole discipline working on this issue [13]. When integration has to be extended to inter-enterprise integration, the issue becomes even more challenging. In this context, topics like supply chain management, e-procurement, and marketplaces are discussed intensively.

T. Härder and W. Lehner (Eds.): Data Management (Wedekind Festschrift), LNCS 3551, pp. 201-213, 2005.

There is much written about EAI; many publications discuss requirements and high-level approaches in general, instead of offering concrete solutions. We do not want to extend this discussion, but want to pursue an approach in this article which seems to contribute considerably to the EAI issue: the message-oriented approach. However, this approach also has to be analyzed thoroughly, before it can be applied. Two aspects have to be considered:

- The message-oriented approach is absolutely compliant with modern architectural approaches, e.g., services-oriented architectures (SOA) or message-oriented middleware (MOM).
- The message-oriented approach is technology (system)-driven; in order to effectively enact it, application knowledge must be incorporated.

SOA is an architectural style [6] whose goal is to achieve loose coupling among interacting programs, here called software agents. A service is a unit of work performed by a service provider to achieve the desired results for a service consumer. Both provider and consumer are roles played by software agents on behalf of their owners. How is loose coupling among interactive software agents achieved? Two architectural constraints have to be employed:

- Simple and ubiquitous interfaces: The interfaces must be available for all providers and consumers.
- Descriptive messages: The messages must be constrained by an extensible schema which limits the vocabulary and the structure of messages.

SOA is based on messages to be exchanged between software agents. MOM is introduced to increase interoperability, portability, and flexibility for message exchange [4], because software agents can be distributed over multiple heterogeneous platforms. MOM reduces the complexity of the development of software agents that span multiple operating systems and network protocols by insulating the application developer from the details of the various operating systems and network interfaces. MOM provides application programming interfaces (APIs) that extend across diverse platforms and networks.

Both SOA and MOM are system-oriented concepts which focus on the provision of architectural constraints and infrastructural means. What is missing—but this is a natural consequence of the system-oriented perspectives of SOA and MOM—are guidelines when to use what messages in order to facilitate the development of an application system.

Since more than a decade, process modeling has been regarded as a most adequate means to model application systems [7]. The behavior of applications participating in a comprehensive process is typically described by their need to exchange messages among each other. Thus, process modeling (and enactment) ideally completes the message-oriented approach by identifying messages that are produced and consumed by applications. For example in [5], workflow management—which represents a special form of process modeling and enactment Sect. 9—is regarded as the top of a stack of messaging methods to support enterprise application integration. It refines techniques like basic asynchronous messaging, message brokering, and message transformation.

Workflow management must be analyzed when process-oriented applications have to be investigated.

Workflow management is not the only infrastructure to enact workflows, however, it is a very prominent one [8]. Not before the advent of Web services [1], it seemed to embody the only feasible infrastructure for process enactment. Of course, there were other concepts like ECA rules (event-condition-action rules); however, these concepts were only of limited use to implement complex processes. Then with Web services, Web service flow languages have entered the picture. Those languages aim at the enactment of process-oriented applications implemented in form of Web services. From that time on, workflow management more and more has been ignored and Web service flow languages have overtaken the role of workflow management for processes, especially in the academic literature. There are a couple of reasons why this happened:

- Workflow management was not as successful as it was forecasted. However, this is not a failure of this technology but it is due to un-reflected predictions given by many researchers and industrial representatives at the beginning of the nineties. Workflow management was praised as a panacea. It was not taken into account that, firstly, workflow management is a complicated technology and, secondly, workflow management only fits specific applications. Because workflow management was very often applied in applications which were not suitable for that technology, many workflow projects were failing. Instead of blaming the responsible project leaders, the technology was blamed which ended up in a bad reputation of workflow management.
- Each (modern) time needs its hype topic. So, as we experienced it with workflow management a dozen years ago, Web service flows are now praised as a next sort of panacea. They seem to successfully be workflow management's heir with respect to process enactment. However, Web service flow languages still lack the proof of broad applicability.

What are our consequences from these observations and developments? Shortly spoken, we consider both workflow management and Web service flows as powerful technologies. Although we see fundamental differences in their deployment areas, and we believe that they can ideally leverage on each other. To identify their areas of deployment, we are reconstructing both technologies in this paper. As a result, we want to contribute to their adequate usage, such that they are not neglected due to unprofessional use and consequently unsuccessful projects.

Workflow management and Web service flows are not the only techniques that are able to enact processes. Processes could also be enacted in conventional programming languages. However, in contrast to programming languages, workflow management and Web service flows incorporate a process model which programming languages do not have. This allows describing processes at a more abstract level and so the usage of this process technology is much more comfortable.

This article shows the following structure. After the introductory remarks of this first section, we briefly introduce processes in Section 2. The area of workflow management is reconstructed in Section 3, whereas in Section 4 the same is done for Web service flows. Section 5 compares workflows and Web service flows and reveals similarities, differences, and complementary features of both technologies. It provides some practical guidelines when to use what of these alternative and complementary techniques. To convey this recommendation is the major contribution of this article. Finally, Section 6 is concluding our considerations.

2 A General Model for Processes

Before we are going to reconstruct both workflow management and Web service flows, we introduce a general model for processes used to describe and compare both technologies. This model is derived from the Mobile process model [8] which is a very general one and, therefore, is suitable to represent a framework for process modeling.

The Mobile model defines a conceptual model and syntax for processes. The goal of the model is to provide a framework for process descriptions. Therefore, it is defining processes in terms of several aspects, the so-called perspectives. The feature which translates Mobile from a normal process model into a framework is its ability to be customized to different application areas. In order to do so, new aspects can be added, existing aspects can be modified (e.g., by changing its attributes) or can be discarded. Mobile regards the following five aspects as important but not as mandatory (this is a simplified description; for details refer to [8]):

- *Functional perspective*: It describes which steps have to be performed in a process; composite processes consists of further (sub-)processes, elementary processes represent tasks to be executed.
- *Operational perspective*: This dimension is introduced to determine the application programs and resources called to execute an elementary process.
- *Behavioral perspective*: Here, the control flow of a process is defined. It specifies in what order sub-processes are executed.
- *Data perspective*: Data flow defines the way data is exchanged among processes.
- *Organizational perspective*: This dimension identifies the agents that are responsible to execute a certain process.

Figure 1 shows a simple example of a Mobile process (modeled with the i>ProcessManager [14], a process modeling tool, completely based on the aspect-oriented modelling paradigm). On the left hand side of the i>PM modeling tool in Figure 1, the five perspectives from above can be found: processes (here: Prozesse), organization (here: Organisationen), flows (control and data flows) (here: Flüsse), data (here: Daten), applications (here: Werkzeuge/Systeme). The process modeled (here: Bauteilkonstruktion) comprises a couple of sub-processes (white rectangles). Data flow is represented by arcs with connected data (colored rectangles) between the processes. Some processes show an organization responsible to execute it (lower left corner of the rectangle), some of them show tools to be used when a process step is executed (upper left corner of the rectangle). To execute the top-level process “Bauteilkonstruktion”, its components, i.e., its sub-processes, must be performed. “Eingang” illustrates the start of this

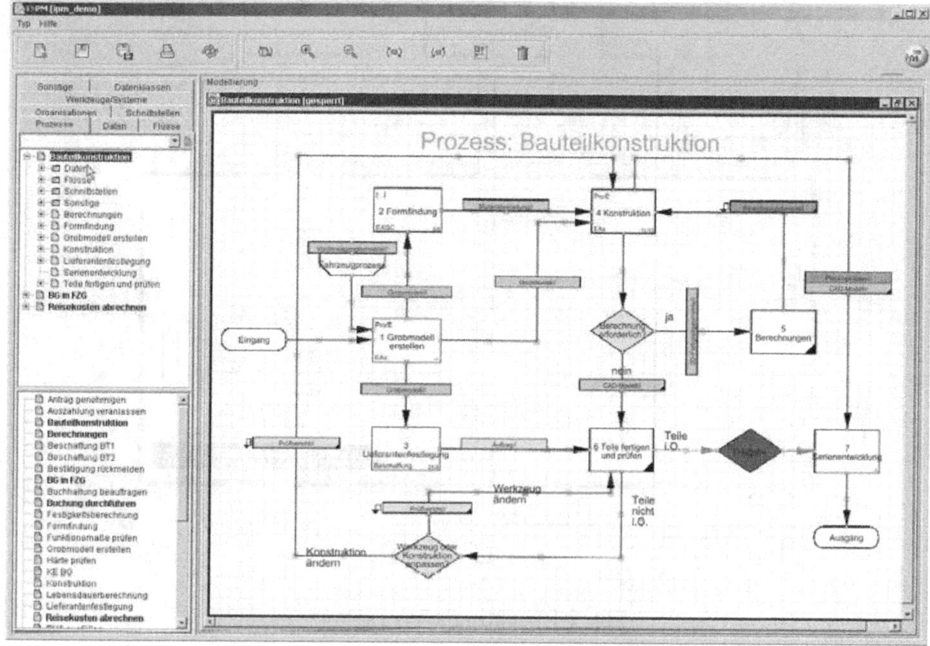

Fig. 1 An Example Process

execution, "Ausgang" its end; both constructs are optional; they are used here to indicate starting and ending points of the depicted process.

3 Workflow Management — Revisited

The Workflow Management Coalition defines a workflow as an automation of a business process, in whole or part, during which documents, information or tasks are passed from one participant to another for action, according to a set of procedural rules [18]. This is some acceptable characterization of a workflow, sufficient for the upcoming discussion. Before we are going to analyze the content of workflow models, we firstly want to demonstrate how the example process of Figure 2 is enacted by workflow management. This is accomplished by illustrating the participants such an enactment is requiring. Therefore, we are using (simplified) sequence diagrams showing either active objects (participants) involved in an enactment and the messages that have to be exchanged between them.

A user starts the execution of a workflow (step 1 in Figure 2). This is done via the worklist which is the usual user interface of a workflow management system (WfMS). The worklist notifies the WfMS to start the corresponding workflow (step 2). The start of a workflow happens once. For each step within the workflow, the now following actions take place. When a certain workflow is ready for execution, the WfMS puts a task,

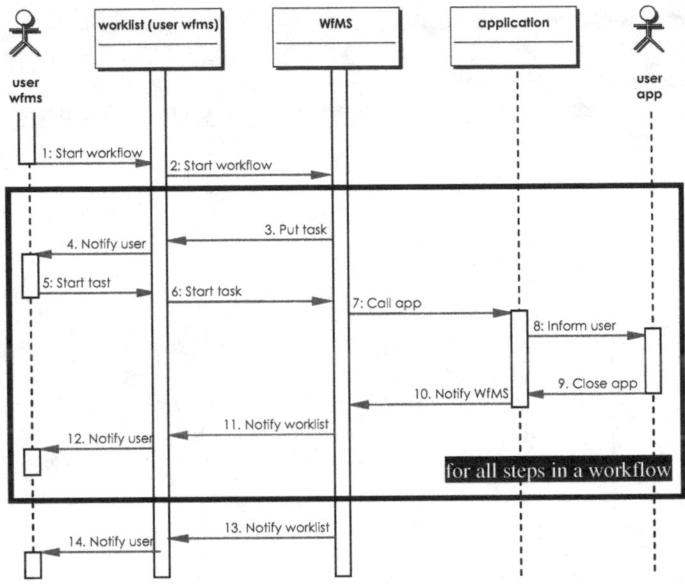

Fig. 2 Executing a Workflow

i.e., a workflow to be executed, back into the worklist of the corresponding user (step 3). The user is notified about this event (step 4) and can start the related task (step 5). This is transmitted to the WfMS (step 6) which now launches the application associated with the task (step 7). The user is notified (step 8) and interacts with the application until (s)he closes it (step 9). This is communicated to the WfMS (step 10) and further to the worklist (step 11). Finally, the user is notified about the end of the task (step 12). Subsequently, the same scenario could be repeated for each task within a workflow. After the whole workflow is performed, the WfMS might inform the user about the end of processing (step 13 and step 14).

The attentive reader might have encountered some inaccuracies in the above description which now have to be cleared up. A first remark is very important, but is not so relevant for the discussion in this article. In Figure 2, we just show one possible execution semantics for a workflow. However, there are many valid alternatives possible. For example, it might be the case that the worklist directly starts an application or an application directly communicates with the worklist when it terminates.

A second remark is essential for our reconstruction. In the description of the workflow execution above, we have just talked about a single user. Conversely, in Figure 2 we distinguish between several users: on the left side, a so-called "user wfms" is shown, and on the right side, a so-called "user app" is identified. By this distinction we want to express that—in principle—the users of the WfMS and the application could be separate entities. However, in the normal case, the two users will be the same.

In Figure 2, some major characteristics of workflow management can be identified. First, a WfMS provides a special interface to their users, the worklist; this also implies that users are expected to directly interact with a WfMS. Normally workflow execution is explicitly initiated and initialized by them. Indeed, the Workflow Management Coalition regards the worklist as one of the basic concepts [18].

In the context of a WfMS, users are frequently humans, although technical artifacts like programs or robots may play the role of a user, too. Another feature of a WfMS is that tasks are executed which typically are applications called from these tasks. Applications are often interactive, i.e., users are again expected to cooperate with them directly.

Without going into details, a workflow comprises all the aspects that are introduced in section 2. This can also be derived from the definition of a workflow by the Workflow Management Coalition (W3C) presented at the beginning of this section. We will discuss this issue further in section 5.

4 Web Service Flows — Revisited

According to the W3C, a Web service is a software system designed to support interoperable machine-to-machine interaction over a network. It has an interface described in a machine-processible format (specifically WSDL). Other systems interact with the Web service in a manner prescribed by its description using SOAP-messages, typically conveyed using HTTP with an XML serialization in conjunction with other Web-related standards [10] [17]. Here, it becomes very obvious that Web services are designed for cooperation between machines.

Business or other activities that involve multiple kinds of organizations or independent processes that use Web service technology to exchange information can only be successful if they are properly coordinated [16]. This means that a sender and a receiver of a message know the sequence and conditions in which messages are exchanged. A shared common or "global" definition of the sequence and conditions is provided by the Web service choreography [16]. We call such a sequence of Web services to be choreographed a Web service flow. Modelling languages for Web service flows are BPEL [2] and BPML [3], for instance.

Similar to the previous section, we want now explain how processes are executed as a Web service flow. We again use sequence diagrams to illustrate this.

A Web service flow is started by a user (step1 in Figure 3). The Web service execution environment (WSEE) is responsible to execute a Web service flow (see section 5 for more details). Each Web service flow is started once. Then the following actions take place for each step within this Web service flow. Normally, the execution of a step involves the launch of an application (step 2). An application might interact with a user (step 3 and step 4). When the application is terminated, the WSEE will be notified by the application (step 5). If all steps of a Web service flow are executed, the user might be notified about the termination (step 6).

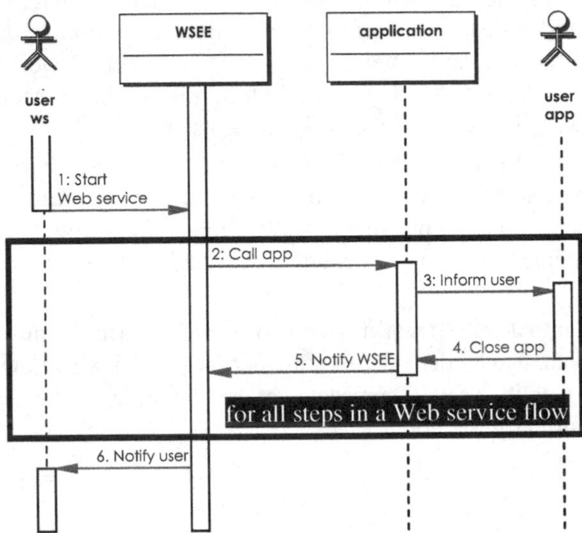

Fig. 3 Executing a Web Service Flow

Symmetrical to the discussion of execution semantics for workflows in the former section, there are also alternative execution semantics for Web service flows. Because this is not so relevant for this article, we omit an extended discussion. Comparing Fig. 2 and Fig. 3, the reader recognizes a couple of major differences between workflow management and Web service flow execution. Although this discussion is up to the next section, we must anticipate some of the observations right away. A WSEE does not provide a component analogous to the worklist of a WfMS. Furthermore, there is a major difference in the interpretation of users in a Web service environment. A (simple or compound) Web service is typically initiated by a program, i.e., "user ws" typically is a piece of software. In contrast, applications frequently do not interact with human users, i.e., they are typically not interactive, but are running in a kind of batch mode. This observation is affirmed by the definition of Web services, where the machine-machine interaction is put into the center of interest.

With the exception of the special design of the organizational aspect, Web service flows comprise principally all aspects of the general process model of section 2. However, the special definition of the organizational aspect will be considered further in the following section.

5 Comparison and Assessment

In this section, some fundamental differences between workflow management and Web service flows are elaborated. In addition, we discuss at the end of this section how both techniques can leverage on each other in a synergetic way.

5.1 The Approach

This first criterion reflects the global approach for workflow management and Web service flow applications, respectively. It has to be considered that our observation is a principle one which reproduces the current and typical usage of both techniques. There are always forms of usage which deviate from this principal one.

Due to the sequence of their advent we start with workflow management. Also due to its development more than a decade ago, workflow management is now a kind of "normal" application in the sense that it is an installed software component and selected users have access to it. The selection of users is determined by the process definitions (organizational perspective) intended to be performed on the WfMS. Thus, we would like to call this application a "closed" one, because there is a clear and sharp perception of who should participate in the workflow management application.

Another criterion for the delimited scope of workflow management applications can be seen in the missing technical standards besides direct process-related standards: above them, no more technical standards are defined such as access protocols or data formats that would support the rapid incorporation of participants. The disregard of these issues does not mean that workflow technology is not complete, rather, it means that quick incorporation of arbitrary users is not the primary issue: if a user wants to participate in a workflow management application, it has to study and to adopt the required protocols and data formats first. Only if both issues were completely based on general standards, this incorporation could be facilitated very quickly.

In contrast to the closed world of workflow management, we tend to characterize Web service flow applications as "open". The Web service approach is totally different in comparison to the workflow approach. We assume to have a Web service execution environment with SOAP as a protocol, WSDL and, for example, BPEL as specification languages, and—what is most decisive—UDDI as registry for Web services [11]. Who is then eligible to participate in a Web service flow execution? All participants who can principally reach the UDDI registry and can, therefore, offer or use Web services, are desired to take part in a Web service application—access rights and payment for the use of Web services have to be taken into account of course. Therefore, the Web service application is open to all participants that can reach the UDDI registry. This set might be restricted, because a UDDI registry can be installed within an intranet solely for some division of a company; nevertheless, for all participants of this division the participation in the Web service application is possible. As a consequence, the eventual users cannot be determined in advance. In contrast, it is desired that many users are participating: also users that are deciding to participate in an ad hoc manner are welcome. In order to alleviate rapid access to Web service flow applications, it is necessary not just to foster standardized concepts for process modelling, but also data and protocols necessary to locate, to identify, and to call a Web service must comply to standardized formats (e.g., WSDL, UDDI, SOAP).

It is quite obvious that the closed and the open character of workflow management and Web service applications, respectively, can be loosened; nevertheless, it is recommended to take this difference into consideration when applications are going to be designed and a technology to enact these applications is choosen. To make a fully closed system out of a Web service application is cumbersome to achieve and, vice versa, to build a fully open system out of a workflow management application is also burdensome to accomplish. Therefore both attempts are not recommended.

5.2 The Implementation

The different character of workflow management and Web service flows also is revealed by analyzing their way how they are implemented. We again start this investigation by looking onto workflow management first.

The normal way to implement a workflow management application is to install a WfMS—hereby, it is not relevant whether it is a centralized or distributed installation. Then, processes, applications, data, and users are made known to it. Next, the WfMS is performing processes, utilizing all these known artifacts.

Aiming at the execution of a Web service flow application, the proceeding is totally different. Web service execution infrastructure is considered to be a common shared middleware. So, (almost) each application server is bearing infrastructure for Web service execution, e.g. [15]. So a Web service application can be set up in an ad hoc way. Since application server are aiming to support standardized techniques the rapid enactment of Web service applications is facilitated.

5.3 The Content

We talked about the contents of either workflow-oriented process models and Web service flow-oriented process models already in Sections 3 and 4. It is common to both approaches that the functional, the behavioral, the data, and the operational aspect of a process model are implemented. However, the two approaches differ drastically in the organizational aspect. Figure 2 and Figure 3 depict the difference in an illustrative way. While in the concept of workflow management a user is explicitly anticipated, Web service flows do not emphasize this. This can best be exemplified by the notion of the worklist. In a workflow management scenario, a workflow is explicitly introduced as an interface between the WfMS and (often human) users, there is nothing comparable for Web service flows.

As was discussed already, Web service flow applications do mostly anticipate the inclusion of batch programs while workflow management applications do support interactive applications in a much more intensive manner. A usual scenario is to perform

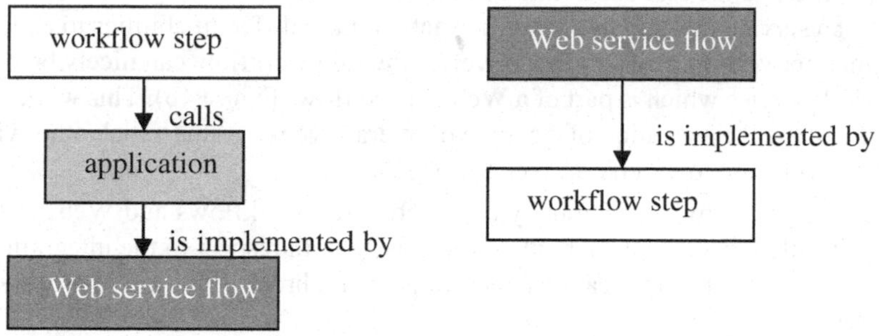

Fig. 4 Integration of Workflow and Web Services

a task that is listed in the worklist which results in the execution of an application that has to be served by a (human) user, typically the same user having issued the task execution request.

5.4 The Synergy

We consider the dissimilarity of workflows and Web service flows as advantageous. It is extremely good that the one technology (Web service flow) is not just the successor of the other technology (workflow management) but is conceptually seen something innovative. This difference offers opportunity for synergy. Synergy between workflow management and Web service flow will be discussed in this subsection.

There are a number of places where Web service technology can be used in workflow management environments. Firstly, there are spots where supporting technology for Web service flow execution can be used. SOAP as a standard communication protocol is suited to support all communication tasks in a WfMS. We might even use an UDDI-like registry to register all workflows of an application realm. Up to a certain degree, WSDL and BPEL can be used to describe workflows, although there might be language features missing sometimes (e.g. to specify the organizational perspective).

Even when we discuss different opportunities for synergy here, we assess the following category of synergy as most relevant. Because Web service flows are an adequate means to describe a sequence of executions of batch programs, we could regard such a flow as workflow application that is called from a certain workflow step (Figure 4a). Having to model a sequence of batch applications in a workflow—without having the concept of Web services at hand—is often very cumbersome: a pseudo worklist must be defined for each batch application; a pseudo agent is then calling the application. From the WfMS point of view, such a Web service flow corresponds to a workflow application that is to be called. Figure 4 summarizes the results of this last point of discussion.

Symmetrical to the last observation, there is another nice synergy between workflows and Web service flows that leverages exactly on the different abilities to execute batch and interactive applications, respectively. A whole workflow can nicely be considered as a Web service which is part of a Web service flow (Figure 4b). This workflow could best facilitate the execution of a couple of interactive programs which otherwise would be very awkward to specify as Web services.

The capacity to bidirectionally call each other, workflows and Web service flows could ideally leverage on each other. Especially with respect to the integration of both batch and interactive applications, they can cover a broad spectrum of process-oriented applications.

6 Conclusion

In principle, the last section summarizes the conclusions of this article: workflows and Web service flows are different in nature. Although, they can nicely complement themselves in a synergetic way.

In this article, we were reconstructing workflows and Web service flows with the intention to help application designers to choose the right technique. We also wanted to contribute to the actual discussion of Web services that workflows are still not obsolete but are complementary to Web service flows.

References

[1] Alonso, G., Casati, F., Kuno, H., Machiraju, V.: Web Services. Concepts, Architectures, and Applications. Springer-Verlag, 2004

[2] Business Process Execution Language (BPEL) for Web Services Version 1.1, http://www-106.ibm.com/developerworks/library/ws-bpel/, 2003

[3] Business Process Modeling Language (BPML), http://www.bpmi.org/bpml.esp, 2004

[4] Carnegie Mellon, Software Engineering Institute: Message-Oriented Middleware. http://www.sei.cmu.edu/str/descriptions/momt.html, 2004/10/28

[5] Cummins, F.A.: Enterprise Integration with Workflow Management, Presentation on November 1,1999, http://www.bijonline.com, 2004/10/14

[6] Erl, T.: Service-Oriented Architecture. Prentice Hall, 2004

[7] Hammer, M., Champy, J.: Reengineering the Corporation. HarperBusiness, 2004

[8] Jablonski, S., Bussler, C.: Workflow Management: Modeling Concepts, Architecture and Implementation. International Thomson Publishing, 1996

[9] Jablonski, S., Bussler, C.: Process Modeling and Execution in Workflow Management Systems. Proceedings 3rd International Workshop on Information Technologies and Systems, Orlando, FL, Dec. 1993

[10] Jablonski, S., Petrov, I., Meiler, C., Mayer, U.: Guide to Web Application and Plattform Architectures. Springer-Verlag, 2004

[11] Jeckle, M.: Techniken der XML-Familie zur Systemintegration. IT-Information Technology, Heft 4, 2004

[12] Linthicum, D.S.: Enterprise Application Integration. Addison Wesley, 1999

[13] Linthicum, D.S.: Next Generation Application Integration. From Simple Information to Web Services. Addison-Wesley, 2003

[14] ProDatO: i>PM, integrated ProcessManager. White Paper. http://www.prodato.de, 2004/10/28

[15] The Apache Cocoon Project, http://xml.apache.org/cocoon/, 2004

[16] WS Choreography Model Overview, W3C Working Draft, 24 March 2004. 2004/10/28

[17] W3C: Web Services Glossary, W3C Working Group Note, 11 February 2004, 2004/10/28

[18] WfMC: Terminology & Glossary. Document Number WFMC-TC-1011, Document Status - Issue 3.0, Feb. 99

Pros and Cons of Distributed Workflow Execution Algorithms

Hans Schuster

Consileon Business Consultancy GmbH, Germany
hans.schuster@consileon.de

Abstract. As an implementation of business processes workflows are inherently distributed. Consequently, there is a considerable amount both of commercial products and research prototypes that address distribution issues in workflow execution and workflow management systems (WfMS). However, most of these approaches provide only results focussed on the properties of a specific workflow model, workflow application, and/or WfMS implementation. An analysis of generic requirements on distributed workflow execution algorithms and their applicability, advantages, and disadvantages in different workflow scenarios is still missing but will be shown in this paper. A comprehensive requirements analysis on distributed workflow execution forms the basis of our discussion of distributed workflow execution. In contrast to existing work that primarily focuses on non-functional requirements, this paper explicitly considers issues that originate in the workflow model as well. Subsequently, four basic algorithms for distributed workflow execution are presented, namely remote access, workflow migration, workflow partitioning, and subworkflow distribution. Existing WfMS approaches use combinations and/or variants of these basic algorithms. The properties of these algorithms with respect to the aforementioned requirements are discussed in detail. As a primary result, subworkflow distribution proves to be a well-suited application-independent and thus generally applicable distributed execution model. Nevertheless, application-specific optimizations can be accomplished by other models.

1 Motivation

Today's enterprises are highly distributed. The trend to enter cooperations among different enterprises in order to build virtual enterprises even intensifies this distributed nature. Workflow management is a promising technology to implement business processes in traditional as well as virtual enterprises through workflows that are enacted by workflow management systems (WfMS). WfMS integrate both human and fully automated activities within workflows [17].

T. Härder and W. Lehner (Eds.): Data Management (Wedekind Festschrift), LNCS 3551, pp. 215-234, 2005.

Due to the distributed nature of the application environment, workflows, i.e. their executions, have to be distributed themselves. Hence, there is a strong need for suitable methods for distributed workflow execution. Although, there are many commercial workflow products and academic WfMS prototypes that all support some kind of distributed workflows, there is still no commonly agreed upon workflow model although the Business Process Execution Language for Web Services (BPEL4WS, [1]) is on a good way to establish an agreed standard for fully automated workflows. There is also no commonly agreed distributed execution model for workflows The existing approaches address only specific problems of distributed workflows in the context of a particular workflow model without tackling the general problem. A comprehensive analysis of the basic requirements on distributed workflow execution and alternative solutions is still missing. However, only such an analysis can build up a solid foundation for a decision how to implement a workflow application in a particular (virtual) enterprise. A taxonomy for the suitability of distributed workflow execution algorithms in specific application scenarios is highly desirable.

The main contribution of this paper is the identification of four generic algorithms for distributed workflow execution, and their thorough discussion with respect to a comprehensive list of requirements covering model-related (e.g., synchronization of activities) and behavioral (e.g., performance, scalability) requirements. 'Generic' in this context means that—in contrast to other work done in this area—we do not assume a specific workflow model and/or WfMS implementation. In contrast, this work is based on a set of rudimentary assumptions that are fulfilled by virtually all existing workflow models. Distributed workflow execution algorithms proposed in the literature [3, 16, 4, 5, 6, 10, 11, 14, 21, 22, 27, 25] are a combination of the four generic algorithms. Therefore, it is not our objective to propose a new way to implement distributed workflows but to improve the understanding of the problem of distributed workflow execution. The results of this paper can serve as a foundation when deciding which approach to chose in a concrete workflow application scenario.

The next section presents the requirements that have to be fulfilled by distributed workflows. Section 3 introduces the four basic distributed workflows execution algorithms and discusses their general properties and combinations. The efficiency of these algorithms is the focus of section 4. Finally, section 5 presents a brief overview on existing work in analyzing distributed workflow approaches and Section 6 gives a short conclusion.

2 Requirements on Distributed Workflow Execution

Distributed workflow execution is not an end in itself. On the contrary, it is the answer on the demand for the adaptation of workflow execution to the distributed nature of the application environment in today's enterprises. This answer is naturally constrained by requirements that result from the workflow model used in a WfMS. Additionally, a distributed WfMS has to meet the non-functional requirements of application, like scalability and efficiency. section 2.1 defines the terminology used in this paper and our assumptions with respect to workflow models. section 2.2 presents the functional requirements originating from the workflow model, section 2.3 is dedicated to the non-functional ones.

2.1 Definitions

According to [13, 17, 31, 32], a workflow is a set of computer-supported activities which implement parts of one or more business processes. A workflow has a well-defined start, an automatically coordinated process, and a well-defined end. A workflow is not restricted to automatically executed processes, like multi-system transactions, but can also coordinate the actions of human participants in complex enterprise scenarios or be a combination of both. The coordination of a workflow's execution is established by a WfMS. Although workflows are in fact processes, they are also (data) objects from the implementation's point of view. The workflow execution is driven by operations on the workflow instance data [17], e.g., to create, start, and terminate workflow instances.

Definition 1: Workflow type, workflow instance

Each workflow type (workflow schema) wt is defined by a workflow specification WF-Spec(wt) that enfolds the algorithmic description of the workflow and a set WF-Op(wt) = $\{op_1, ..., op_n\}$ of workflow operations. A workflow instance wi is an instantiation of a workflow type. The workflow type of a particular workflow instance wi is denoted in this paper as Type(wi), the state of wi as State(wi).

The set of workflow operations WF-Op(wt) of a workflow type wt is subdivided into workflow type operations, e.g. for creating a workflow instance of a workflow type wt, and into workflow instance operations, which operate on the workflow instances, for example to start, stop or destruct workflow instances.

Business processes in real life are often very complex. This is the reason for subdividing work into smaller steps, whereby each step is easier to handle and understand than the whole. In the following, we assume the same for workflows (Definition 2).

Definition 2: Subworkflows, father, top-level, and elementary workflows

Composite workflows are functionally decomposed into a set of subworkflows. A workflow (instance) becomes a subworkflow (instance) by being created in the context of a composite workflow (instance), called father workflow. A workflow (instance) without a father workflow is called top-level workflow (instance). Each subworkflow (instance) in turn is a workflow in its own right, i.e., it has its own workflow type, can be further decomposed in subworkflows, and is represented by its own instance data (e.g. data container and dependencies). The internal instance data is private to the corresponding workflow instance. A (sub)workflow is a unit of work and can be assigned to roles. A workflow (instance) which consists only of invocations of external applications is an elementary workflow (instance).

Functional decomposition of workflows is supported by virtually every commercial workflow model and by many workflow models used in research prototypes. However, there is no commonly accepted terminology. In WebSphere MQ Workflow [16] (formerly called FlowMark), for example, a workflow—called *process*—consists of *activities*. Composite subworkflows are called *process activities* and reference a *process template*, i.e., have a process type. *Program activities* correspond to elementary subworkflows. The Workflow Management Coalition calls a composite subworkflow *subprocess* [34]. Definition 2 assumes role assignment for both elementary and composite subworkflows, which is consistent with the Workflow Management Coalition standard [35, p.168] and many WfMS products, e.g., IBM WebSphere MQ Workflow [16], BEA WebLogic Integration [8], and Oracle Workflow [24].

To enable a coordinated execution of a workflow, additional information besides subworkflows and external applications is required. According to the literature, e.g. [17, 18, 31], a workflow covers at least control and data flow dependencies among subworkflows, workflow-relevant data, and assignment of actors (roles) to subworkflows. This leads to the following refinement of the workflow specification. The state State(wi) of a workflow instance wi can be refined analogously.

Definition 3: Workflow specification

The specification WF-Spec(wt) of a workflow type wt consists of a set of typed subworkflow placeholders SubWF(wt), a set of references to external applications ExtApp(wt), a set of data variables Data(wt) for workflow relevant data, control and data flow dependencies (CFDep(wt) and DFDep(wt)), and a set of role assignment rules RoAss(wt). Thus, WF-Spec(wt) = (SubWF(wt), ExtApp(wt), Data(wt), CFDep(wt), DFDep(wt), RoAss(wt)).

Definition 3 does not define what kind of dependencies are available and how they relate subworkflows. Since existing workflow models differ significantly with respect to dependencies, this paper will stay at this general level to reach results valid for a wide range of existing WfMS.

The execution of workflow operations is usually requested by the player of the role that is assigned to the corresponding workflow instance (called participant in Definition 4). In fully automated workflows the WfMS itself may request a workflow operation to be performed. Based on these prerequisites, Definition 4 introduces the term distributed workflow execution.

Definition 4: Distributed workflow execution

The execution of a workflow instance is called distributed, if at least two workflow operations within this workflow execution are requested by participants in different physical locations or if workflow instance data are distributed among different components of the computing infrastructure.

Note, we do not assume a distributed workflow enactment service as a mandatory prerequisite for distributed workflow execution. The distribution of a workflow's participants already constitutes distributed workflows.

2.2 Model-Related Requirements

The distributed execution of workflows is not straight forward because a composite workflow implements a coordination pattern among its subworkflows. The coordination rules are made up by data and control flow dependencies (CFDep(wt), DFDep(wt)) and by role assignment rules (RoAss(wt)). The WfMS has to ensure that the specified coordination rules are fulfilled in a distributed environment. To illustrate this, Figure 1 shows a simplified workflow specification for a currency trading workflow running in a distributed bank environment, which consists of a set of branches and some departments for asset management and for stock market trading. In larger banks not only the branches are distributed but also the other departments. In Figure 1, the organizations that perform stock market trading are located at different physical locations, e.g., there may be brokers in New York, London, Tokyo, Frankfurt, etc.). In fact, the tasks in some locations may be even sourced out to a different company. For example, the stock market trading may be performed by separate brokering companies, i.e., the bank may be a virtual enterprise.

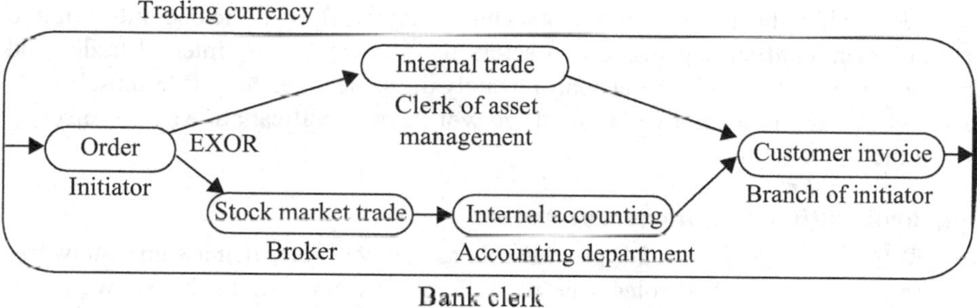

Fig. 1 Distributed Workflow Example

The currency trading workflow is initiated on a customer request by a bank clerk within a branch. The first subworkflow, registering a customer's order to buy or sell a certain amount of currency, is done by the initiating clerk. Depending on the amount of currency and the current situation of the bank, there are two possibilities to proceed: first, the order could be fulfilled by the bank's internal trade. Second, the bank could go to the stock market in order to process the order. The WfMS has to ensure that only one of these variants is chosen. Processing an order twice must be prohibited in all circumstances. However, the decision which variant is to be taken in a workflow instance is done by the human actors within the responsible organization (asset management and broker) and is not predefined by a condition that could be evaluated by the WfMS. In both variants, trading is performed in general at different geographic locations than ordering. After performing the trade the workflow returns to the branch where it has been started, the customer's invoice is determined and the workflow terminates. In the following we briefly discuss the requirements on the distributed execution of workflows in more detail.

Synchronization of Concurrent Subworkflows

Both control and data flow dependencies define a relationship among two or more subworkflow instances within a father workflow. Some of these dependencies, for example the well-known *sequence* control flow dependency [17, 29], imply just an execution order for some workflow instances. Other control flow dependencies influence also the existence of workflow instances, e.g., deadline and delay [17] and the exclusive or (EX-OR) [17, 29]. Data flow dependencies that consume data items from a pool can also entail the existence or non-existence of subworkflows, if there are multiple consuming subworkflows. Petri net based workflow models, e.g., FUNSOFT nets [12], support these kind of data flow dependencies.

During workflow execution, control and data flow dependencies that have impact on the existence of subworkflows imply a strict synchronization on the execution of the affected subworkflow instances' constructor operations. This is necessary to enforce the dependencies in case multiple subworkflow instances are to be created concurrently.

In the example workflow shown in Figure 1, "Internal trade" and "Stock market trade" are two concurrent subworkflows which have to be synchronized. Only one of them is allowed to be executed. Only the actors responsible for the concurrent subworkflows decide if and when they want to execute a subworkflow. If the operations of two or more users conflict, e.g. when two actors try to execute the "Internal trade" and "Stock market trade" workflow at approximately the same time, the WfMS must be able to detect this and prevent a violation of the workflow specification, e.g., by rejecting one of the actors' requests.

Synchronization of Concurrent Actors

Most WfMS, e.g., [8, 16, 17, 24] provide role assignment rules that assign a subworkflow to players of a set of roles. The work item corresponding to this subworkflow therefore appears on the worklists of a set of actors, but only one of them shall perform the subworkflow. This synchronization strategy is called *one out of many*. Depending on the workflow model, other more complicated synchronization policies are possible [9, 30]. To facilitate our analysis of algorithms for distributed workflow execution, we will concentrate on the *one out of many* strategy, because this strategy is mostly used in today's workflow applications. Other synchronization strategies may lead to slightly different results, but in any case the WfMS has to synchronize actors who try to concurrently access the same subworkflow instance.

The aforementioned issue shows up in the example of Figure 1, if the "Stock market trade" subworkflow is analyzed in more detail (Figure 2). There are several major stock markets all over the world and virtually all major banks are working globally. Thus, a customer order can be processed by different brokers located at different places all over the world. The WfMS has to ensure that the order is processed only once by synchronizing the brokers' operations.

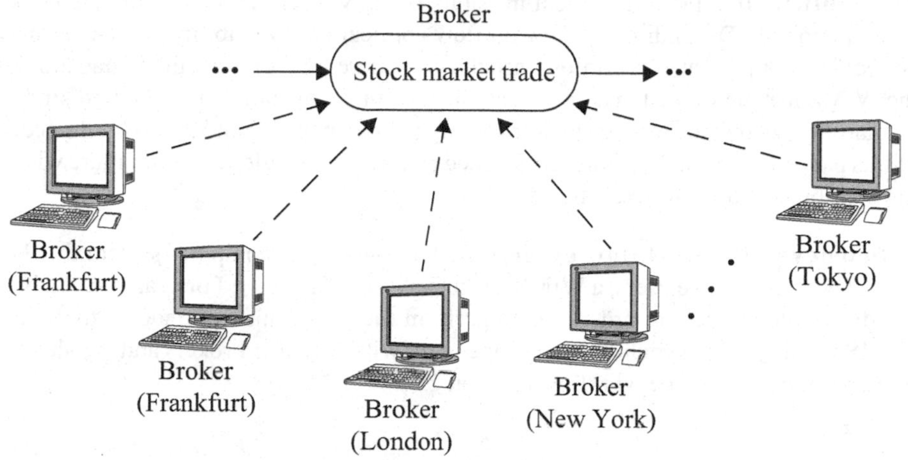

Fig. 2 Concurrent Actors

2.3 Non-functional Requirements

Besides implementing the features of a workflow model, a WfMS also has to meet the non-functional requirements implied by the application environment. An exhaustive coverage of these requirements is not possible here because of space limitations. Thus, only these issues are considered that apply to a wide range of workflow applications [2, 28].

Support for heterogeneous WfMS environments. It is unrealistic to assume a homogeneous WfMS infrastructure in a large company or a virtual enterprise consisting of multiple companies. In the banking example of Section 2, some departments likely have their own WfMS installation depending on a different WfMS as other departments. Independent broker firms that perform the stock market trading will probably use a different WfMS than the bank. Nevertheless, enterprise-wide workflows, like the 'Trading Currency' workflow, have to be executed despite of this heterogeneity. This must be considered when choosing a distributed workflow execution model.

Scalability. In the context of WfMS, two aspects of scalability can be identified. First, a WfMS must be scalable to varying workloads, i.e., independent of the number of active users and concurrently running workflow instances the system should be able to provide approximately the same response time. Second, a WfMS must be scalable to the size and structure of an enterprise. This involves locating and coordinating WfMS users, workflow types and instances, and WfMS computer resources as well as considering locality and control requirements of workflow participants [26]. For example, departments and in particular external companies may insist in having control over "their part" of the workflow.

Availability. If WfMS implement mission-critical workflows availability issues become important. Depending on the workflow application, availability guarantees may be required for particular workflow instances, or some kind of graceful degradation of the WfMS may be wanted in case some system components fail. While the first kind of availability can only be reached by introducing redundancy [20] and is outside the scope of this paper, the second type may be reached by avoiding single points of failure within the distributed workflow execution algorithm.

Efficiency of the workflow execution. Like any other computer system that has to deal with interactive users, a WfMS has to perform efficiently. For example, if a broker decides to execute an order, i.e., to perform the 'Stock market trade' activity, the WfMS has to quickly synchronize this operation with the other brokers and the alternative execution path in the workflow (section 2.2).

3 Approaches to Distributed Workflow Execution

In the system architecture of a WfMS both a client/server and peer-to-peer approach can be taken (section 3.1). However, this architectural decision has only limited impact. The primary issue is the distributed execution algorithm. In section 3.2, four basic algorithms are presented. section 3.3 then provides a discussion of these algorithms with respect to the requirements presented in section 2 and shows that existing WfMS approaches use a combination of these algorithms.

3.1 Client/Server Versus Peer-to-Peer

According to the reference architecture of the Workflow Management Coalition [31] the runtime part of a WfMS consists of workflow enactment service, worklist (i.e. workflow client applications), and invoked (external) applications. A basic design decision for WfMS is the architecture choice for the workflow enactment service. Most approaches, for example [3, 6, 8, 11, 16, 24, 26, 27, 22], implement the workflow enactment service by a set of workflow servers. Each server can be used by multiple users. The users' worklists are clients of these servers. The advantages of this architecture—the general advantages of client/server architectures—are well known. Well-programmed client/server architectures provide good performance and scale well [15]. It has to be emphasized that a client/server architecture does not necessarily imply a centralized workflow execution, i.e., that a workflow instance and also its subworkflows are located at the same workflow server. A distributed workflow execution is also possible in a client/server architecture if a set of servers cooperate and a suitable distributed execution algorithm is deployed. This cooperation among servers can be implemented using again client/server protocols (e.g., [26]) or using a peer-to-peer like communication (e.g., [30]). As a conclusion, the decision whether to use client/server communication and/or peer-to-peer communication within a WfMS has only limited impact on the properties of the implemented distributed workflow execution. The (synchronization) protocols implied by the distributed workflow execution algorithms and workflow models have the primary influence. For this reason, we do not distinguish client/server and peer-to-peer communication in the reminder of this paper. For simplicity, we will call the workflow enactment service components *servers*, even if they interact using a peer-to-peer protocol.

3.2 Basic Algorithms

In the following, four basic approaches for distributed workflow execution are presented.

Remote access. The traditional (and trivial) method for distributed workflow execution is remote access of users, i.e., the users' worklists, to a workflow server. Pure remote access has been used in early versions of commercial and academic WfMS as the only means for distributed workflow execution.

Migration of workflow instances. The key problem of the remote access algorithm are the increasing costs for the communication between remote users and the workflow engine, if they are geographically separated. Migration of workflow instances is an approach to deal with this problem. The primary idea is to migrate the instance data of a whole (top-level) workflow instance to the user(s) who currently work with it or its subworkflows. In other words, the pure migration algorithm moves always the whole workflow tree.

Partitioning of workflows. Another approach to overcome the costs of remote access is partitioning of workflows, strategy is popular in the research community and used for example in [4, 14, 22]. The basic idea is to break a workflow into parts that are performed by people located in physical neighborhood. More detailed, a for workflow specification WF-Spec(wt) = (SubWF(wt), ExtApp(wt), Data(wt), CFDep(wt), DFDep(wt), RoAss(wt)), the set of subworkflows SubWF(wt) (and also ExtApp(wt) and RoAss(wt)) is partitioned in n disjoint sets SubWF(wt)_i. In general, Data(wt) and the dependency sets CFDep(wt) and DFDep(wt) cannot be divided into disjoint sets, because data can be accessed by subworkflows and dependencies in different partitions; dependencies may also relate subworkflows of different partitions. Fig. 3 shows the partitioning of the example workflow introduced in section 2: p_1 = {'Order', 'Customer invoice'}, p_2 = {'Internal trade'}, p_3 = {'Stock market trade', 'Internal Accounting'}. The EXOR control flow dependency is shared between the three partitions. (1) is shared between p_1 and p_2, (2) between p_1 and p_3.

Subworkflow Distribution. Subworkflow distribution [25] is founded on the hierarchical structure of workflows (section 2.1). The granule of distribution are subworkflows. Subworkflow distribution is a generalization of the *nested subprocess* interoperability variant of the workflow management coalition [31, 33]. In general, if a workflow instance wi is to be executed using subworkflow distribution, the following algorithm is applied (assumed a set WS = $\{ws_1, ..., ws_n\}$ of workflow servers is available):

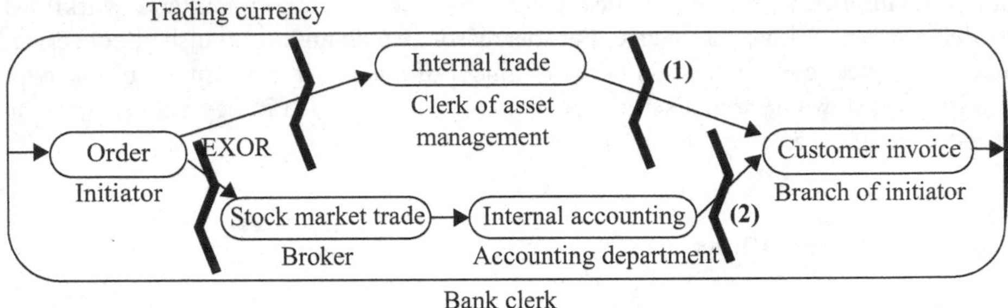

Fig. 3 Distributed Workflow with Partitions According to the Location of Participants

1. If wi is created by invocation of a corresponding constructor workflow operation, select exactly one server s $\in$ WS and assign wi to this server, i.e., server s performs the constructor, stores State(wi), and will perform all subsequent operations on wi, and finally the destructor if wi is deleted (section 2.1). Criteria to be considered for the selection of the server s depend on the concrete implementation.
2. If wi is a composite workflow, i.e., it has a set SubWF(Type(wi)) = $\{sw_1, ..., sw_m\}$ of subworkflows, each $sw_i \in$ SubWF(Type(wi)) is processed as a normal workflow. If sw_i is to be created (according to the specification of wi), the same assignment algorithm is used for sw_i as it has been applied to wi, i.e., sw_i is also treated according to step (1), (2), and (3).
3. If wi is an elementary workflow, no additional actions have to be done with respect to distribution.

Subworkflow distribution enables the usage of the father workflow as a single synchronization point for all of its subworkflows. This may cause the workflow servers involved in the subworkflows' processing to communicate with the father's workflow server. Synchronization with the father workflow is needed, if subworkflows are in competition with each other or if one subworkflow shall be executed by one out of many agents (section 2.2). Using the father's workflow server as a synchronization point for its subworkflows does not mean that there is a central component or a single point of failure in the overall WfMS configuration, because each workflow instance is scheduled separately. As a consequence, the breakdown of a workflow server affects only the workflow instances it is responsible for and partially their subworkflow instances: subworkflows which use the failed workflow server as a synchronization point are affected if they are to be created or to be destructed. During normal processing, a subworkflow needs not to synchronize with the father in most workflow models. Since subworkflows are separate workflows, they can be specified using a different workflow model than the father's.

3.3 Discussion

In section 2, synchronization of concurrent subworkflows and participants have been identified as functional requirements on workflow execution. Support for heterogeneous environments, scalability, availability (i.e., graceful degradation), and efficiency are the non-functional requirements to be considered. In this section, we discuss the properties of the four basic algorithms with respect to these requirements. Tab. 1 summarizes the properties of the algorithms. Assessment of efficiency of the algorithms is more complicated and therefore analyzed separately in section 4.

Algorithm	Concurrent subwork-flows	Concurrent participants	Hetero-geneity	Scalability	Availability
Remote	✔	✔	–	–	–
Migration	–	–	–	✔	✔
Partitioning	✔	–	–	✔	✔
SubWf Distr.	✔	–	✔	✔	✔

Tab. 1 Properties of the Basic Workflow Execution Algorithms

A pure remote access approach, i.e., a single centralized WfMS server, trivially fulfills both functional requirement classes, because the whole workflow instance information is in a single place and accessed by all participants. This algorithm requires a homogeneous system. It provides only limited availability, because the central server is a single point of failure and has poor scalability. In particular, it cannot adapt to the enterprise structure.

The major drawback of the pure migration algorithm is its lack of support for synchronization both of concurrent subworkflows and actors. Because this algorithm always migrates the whole workflow tree to a single location, concurrent subworkflows/ participants located in different places cannot be handled. However, this problem can be overcome by combining migration with remote access. Migration works only between homogeneous WfMS servers. No inherent limitations exist for scalability and also graceful degradation is guaranteed, because the failure of a server affects only the workflow instances of this server. The rest of the system stays operational.

Workflow partitioning divides a workflow's subworkflows into a set of partitions. Each of them is assigned to a workflow engine. Concurrent subworkflows can be synchronized by having the responsible engines communicate with each other. Concurrent participants are not natively supported, because a workflow engine can only be at one participant's place. Again, a combination with remote access solves this problem. Scalability and availability are achievable for the same reasons as in the migration algorithm. Heterogeneous environments are not supported, because all WfMS engines have to use the same workflow model to implement the synchronization protocols between the workflow partitions.

Similar to workflow partitioning, subworkflow distribution enables synchronization of concurrent subworkflows, because the involved subworkflows use the father as a synchronization point. The lack of support for concurrent participants, which is here also due to the fact that a workflow instance can only be at a single location, can be resolved by combining this strategy with remote access. Subworkflow distribution can be used in heterogeneous environments, i.e., subworkflows may be implemented by a different type of WfMS, as long the involved WfMS agree on the basic activity abstraction introduced in section 2.1. In a subworkflow distribution scheme involved WfMS do not share any dependency information. Therefore, the synchronization protocol among the servers is much simpler than for workflow partitioning. Scalability and graceful degradation in case of server breakdowns can also be met with subworkflow distribution for the same reasons as discussed above.

Approach	**Remote**	**Migration**	**Partitioning**	**SubWf Distr.**
Bea WebLogic Integration [8]	✔			(✔)
BPEL [1]				✔
Exotica [3]	✔			
Exotica/FMQM [4]			✔	
INCA [5]		✔		
ADEPT [7]	✔	✔		
Migrating Workflows [10]	✔	✔		
METEOR2 [11]	✔		✔	
METUFlow [14]	✔		✔	
MENTOR [22]	✔		✔	
MOBILE [26, 25]	✔	(✔)		✔
Oracle Workflow [24]	✔			(✔)
WebSphere MQ Workflow [16]	✔			✔

Tab. 2 Use of Basic Algorithms in Existing WfMS

Tab. 2 depicts how distributed workflow execution algorithms proposed in the literature are combined from the four basic algorithms identified in this paper. Space limitations do not allow us to discuss all of these approaches here. We will therefore only point out some interesting observations: Most of these approaches use remote access to workflow servers. This is due to the fact that this is the only strategy that implements synchronization of participants. In addition, it is noticeable that many of the approaches rely on migration and partitioning, although these algorithms are not suitable for the heterogeneous environments usual in today's enterprises. This is even more surprising, since dealing with heterogeneity is absolutely crucial for virtual enterprise and electronic commerce applications. Another special case is BPEL [1]: BPEL is not a general purpose workflow language. It is specialized on fully automated workflows but is does not implement role assignments. A BPEL process can invoke Web Services and is itself a Web Service. In addition, a Web Service provides location transparency and may be implemented by a remote server. This way the BPEL language already contains subworkflow distribution as a model feature. Consequently, BPEL implementations like [23] or workflow engines that support BPEL like [8, 24] have this property as well.

4 Performance Analysis

In the preceding section, the four basic distributed workflow execution algorithms have been evaluated with respect to all requirements identified in section 2 except efficiency. To prepare a performance comparison of these algorithms, a rough estimation of execution costs for the various algorithms is developed throughout this section. This cost estimation seems on first sight to be quite superficial. However, a more detailed one cannot be provided without having additional assumptions regarding the workflow model, the WfMS architecture, and the underlying communication infrastructure. But including additional assumptions would compromise the generality of the analysis. There is a trade-off between generality and accuracy of numbers. The subsequent cost estimations are based on the following assumptions on the execution of workflows and communication costs:

1. Before any operation on a subworkflow of a workflow instance wi can be performed, the responsible actors according to the role assignment rules RoAss(Type(wi)) have to be informed by inserting a corresponding entry into their worklists. Automated subworkflows may be initiated directly by the workflow enactment service without human intervention. Therefore, a worklist entry is not needed in this case.
2. Operations on (sub)workflows—except operations on fully automated (sub)workflows—are initiated by humans interacting with their worklist.
3. The costs for performing a workflow operation op at a workflow engine are denoted t(op).
4. Execution times of external applications are not considered here, because they are completely application dependent. Our estimation is based only on actions between components of the WfMS. This is a very restrictive assumption. However it is justified, because we focus only on the algorithms used within the WfMS. For the same reason, we consider only workflow-internal data in our analysis. Consequently, we do not consider workflow-external data, e.g., documents that are accessed using external applications. In certain application scenarios, execution time for external applications and/or access time to workflow-external data will outweigh any other costs during workflow execution. However, analyzing this effect is fully application dependent and not in the scope of this paper.
5. To simplify the cost estimation, we distinguish only two network zones: local networks (tc_{local}) and WANs (tc_{wan}). For the costs, i.e., times, needed for sending a standard bidirectional message $tc_{local} < tc_{wan}$ holds.

4.1 Estimation of Workflow Execution Costs

In this section the execution costs for workflow operations are estimated for the distributed workflow execution algorithms introduced in section 3.2. Workflow partitioning and subworkflow distribution are analyzed in combination with remote access, because only the combined strategy fulfills the model-related requirements (section 3.3). The discussion of workflow migration is restricted to an estimation of the migration costs. Since a workflow instance usually will not be migrated for every workflow operation, the fraction of the migration costs that apply to a single workflow operation is totally application dependent. Therefore, no reasonable general estimation for the cost of a workflow operation can be made for workflow migration algorithms without making additional assumptions.

Remote Access

If a user wants a workflow operation to be executed, remote access causes the following costs:

1. Communication from worklist to server: $t_1 = c_1 * \{tc_{local}, tc_{wan}\}$; c_1 is a constant capturing the size of a request message.
2. The server performs the operation. This amounts to $t_2 = t(op)$. There is no additional communication effort, because any necessary synchronizations (section 2.2) are performed within the server.
3. A workflow operation may cause modifications of the worklists of several users, e.g. the termination of a subworkflow may enable subsequent workflows and will require the removal of its own work item. This amounts to $t_3 = n * c_2 * \{tc_{local}, tc_{wan}\}$, if n worklist updates with size c_2 have to be performed.

Consequently, a workflow operation causes in the best case a total cost of

$$t_{best} = tc_{local} * (c_1 + n*c_2) + t(op)$$

and in the worst case

$$t_{worst} = tc_{wan} * (c_1 + n*c_2) + t(op).$$

Especially if the users are in physical neighborhood to the workflow server, the communication overhead during workflow operations is quite small; this in particular because no workflow instance state information is transmitted. If subsequent subworkflows are to be performed by actors in different physical locations, like in the example shown in section 2.2, costs increase significantly.

Migration of Workflows

The costs for the migration of a workflow instance wi amount to (x is a placeholder for local and wan)

$$t_{migration} = tc_x * (\text{size}(\text{State}(wi)) + \text{size}(\text{State of all (transitive) subworkflows}(wi))).$$

If we recall that the state of a workflow (section 2.1) contains a considerable amount of data, migration is a very costly operation. In most cases $\text{size}(\text{State}(wi)) >> c_i$ will hold. A migration operation is much more expensive than communicating to a server. Therefore, migration is only beneficial from the viewpoint of costs, if several subsequent operations are performed at the place where the workflow is migrated to.

Partitioning of Workflows Combined with Remote Access

The sharing of data and/or dependencies among partitions causes the need of information exchange during the workflow execution. The following cost estimation for the execution of a workflow operation results:

1. Communication from worklist to the server responsible for the respective partition:
   $t_1 = c_1 * \{tc_{local}, tc_{wan}\}$
2. If the operation has impact on a shared dependency and/or data, the server has to synchronize with the other partitions (assumed number: m). This amounts to
   - $t_2 = c_3 * m * \{tc_{local}, tc_{wan}\}$ (c_3 is the assumed message size), if no synchronizing dependency (section 2.2) is involved.
   - If a synchronizing dependency, e.g., the EXOR dependency in Fig. 3, is involved: $t_{2,\ best} = t_2$, if no other operation is executed concurrently and $t_{2,\ worst} = t_2 * m$, if concurrent operations occur in all affected partitions.
3. The execution of the workflow operation may be split into several parts according to the partitioning of the workflow specification. But this generally has no noteworthy impact on the cost of the operation. Therefore this amounts to $t_3 \cong t(op)$ as in the centralized case. The execution time may be even smaller because the involved servers might work in parallel on their partitions, but this heavily depends on the workflow model.
4. The modifications of the users' worklists are the same as in the centralized case: $t_4 = n * c_2 * \{tc_{local}, tc_{wan}\}$, if n worklist updates with size c_2 have to be performed.

The total estimated cost for a synchronizing workflow operation is in the best case

$t_{best} = tc_{local} * (c_1 + c_3*m + n*c_2) + t(op)$
(for non-synchronizing operations: $t_{best} = tc_{local} * (c_1 + n*c_2) + t(op)$)

and in the worst case

$t_{worst} = tc_{wan} * (c_1 + c_3*m^2 + n*c_2) + t(op)$
(for non-synchronizing operations: $t_{worst} = tc_{wan} * (c_1 + n*c_2) + t(op)$)

This means that partitioning is better than remote access, if the physical proximity of the partition servers to the users outweighs the additional effort for synchronizing the partitions. As long as all users eligible to execute a workflow are approximately at the same location and there are no synchronizing dependencies, this assumption is surely fulfilled. The example shown in Fig. 3 however, is a hard scenario for workflow partitioning: partition p_2 and p_3 are at different locations and contain concurrent subworkflows, which have to be synchronized. 'Stock market trade' can be performed by brokers at different geographic locations and communication over WAN cannot be avoided.

Subworkflow Distribution Combined with Remote Access

The costs for the execution of a workflow operation using this execution strategy are:

1. Communication from worklist to the server: $t_1 = c_1 * \{tc_{local}, tc_{wan}\}$.
2. If the operation has to be synchronized with the father, a message is sent to the father's server: $t_2 = c_3 * \{tc_{local}, tc_{wan}\}$; we assume that the size of the synchronization message is comparable to the one used in section .
3. Performance of the operation, i.e., the part at the local server plus the part at the father, amounts to $t_3 \cong t(op)$.
4. The closing modifications of the worklists require $t_4 = n * c_2 * \{tc_{local}, tc_{wan}\}$, if n worklist updates with size c_2 have to be performed.

Consequently, a workflow operation which needs synchronization causes in the best case a total cost of

$$t_{best} = tc_{local} * (c_1 + c_3 + n*c_2) + t(op)$$

and in the worst case a total cost of

$$t_{worst} = tc_{wan} * (c_1 + c_3 + n*c_2) + t(op).$$

This shows that subworkflow distribution will in general perform better than partitioning of workflows for synchronizing workflow operations. If we reach good locality of the selected workflow servers with respect to the users it will also beat the plain remote server approach. However, there is one (minor) drawback: need for synchronization in subworkflow distribution is a property of a workflow operation. These operations will always cause a message to be sent to the father, even if it is not required because of the structure of the father workflow. In this case workflow partitioning is better because it does not send messages for operations within a partition. In the following section, the performance behavior of the various algorithms is discussed in more detail.

4.2 Discussion

Tab. 3 summarizes the estimated costs of a workflow operations execution for the combination workflow partitioning + remote access, and the combination subworkflow distribution + remote access. Pure remote access is not included, because this strategy has severe scalability limitations (section 3.3); Migration is not considered because there is no application-independent scheme to assign a fraction of the migration costs to a single workflow operation (see section 4.1).

Algorithm	Best case	Worst case
Workflow partitioning + remote access	$t_{best} = tc_{local} *(c_1 + c_3*m + n*c_2)+t(op)$ (non-synchronizing operations: $t_{best} = tc_{local} * (c_1 + n*c_2) + t(op)$)	$t_{worst} = tc_{wan} *(c_1 + c_3*m^2 + n*c_2)+ t(op)$ (for non-synchronizing operations: $t_{worst} = tc_{wan} * (c_1 + n*c_2) + t(op)$)
Subworkflow distribution + remote access	$t_{best} = tc_{local} * (c_1 + c_3 + n*c_2) + t(op)$	$t_{worst} = tc_{wan} * (c_1 + c_3 + n*c_2) + t(op)$

Tab. 3 Summary of costs per workflow operation

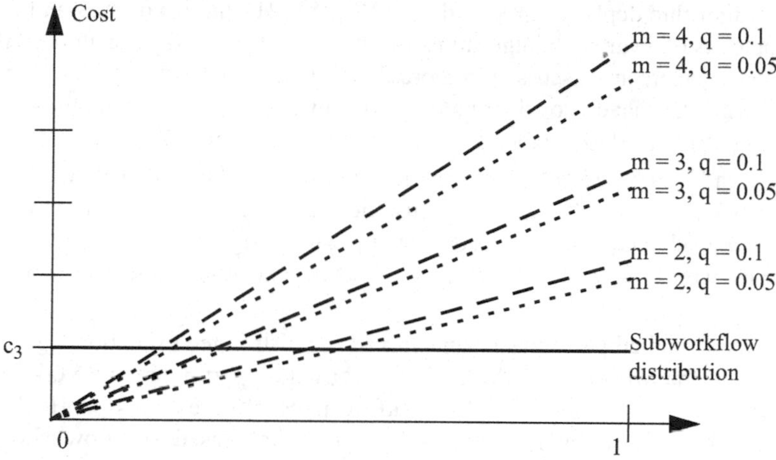

Fig. 4 Estimated Cost per Workflow Operation in Specific Application Situations

If we look at the costs depicted in Tab. 3, it is obvious that both variants differ only in the effort for synchronizing the workflow partitions in the first case and synchronizing with the father in the second case. For workflow partitioning, this results to the term c_3*m (best case) or c_3*m^2 (worst case) if synchronization is needed, otherwise the additional cost is 0. Subworkflow distribution has a constant distribution overhead of c_3 for operations that potentially need to be synchronized, like the start operation of a workflow. In contrast to workflow partitioning, in subworkflow distribution a server performing an operation on a subworkflow cannot decide whether it needs synchronization because the server has no knowledge of the father's dependencies.

Fig. 4 illustrates the trade-off between subworkflow distribution and workflow partitioning. For simplification, we estimate the expected cost for an operation using the partitioning strategy is: $p * ((1-q)*c_3*m + q*c_3*m^2)$ where p is the fraction of workflow operations that need synchronization, q is the probability for the worst case to happen, and m is the number of partitions to be synchronized. I.e., we neglect the cases where the cost for partitioning is between the best and the worst case. Nevertheless, Fig. 4 shows that the cost for workflow partitioning grows enormously, if the workflow specification requires a lot of synchronization either because of synchronizing control flow or because subworkflows concurrently access data of the father workflow.

5 Related Work

Although many commercial and academic WfMS deal with distribution, there is only few work that analyzes distribution strategies in some detail and/or compares different strategies for distributed workflows execution. [7], [19], and [21] concentrate on the behavior of an algorithm deployed in a particular WfMS; [21] and [6] discuss and compare the properties of a variety of algorithms for distributed workflow execution. In the following, these papers are discussed in more detail. Other approaches [3, 16, 4, 5, 7, 10, 11, 14, 22, 26, 25] that deploy distributed workflow execution but do not provide an analysis have been related to the four basic algorithms in section 3.3.

The work in [7] is based on a workflow migration algorithm and deals with overloading of subnets by a WfMS. Workflow instances are migrated between servers located in different subnets to balance load. The approach is tightly coupled with the assumed ADEPT workflow model. Alternative workflow execution models are not considered.

[22] shows a detailed performance analysis of the distributed execution algorithm for workflows in the MENTOR WfMS, which is based on partitioning of workflows. Several alternatives for synchronizing the workflow partitions are discussed. However, the result are tightly coupled with the activity and state chart based workflow model of MENTOR. Other distributed execution models besides partitioning are not discussed.

Several architectures to implement the METEOR workflow model are presented in [21], starting with a centralized architecture and ending with a fully distributed architecture. The properties of these architectures are discussed in detail. A comparison of the approaches based on a cost estimation is not provided. In addition, the impact of the METEOR workflow model on the behavior of the architecture variants has not been considered in the discussion.

A comprehensive classification of distributed WfMS architectures and a simulation of their behavior is presented in [6]. In contrast to our approach, [6] does not provide basic algorithms from which the existing algorithms can be derived by combination. The simulation is based on particular workflow examples and focuses on the resulting load in the WfMS components. The impact of workflow model on the performance of the algorithms not covered.

6 Conclusion

Distributed workflow execution is a mandatory feature for WfMS. Based on a comprehensive list of requirements which have to be fulfilled by a distributed WfMS we have introduced four basic strategies for the distributed workflow execution. It turns out that subworkflow distribution is an algorithm that is best for general-purpose WfMS with a workflow model containing modeling primitives that require the synchronization of subworkflows, like the *MOBILE* workflow model [17]. Application-specific WfMS or workflow models that do not contain synchronizing primitives, e.g., WebSphere MQ Workflow's workflow model [16] and email-based workflow approaches, can be enacted more efficiently, if a partitioning strategy is deployed for the workflow execution. However, if a WfMS installation is used in a heterogeneous environment subworkflow distribution is a must, because this is the only distributed workflow execution algorithm that can tolerate heterogeneous workflow servers.

References

[1] Andrews, T., Curbera F., Dholakia, H., Goland, Y., Klein, J., Leymann, F., Liu, K., Roller, D., Smith, D., Thatte, S., Trickovic, I., Weerawarana, S.: *Business Process Execution Language for Web Services.* Version 1.1. 2003

[2] Alonso, G., Agrawal, D., El Abbadi, A., Mohan, C.: Functionality and Limitations of Current Workflow Management Systems. In: *IEEE Expert, Special Issue on Cooperative Information Systems*, 1997

[3] Alonso, G., Kamath, M., Agrawal, D., El Abbadi, A., Günthör, R., Mohan, C.: Failure Handling in Large Scale Workflow Management Systems. *Technical Report, IBM Almaden Research Center*, 1994

[4] Alonso, G., Mohan, C., Günthör, R., Agrawal, D., El Abbadi, A., Kamath, M.: Exotica/FMQM: A Persistent Message-Based Architecture for Distributed Workflow Management. In: *Proc. IFIP Working Conference on Information Systems for Decentralized Organzations*, Trondheim, 1995

[5] Barbara, D., Mehrotra, S., Rusinkiewicz, M.: INCAs: Managing Dynamic Workflows in Distributed Environments. In: *Journal of Database Management, Special Issue on Multidatabases*, 7(1), 1996

[6] Bauer, T., Dadam, P.: Verteilungsmodelle für Workflow-Management-Systeme - Klassifikation und Simulation. *Ulmer Informatik-Berichte*, Nr. 99-02, Universität Ulm, 1999

[7] Bauer, T., Reichert, M.: Dynamic Change of Server Assignments in Distributed Workflow Management Systems. In: *Proc. 6th Int'l Conf. Enterprise Information Systems (ICEIS'04)*, Volume 1, Porto, 2004

[8] *Bea Weblogic Integration.* Version 8.1, http://www.bea.com/framework.jsp?CNT=index.htm&FP=/content/products/integrate/, 2005.

[9] Bußler, C.: *Organisationsverwaltung in Workflow-Management-Systemen.* Dissertation, Universität Erlangen-Nürnberg, 1997

[10] Cichocki, A., Rusinkiewicz, M.: Migrating Workflows. In: Dogac, A. ; Kalinichenko, L. ; Ozsu, T. ; Sheth, A. (Eds.): *Advances in Workflow Management Systems and Interoperability.* NATO ASI Series F, Springer Verlag, 1998

[11] Das, S., Kochut, K., Miller, J., Sheth, A., Worah, D.: ORBWork: A Reliable Distributed CORBA-based Workflow Enactment System for METEOR2. *Technical Report UGA-CS-TR-97-001*, Department of Computer Science, University of Georgia, 1997

[12] Deiters, W., Gruhn, V.: The FUNSOFT Net Approach to Software Process Management. In: *International Journal of Software Engineering and Knowledge Engineering*, 4, 1994

[13] Georgakopoulos, D., Hornick, M.F., Shet, A.: An Overview of Workflow Management: From Process Modeling to Workflow Automation Infrastructure. In: *Distributed and Parallel Databases*, 3, 1995

[14] Gokkoca, E., Altinel, M., Cingil, I., Tatbul, E.N., Koksal, P., Dogac, A.: Design and Implementation of a Distributed Workflow Enactment Service. In: *Proc. Int. Conf. on Cooperative Information Systems*, Charleston, 1997

[15] Gray, J., Edwards, J.: Scale Up with TP Monitors. In: *Byte*, April 1995

[16] *IBM WebSphere MQ Workflow.* http://www-306.ibm.com/software/integration/wmqwf/, IBM, 2005

[17] Jablonski, S., Bußler, C.: *Workflow Management - Modeling Concepts, Architecture and Implementation.* International Thomson Computer Press, 1996

[18] Jablonski, S., Böhm, M., Schulze, W. (Hrsg.): *Workflow-Management: Entwicklung von Anwendungen und Systemen - Facetten einer neuen Technologie.* dpunkt Verlag, 1997

[19] Jin, L., Casati, F., Sayal, M., Shan, M.-C.: Load Balancing in Distributed Workflow Management System, Proceedings of the 2001 ACM symposium on Applied computing, 2001

[20] Kamath, M., Alonso, G., Günthör, R., Mohan, C.: Providing High Availability in Very Large Workflow Management Systems. In: *Proc. 5th Int. Conference on Extending Database Technology*, Avignon, 1996

[21] Miller, J.A., Sheth, A.P., Kochut, K.J. ; Wang, X.: CORBA-Based Run-Time Architectures for Workflow Management Systems. In: *Journal of Database Management, Special Issue on Multidatabases*, 7(1), 1996

[22] Muth, P., Wodtke, D., Weissenfels, J., Kotz Dittrich, A., Weikum, G.: From Centralized Workflow Specification to Distributed Workflow Execution. In: *JIIS - Special Issue on Workflow Managament*, 10(2), 1998

[23] *Oracle BPEL Process Manager.* http://www.oracle.com/appserver/bpel_home.html, Oracle, 2005

[24] *Oracle Workflow.* Developer's Guide, Version 2.6.3, http://download-west.oracle.com/docs/cd/B14117_01/workflow.101/b10283/toc.htm, Oracle, 2005

[25] Schuster H.: *Architektur verteilter Workflow-Management-Systeme.* DISDBIS 50, Infix, 1998

[26] Schuster, H., Neeb, J., Schamburger, R.: A Configuration Management Approach for Large Workflow Management Systems. In: *Proc. Int. Joint Conference on Work Activities Coordination and Collaboration (WACC'99)*, San Francisco, February, 1999

[27] Schuster, H., Neeb, J., Schamburger, R.: Using Distributed Object Middleware to Implement Scalable Workflow Management Systems. In: *Journal of Integrated Design & Process Science*, 1999

[28] Sheth, A., Kochut, K.J.: Workflow Applications to Research Agenda: Scalable and Dynamic Work Coordination and Collaboration Systems. In: *Proc. of the NATO ASI on Workflow Management Systems and Interoperability*, Istambul, 1997

[29] Singh, M.P.: Formal Aspects of Workflow Management - Part 1: Semantics. *Technical Report*, Department of Computer Science, North Carolina State University, June, 1997

[30] Weissenfels, J., Muth, P., Weikum, G.: Flexible Worklist Management in a Light-Weight Workflow Management System. In: *Proc. of the EDBT Workshop on Workflow Management Systems*, Valencia, Spain, March 1998

[31] Hollingsworth, D.: *Workflow Management Coalition The Workflow Reference Model.* Workflow Management Coalition, Document Number TC00-1003, 1994

[32] Hollingsworth, D.: The Workflow Reference Model: 10 Years On. Workflow Management Coalition, 2004

[33] *Workflow Management Coalition Workflow Standard - Interoperability Abstract Specification.* Workflow Management Coalition, Document Number WFMC-TC-1012, Version 1.0, 1996

[34] *Workflow Management Coalition Terminology & Glossary.* Workflow Management Coalition, Document Number WFMC-TC-1011, Document Status - Issue 2.0, 1996

[35] *Workflow Management Coalition Workflow Client Application (Interface 2) Application Programming Interface (WAPI).* Workflow Management Coalition, Specification Document Number WFMC-TC-1009, Version 2.0e (Beta), October, 1997

Business-to-Business Integration Technology

Christoph Bussler

National University of Ireland
Digital Enterprise Research Institute (DERI)
chris.bussler@deri.org

Abstract. Business-to-Business (B2B) integration technology refers to software systems that enable the communication of electronic business events between organizations across computer networks like the Internet or specialized networks like SWIFT [19]. A typical example of business events is a *create purchase order* sent from a buyer to a seller with the intent that the seller delivers the ordered products eventually, or a *post invoice* sent from a supplier to a buyer with the intent that the buyer fulfills his obligation to pay for delivered products. Business events carry business data as such and the sender's intent about what it expects the receiver to do. As business events are mission critical for the success of private, public, and government organizations, their reliable and dependable processing and transmission is paramount.

Database technology is a platform technology that has proven to be reliable and dependable for the management of large sets of dynamic data across a huge variety of applications. In recent years, functionality beyond data management was added to database technology making it a feasible platform for business event processing in addition to data processing itself. New functionality like complex data types, audit trails, message queuing, remote message transmission or publish/subscribe communication fulfills basic requirements for business event processing and are all relevant for B2B integration technology.

This contribution investigates the use of database technology for business event processing between organizations. First, a high-level conceptual model for B2B integration is introduced that derives basic business event processing requirements. A B2B integration system architecture outline is provided that defines the B2B integration system boundaries, before specific database functionality is discussed as implementation technology for business event processing. Some future trends as well as some proposals for extended database functionality is presented as a conclusion of this chapter.

T. Härder and W. Lehner (Eds.): Data Management (Wedekind Festschrift), LNCS 3551, pp. 235-254, 2005.

1 Business Events

The core concept of B2B integration is the business event. It is the main element of concern and all other concepts are subordinate to it. An organization that communicates with another organization has to define which business events are communicated and in which order they are sent by it or are expected to be received by it from the partner organization. The business event is therefore the main carrier of the communication semantics between organizations.

A B2B integration architecture is the system conception for executing business event communication between organizations over networks. It also has to connect to the organization internal business application systems. This is important, because business application systems manage the business data that are communicated through business events by the B2B integration technology.

This initial section introduces both, the concepts of B2B integration with business events as the main concept as well as a B2B integration architecture overview.

1.1 Concepts

The main concepts are introduced in this section in more detail. Based on these concepts the B2B integration architecture is introduced that will be the basis for discussion how database technology can implement its components. In [3], the conceptual model of B2B integration is described in a lot more detail and so is the corresponding B2B integration architecture.

Business Event. The main concept of B2B integration is the business event which has a name, an intent, and carries business data. For example, *create purchase order* is a name of a business event. That name by itself indicates the intent *create* and the business data that are carried by it *purchase order*. When defining a business event, it is mandatory that all necessary business data are included so that the recipient of the business event can fulfill the intent by executing an appropriate business function.

For example, in case of creating a purchase order the intent of the buyer is to receive certain goods by a certain time for a specific price and a given quality, amongst other properties. The supplier executes a business function that either determines that it can deliver the products as specified by the *create purchase order* event, that it can deliver the ordered products with different parameters from those defined (for example, the delivery will be later as requested), or it cannot deliver those at all. Whatever the outcome of the business function is, it returns an event *notify purchase order acknowledgement* that specifies the outcome of the business function for the buyer. The intent of this business event depends on the outcome. If the supplier can ship the products as ordered by the buyer, then this is a true notification. And the expectation is, that the products are going to be built and delivered as specified. If the outcome is that in principle the products can be delivered, however, with different parameters, then the buyer is expected to agree to this change or to disagree with it. If the outcome is that the supplier cannot deliver at all, the intent is again that of a notification. Implicitly, however, the buyer has to look for an alternative supplier.

It is important to note at this point that a business event is different from a message. A message is a particular data structure with an associated behavior defined by a queuing system [7]. The basic behavior of messages is enqueue, dequeue and lookup. A message does not have an intent. However, a messaging system can be used as an implementation technology to implement certain aspects of a business event. This is discussed in section 3 in more detail.

Another important note is that in real implementations of business data sometimes the intent is not explicitly defined, but has to be implicitly derived from the business data itself. For example, the existence of a *purchase order number* in a *purchase order* implies that this is an update of a purchase order rather then the creation of a new purchase order. However, for the purpose of the discussion in this chapter, this difference is not essential and therefore not further called out in the following discussion.

Party. As the purchase order example has shown, the involved organizations are identified organizations and not anonymous organizations. For example, a buyer directs the business event to a specific supplier and the supplier responds back to the buyer that sent the business event. A business event, therefore, is directed at one target organization (called party in the following). A party is an organization that can send and receive business events. In general, a party does not send and receive arbitrary business events but only those that are vital and important for its business. For those business events that it receives it implements the intent in form of a business function.

A business event can be directed at several identified parties. For example, a *request for quotation* is sent to a set of suppliers with the intent that they respond with quotes. In this case, the business event is sent to each of the named suppliers and each of the suppliers can send back a quote if it is interested in bidding for the potential order. A consequence of a quote might be the receipt of the subsequent *create purchase order,* if the quote was the best from the viewpoint of the buyer.

Because a business event is sent by a party, it has a particular party as source. In summary, each business event has one source party and one or many target parties.

Process Management. As above examples of a purchase order or quotation process have shown, there is a business event conversation going on between two or more parties. It is important that this conversation follows particular rules so that the conversation terminates successfully. The rules are that each party needs to send the business events that the other party expects and that the intent is executed correctly. This conversation itself has to be modeled and the means for this is a choreography.

A choreography of a party defines the business events it is going to send, the business events that it is going to expect and their relative order or sequence. Because each party has a choreography, it can be determined whether or not the choreographies match and the conversation derives to a successful end. A perfect match is given if all possible conversations of the involved choreographies terminate. Each possible execution path has to match in the sense that all business events sent by a party have to be received by the other party and vice versa. If there is a business event sent, but the other party does not expect it, then this is the case of a mismatch and the choreographies will not work (at least not for this case).

For example, after sending a *create purchase order* event a *notify purchase order acknowledgment* event is expected. While this is a simple conversation, the buyer and the supplier both have a choreography. The buyer sends a *create purchase order* first and then expects a *notify purchase order acknowledgment*. The supplier has the complementary choreography. First, it expects a *create purchase order* and after executing the appropriate business function returns a *notify purchase order acknowledgment*.

While the choreography defines the conversation on a per-party basis, sometimes more then one party is involved overall. In this case, another concept applies that deals with more than one party. For example, if the notify purchase order acknowledgment event says that the supplier will not deliver the products; another supplier has to be found subsequently. In general this finding of a new supplier requires communication with other parties through appropriate choreographies. That overall process involving several choreographies is implemented by orchestration.

Orchestration implements business logic by defining how several parties are involved in the communication, each with its own choreography. Orchestration 'orchestrates' several parties in order to achieve a final outcome.

As a note, it is important to point out that application systems are in general the location of business logic. Business events that are sent out by a party usually originate in application systems and business events that are received are usually forwarded to application systems. This requires the B2B integration system to connect to the application systems in order to make this communication happen. In section 2.1, we discuss the connectivity with application systems in more detail and show how this is achieved in general.

Data Mediation. When parties are communicating with each other by means of business events they basically send data to each other. In the general case, each party has its own conceptualization of its business data. For example, a buyer identifies its products and product parts in its way. This might include part numbers and other identifiers. A supplier does the same, it defines the parts it can supply in its way. When a buyer orders parts, the question arises how the buyer communicates with the seller. Does it use its own way of identifying the supplier's parts or the way the supplier identifies its parts? When there are different conceptualizations, a mismatch exists that requires resolution.

The concept that achieves this resolution of data mismatch is called data mediation. Data mediation defines the transformation rules necessary to ensure that the source and the target party send and receive business events in their conceptualization. This is achieved by intercepting each business event sent by the source party and transforming it into the business event as understood by the target party. In the easiest case, both are identical and this is possible, if source and target party have the exactly same conceptualization. If they differ, then the transformation rules ensure that the difference is bridged.

For example, the source party might have three different attributes to identify a part that it wants to order from a supplier. The supplier, however, has only one attribute containing the same information. In order to establish semantic equivalence, the transformation rules have to take the three attributes and derive the value of the one attribute. After this is done the buyer and supplier semantically understand each other, while the data representations in the business events are different.

The conceptualization of a party is called the internal conceptualization and the data is in the internal data format. The conceptualization of a remote party is called external conceptualization and the data format is called the external data format. Transformation rules therefore ensure that there is a way to transform the internal to the external data format without changing the semantics of the data in case of an outbound event (i.e., one that is sent out to an organization). In the case of an inbound event, the opposite transformation happens.

External data formats are often implemented by B2B standards like EDI [2] or RosettaNet [17]. In case a party uses a B2B standard, it decided not to define and implement its own proprietary format, but to follow a standardized one that is shared across many organizations. While B2B standards play an important roles in the business world [4] they are not relevant for the subsequent discussion as the B2B integration concepts and architecture can deal with any format, proprietary or standardized.

Process Mediation. As data formats can mismatch between parties, so can choreographies. Two choreographies might not be directly complementary in themselves. For example, a party might send back one *notify purchase order acknowledgment* while the other party expects one for each line item in the original *create purchase order*. There is no direct match; however, in principle all the data necessary for a direct match are being communicated. In this example, it is possible that a mediator splits the one *notify purchase order acknowledgment* business event into as many as there are line items. After this transformation the choreographies match.

This transformation is called process mediation as the number and order of business events are changed between two choreographies in order to make them match. The concept of process mediation is fairly new and not a lot of research results are available yet. Therefore, it will not receive further discussion in the reminder of the chapter.

1.2 Non-functional Requirements

In addition to the concepts that define the functionality of a B2B integration system, there are non-functional aspects. These are listed briefly in the following.

- **Status**. At any point in time it must be possible to determine the status of a business event as well as all other business events related to it through choreography and orchestration, i.e., the current state of execution.
- **History**. At any point in time it must be possible to see the history of the execution up to a given point. This is interesting in order to figure out the path of execution one or several business events took. Sometimes the history allows determining the cause of failures after they happened as it can show what data has been sent around and which parties have been involved.

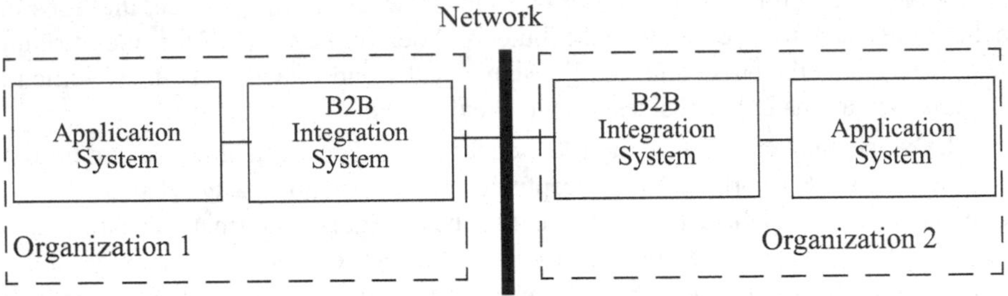

Fig. 1 Overall System Placement

- **Security**. Security is an important aspect of B2B integration. Communication must be secret between parties so that no unauthorized and unauthenticated party can participate or even just listen to the data sent. In addition, non-repudiation, authentication, as well as authorization play a big role in system security.
- **Business Data Context**. When business events are executed, application systems access business data. In order to after-the-fact of execution understand decisions that have been taken it is necessary to capture the state of business data at that point in time. This means that for example exchange rates, or schedules are available or recorded into history so that they can be accessed later on for inspection.
- **Reporting**. Reporting is an important functionality for organizations. All the history data of a B2B integration system must be available so that reports like the number of business events processed or the number of failures encountered can be established and executed.

1.3 System Overview

B2B integration technology is the enabler of communication between organizations. In addition, it needs to extract and insert business events into application systems. Fig. 1 shows the overall system placement of application systems, B2B integration systems, organizations, as well as networks in order to provide an overview.

An organization has a B2B integration system for communication and at least one application system. Both are integrated as the vertical line in the figure indicates. Organizations communicate business events over networks by means of their B2B integration systems. A network is represented as a vertical bar and the fact that the two B2B integration systems communicate is indicated by the vertical line between them that crosses the network.

This system arrangement is assumed throughout the remainder of this chapter.

2 B2B Integration Technology Architecture

This section introduces a generic and common software architecture for B2B integration systems. The architecture is generic in the sense that it establishes a generic system boundary. It defines the input and output behavior of the system from an architectural viewpoint. Furthermore, it contains all necessary internal software components in order to address all the business event execution requirements outlined in the previous section.

The generic system architecture abstracts from specific architecture choices and implementation decisions that the various existing vendor products as well as research prototypes have had to make. It does not make any implementation-specific prescriptions. These concrete B2B integration systems are usually implemented with a specific implementation philosophy in mind and, hence, they might vary significantly in implementation details. On a more abstract level, however, their architecture and system boundaries are very similar to the presented generic and common software architecture. It therefore can represent them accurately.

This section will start with defining the B2B integration system boundary in a defined architecture context. Afterwards the architecture components are introduced followed by a discussion of how the architecture executes specific business events involving the various architecture components.

2.1 Architecture Context

B2B integration technology is not a stand-alone software system. Instead, it interfaces with two distinct type of systems, namely data communication software and application systems. Data communication software supports the remote communication over data networks and, through it, B2B integration technology supports the data communication with remote organizations. Application systems like Enterprise Resource Planning (ERP) systems manage enterprise data. B2B integration technology must interface with application systems for extracting data that require transmission as well as inserting data after receipt from other cooperating organizations.

Each piece of communication software and each application system in general has a different application programming interface for accessing it. For example, some provide a set of methods, some a queuing interface, some a standard interface following the J2EE Connector Architecture [9] and so on. Interfacing with communication software as well as application systems means therefore that for each new network and each new application software an adapter has to be built that bridges their interface with the interfaces of the B2B integration technology. This is not a once-off development for all application systems or all communication software, but requires a special implementation for every new communication software or application system that needs to be integrated.

From an architectural viewpoint the question arises whether these adapters that are part of the overall context are considered part of the overall B2B integration system ar-

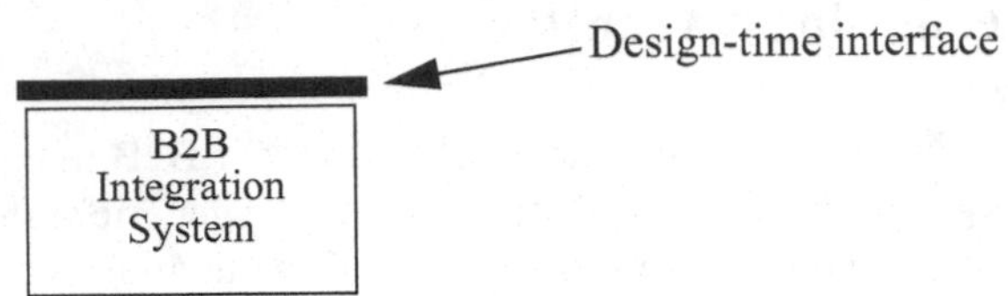

Fig. 2 Design-Time Interface

chitecture or whether they are outside the architecture and are seen as components external to it (and consequently are not part of the architecture discussion).

An argument to exclude them is that these are 'auxiliary' components that do not provide business event functionality itself but provide infrastructure to connect to existing software components required for communication with networks and application systems. Furthermore, depending on the number of networks and application systems, the number of these auxiliary components can be quite high causing the architecture to expand significantly over time.

While these are compelling arguments to exclude adapters, a different choice was made. In the following they are included in the architecture. The reason for including them is that database technology exists that can implement this adaptation functionality for specific cases of application systems and communication networks directly. In order to be able to use this native database functionality, these components are included in the B2B integration technology architecture.

2.2 System Boundary

B2B integration systems in general provide two different types of functionality. One is design-time functionality and the other one is run-time functionality. Both of these require different application programming interfaces as the objects that are passed through these interfaces are different: types and instances, respectively. The design-time interface and the run-time interface together define the overall B2B integration system boundary.

The design-time interface provides functionality for managing the definition data (types) of B2B integration concepts as introduced in section 1. For example,

- creating a new business event definition
- deleting an existing business event definition
- updating an existing business event definition or
- creating a new version of an existing business event definition

are all part of the design-time interface. Fig. 2 shows an abstraction of the design-time interface of the B2B integration system. The B2B integration system is represented as a self-contained 'box' that contains all functionality including any data storage facility necessary. The design-time interface is represented as a black bar. It provides the application programming interface (API) that can be accessed by various modeling user in-

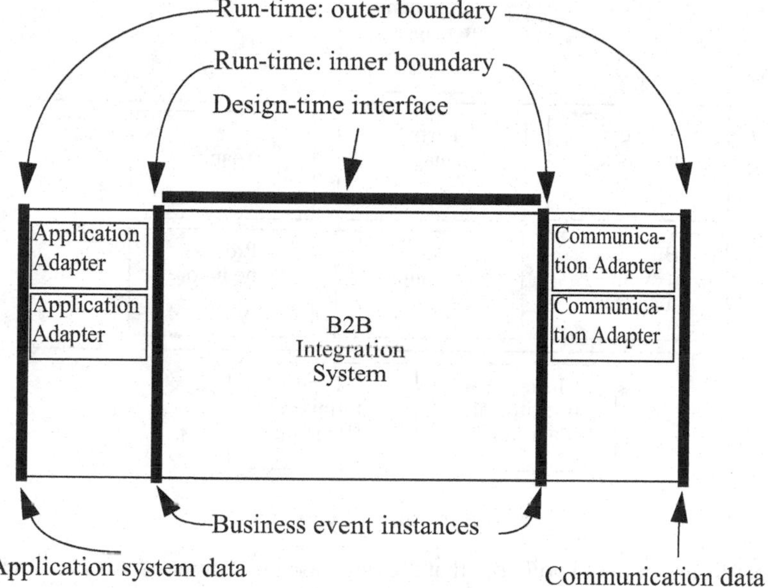

Fig. 3 Run-Time Interfaces, Inner and Outer Boundary

terface tools in order to provide designers an appropriate access to the B2B integration system.

The run-time boundary of the B2B integration system is multi-layered. The inner boundary is providing and receiving business event instances. The outer boundary is communicating to the APIs of the application systems and the communication components for the various networks. The object instances of the outer boundary are defined by the communication software or application systems that are connected to the B2B integration technology through adapters. Fig. 3 shows the graphical representation (that also includes the design-time interface for clarification). The components between the inner and outer boundary are adapters. By convention, the left side of the graphical representation is connecting to application systems whereas the right side is connecting to other organizations via networks. This is a convention in order to keep the interpretation of the figures uniform. In consequence, application adapters and communication components are shown on the left and right side, respectively.

By implication, application adapters 'mediate' between the application system interface and the business event interface. In analogy, communication adapters are mediating between the business event interface and the communication software interface communicating data as required by remote organizations. In both cases, 'mediation' means that syntactical serialization might have to be rewritten, for example, from a Java API of an application system to an XML representation of business event instances. On the network communication side, it might be a mediation for example between the XML serialization of the business event instances to EDI [2].

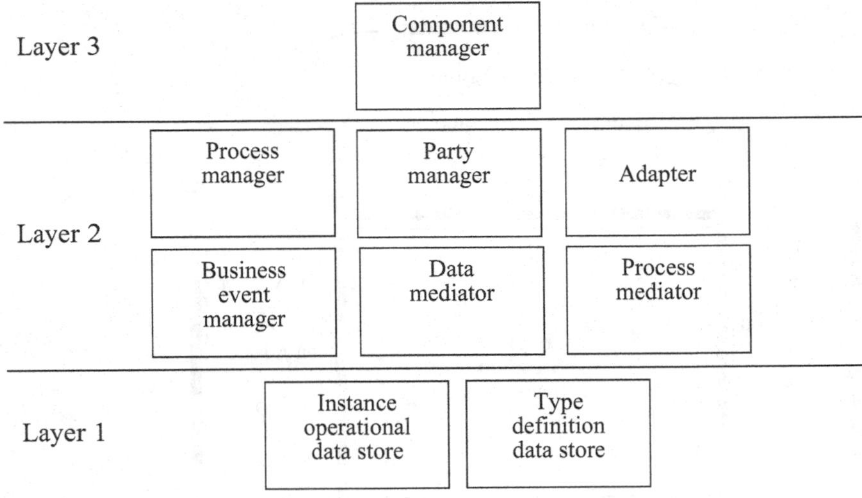

Fig. 4 Architecture Layers

As a note, it is important to point out that the database as a component is considered to be within the system boundary of the B2B integration system. In many architecture representations, databases are placed outside the system boundary. However, here the view is supported that the database technology is yet another component in the set of all components of the B2B integration system. The architectural components are discussed next.

2.3 Architecture Components

The B2B integration system architecture is a layered architecture. Each layer provides a specific functionality the layer above it can use to implement its functionality. The layers and their architectural components are shown in Fig. 4 and discussed next.

- Layer 1. This layer consists of two components, an instance operational data store and a type definition data store. The instance operational data store stores all instance data like business event instances, process instances, and so on. It is optimized for instance processing in the sense that throughput and performance are key criteria. The definition data store contains the definition data necessary to run the system. This includes business event definitions, process definition, party definitions, and so on. Both stores provide of course basic functionality like transactions, save points, backup, and retention. The definition data store might in addition provide versioning and variant management functionality and design staging, i.e., functionality especially relevant for design activities.
- Layer 2. This layer consists of components that implement the specific B2B functionality. This includes a business event manager, a data mediator, a process mediator, process management for choreography and orchestration as well as party man-

agement. These components interact with layer 1 in order to provide their functionality. For each concept described in section 1.1, a separate component is introduced that encapsulates the specific functionality. Adapters fall also in this layer and as discussed previously, the number of adapters depends directly on the number of networks and application systems.

- Layer 3. This layer introduces a management component that invokes the components of layer 2 in the appropriate order in order to execution business events. It passes context and identification information around in order to ensure proper relationship between the data in processing.

2.4 Execution Model

The execution model of the B2B integration system architecture is fixed in the sense that all business events are executed in the same way and therefore all components are invoked in the same order. Data enters and leaves the system through adapters to either application systems or networks. Adapters establish the outer system boundary.

The inbound processing works as follows. When data comes in, it first is checked whether or not the source and target parties are known and correct by invoking the party manager component. Afterwards the data mediator and the process mediator is invoked in order to derive to the correct business events. This establishes the inner system boundary.

At this point, the process manager advances any choreography and/or orchestration that is under execution in order to establish that the business event matches. At this point, a correct business event has been received and it now has to be passed on to a network or an application system depending on the target party.

The outbound processing works very similar. In order to send out a business event the same functionality as in the inbound case is invoked, however, in the opposite order. First, the process manager advances choreographies and orchestration as needed. Then data and process mediators are invoked in order to transform the business event into the external format. The transformed data is passed on to the appropriate adapters as required to communicate with the target party.

3 Database Support for B2B Integration Technology

Database technology provides quite an impressive array of functionality today that can implement directly some of the components outlined in the previous section. This is shown in the following by mapping components of the generic and common architecture components to database technology functionality.

However, some of the functionality required for business event processing cannot be directly implemented with today's database technology and a discussion follows that outlines the missing functionality. If this functionality were available, the complete business event processing could be directly implemented in a database and the complete B2B integration technology could be mapped to a pure database implementation.

3.1 Component Implementation

This section lists the components of the B2B integration system as introduced in section 2.3 that can be implemented directly with native database functionality. A brief discussion is included to show a possible concrete way. As it will turn out, some of the database functionality can be used for the implementation of several different components. Components that cannot be implemented with native database technology directly or only in part are still mentioned for completeness reasons.

Instance Operational Data Store and Type Definition Data Store. These two components are 'classical' database functionality: processing large sets of data. For instance data as well as type data, a data model has to be developed and then implemented as a database schema. The type definition store typically holds the definition of business events, choreographies, orchestrations, and all the other definition data that is required to establish a complete definition of B2B integration, including the identification of the participating organizations.

The instance operational data store holds the instance of the concepts like business events or choreographies. As the execution progresses the instance data is updated accordingly. In addition, this store needs to provide, besides the current execution status, also the history of all executions so that at any point in time it is possible to query all past executions. Again, native database technology can capture history through various means like, for example, avoiding update in place but additive status change. Whenever an instance changes, instead of changing the data representation in place, a new entry is created with the new status data. An alternative way are triggers that write history information on updates of the instance data.

Business Event Manager. The business event manager is implementing the business event functionality. Business events are received as well as sent by the B2B integration technology. This behavior can be implemented with queues where business events are represented as messages. A receipt of a business event results in an enqueue of an equivalent message, whereas the sending of a business event is the result of a dequeue. In this sense, the implementation can be achieved with native database functionality [13].

Component Manager. The component manager in layer 3 is steering all the components of layer 2 of the architecture in such a way that they are invoked in the order necessary to execute business events. The component manager has to pass identifiers to the components in order for them to retrieve the appropriate instances from the instance operational store. These instances are then executed on, whatever the component requires to do. Once a component finishes its task, it reports back to the component manager that it is done and it also returns relevant identifier information. This is then picked up by the component manager to make a decision which component has to work next. This is a 'classical' processing cycle that can be found in many architectures.

Implementing this invocation sequence can be achieved by using queues [13] combined with publish/subscribe technology [15]. Whenever a component is done with processing, it puts a message on a queue with the corresponding identification data in the message body. Components that subsequently have to process that data next subscribe to these messages. Once the subscription applies the appropriate component is notified, it then can dequeue the message and start processing. After processing the result is put on the queue as a message again and the cycle starts over.

At any point in time the messages on the queue reflect the overall system processing status. If the messages are retained, the temporal processing history can be retrieved and analyzed. As queues are persistent and transactional, no further effort has to be spent making the system reliable.

Adapter. Compared to the components discussed so far, adapters are not that straight forward to implement with native database technology. The reason is that interfaces of software components can follow many different approaches and not all of them are known to a database. For example, if an application system follows the J2EE Connector Architecture standard [9] then the database does not have a chance to connect to this natively as it does not implement this standard. However, there are some interfaces that a database can connect to directly and those are discussed in the following. This is an example where database technology can implement a component of the B2B integration architecture to some extent, but not completely. The missing required functionality in this case has to be implemented outside the database management system.

- Messaging interface. If the application system or communication software component has a messaging interface, then the database can directly enqueue or dequeue from the queues provided by the application system or communication software component. A native implementation is achieved easily here.
- Messaging communication. In the special case where the remote organization implements a message queue, the database can connect directly to it over the network. No adapter is required in this case and the native database functionality covers the complete communication functionality [13].
- Interface tables. Some systems to be integrated implement their interface as so-called interface tables. Interface tables belong to the database schema of the system to be integrated and contain the data that the system provides and provide a place where data can be put to pass it to the system. In this case, native querying functionality is sufficient to connect and this way the B2B integration system can adapt natively.
- Stored procedures. Some systems that require integration provide stored procedures as interfaces. The communication with the system is achieved by the B2B integration architecture calling stored procedures provided by the system to be integrated. Because a database can call stored procedures this is straightforward to implement.

In summary, there are several possibilities for a database to connect to application systems or communication software using database native functionality. This is especially simple if those use the same database technology from the same vendor. If a database from a different vendor is used, then it might or might not be possible to follow the same approach. Some databases provide access to competitive products seamlessly and in this case it works, too. Otherwise, the traditional way must be followed, i.e., the adapter functionality is implemented outside the database.

Party Manager. Databases have natively user management functionality built in. With the integration of directory services more expressive user management is possible. In the simplest case, each party is represented as a user with its credentials and hence the party management can be implemented natively through the given database functionality.

If the functionality needed in a specific implementation of B2B integration technology exceeds the provided functionality, then an external implementation might be necessary.

Process Manager. Database management systems' origin is data processing, not workflow processing. Therefore process management functionality cannot be found as a general functionality as such that is native to a database management system. However, with the advent of publish / subscribe functionality [15] it is possible to implement a subset of process management functionality directly.

- Sequencing. One important process functionality is sequencing of tasks. It is possible to sequence tasks by coordinating them through queues. Once one task is finished it places its result in a queue. The next task picks up the data from a queue and therefore sequential processing is achieved.
- Conditional branching. Conditional processing can be achieved through publish / subscribe functionality. A subscription can examine the attributes of a message body and decide wether the message is applicable. A task subscribing to a message can therefore decide which messages are relevant—this is conditional behavior.
- Broadcasting. Broadcasting out data to many subscribers is possible. The example is the *request for quotation*. The request needs to be sent to many organizations. This can be directly implemented through multi-consumer queues where one message can be consumed by many recipients. The subscription in this case would ensure that all recipients are subscribed and consequently will send the message to those.

In summary, the process manager is a component that in part can natively be implemented through database technology. Other functionality has to be implemented outside of it.

Process Mediator and **Data Mediator.** Both, process mediation and data mediation is currently outside of native database functionality. This means that this functionality has to be implemented outside the database as normal programs accessing the database.

3.2 Missing Functionality

While there is an impressive array of database functionality that can implement some of the B2B integration system components directly, some major functionality is missing in order to implement the complete set of B2B integration system components. This discussion is to some extent hypothetical as it is not clear whether the implementation of this functionality is desirable at all—from a database technology viewpoint. However, from a B2B integration technology viewpoint it is certainly interesting as its implementation would be seamless.

Business Event Mediation. As it was discussed before, data retrieved from application systems that have to be sent to remote organizations might vary significantly in their syntactical structure as well as their conceptualization of the business data content. This requires transforming the data in their syntactical form as well as their semantic conceptualization ensuring that the intended semantics is not changed whatsoever under any circumstances during transformation. Transformation rules are the mechanism that rewrites a business event in a different conceptualization.

Database technology does not implement transformation rules as a database native concept. As such, no direct support is provided by it. Instead, an implementation of the B2B integration system architecture has to implement the transformation rules 'outside' or 'on top of' the database management system in a programming language of choice.

Process Management. Choreography and orchestration are both necessary in order to define the proper integration behavior of the communicated business events between two or more organizations. While choreography supports the definition of the business event exchange between two organizations, orchestration supports the definition of the interaction order across several organizations.

Database technology does not implement process management functionality directly as database native concepts. Any process functionality required has to be implemented as programs outside the database itself (and this includes stored procedures as a very specialized programming language).

A specific exception is the multi-consumer functionality of publish/subscribe that can, for example, implement the *request for quotation* scenario. This broadcast of business events to several organizations can be natively implemented already today. However, the inverse operation, for example, that collects the *quotes* as responses of a *request for quotation* is already outside today's native database functionality.

Semantic Web Technology. The representation of business events with Semantic Web technology like ontology languages like RDF, RDFS, or OWL, and their concepts is not supported natively in database technology. As a non-proprietary format only XML is supported. However, from a conceptual viewpoint the definition of data in form of ontology language concepts like classes, relationships, and attributes is not possible in databases today. Semantic Web technology inherent concepts like subsumption or logical constraints are missing.

Adapters. Adapters are essential to connect from the inner system boundary to the outer system boundary. The outer system boundary is the interface to application systems and communication software and therefore essential for making the B2B integration possible.

Specific application systems can be interfaced with directly through database technology. For example, if the application system is a relational database itself (called application database in the following), then so-called database gateways can directly execute queries on it. This means that the adapter implementation is at the same time a client of the application database. In this case, the adapter can be directly implemented by database technology and no separate program outside the database is necessary.

The same applies if the application system presents its interface as stored procedures. Again these can be directly invoked and, also in this case, no separate adapter has to be implemented. And if the application system presents itself as a message queue the same situation exists. Here database technology can also directly implement the adapter by connecting to the message queue through its built-in message concepts.

A big caveat, however, is that different database vendors support the interoperability with competitive database products to a different extent. In a specific case when the B2B integration system is implemented with a specific database product, it might not be possible to implement adapters at all or only when the application database is from the same vendor.

General adapter support is not available natively in database systems as such and therefore adapters have to be implemented outside database technology, in general.

Transactional Remote Communication. The ultimate goal for B2B integration systems must be to provide reliable and transactional communication over any network between organizations that are engaged in B2B interaction. This is a must due to the nature of the mission-critical data that is communicated. Currently, the implementation of remote transactional communication is possible with database technology if the communicating organizations use database technology from the same vendor. Functionality like message propagation can achieve transactional and reliable communication.

Distributed transactions are possible, too, but due to the nature of B2B interactions (where one organizations does not like at all that their data resources are locked by another organization) distributed transactions are not a serious alternative.

In general, however, database technology does not provide transactional connectivity to any network that exists like SWIFT [19] or remote invocation technology like Web Services in the form of SOAP [8] and WSDL [5]. In those cases, separate communication software has to be linked to the B2B integration system to enable the communication of organizations over that specific network. And this means non-transactional and non-reliable remote communication.

4 Future Trends and Extended Database Technology

Current database technology is a very important platform for B2B integration technology. It is a proven and dependable technology, and with new functionality being incorporated continuously more and more business event requirements can be directly implemented with current database technology.

As the discussion in the previous chapter has shown, some required functionality is not yet available directly at the database interface. While it is not clear that it ever will be, this section makes the case that it would be advantageous, at least for B2B integration technology.

After the discussion of additional required database technology functionality, future trends in B2B integration technology are discussed. Areas such as Web Services as well as Semantic Web Services are currently at the stage of research investigation and first industry implementations can be found.

4.1 Extended Database Technology

The discussion of the B2B integration system architecture has shown that a variety of native database functionality is missing (see section 3.2). To summarize, this is native database technology support for

- Data transformation rules
- Semantic Web technology
- Transactional and reliable communication over any network
- Process management
- Generic adapter technology.

This additional functionality, if directly supported, would allow a completely native implementation of B2B integration technology within a database platform. The benefit would be that the complete processing would be reliable and powerful, transactional, recoverable, and backups as well as save points would be available by default. Because all definition as well as execution data would be under the management control of the database technology itself, optimization would be possible across all stages of processing. Furthermore, any future optimization work or extended functionality of the database technology would directly and immediately benefit the B2B integration functionality.

4.2 Future Trends

Two significant future trends that are related to each other are Web Services and Semantic Web Services. While Web Services are syntactic in their nature, Semantic Web

Services are emphasizing the semantic description of remote functionality and are the future of B2B integration.

Web Services. A very definitive trend for remote invocation of functionality over the Internet currently is Web Service technology. There is a general expectation that remote functionality is encapsulated and accessible through Web Services. The basic Web Service technology is a combination of the implementation of two standards, SOAP [8] and WSDL [5]. SOAP (Simple Object Access Protocol) is the definition of a message serialization layout. A message that is SOAP compliant follows this message layout definition. It consists of a header and a body. The header contains management data while the body contains the business data that is transmitted. In terms of business events, the header could carry the intent while the body of the message carries the business event data. A SOAP message is represented as an XML instance and transmitted as such. If both, sender and receiver are SOAP compliant, then both interpret the various parts of the message the same way in terms of its syntax.

WSDL (Web Service Definition Language) is a methodology for describing a server interface in terms of operations. Each operation has input and output parameters and, based on the concrete input, provides a concrete output. Operations are the way for a server to provide functionality. Operations and their details are defined in a so-called WSDL file. The specific definition of operations is expressed in XML.

The relationship between SOAP and WSDL is that in a WSDL file the operations are declared. An operation has at most one input and one output message. The message structure is defined in the WSDL file itself. A client accessing the server must ensure that the SOAP message body follows the definition of the WSDL operation's input message. After the operation is executed, the output message of the WSDL operation is sent back as a separate SOAP message to the client. In such a way, SOAP and WSDL are complementary and both are the basic Web Service functionality.

For database technology—assuming that it plans to natively support Web Services—this means that it has to provide its functionality as Web Services. Its functionality would have to be defined as WSDL operations and it could be accessed by sending it SOAP messages. In turn, if database technology wants to incorporate Web Service functionality, it must be able to send and receive SOAP messages as defined by WSDL operations.

Semantic Web Services. A more advanced approach of defining and executing remote functionality is Semantic Web Services. In this case, the service definition is described through Semantic Web technology like ontology languages instead of solely XML. Once remote functionality is described using Semantic Web Services, technology services can be searched, too, as the search terms are semantically defined. Furthermore, the semantic integration is enabled as mediation technology can make use of semantic descriptions in contrast to syntactic descriptions in 'traditional' Web Services. Transformation rules can refer to semantic concepts, relationships, and attributes ensuring that after transformation the business events have the exactly same semantics. In addition, for establishing the transformation rules, a semantic definition of the functionality helps as the concepts can be identified easily.

Currently relevant Semantic Web Service working groups are WSMO [16], WSML [21], and WSMX [22]. These efforts are established through several European Union IST projects and across several research institutes, universities, and commercial companies. The outcome of these projects is already being used and deployed in various projects like DIP [6], KW [10], ASG [1], Lion [11], and SWWS [20]. Initial industrial efforts are taking place implementing Semantic Web Services technology. Other efforts in this area are OWL-S [12] and METEOR-S [14] following different approaches.

Semantic Web Services are already being discussed in a standards effort called SWSI (Semantic Web Service Initiative) [18]. This clearly shows that there is an enormous interest as well as significant progress.

Semantic mediation is another area that receives a lot of attention currently in research projects. Here the semantic description of data is key in order to provide mediation technology that allows defining transformation rules that preserve semantics.

5 Conclusion

The current efforts of Web Services and Semantic Web Services have a potentially big impact for database technology. For database technology, this means that it has to uptake Semantic Web and Semantic Web Services technology if it wants to continue to be the implementation platform of choice for B2B integration technology in the long run. From an integration perspective, this is certainly desirable in order to fully implement B2B integration technology natively in database technology.

Acknowledgement

The personal discussion with Dieter Gawlick had significant influence in my way of thinking about database technology as a platform for B2B integration technology rather then as a pure data processing technology. I would like to acknowledge this here with appreciation.

The work is funded by the European Commission under the projects DIP, Knowledge Web, and SWWS; by Science Foundation Ireland under the DERI Lion and M3PE project.

References

[1] ASG. Adaptive Services Grid. http://asg-platform.org

[2] The Accredited Standards Committee (ASC) X12. http://www.x12.org/x12org/index.cfm

[3] Bussler, C.: *B2B Integration.* Springer-Verlag, 2003

[4] Bussler, C.: B2B Protocol Standards and their Role in Semantic B2B Integration Engines. *Bulletin of the Technical Committee on Data Engineering* 24(1): 3-11, March 2001

[5] Christensen, E., Curbera, F., Meredith, G., Weerawarana, S. (eds.): Web Services Description Language (WSDL) 1.1, W3C Note, March 2001, http://www.w3.org/TR/wsdl

[6] DIP. Data, Information and Process Integration with Semantic Web Services. European Union IST project. http://dip.semanticweb.org

[7] Gray, J., Reuter, A.: Transaction Processing: Concepts and Techniques. Morgan Kaufmann, 1993

[8] Gudgin, M., Hadley, M., Mendelsohn, N., Moreau, J.-J., Nielsen, H. F. (eds): SOAP Version 1.2 Part 1: Messaging Framework. W3C Recommendation, June 2003, http://www.w3.org/TR/soap12-part1/

[9] J2EE Connector Architecture Specification. Version 1.5. Sun Microsystems. Final Release, November 2003

[10] KW. Knowledge Web. European Union IST project. http://knowledgeweb.semanticweb.org

[11] Lion. DERI Lion. http://lion.deri.ie

[12] Martin, D., Burstein, M., Hobbs, J., Lassila, O., McDermott, D., McIlraith, S., Narayanan, S., Paolucci, M., Parsia, B., Payne, T., Sirin, E., Srinivasan, N., Sycara, K.: OWL-S: Semantic Markup for Web Services. http://www.daml.org/services/owl-s/1.1/overview/

[13] Oracle Streams. Advanced Queuing User's Guide and Reference. Release 10.1. Part No. B10785-01, December 2003

[14] Patil, A., Oundhakar, S., Sheth, A., Verma, K.: METEOR-S Web Service Annotation Framework. In: Proceeding of the 13th Conference on World Wide Web, New York, NY, July 2004, pp. 554-562

[15] Publish/Subscribe. Oracle Database. Application Developer's Guide—Fundamentals. 10*g* Release 1 (10.1), Part No. B10795-01, December 2003 (Chapter 11)

[16] Roman, D., Lausen, H., Keller, U. (eds.): D2v1.0. Web Service Modeling Ontology (WSMO) WSMO Working Draft, September 2004, http://www.wsmo.org/2004/d2/v1.0/

[17] RosettaNet. http://www.rosettanet.org

[18] Semantic Web Services Initiative (SWSI). http://www.swsi.org/

[19] S.W.I.F.T. SRCL. http://www.swift.com

[20] SWWS. Semantic Web Enabled Web Services. http://swws.semanticweb.org

[21] Web Service Modeling Language. http://www.wsmo.org/wsml/

[22] Zaremba, M. (ed.): D13.4v0.1 WSMX Architecture. WSMO Working Draft, June 2004, http://www.wsmo.org/2004/d13/d13.4/v0.1/20040622/

Part IV Application Scenarios

Information Dissemination in Modern Banking Applications

Peter Peinl, Uta Störl

Fachhochschule Fulda, Germany / Fachhochschule Darmstadt, Germany
peter.peinl@informatik.fh-fulda.de, u.stoerl@fbi.fh-darmstadt.de

Abstract. Requirements for information systems, especially in the banking and finance industry, have drastically changed in the past few years to cope with phenomena like globalization and the growing impact of financial markets. Nowadays flexibility and profitability in this segment of the economy depends on the availability of ready, actual and accurate information at the working place of every single employee. These theses are exemplified by outlining two modern real-life banking applications, each different. Their business value is founded on the rapid dissemination of accurate information in a global, distributed working environment. To succeed technically, they employ a combination of modern database, networking and software engineering concepts. One case study centers on the swift dissemination of structured financial data to hundreds of investment bankers; the other deals with the rapid dissemination of semi-structured and/or unstructured information in a knowledge retrieval context.

1 Introduction

The past decade has been characterized by the economic phenomena of globalization, a shift from production oriented industries to service oriented industries, and the ever growing importance of information technology. In particular, this has brought about a dramatic change in the attitude towards and the requirements for the information systems in the banking and financial services industries. Originally, information systems in these industries were vehicles to automate high-volume business processes (accounts, credit cards, …). Yet their complexity was low or medium. Systems of that kind were built on top of a database system, and a transaction processing monitor skilfully exploited the available computing resources to maximize throughput in terms of standardized, simple transactions. Though it is arguable, whether these types of systems still dominate the banking IT environment, certainly they still play an important role. Nowadays and even more in the future, flexibility and profitability of this segment of the economy crucially depends on the immediate availability of accurate information at the working place of every single employee. Information has undoubtedly become one of the most valuable resources in the banking industry.

T. Härder and W. Lehner (Eds.): Data Management (Wedekind Festschrift), LNCS 3551, pp. 257-276, 2005.

Due to business requirements and the rapidness of decision-making, the information technology landscape is best characterized by a high degree of heterogeneity, the physical and logical distribution of the application systems and the availability of high-end technology. From an operational perspective, demands on information system reliability, speed and accuracy are challenging. Likewise, this applies to development cycles resulting in the need for rapid development and speedy introduction of new technology and operational systems into the business environment.

We exemplify these theses by outlining two modern real-life banking applications, each representing one of a kind. Their business value is founded on the rapid dissemination of accurate information in a global, distributed working environment. Though we also point out the potential economical benefits, naturally the article focuses on technologies employed, the technical problems overcome and some lessons learnt in the process of implementing applications of that type. One case study centers on the swift dissemination of structured financial data to hundreds of investment bankers. The brokers' decisions are based on real-time data and a very specific financial calculus. From the technical and science perspective, the system makes use of a very intriguing combination of database, network and software engineering techniques. The other case study focuses on the rapid dissemination of semi-structured and/or unstructured information in a large banking environment. Its architecture as well as an integrated framework based on text mining technologies for efficient knowledge retrieval are presented. One of the key modules consists of a browsable, automatically generated semantic network, extracted from various document sources (in-house as well as external) without any need for expensive human modeling or supervision.

2 A Large Scale Real-Time System for FX Trading

2.1 Motivation

Global networks had been effecting large scale transactions between financial institutions for a long time before E-commerce or the WWW came to everyone's attention. Knowledge about the intricacies of securities and derivatives is shared among just a few professionals within each bank. The profitability of the traded products remains high as long as only few players understand their real mechanisms and implications. Striking successful deals depends on the availability of consistent and current market prices. A combination of well conceived trading strategies, the availability of current market data and sophisticated tools for their interpretation and evaluation constitute a sound basis for high profitability in the business.

The case study outlines the design and implementation of a large scale online/real-time system for the foreign exchange (FX) division of a world-wide investment bank with hundreds of brokers employed in several trading rooms in various countries. In the design phase, major issues, such as parallelism, representation and location of data, techniques for their replication and the distribution of work between client and server had to be deliberated and appropriate solutions to be found. Common issues like reliability, availability and accountability had to be addressed, too. As the system comprises more than half a million lines of code and commensurate functionality, only some of the more interesting aspects of distribution, replication, and the particular way of partitioning the calculation functionality between the client and the server side can be expounded here.

2.2 Some Basic Terms of FX Trading

FX trading [17] is the business of exchanging currencies, the most actively traded being the US Dollar (ISO code USD), Euro (EUR), Japanese Yen (JPY) and British Pound (GBP). In inter-bank trading the typical transaction amounts to several million USD. Mostly, banks act as intermediaries between the actual buyer and the seller of a currency, thereby earning a commission. Therefore, two rates (prices) are quoted for a currency, i.e., the offer rate (sell price) and the bid rate (buy price). The commission results from the difference between those rates (spread). Moreover, trades may be distinguished into types depending on the effective exchange date and whether it is mandatory or optional to complete the exchange.

- The simplest type is called *spot contract*, because it is effected immediately[1].
- The effective date of exchange in a *forward contract* [9] lies in the future[2]. But both parties agree on a fixed price in advance. Thereby an export company might hedge against currency fluctuations. The "insurance premium" is charged in the form of a swap rate[3]. Market rates for swaps are quoted for standard value dates[4], such as 1, 2, 3, 6 or 12 months, any dates in between are interpolated by various techniques.
- An *option* has some commonality with a forward contract. However, one party may unilaterally decide to (not) complete the exchange at the predetermined date (expiry date) and price (the strike price)[5]. Naturally, that heightened degree of freedom has its price. Complex formulas guide the calculation of the option price[6], based on parameters such as spot, swap and interest rates, plus the so called volatility.

Much more could be said with respect to the FX calculus, but there is no room to explain anything close to the real complexity in a paper as this[7].

---

1. Reality is a bit more complex. It takes one or two days to settle the deal.
2. maybe even years
3. which reflects expectations of the future spot rate plus interest
4. effective date of the exchange, i.e.settlement
5. Again, for the sake of brevity reality has been grossly simplified—for details see [9]
6. Beware that option price and strike price are different notions.
7. The underlying rules have evolved in the past 100 years and are known to a few specialists and are far from trivial and systematic.

2.3 Trading Room and Communication Infrastructure

Even being implemented from scratch, the system had to fit into an existing IT infrastructure. To comprehend some of the design decisions and receive an impression of the working environment of a trader, the typical trading room information and communication infrastructure is sketched in Fig. 1.

A trading room, potentially separated into several compartments, may house hundreds of persons. Each workplace is equipped with at least one powerful workstation and two or even three large colour screens to display the various (real-time) data a trader is interested in. Often a commercial UNIX is the operating system of choice and, naturally, the GUI is window-based.

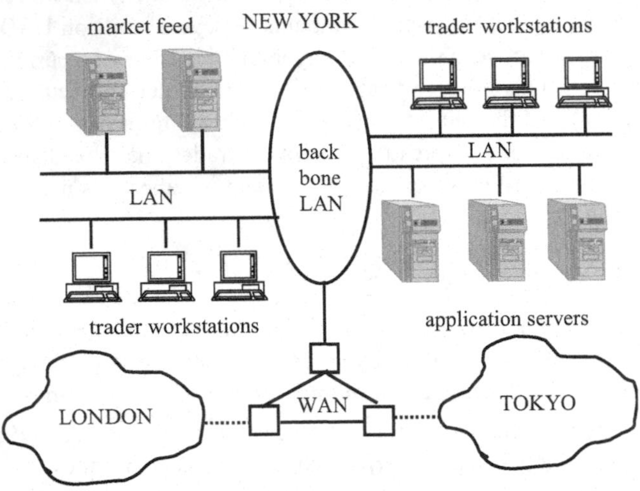

Fig. 1 Trading Room Infrastructure

Communication software and protocols in these environments always have been from the Internet stack (TCP/UDP/IP), even years before these protocols became the communication system of choice in the consumer market (WWW). Communication on the physical layer is enabled by a high-speed local area network in the trading room (compartments). The latter may be segmented and interconnected through an extremely high-speed backbone. Global distribution of trading rooms (a popular setup being London, New York, Tokyo), which are connected through a private wide area network, enables continuous trading. The bandwidth of those networks is shared between various (bank internal) information systems, each typically running on one or more servers. Real-time market data for a plethora of tradable financial products is gathered externally by one or more external information providers (the market feed in Fig. 1), such as Reuters, Bloomberg and Dow Jones/Telerate, and made available through proprietary software and communication protocols [19]. In the system described here, as is common for many other bank internal information systems, the raw market data may be modified to a certain extent before being used within the bank internal information system, for instance to implement a consistent and successful trading strategy.

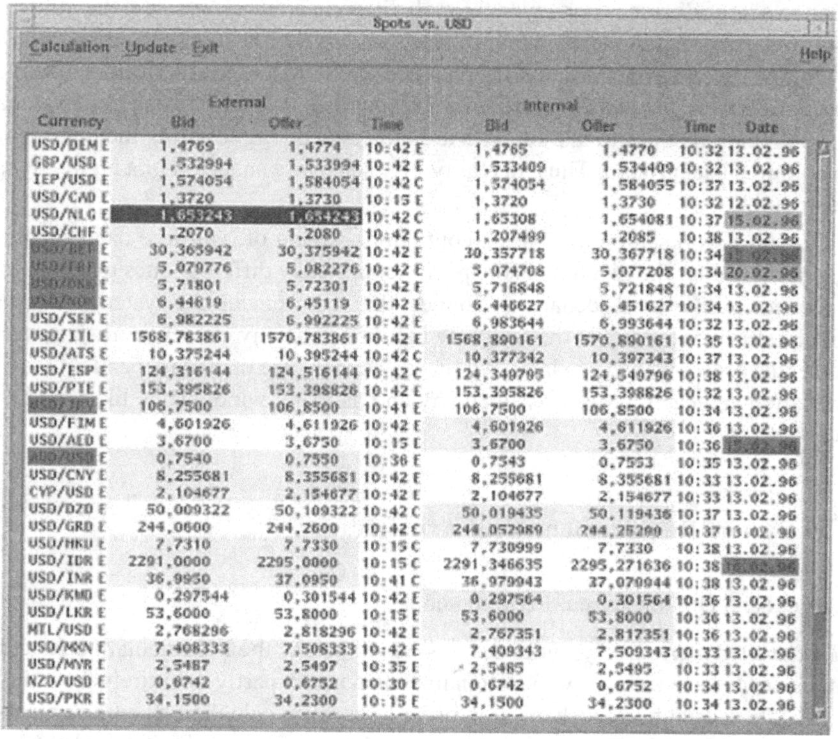

Spots vs. USD

Calculation Update Exit Help

Currency	External			Internal			
	Bid	Offer	Time	Bid	Offer	Time	Date
USD/DEM E	1,4769	1,4774	10:42 E	1,4765	1,4770	10:32	13.02.96
GBP/USD E	1,532994	1,533994	10:42 E	1,533409	1,534409	10:32	13.02.96
IEP/USD E	1,574054	1,584054	10:42 C	1,574054	1,584055	10:37	13.02.96
USD/CAD E	1,3720	1,3730	10:15 E	1,3720	1,3730	10:32	12.02.96
USD/NLG E	1,653243	1,654243	10:42 C	1,65308	1,654081	10:37	15.02.96
USD/CHF E	1,2070	1,2080	10:42 C	1,207499	1,2085	10:38	13.02.96
USD/BEF E	30,365942	30,375942	10:42 E	30,357718	30,367718	10:34	[illegible]
USD/FRF E	5,079776	5,082276	10:42 E	5,074708	5,077208	10:34	20.02.96
USD/DKK E	5,71801	5,72301	10:42 E	5,716848	5,721848	10:34	13.02.96
USD/NOK E	6,44619	6,45119	10:42 E	6,446627	6,451627	10:34	13.02.96
USD/SEK E	6,982225	6,992225	10:42 E	6,983644	6,993644	10:32	13.02.96
USD/ITL E	1568,783861	1570,783861	10:42 E	1568,890161	1570,890161	10:35	13.02.96
USD/ATS E	10,375244	10,395244	10:42 C	10,377342	10,397343	10:37	13.02.96
USD/ESP E	124,316144	124,516144	10:42 C	124,349795	124,549796	10:38	13.02.96
USD/PTE E	153,395826	153,398826	10:42 E	153,395826	153,398826	10:32	13.02.96
USD/JPY E	106,7500	106,8500	10:41 E	106,7500	106,8500	10:34	13.02.96
USD/FIM E	4,601926	4,611926	10:42 E	4,601926	4,611926	10:36	13.02.96
USD/AED E	3,6700	3,6750	10:15 E	3,6700	3,6750	10:36	[illegible]
AUD/USD E	0,7540	0,7550	10:36 E	0,7543	0.7553	10:35	13.02.96
USD/CNY E	8,255681	8,355681	10:42 E	8,255681	8,355681	10:33	13.02.96
CYP/USD E	2,104677	2,154677	10:42 E	2,104677	2,154677	10:33	13.02.96
USD/DZD E	50,009322	50,109322	10:42 C	50,019435	50,119436	10:37	13.02.96
USD/GRD E	244,0600	244,2600	10:42 C	244,052989	244,25200	10:37	13.02.96
USD/HKD E	7,7310	7,7330	10:15 C	7,730999	7,7330	10:38	13.02.96
USD/IDR E	2291,0000	2295,0000	10:15 C	2291,346635	2295,271636	10:38	[illegible]
USD/INR E	36,9950	37,0950	10:41 C	36,979943	37,070944	10:38	13.02.96
USD/KWD E	0,297544	0,301544	10:42 E	0,297564	0,301564	10:36	13.02.96
USD/LKR E	53,6000	53,8000	10:15 E	53,6000	53,8000	10:36	13.02.96
MTL/USD E	2,768296	2,818296	10:42 E	2,767351	2,817351	10:36	13.02.96
USD/MXN E	7,408333	7,508333	10:42 E	7,409343	7,509343	10:33	13.02.96
USD/MYR E	2,5487	2,5497	10:35 E	2,5485	2,5495	10:33	13.02.96
NZD/USD E	0,6742	0,6752	10:30 E	0.6742	0,6752	10:34	13.02.96
USD/PKR E	34,1500	34,2300	10:15 E	34,1500	34,2300	10:34	13.02.96

Fig. 2 Example of Information Presented to the User by the GUI

2.4 The Trader Interface

The overall goal of the system is to give the traders access to all standard FX market rates, and to equip them with a powerful financial calculus heeding all FX intricacies. This calculus determines the prices of non-standard FX products, for which there are no market prices and typically incorporates confidential pricing models. Basic rates are mostly taken from real-time market feeds, for instance Reuters, and relayed to the trader workstations, potentially after applying some modifications. Those modifications reflect the trading policy and are determined by authorised traders. Once the policy has been altered, the stream of real-time data relayed to the trader workstations has to be altered accordingly, and mirrored on the workstations with as small a delay as possible. Obviously, the whole process has to be secure, reliable and accompanied by audit capabilities, among other considerations.

The trader sees the result of this process through a number of windows, each of which either assembles the data particular to a financial product or displays an overview of a specific market. In total, the system comprises about 100 different windows. Fig. 2 shows a screen dump of the simpler kind, the so called spot window, that groups the spot rates of the traded currencies. In reality, apart from the numbers, additional information to a large degree is conveyed through different colours, which in the printed version of this paper is transformed into more or less intense shading. The first column of the window specifies the currencies exchanged, the third and fourth display the external bid and offer rates, the last column shows the spot date. For a more detailed explanation see [18]. Value changes to market rates are indicated by highlighting them temporarily on a coloured background. Thus, in reality Fig. 2 shows a snapshot of a highly dynamic data stream.

Though a workstation accesses a continuous stream of real-time data, each trader might wish to alter the given rates or specify completely different ones to evaluate certain alternatives (what-if scenarios). To meet this requirement, the system allows to selectively freeze or overwrite the real-time input rates on any chosen workstation and to reverse this decision any time later. All those decisions are made independently on each workstation and each trader may open any and as many windows he likes, and at any time.

2.5 System Requirements and Architecture

Technical and Organizational Requirements.

- *Trader autonomy.* Every trader decides which part of the FX calculation functionality is needed at a time. A workstation may disconnect partly or entirely from the real-time rate distribution mechanism in order to perform calculations based on a mix of trader specific and real-time rates to assess what-if scenarios. Switching back to real-time rates should be effected with minimal delay.
- *Centralized policy making.* Trading policy is governed by rules and parameters applied to market rates and calculation models. Changes in policy have to be delivered to all workstations without loss, duplication or reordering as speedily as possible.
- *Integrity and accountability.* All changes to the trading policy and the system configuration have to authorised and logged.
- *Recoverability.* Recovery of a single workstation or the central policy setting instance should be swift, automatic and transparent to the user. In particular, policy related information must not be lost in a failure of the system.
- *Coupling modes* between *trading rooms.* Certain policy aspects are common for all trading rooms. The system has to provide an appropriate replication mechanism.

Architecture—Functional View. The functional decomposition of the system is laid out in Fig. 3. The example system interconnects two instances, i.e., trading rooms in Frankfurt and London. The diagonal line illustrates the geographical separation, but should not be mistaken to signify any logical separation or lack of integration among the software elements in the trading rooms

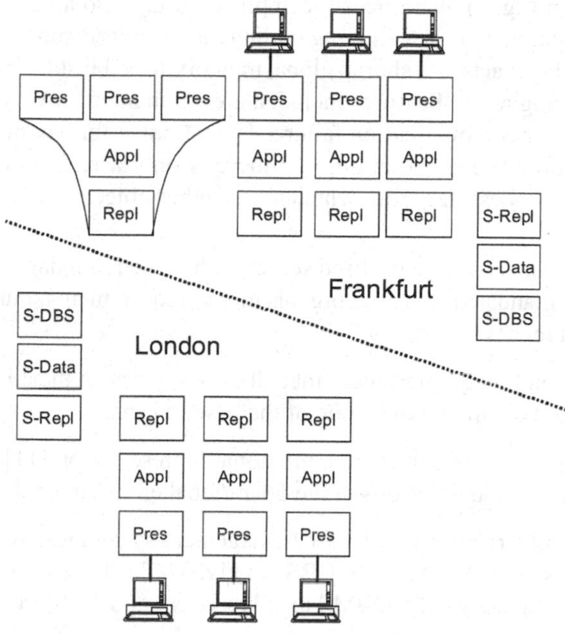

Fig. 3 Architecture—Functional View

Client and server side of the FX system have been structured into a number of respective software layers. The server side of the Frankfurt part of Fig. 3 consists of the three boxes above the right end of the diagonal line (labels starting with "S-").Their counterparts in London are positioned close to the left rim just below the line. All other boxes in Fig. 3 represent the client sides of the system. A vertical arrangement of boxes typically groups the components running on a single machine.

Subsequently, purpose and functionality of each layer will be explained, starting on the client side, and some of the salient features will pointed out.

- The *presentation layer* ("Pres" in Fig. 3) comprises all the input and display functionality, but does not include any of the functionality related to the FX calculus. The box in Fig. 3 stands for a number of different and independent elements implementing interfaces to the user, for example the graphical interface of the TIS (Trader Interaction System) depicted in Fig. 1. Other elements of the presentation layer interact with specific information systems of the banking environment that need a particular set and representation of the FX data. Typically these elements operate as background processes in batch mode (see the upper left corner of Fig. 3) and have custom-made interfaces to the applications.

- The *application layer* ("Appl" in Fig. 3) implements the entire functionality of the financial calculus (see Sect. 2.4). Following the rules of object-oriented design, all the complexities of the FX calculus are effectively encapsulated. Increasingly complex financial products have been modelled as objects (implemented in C++), are organized into a hierarchy and are calculated as necessary, i.e., on demand, from the more basic ones. The highlights of this dynamic, on-demand, graph-based real-time recalculation scheme will be elaborated in Sect. 2.6. All objects are made accessible to the presentation layer by means of a publish-and-subscribe [6] interface. The clear functional separation resulting from the layered approach entails great freedom and flexibility for the distribution of instances to machines.

- The *replication layer* ("Repl" in Fig. 3) guarantees the application layer to always have up-to-date basic rates and parameters determining trading policy at its disposal. For this purpose the replication layer acts as a shared global memory for all instances of the application layer in a trading room. Features included are automatic recovery in case of partial or total system or communication failure. The rationale for having the replication layer is founded on the observation, that there is only a relatively small number of base objects of modest size from which all the other objects can be dynamically calculated.

The server side is also built in three layers. A centralised server with some redundancy for reasons of fault-tolerance was mandated by some organisational requirements, but the approach also has its technical merits.

- The *replication layer* ("S-Repl" in Fig. 3) guarantees that all counterparts on the client and server side always have the same set and state of the base objects.
- The *data layer* ("S-Data" in Fig. 3) maps objects to a relational representation [11], which was necessitated by organizational reasons in the operational environment.
- For the same reasons, a commercial relational database management system was selected to hold the persistent parts of the FX data ("S-DBS" in Fig. 3). The FX system relies on the integrity preserving functions of a DBMS to aid recovery and enable audits, among others.

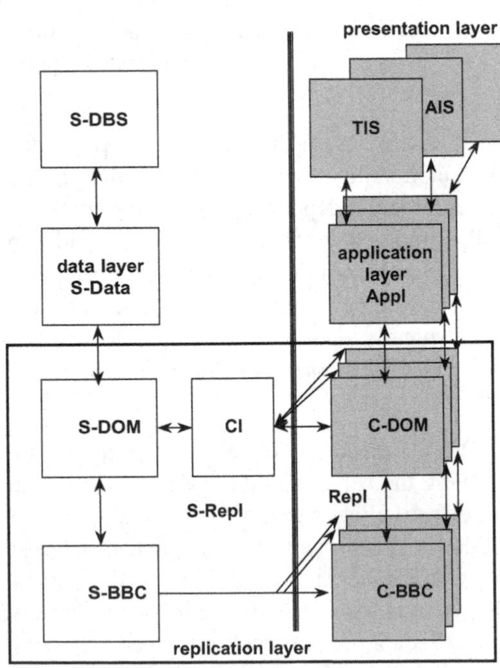

Fig. 4 Architecture—Dynamic View

As neither a single system on the market nor an easy combination of common off-the-shelf tools could be identified, that would technically fulfil all requirements, it was decided to build some critical mechanisms and components as a proprietary solution. Off-the-shelf commercial software products and components were employed wherever feasible and in conformance with bank procurement standards.

Architecture—Dynamic View. Fig. 4 depicts the dynamic aspects of the FX system. Every box corresponds to an operating system process. In many cases there is a one-to-one mapping between processes and instances of the functional layers introduced in the preceding section, the only exception being the replication layer. All the processes constituting the server side are arranged on the left of Fig. 4 and the respective client side processes on the right. In total three client instances, running on different workstations, are shown.

When a policy change or a new value of a base rate enters the system (for example via an external data feed), the data layer on the server side records it in the database and forwards it to the distributed object manager on the server side (S-DOM). S-DOM always holds the master copy of the up-to-date versions of all base objects in volatile memory. After changing the objects in the S-DOM, they are relayed to the server side object distribution component (S-BBC[8]), which multicasts them to the corresponding client side (C-BBC). From here, they are relayed to their respective C-DOM. Changes to objects in the C-DOM automatically trigger the dynamic recalculation scheme in the application layer (see Sect. 2.6). Thus, the replication system is the vehicle to maintain current and consistent mirrors of all base objects in all clients. The CI (client initialize) process, also part of the replication layer, establishes an up-to-date replica of all base objects during recovery or the regular start-up sequence of a client. There is a lot of flexibility with respect to the distribution of system components. Depending on the actual environment, multiple instances of these processes might be used to serve each compartment of a segmented trading room. Thus a lot of communication bandwidth can be saved.

2.6 Implementation of FX Calculus

General Aspects. Two big decisions were to be made during the design phase of the system.

- Where and how to perform the calculations respecting all FX peculiarities?
- How to deal with the more or less continuous real-time updates of some basic rates?

Even a cursory analysis of the FX calculus and the dependencies among the diverse financial products clearly revealed that there was only a relatively small set of basic financial objects, depending on which a potentially huge number of other objects were calculated. The objects to be calculated were determined by the specific task of a trader, and never were major parts of the object set required by a single workstation. Yet, the set of objects needed per workstation might change from time to time. As a consequence, centralised calculation of all possible rates was discarded as an option, due to the expected server and network load and the futility of calculating values not needed by any client. Hence by design, all the calculations were shifted to the client side and only those values are recalculated that directly or indirectly depend on changed input.

Dynamic Recalculation Mechanism. Analysis of the structural and mathematical dependencies between the various FX products revealed, that all objects representing financial products could be arranged into an acyclic graph. Links between nodes signify rates that have to be calculated as a prerequisite to the calculation of others. An excerpt

8. Basic Broadcasting Component (client and server)

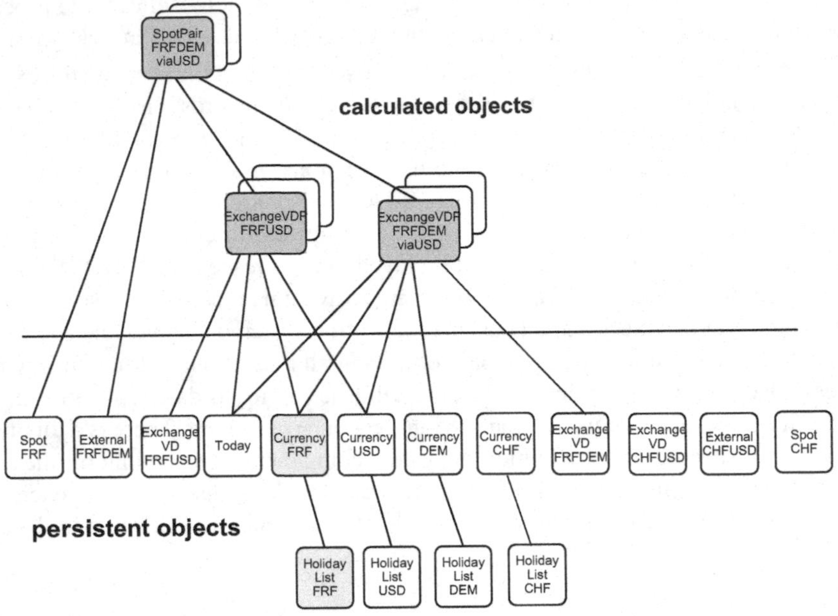

Fig. 5 Dynamic Recalculation of Objects

of this graph is drawn in Fig. 5. Primarily, the entire concept of the novel recalculation algorithm is founded on the ability to disjointly classify the objects as either base or calculated and secondly that all base objects by the nature of the application are arranged below all calculated objects. The horizontal line in the middle of Fig. 5 symbolizes this conceptual boundary. Two layers of base objects can be seen below two layers of calculated objects. The values and states of the base objects are held on the server side of the system using standard transactional features [13, 14] of a commercial database system and the replication mechanism implemented within the FX system maintains an up-to-date, exact replica of this state in every client connected. Every modification of the state or value of a base object detected by the replication system on the client side automatically triggers the recalculation of all its dependent objects.

In the example of Fig. 5 one of the base objects (labelled “Holiday List FRF”) is changed by the replication system. As a consequence, all dependent objects first have to be determined and subsequently recalculated. One of the virtues of the mechanism is its object-oriented implementation. Thereby each object inherits and overwrites abstract methods for the recalculation, connection and disconnection to the overall graph. The objects are controlled by an engine, which drives the evaluation by first arranging the objects concerned into layers and then invoking the recalculation methods of the respective objects. Because of this, the system can be extended easily to incorporate new object types, which just need to re-implement the connect and disconnect methods and to specify the recalculation method that is particular to the financial product modelled by the object.

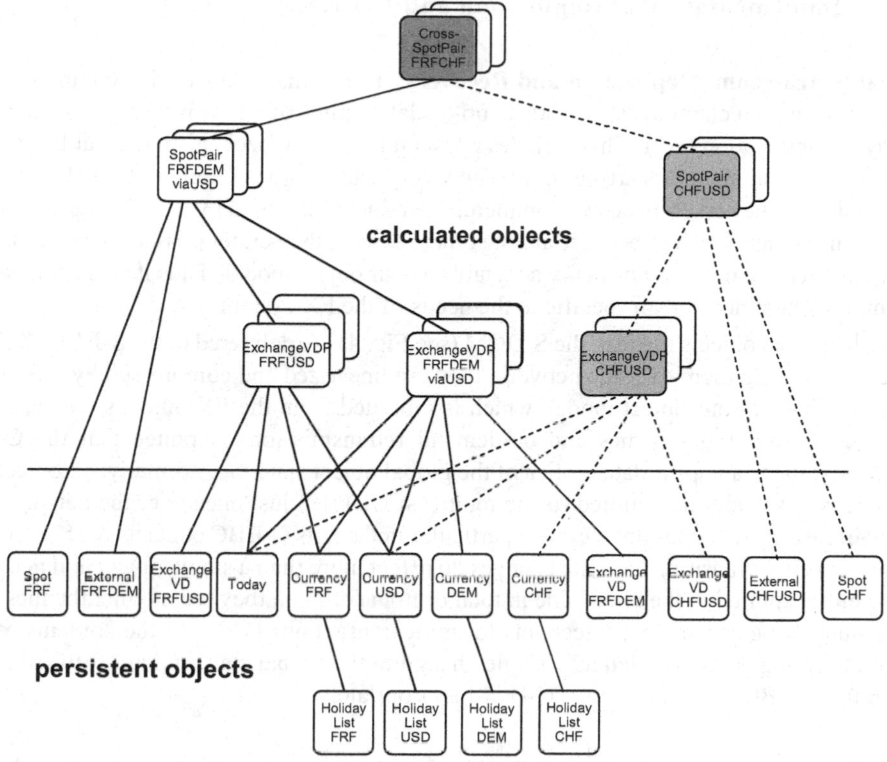

Fig. 6 Dynamic Restructuring of Object Dependencies

Dynamic Restructuring Mechanism. Another virtue of the mechanism lies in its distribution properties. The graph is dynamic and only comprises the calculated objects actually needed by a particular client instance. In any case, only the minimum computation effort is required. This is achieved by calculating the dependency graph on demand.

In the following a scenario is presented in which a trader opens an additional window to display, for instance, cross spot rates. During initialisation the presentation layer issues a subscription to the application layer referring to the cross spot rate of French Francs versus Swiss Francs (FRF/CHF). The application layer detects that this rate so far has not been calculated on the particular workstation and thus creates an instance of the object. The new object recursively tries to locate all objects in the application layer that are needed for the calculation, creating them if necessary. The starting point of this scenario shown in Fig. 5, whereas Fig. 6 depicts objects and dependencies after the completion of restructuring. As can be seen in Fig. 6, two more objects have been created recursively, in addition to the (root) object originally requested. Technically, restructuring is supported by a general addressing and location mechanism in the application and the replication layer, as well as a generic connect and disconnect mechanism which can be invoked by each object.

2.7 Implementation of Replication and Recovery

Local (Intra-room) Replication and Recovery. The primary task of this component is to provide each client instance with an up-to-date replica of all the base objects needed by the application layer. This includes a fast and efficient mechanism to establish an initial state in a client at start-up or after recovery and the speedy relay of all changes forwarded by the server instance. Commercial products examined [3, 2] did not provide the required functionality, because among other reasons, they either missed a broadcast/multicast feature or were not easily adaptable to our object model. Thus it was decided to implement a mechanism specific to the needs of the FX system.

Changes to objects made in the S-DOM (see Fig. 4) are delivered to the S-BBC. Before multicasting them over the network, they are linearized and compressed by one or more methods of our object model, which is inherited from the FX-object superclass. Message numbering schemes and on-demand retransmission guarantee that the C-DOM maintains an up-to-date replica of the global object state. So, normally, an object change is physically transmitted (using multicast UDP/IP) just once over the network. Only in case a client does not receive a particular update, its C-BBC contacts the S-BBC to selectively retransmit. As some changes do affect more than a single object and need to be either applied to the client side in total or not at all, i.e., they are atomic, the message numbering scheme even accounts for mini-transactions [10], i.e., the contents of several messages are handled as a single change to the global state and are forwarded from the C-BBC to the respective C-DOM appropriately.

Distributed (Inter-trading Room) Replication. Little mention has been given to the interaction between geographically distributed elements of the FX system, except for depicting two trading rooms in Fig. 3. The chosen solution for the implementation of inter-trading room replication again depended on some of the specific requirements of the application. First of all, two or more geographically distributed trading rooms operate in a relatively autonomous mode. The overwhelming part of the calculation of rates is determined by a "local" (trading room specific) policy, because the entire calculus is based on a (in our jargon) "home" currency. Typically this is the economically most important currency in the geographic area. As a consequence of these observations, only a few parameters of the trading policy are global and to be maintained consistently in a replicated fashion. For implementing the replication functionality between trading rooms, a few options were evaluated.

- A proprietary scheme was ruled out for technical and practical reasons. The implementation of the local replication system, necessitated by functional and performance reasons, already amounted to a big effort. However, this would not be justified for the global one. Furthermore, the global replication scheme required the entire set of properties (ACID) normally associated with (database) transactions [14].
- A second alternative was seen in using one of the commercially available message queuing systems [1, 12] to transmit changes reliably between the trading room systems. However, this would not have provided for the reliable transmission of the

changes end-to-end, i.e., from on FX system to another. Fortunately, the database system employed provides a very powerful replication mechanism [8], by which either data, i.e., tables and/or rows, or the execution of stored procedures can be replicated. As the number of FX objects and hence object types to be replicated is small, procedure replication was elected as the replication mechanism. In fact, procedure replication, apart from reasons of performance, was much better suited to the task.

2.8 Lessons Learnt

The design and implementation of a large software system often resembles a journey into unsurveyed territory. To succeed it is paramount, that requirements have been properly understood. This knowledge enables the implementor to make his own judgement as to the real needs and priorities of the system's features. Also, commercial software engineering in general implies that as much standard software as feasible is employed. This minimizes costs and duration of system development. Proprietary solutions should only be considered where available commercial software does not comprise required features[9] or is utterly expensive[10].

One of the big challenges in the FX system described was to implement all the peculiar rules and usances of FX trading, including mechanisms that allow to adapt existing FX products and to incorporate novel FX products. Another big challenge was posed by the need to effectively support the trading policy within the bank, resulting in very particular requirements for the distribution and replication of the data.

Among others, the first objective was achieved by the encapsulation of all the calculus pertaining to a particular FX product into an object, and the structuring of those objects into an acyclic graph that could be exploited for our on-demand recalculation mechanism. That mechanism plus the decision to perform all the calculations on the client side is one of the major assets of the system, from the performance point-of-view as well as with respect to its extensibility. Insofar, object-orientation served quite well for that purpose. Even though the mapping of the base objects to relational data structures incurred some of the usual problems, this drawback was by far offset by the ability to fit into the established infrastructure of commercial database systems within the bank.

Furthermore, the standard replication mechanisms of the database system provided all the features that were needed to implement the particular replication strategy between the trading rooms that was mandated by the trading policy. The missing parts were implemented with relative ease in the form of stored procedures, which proved to be an extremely useful feature. A lot of thought went into the design and implementation of the local replication mechanism, i.e., the replication of on-line rates within a single trading room. A profound study of distributed messaging algorithms [7], especially those including atomic multi-cast, and a survey of available products did not come up

9. avoiding what is usually—quite appropriately—called the NIH (Not Invented Here) syndrome

10. Costs must be stated honestly, i.e., licence and maintenance costs of standard software vs. development and maintenance cost, especially personnel, of the proprietary software.

with a single one that would satisfy all our needs. Mostly, our very particular multi-cast semantics in conjunction with atomicity properties and the need for proper recovery would not be supported. As a consequence, there was no choice but to opt for a proprietary implementation of such a mechanism. From the engineering point-of-view this turned out to be quite a challenge, because of all the intricacies of concurrency, fault-tolerance and atomicity in distributed systems. It was worth the effort, because there was no choice. However, this dissemination mechanism is relatively small compared to the generic infrastructures provided by companies like Reuters[19], DowJones or Bloomberg, and shows the business value of the latter.

After describing challenges from and solutions to the rapid dissemination of structured financial data, the focus now shifts to the processing of the huge amounts of semi-structured and unstructured information, which exists today and will dramatically increase in volume in the future.

3 Setting Up an Infrastructure for Efficient Retrieval of Unstructured Information

3.1 Motivation

Alongside structured information, a primary means of recording, transporting, and storing knowledge is the document, be it a letter, an invoice, an internal memo, or information provided by internal or external market research, to cite a few examples. Within big financial service companies an estimate for the number of document pages containing valuable information will probably amount to be in the range of billions of pages. Thus, the main issue associated with information retrieval in today's working environment is the enormous amount of data to be searched. The engineering progress that has made those vast repositories of data possible has no real counterpart in the semantics of the resulting systems. Nowadays, information retrieval primarily still means keyword-index-based or full-text search on the data (i.e., the signal) itself. An evaluation of the statistics of one such retrieval mechanism – the keyword-index-based search engine implemented on the Dresdner Bank corporate intranet – has revealed that a very high percentage of users just specify a single keyword in their search, which generally leads to a very unspecific and usually huge result set. To identify the relevant items it is still inevitable to manually browse through the entire result set, unless the documents are really well annotated, which usually is not the case.

A core factor of today's document or even "knowledge"-management systems is its dependency on some sort of structural input. Be it pre-clustering, providing keywords or developing a structure which documents may fit into, most commercial systems are not able to generate real benefit for retrieval without manual effort. Therefore organizations, whose primary business asset is information, are facing a somehow paradoxical situation. On the one hand information is available in ever greater quantity and variety; however, on the other hand the probability that one can find and utilize this information is decreasing. As information is to a great extent available textually in natural language, and as such in unstructured or only partially structured form, natural language technology can play an important role in dealing with this flood of information.

3.2 Architecture Principles

The main idea of the approach presented was derived from the observation, that the typical knowledge worker is not willing or simply does not have the time to do extra work (for example to specify and maintain keywords, integrate documents into pre-existing structures, etc.) to facilitate knowledge sharing with colleagues. Therefore, it is necessary to provide a set of tools that on the one hand do all the extra work without requiring intervention or even attention by the knowledge worker, and that on the other hand will provide him with an easy to work retrieval tool so he can efficiently find his way through the growing knowledge repository.

An integrated framework built on these tools would enable every employee to use as well as to contribute to the company's "digital organizational memory" without having to acquire beforehand special skills or knowledge. Hence, compared to today's systems the threshold for effective knowledge management will be drastically lowered.

One of the prerequisites for knowledge management is to get access to and incorporate those vast document repositories. The automatic creation of a simple syntactic index of all electronically available documents is a first approach. This initial solution has the advantage of being simple and cheap. But its shortcoming is low quality, i.e., an unspecific and usually huge result set. Because of this much research is oriented towards conceptualizing knowledge in order to abstract a model (pre-clustering, building ontologies, etc.). However, most of these approaches are very expensive because they typically entail a big manual effort.

Taking this into account, the benefit of an automatically generated and semantically enriched search mechanism becomes obvious. The concept presented combines the low initial effort required by an indexing approach with several methods of automated implicit model building and a retrieval mechanism, which smoothly fits into the individual desktop workspace [16]. On the retrieval side term correlation measure is used to extract some semantic information from large corpora of documents that are already available in the intranet or other large document repositories [15]. This information is then taken to draw a semantic network (see Fig. 7 and Fig. 8) that allows associative search and retrieval of documents. On the other end we automatically enrich documents semantically, using term extraction methods and term frequency analysis to determine the most relevant keywords [4]. These constitute important meta-information for a given document to facilitate and improve indexing and retrieval.

The common principle guiding the various approaches is our notion of "minimal invasive knowledge management", which may be summed up as an IT-driven knowledge management infrastructure, which smoothly integrates itself into the personalized workspace and workflow of each individual knowledge worker without any need to learn new tools, change habits or even be aware of its functionality [5]. To accomplish this, the whole knowledge management process must be effected in the background and run automatically without the need of human interaction. Widely used applications like word-processors, e-mail, or presentation graphics are the primary means for work with knowledge. The integration of these standard applications into the framework permits easy and efficient knowledge collection. Ideally, the introduction of a new item into the knowledge base must not cause any additional effort to the usual daily work. On the retrieval side a semantically rich presentation layer is provided.

3.3 Modules

Several modules, representing the respective parts of the framework have been implemented or are currently under development. The main building blocks that constitute a knowledge management tool-set are described in this section.

Term Extractor. To support the intelligent indexing part of our framework, a natural language term extractor[11] is employed. This tool applies methods from linguistic analysis to extract tagged terms from given documents and is driven by a task specific grammar [20]. Based on this component two high level applications have been developed in Dresdner Bank: the Knowledge Net and an Automated Meta-tagging Engine. These tools address the different aspects of indexing and semantic enrichment of documents that have been described previously.

Knowledge Net. The goal of the "Knowledge Net" (kNet) application is to improve the usability of the search interface and the quality of search results. It defines a general architecture for knowledge retrieval based on text mining technologies by automatically generating a browsable semantic network of terms extracted from the document repository without any need for expensive human modeling or supervision [5].

The indexing engine is based on a term correlation grammar, which extracts pairs of named entities and calculates two correlation measures.

- A syntactic distance measure shows an untyped relation between two terms within a document or document part.
- The second, paradigmatic measure, is drawn from statistical analysis of context similarities.

On the retrieval side the kNet has a visual search interface that implements our idea of an implicit knowledge model. Based on the two correlation measures a semantic network is drawn, representing the terms as nodes and weighted, coloured edges the two types of correlation. Fig. 7 shows the search result for "Dresdner Bank" in autumn 2001. A strong syntactic relation exists between Dresdner Bank and Allianz—not a surprise considering the fact that Dresdner Bank was taken over by Allianz in Spring, 2001. Having discovered that relationship, the user can easily restrict the search to doc-

11. Currently we use the Insight Discoverer Extractor of Temis SA (http://www.temis-group.com)

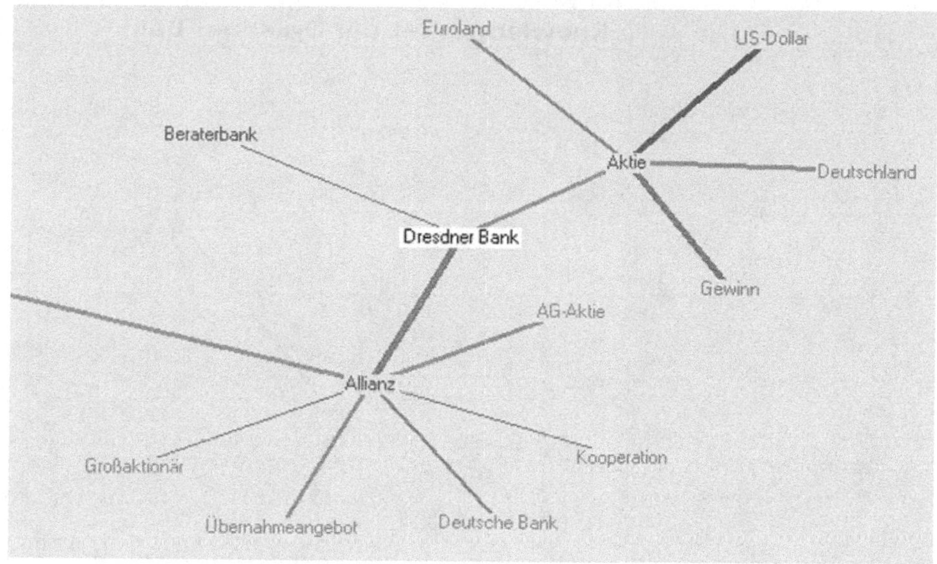

Fig. 7 kNet Example: Search Result for "Dresdner Bank"

uments containing the term "Dresdner Bank" as well as the term "Allianz", just by one mouse click—adding "Allianz" to the search phrase. Moreover, this example illustrates another feature of the kNet—the ability to extract named entities, e.g., company names like "Dresdner Bank" or names of persons. Furthermore, this kind of graphical representation indicates whether terms occur in different typical contexts. An example—the search result for the term "PKI"—is shown in Fig. 8. Even though the term "PKI" mostly stands for Public Key Infrastructure it has two completely different meanings inside Dresdner Bank:

There is a strong syntactic relation between "PKI" and "GB". In this context, "PKI" stands for "Private Kunden Inland" (private customers inland) and "GB" means "Geschäftsbereich" (business division). So the solution is: "PKI" is the name of a business division of Dresdner Bank. There is also a strong syntactic relation between "GB" and "PVK" and a strong paradigmatic relation between "PKI" and "PVK". However, there are not many documents containing "PKI" as well as "PVK" yet there must be a correlation between PKI and PVK. Well, PVK is the former name of the business division PKI. So it is possible to detect interesting correlations between terms and exploit this information for a refined, more successful search: "PKI" as well as "PVK" are included into the search phrase to find all relevant documents—independent from the current name of the business division.

However, "PKI" and terms like "Hauptspeicher" (main memory), "RAM" and "MByte" are also interrelated. What does this mean? Answer: "PKI" is also the name of an in-house application of Dresdner Bank and existing documents describe the parameters to configure the computer for this application. Again the search criteria may be refined by including relevant terms and by restricting the search to the relevant context at the same time.

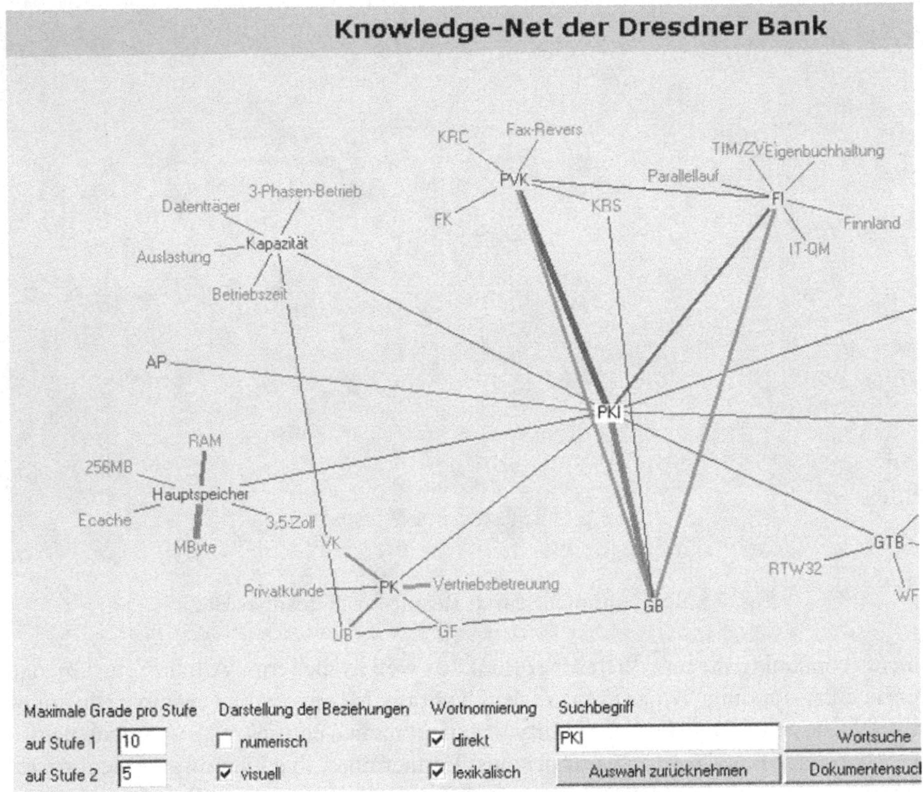

Fig. 8 kNet Example: Search Result for "PKI"

While the kNet[12] increases the quality of search results on the client side, quality, i.e., the semantic richness of documents, can also be improved on the "backend" side. One possibility is the usage of meta-information. In the next section a prototype is described, which permits one to automatically extract keywords from documents of almost all formats. Both concepts are orthogonal but can (and should) be used jointly.

Automated Meta-tagging Engine. Meta-information, e.g., topic or keywords, assigned to documents, helps to determine the relevant ones in search and retrieval processes. However, to assign meta-information in the form of keywords and topics to documents is a very tedious task. On the one hand, the specification of keywords pertaining to a document burdens the author with a cognitive effort that consumes too much time and energy. On the other hand, the keywords assigned seem to be sensitive to personal disposition, varying with the situation of the author, etc. Because such keywords often tend to be too general, their value in the search process is extremely reduced. Further-

12. Currently the kNet is being enhanced and developed into a commercial solution by H.A.S.E. GmbH (http://www.h-a-s-e.org) and Temis SA (http://www.temis-group.com)

more, it seems difficult to establish a unified linguistic basis (e.g., some keywords appear preferably in their plural form, others in singular etc.).

To address these problems an automated meta-tagging engine was implemented, based on another specialized grammar for the term extractor. It computes a set of statistically selected lemmatized keywords for a given document. At present we are evaluating different algorithms, using text frequency combined with document frequency as statistical measure, as well as clustering- and categorizing-based approaches.

Moreover, the meta-information generated about the document content needs to be stored and managed appropriately. With respect to the format, the goal was to make use of non-proprietary standards which are supported by different search and retrieval engines. Besides the established meta-tags for HTML documents, we decided to use XML-based Semantic Web Technologies, i.e., RDF (http://www.w3.org/RDF/) and Dublin Core Metadata Initiative (http://dublincore.org/) for all document formats. Also, some document formats (e.g., MS Word) allow one to store meta-information inside the document in the proprietary meta-data format.

To achieve the most seamless workspace integration the engine is implemented as a Java-based web service with several clients, one of which—as an example—is automatically invoked when a document is saved by the commonly used word-processor. This client is .Net/C#-based, whereas other clients, i.e., for batch processing of huge amounts of documents, are implemented in Java [4]. Even though there are some teething troubles, web services seem to offer great opportunities for easy and efficient enterprise application integration in certain use scenarios.

As one of the next steps, the automated meta-tagging engine will be integrated with the content management system of Dresdner Bank. Thereby the content creating authors are supported to enhance the quality of meta-tags used within the Intranet without additional effort and as a consequence to improve the quality of search results.

4 Summary and Conclusion

In the first part, we presented a large-scale system for FX traders. The salient features are a very peculiar distribution and replication mechanism for structured on-line rates needed in the calculation of the prices of FX products, plus the object-oriented implementation of the rules and usances in FX trading. It was shown that a clever combination of state-of-the-art communications, database and software engineering products and technology and a peculiar partitioning of the functionality between the client and the server side could result in an efficient, scalable, distributed system supporting hundreds of trader workplaces.

In the second part we presented an architecture for efficient retrieval of huge amounts of unstructured information. The architecture and the implemented modules comprise indexing tools based on linguistics, and a visual retrieval interface to integrate pre-existing document repositories, as they are always found in large companies. On the knowledge creation side of the process those tools liberate the author of a document from annotating it, by extracting keywords automatically. These tools allow for nearly maintenance free indexing, and do not necessitate previous model building or continuous supervision by expensive experts. Natural language technology is the main enabling factor, which together with an intuitive graphical visualization makes the described tools a valuable instrument in a knowledge intensive working environment.

References

[1] Bernstein, P.; Hsu, M.; Mann, B.: Implementing Recoverable Requests Using Queues, in: ACM SIGMOD Conference, 1990, pp. 112-122

[2] Birman, K.: Replication and Fault-Tolerance in the ISIS System, in: Symposium on Operating Systems Principles (SOSP), 1985, pp. 79-86

[3] Birman, K.; Schiper, A.; Stephenson, P.: Lightweight Causal and Atomic Group Multicast, in: ACM Transactions on Computer Systems, Vol. 9, pp. 272-314, August 1991

[4] Brandt, S.; Cavar, D.; Störl, U.: A Real Live Web Service using Semantic Web Technologies: Automatic Generation of Meta-Information. Proc. On the Move to Meaningful Internet Systems (DOA, CoopIS, ODBASE 2002), Irvine, CA (2002)

[5] Cavar, D.; Kauppert, R.: Strategien für die Implementierung IT-basierter KM-Lösungen: Minimal invasive Systeme. In Ch. Prange (Ed.): Organisationales Lernen und Wissensmanagement – Fallstudien aus der Unternehmenspraxis. Gabler Verlag (2002)

[6] Chan, A.: Transactional Publish/Subscribe: The Proactive Multicast of Database Changes, in: ACM SIGMOD Conference, 1998, p. 521

[7] Coulouris, G.; Dollimore, J.; Kinderberg, T.: Distributed Systems: Concepts and Design, Addison-Wesley, 1994

[8] Daniels, D.; Doo, L.; Downing, A.; et al.: Oracle's Symmetric Replication Technology and Implications for Application Design, in: ACM SIGMOD Conference, 1994, p. 497

[9] DeRosa, D.: Options on Foreign Exchange, John Wiley & Sons, 1999

[10] Elmagarmid, A.: Database Transaction Models for Advanced Applications, Morgan Kaufmann Publishers, 1992

[11] Freytag, J.C., Manthey, R.; Wallace, M.: Mapping Object-Oriented Concepts into Relational Concepts by Meta-Compilation in a Logic Programming Environment, in: Advances in Object-Oriented Database Systems, LNCS, Springer, Vol. 334, pp. 204-208

[12] Gawlick, D.: Message Queuing in Oracle8, in: ICDE Conference, 1998, pp. 66-68

[13] Gray, J.; Reuter, A.: Transaction Processing Systems, Morgan Kaufmann Publishers, 1993

[14] Härder, T.; Reuter, A.: Principles of Transaction-Oriented Database Recovery, in: ACM Computing Surveys, Vol. 15, No.4, 1983, pp. 287-317

[15] Lebeth, K.: Semantic Networks in a Knowledge Management Portal. Proc. Advances in Artificial Intelligence (KI/ÖGAI 2001), Vienna, Austria (2001) 463-366

[16] Lebeth, K.; Lorenz, M.; Störl, U.: Text Mining based Knowledge Management in Banking. In: Zanasis, A. (Ed.): Text Mining and Its Applications. WIT Press, April 2005

[17] Luca, C.: Trading in the Global Currency Markets, Prentice Hall, 1995

[18] Peinl, P.: Design and Implementation of a Large Scale Online/Real-time Information System for Foreign Exchange Trading, Technical Report, University of Stuttgart, 1999

[19] Reuters: Reuters Market Data System, http://about.reuters.com/productinfo/rmds/

[20] Zanasis, A. (Ed.): Text Mining and Its Applications. WIT Press, April 2005

An Intermediate Information System Forms Mutual Trust

Dieter Steinbauer

Schufa Holding AG, Germany
dieter.steinbauer@schufa.de

Abstract. On the Internet, business transactions between anonyms are being made on a minute cycle. How can confidence between such business partners be obtained? For this purpose, an organization called the "credit bureau" exists in all countries having a functioning free market. In Germany, the leading credit bureau is the SCHUFA.

On the one hand, a credit bureau operates an information system which supplies for the credit grantor data about the credit-worthiness of his clients. On the other hand, the credit bureau offers the customer the possibility to document his reliability to the contractor or the credit grantor, respectively. Of its own accord, the credit bureau strictly commits itself to neutrality and only gives data to credit grantors that are relevant for the credit granting itself. This procedure prevents the system from being abused thereby alienating customers.

In many branches, the credit-granting process is highly automated. Via statistical methods the data of the credit bureaus are condensed into scoring systems. Via correlation of scores, equivalence classes of customers are being formed according to their non-payment risk.

The final credit decision is not only based on the data and the score of the customer in question but obviously also on the data which the credit grantor already possessed or which he was collecting since the contract was concluded. An integrated decision support system for credit processing starts at the point of sale. It supports an appropriate computer-based dialogue and it includes a rule engine in which the rules for risk assessment are integrated. The information system of the credit bureau can be used in an interactive way.

While a credit is used, the non-payment risk and its probability are of substantial interest. For this purpose, a special monitoring process has to be established.

In summary, the credit-bureau system combines several techniques of computer science in an interesting way. You will find everything from database technology, via mathematical/statistical methods and rule-based systems to Web-based communication.

T. Härder and W. Lehner (Eds.): Data Management (Wedekind Festschrift), LNCS 3551, pp. 277-292, 2005.

1 Introduction

A credit bureau is the ancestral model of a commercial data base. The data collection concerning the credit-worthiness and credit standing is almost as old as trade itself.

In a free market economy, granting a credit to a business partner and relying upon the repayment belongs to the basic principles of economy. Originally, trade was the only area where you could find consumer credits, the granting of a credit relying upon the settlement of the debt.

In former times, you could drink on tick in your local pub, where a chalk board was placed on the wall on which the regular customer´s debt was openly written. Visitors could immediately find out who was well known and thus was creditworthy. There were negative entries (the debt had not been paid back on pay-day) and positive entries (one actually was on the list). Not being on the list meant that you were not creditworthy, either because you were not known or because you were not trustworthy.

Today, we make business on the internet. How well acquainted are business partners there? At ebay's, for example, there is a rating system working with asterisks showing the performance of buyers and sellers; but can we confide in this system?

When two parties close a deal and money and goods are not being exchanged at the same time, a credit or economic risk is being created. Obviously, the party which delivers in advance wants to minimize this risk or at least wants to take the risk consciously, thereby following one of the slogans "nothing ventured, nothing gained" or "there is no chance where there is no risk".

In order to meet these requirements, in market economies all over the world credit bureaus are being established providing potential credit grantors with credit biographies of their customers [3]. Credit bureaus of this type are working on a commercial basis which means one has to pay for the information which is basically related to private persons. The first credit bureau was founded in New York around 1830. In Germany, SCHUFA ("Schutzgemeinschaft für allgemeine Kreditsicherung") as the first credit bureau was founded in Berlin in 1927 [7].

2 The Credit Bureau — Benefits for the Credit Grantor and the Consumer

The basic purpose of this business does still not have changed: A credit bureau protects a credit grantor against default risk and a consumer against over-indebtedness. The credit bureau creates confidence between credit grantor and client, which is essential for a credit business. Using this procedure the credit grantor is protected against undesired default risks which helps to minimize the interest rates as the criterion default risk has to be taken into less consideration. Another advantage is the increasing mobility. Via the information exchange between the various credit grantors, the consumer is able to prove his credit-worthiness anywhere at any time (see Fig. 1).

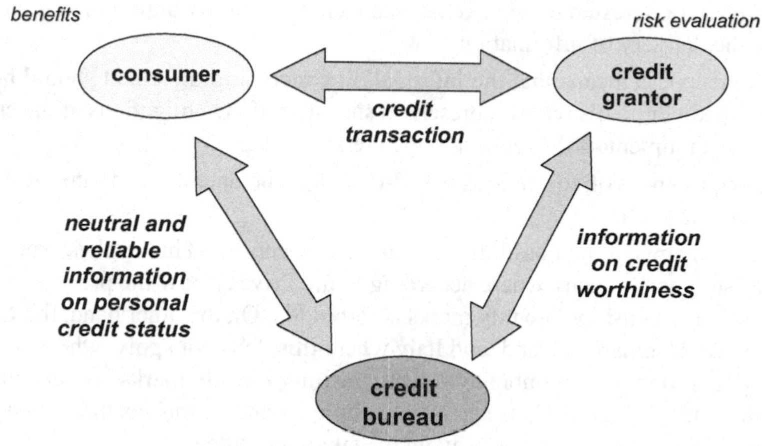

Fig. 1 Interdependency between Consumer – Credit Grantor – Credit Bureau

3 Data Base as Mutual Trust — The Principle of Reciprocity

The main core of a credit bureau is its data base where the credit history of a consumer is being stored. This data base forms the basis for all further processes referring to the risk evaluation of future credits and possible defaults [8].

Additionally to the master data referring to persons (first name, surname, name of birth, birth date, birth place, current and previous addresses), information is also stored on current and past contractual relationships (credit grantor, type of credit, duration of credit, status of credit) in this data base.

The data is completed by third-party information provided by public registers such as the Local Court (affidavits, detention orders to enforce affidavits) or the German Federal Gazette (i.e., bankruptcy proceedings). Additionally, information of persons provided by contractual partners or third parties is maintained, e.g., change of address. In contrast, information related to assets, income, profession, social class, marital status, religious or political attitude, etc. is not being stored.

As far as data in the data base is concerned, we demand the following quality requirements:

- completeness
- up-to-dateness
- correctness
- clearness
- availability

Referring to the single quality characteristics the following is to be added:

Completeness means that, using the given data basis, the credit grantor has to be able to get a complete picture of the current obligations of the consumer. Therefore, a credit bureau is interested to win over as many credit granting branches of trade as possible for the delivery of information.

Up-to-dateness means that the information concerning the client should be up-to-date. The credit bureau´s report represents a snapshot of the obligations of the credit applicant at the moment of the request to the credit bureau.

The requirement of correctness is self-evident. The data entered into the data base has to meet the truth.

Clearness aims at the possibility of mistaken identities. This applies especially for countries such as Germany where according to the Privacy Law the processing of non-ambiguous distinguishing identity marks is forbidden. On the other hand, there are EU-countries like Denmark, Poland, and Italy where this does not apply, whereas the positive identification via non-ambiguous distinguishing identity marks is even compellent in Sweden and Belgium. Consequently, complex search- and postprocessing procedures are necessary in Germany to avoid mistaken identities.

Availability of information results from the need to offer a twenty-four-times-seven credit granting. Due to Internet trade, break times in which credit granting is not possible cannot be tolerated.

The principle of reciprocity is the practical and theoretical basis for the information structure in the data base, where information of various credit granting institutes is consolidated. The principle of reciprocity assures that only the contractual partners who report information will as well receive information. This also applies for the granularity and the semantic content of this information. As a consequence, a contractual partner who reports credits (positive information) will also receive information on current credits (primarily banks). A contractual partner who only reports the non-compliance with contractual obligations (negative information) will only receive this sort of information (generally retailers).

Which branches are partners of the credit bureau? Typically, the partners are among the following kinds of institutions or organizations:

- banks and credit institutes
- trade and mail order companies
- telecommunication companies
- power authorities
- housing associations
- insurance companies
- collection agencies
- eCommerce companies

It should be especially emphasized that information concerning a consumer in a report to the credit grantor has to be filtered according to strict rules. As mentioned above, contractual partners of a credit bureau do not receive **all** information related to the consumer. Additionally, the name of another contractual partner is never disclosed in the report—only the very existence of a business connection as well as the status and the type of credit relation are being revealed. This is simply a question of discretion: The credit grantor who made the request will not find out which other companies also have this

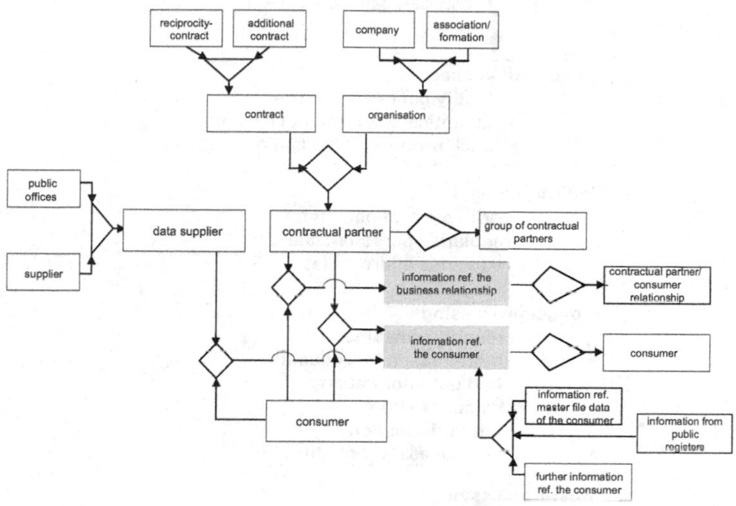

Fig. 2 Excerpt from the Data Model of a Credit Bureau

prospective credit client among their clientele. Anonymity and neutrality are very important in order to prevent the customer to become the target of competing marketing campaigns.

3.1 Structure and Restriction of the Information

Of course, the central issue of a credit bureau pertains to the contracts of loans respectively the business relationship between the consumer and a contractual partner of the credit bureau. This business connection has to be considered in a chronological perspective: it has to go through a sequence of phases such as the actual request for the credit, the credit decision, the paying off, and the debt settlement. Additionally, the terms consumer, borrower, and client, respectively, are of interest because they cover interesting criteria concerning the credit-worthiness.

For the credit bureau, the contractual partner possesses another quality than the consumer as there exists an actual business relationship between both of them. In this relationship, especially access control and information rights have to be regulated. Fig. 2 shows a simplified extract of the data model of a credit bureau. A simplified notation of the object-type method was used [4, 5].

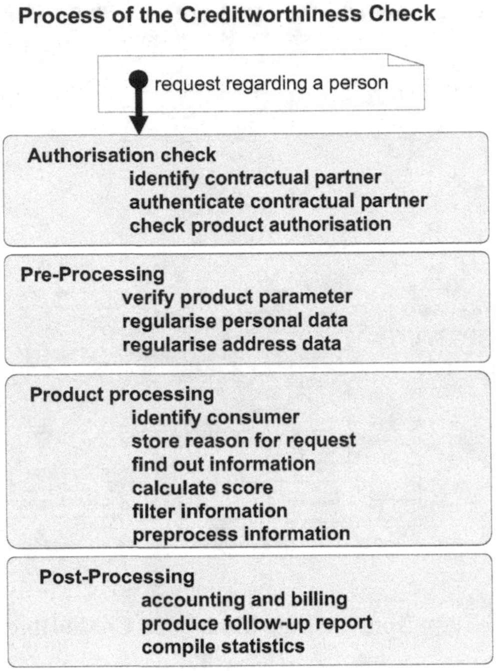

Process of the Creditworthiness Check

request regarding a person

Authorisation check
identify contractual partner
authenticate contractual partner
check product authorisation

Pre-Processing
verify product parameter
regularise personal data
regularise address data

Product processing
identify consumer
store reason for request
find out information
calculate score
filter information
preprocess information

Post-Processing
accounting and billing
produce follow-up report
compile statistics

Fig. 3 Process of the Credit-Worthiness Check

3.2 Gain of Information

Gaining information is achieved on the basis of the principle of reciprocity. Contractual partners automatically report to the credit bureau the credit information referring to the appropriate consumer. The single phases of the credit history are being checked on plausibility and afterwards are stored in the data base.

It is obvious that the close interaction between the credit decision system and the credit monitoring system of the credit grantor on one side and the application system of the credit bureau on the other side leads to cost-effective solutions. In contrast, the data delivery of third parties like the Local Court, etc. is more complex as the necessary process integration is often missing in such cases.

3.3 Transfer of Information

The transfer of information is along these lines. Enabled by their authorization and service profiles, the contractual partners have access to the information. Thus, the usual chronology has to be implemented: identification, authentication, and proof of the service profiles. As already mentioned, the information for the contractual partner is especially filtered. As a consequence, the appropriate profiles have to be lodged in the con-

Score Card Development

- **Credit-Scoring is the quantitative, resp. objektive risk measurement** compared to
- **the qualitative risk definition during the manual credit processing:**

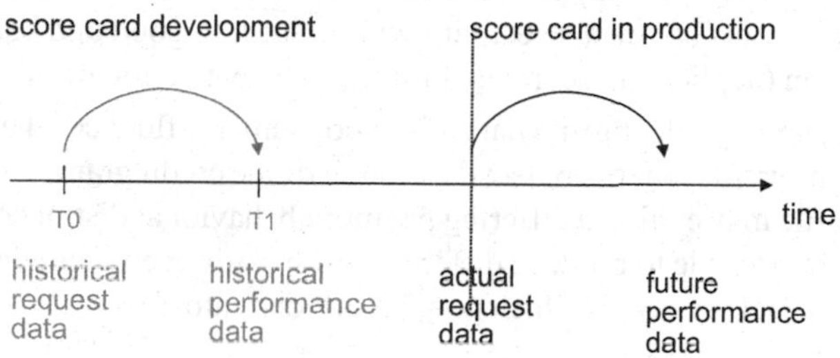

credit score = probability of default (PD)

Fig. 4 Score Card Development

tractual partner´s administration and have to be activated, if needed. This process is completed by quality-securing pre-processes referring to identification and address normalization, as illustrated in Fig. 3.

After the pre-processing phase, the actual access to the information, the credit-worthiness evaluation (score), and the contract-specific filtering can take place. During the post-processing phase, the information necessary for billing and for proof of truth and fairness, etc. are edited. The follow-up reports which are automatically sent to other contractual partners will be explained later.

4 Scoring – Risk Evaluation Based on the Common Data Base

So far, we have described the various aspects of the data base of a credit bureau where the credit histories of consumers are maintained. How is this sensitive data used? Therefore, the introduction of scoring systems was an important development in order to evaluate credit-worthiness. Actually a scoring system is nothing more than a probability index for possible debt losses. The tantalizing question is how this probability index is being appraised?

In an early stage, so-called generic scores were created which were only based on the experience of risk managers. Special rating agencies still do possess the necessary knowledge which is being lodged in score cards in the form of decision and evaluation rules. Based on their own data stock, credit bureaus developed their own scores in order to forecast the credit-worthiness in the new- and stock-customers business.

The development of a score card (see Fig. 4) as probability index for a possible debt loss is based on mathematical/statistical methods. Via regression calculations, equivalence classes can be generated which are significant for the non-payment risk of a credit. To improve their accuracy, a large amount of spot checks can be drawn (up to 2 million records). This is followed by a $t_0 - t_1$ analysis which computes certain criteria indicating that a borrower will or will not pay back his credit. This mere mathematical/statistical process allows an exact contract selectivity with respect to good and bad risks both for the credit decision (application score) and for the risk evaluation of the credit stock.

Obviously, not only the profile data of the consumer influences the score, but also the purpose of the credit and, of course, the branch of the credit grantor. Customers with an identical profile may exhibit a differing payment behavior at distinct credit institutes. Therefore, it is reasonable to produce different score cards even within one branch like, for example, the banking sector which may be divided into

- major and private banks,
- savings banks,
- cooperative banks, and
- mortgage banks.

Fig. 5 tries to indicate the conceivable benefits to be accomplished when the selectivity of the risk assessment can be improved.

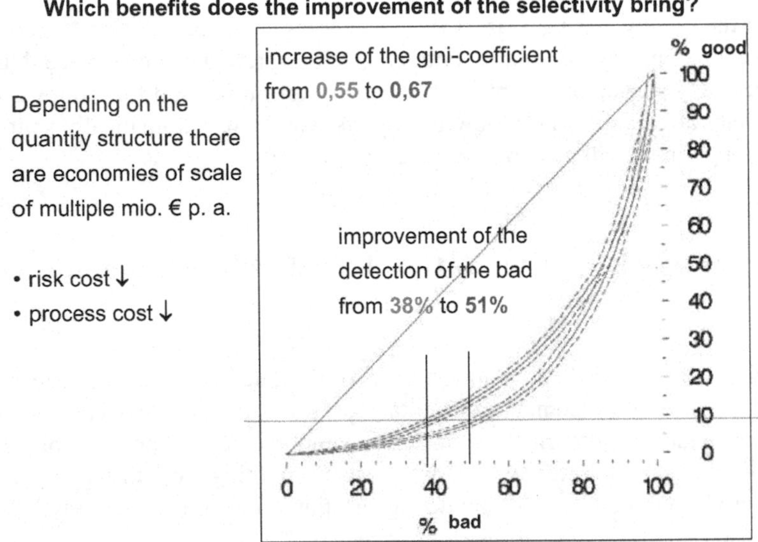

Fig. 5 Benefits of the Selectivity Improvement

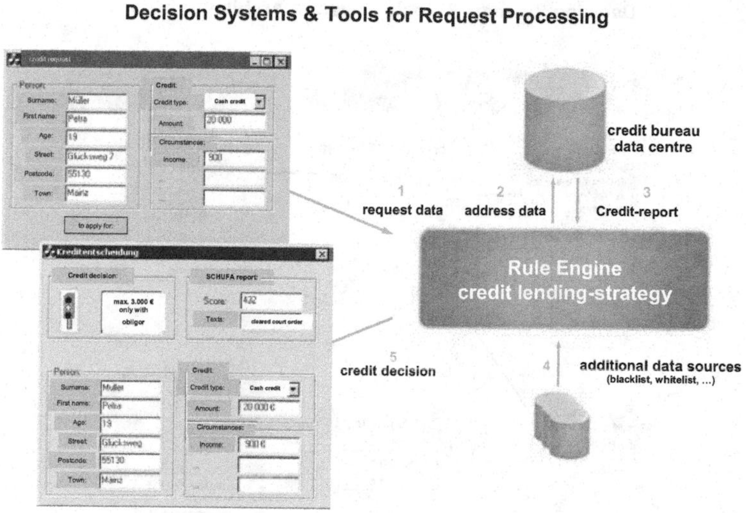

Fig. 6 Decision Systems & Tools for Request Processing

5 Decision Support at Point of Sale

After having sketched the risk evaluation procedure, we will briefly outline the process leading to a credit decision. Using the institution "credit bureau", the credit decision process is facilitated and accelerated not only for the contractual partner but also for the consumer. This applies for credits at banks, online orders at mail order companies as well as mobile phone contracts.

The application scoring allows an efficient execution of the credit processing. Its central mechanism is a high-capacity rule-engine which contains the credit granting-policy of the credit grantor. The credit bureau´s data, its score or the score variables form the basic contribution to the accuracy of the credit decision—this process is visualized in Fig. 6.

6 Integrated Scoring Systems

The development of integrated score cards in which the selective variables of the credit bureau are combined with the information delivered by the consumer in his credit request (e.g., income) and the information already stored at the bank (e.g., assets) increase the forecast's accuracy.

Integrated scoring systems evaluate this information and, thus, allow a more precise credit granting-policy in order to reach a justified decision. Via score cards, the non-payment risk of a certain customer is forecasted. All customers are divided into equiv-

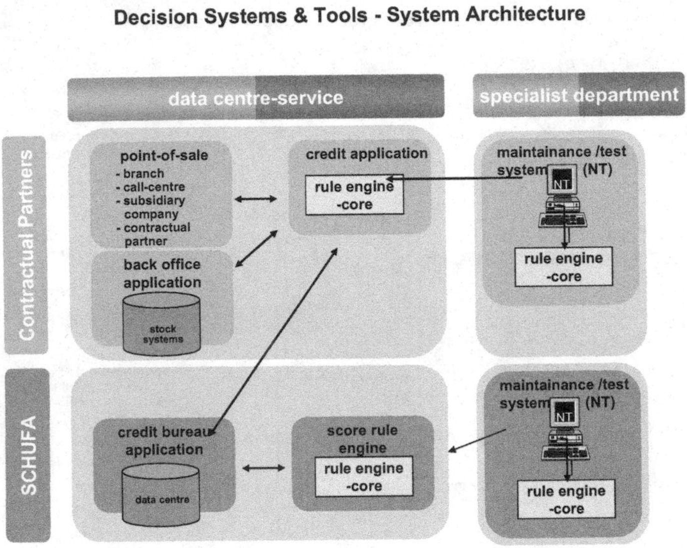

Fig. 7 Decision Systems & Tools—System Architecture

alence classes. According to the non-payment risk, each of these equivalence classes correspond to a certain type of credit offer.

In order to react on current market developments, it is essential for the credit grantor to have simple tools with which he can easily administer and change his credit granting strategy—for example, which credit offer will be assigned to which equivalence class. The system architecture enabling this required flexibility is sketched in Fig. 7.

7 Automation of the Credit Transaction Process

In order to demonstrate the various possibilities of automated credit transaction processes, it is best to have a closer look at the online credit granting of a direct bank. As illustrated in Fig. 8, such a system consists of two central components: the Web interface incorporating the presentation component which processes the dialogue with the users and the credit application with the rule engine. In this way, a user-friendly access to the bank is guaranteed for the customers. A credit request is immediately possible at any time. Additionally, the system operates via the Internet and, thus, its connectivity may be exploited as well.

The application enables a flexible and fast reaction to changing market situations and thus the bank can easily update its conditions. Furthermore, the process flow and the decision rules can be monitored; in this way, adaptations / changes can be quickly accomplished.

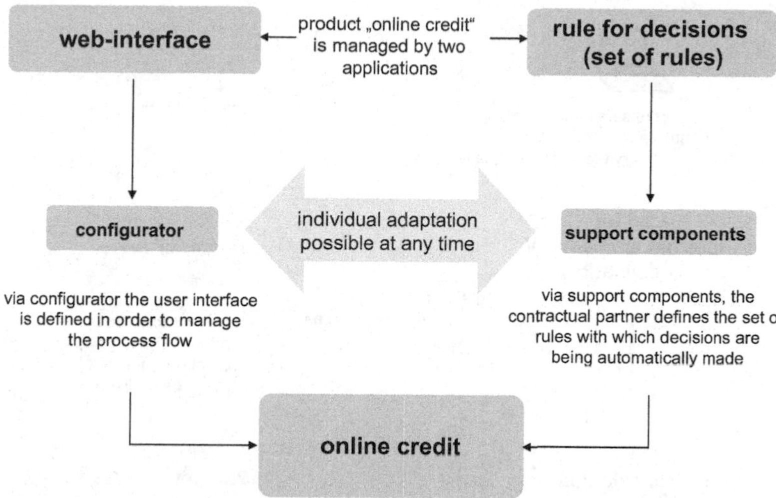

Fig. 8 Automation Phase I

To start a credit application, the personal data of the consumer is collected. For this purpose, the compulsory household calculation is relevant. The applicant is also compelled to present his credit obligations and his earning capacity. Of course, information concerning the credit itself like amount, duration, payment terms are also needed (see Fig. 9).

Having this information available, the bank can evaluate the credit request by means of a decision system. The basis for this evaluation is formed not only by the information delivered by the client himself but also via information already contained in the bank's data base concerning this client and additionally via the credit bureau's information on further obligations of the customer. According to the information resulting from these three data sources combined with the bank's credit granting strategy, the bank submits an offer to the customer. Of course, the bank will not take the credit risk, if a so-called "hard" negative criterion exists like, for example, a private insolvency proceeding. For the credit evaluation, the only relevant factor interesting for the bank is the non-payment risk for the credit request in question.

The acceptance of the credit bureau's clause (SCHUFA clause) is important, because the consumer hereby accepts the receipt and transfer of information to/from the credit bureau (SCHUFA) according to the regulations of the Privacy Law (see Fig. 10). After the information delivered by the consumer and by the credit bureau is available, usually an individual score for this specific credit decision situation is being generated thereby also referring to information in the bank´s data base. As a result, a direct and binding credit offer is submitted to the consumer. An individual evaluation of the non-payment risk for a certain credit request enables the bank to consciously control this risk. Hence, decisions formerly based on the experience of a loan officer are made on the basis of fixed rules combined with the extra information of integrated score cards.

Finally, the credit is being granted according to the proposed conditions.

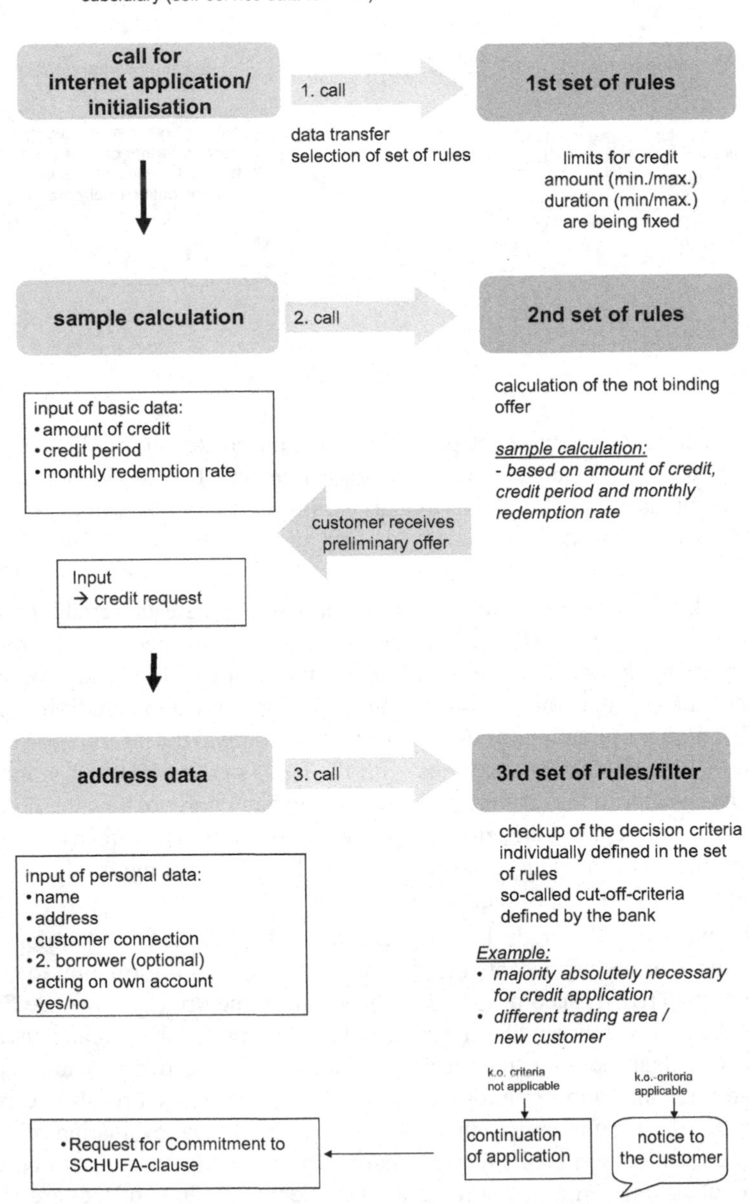

point of sale (salesman)
internet
subsidiary (self-service data terminal)
call for internet application/ initialisation
1. call
data transfer
selection of set of rules
1st set of rules
limits for credit amount (min./max.) duration (min/max.) are being fixed
sample calculation
2. call
2nd set of rules
input of basic data:
• amount of credit
• credit period
• monthly redemption rate
calculation of the not binding offer
sample calculation:
- based on amount of credit, credit period and monthly redemption rate
customer receives preliminary offer
Input → credit request
address data
3. call
3rd set of rules/filter
checkup of the decision criteria individually defined in the set of rules
so-called cut-off-criteria defined by the bank
input of personal data:
• name
• address
• customer connection
• 2. borrower (optional)
• acting on own account yes/no
Example:
• majority absolutely necessary for credit application
• different trading area / new customer
k.o. criteria not applicable
k.o.-criteria applicable
• Request for Commitment to SCHUFA-clause
continuation of application
notice to the customer

Fig. 9 Automation Phase II

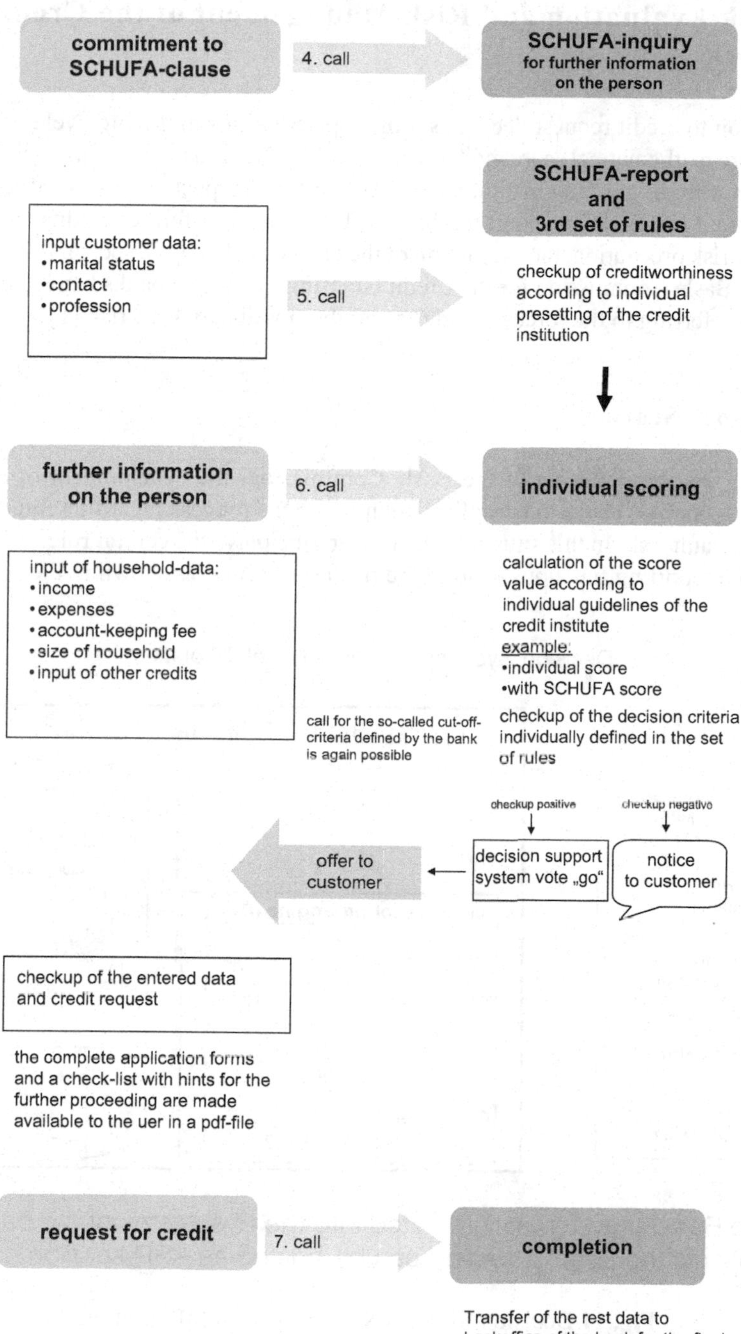

Fig. 10 Automation Phase III

8 Risk Evaluation and Risk Management of the Credit Stock

In addition to credit request decisions, other opportunities in the life cycle of a credit exist where mathematical score models can be useful. Next to the evaluation of the credit stock of a credit granting institute, forecasts for the prospect of success of reminders are important in case of payment troubles or the affinity for further credits. Due to the necessary risk precaution, the evaluation of the credit stock plays a special role. According to the Basle Commission for the Credit Granting Economy, banks have to obey certain rules referring to the forecast horizon and the possible default risk [1].

8.1 Stock Scoring

Following the requirements of the Basle Commission, the development of Basle II-score cards enables banks to periodically automate the process regarding forecast horizon and default risk. In this situation, the rule engine plays the central role. Additionally, flexible reporting functions support the risk controlling (as shown in Fig. 11).

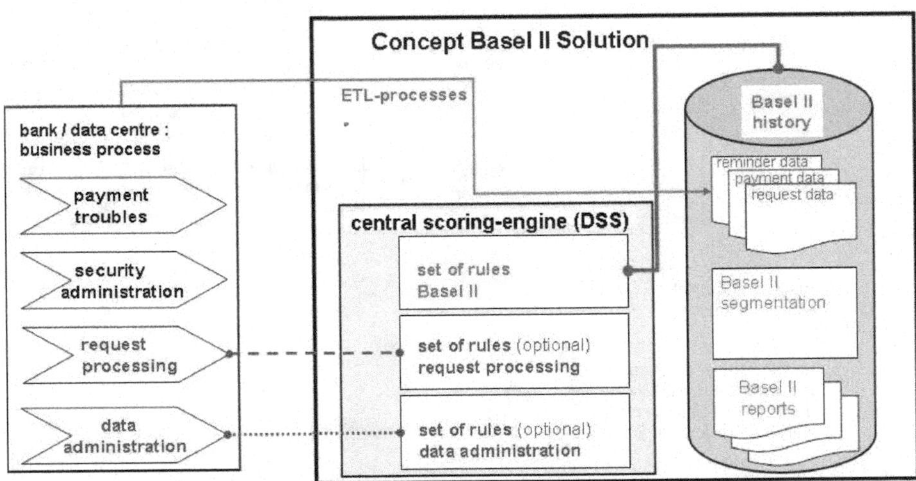

Fig. 11 Decision Systems & Tools—Basel II Solution

8.2 Follow-Up Report

The evaluation of the credit stock uses a statistical analysis. Additionally, the credit grantor still needs the individual examination of the single credit risk. Therefore, credit bureaus offer so-called follow-up reports. The credit bureau informs all contractual partners who have granted credits to a consumer on payment troubles or a significant score pejoration of this certain consumer. Via this triggered information, the credit grantors are able to individually adjust their risk evaluation of this credit and to take steps to minimize their risk, respectively. Technically speaking, these follow-up reports correspond to the normal reports. The only significant difference consists in the information being triggered by the credit bureau itself.

9 Perspective: "Glass Citizen" or "Mobile Trust"

This article shows that it is essential for the economy in a mobile world to create mutual trust between business partners. Ages ago people followed the slogan: "One knows each other and one helps each other". But times have changed. The high profile of each other is now replaced by the risk evaluation of a neutral trust-worthy institute. The reliability of the credit bureau´s data and the due diligence necessary are basic requirements for this procedure. Obviously, a credit grantor will only put trust in someone who deserves it, that is, who will settle his debts. It is always the solidarity community of all borrowers who will have to bear the expenses for increased credit cost caused by the non-payment mentality of single consumers. Thus, for the good of all concerned parties, the credit bureau supports the credit grantor in the evaluation of credit-worthiness and willingness to pay. Obviously, only correct information provides trust.

The keyword "Glass Person or Citizen" meaning the absolute transparency, the loss of privacy is the counter-value to information. Obviously, it is a question of morale and ethics in many areas of life, whether or not we will be allowed to withhold information or even deceive someone. Of course, in certain situations of life everybody has the right to consciously do this. But the individual protection of the consumer's concerns postulated in the Privacy Law must not lead to a protection of criminals. Therefore, we always have to balance between the individual protection of the consumer's concerns and the legitimate interest of the credit grantor. As a consequence, the credit grantor should only receive the information he will need for a proper credit decision and risk evaluation. Additional information is simply not to be granted. On the other hand, the credit grantor has a highly legitimated interest to minimize his risks.

Considering the above mentioned balance of interests, the protection against misuse of the credit bureau's data is a top-ranking issue. In order to achieve this goal, all appropriate technical, organizational, and legal precautions have to be taken [2].

It is helpful if everyone knows which data is being stored on him personally. Additionally, the information flow concerning a consumer has to be strictly processed according to fixed rules. The consumer should be able to put trust in the institution of the credit bureau which always strives for mirroring a correct picture of his credit-worthiness. The credit grantor should trust in getting a sufficiently correct and complete picture of the credit-worthiness of the consumer. Incorrect entries need a fast correction; such an action should always be combined with a consultation of the credit grantor who originally gave the wrong data input.

Careful handling and maintenance presumed, the data base of a credit bureau creates a real win-win-situation for both the credit grantor and the consumer [6]. Thus, consumers are enabled to act in economic freedom and credit grantors are enabled to put trust even in unknown clients.

Acknowledgement

Many thanks to Mrs. Sibylle Weisenborn for editing, translating, and formatting this text. Without her dedicated efforts this contribution would not have been possible.

References

[1] Basle Committee on Banking Supervision: New Capital Adequacy Framework. Consultative Paper. Mimeo, Basle (1999)

[2] Klöpfer, M.: Informationsrecht. C.H. Beck-Verlag, München (2002)

[3] Miller, M.J. (Editor): Credit Reporting Systems and the International Economy. MIT-Press, Cambridge MA (2003)

[4] Ortner, E.: Fachsprachlich normierte Anwendungssysteme – Eine neue Generation von Applikationssoftware für Unternehmen mit globalen Geschäftsbeziehungen. In: Information als Erfolgsfaktor. Bernd Britzelmaier / Stephan Geberl (Hrsg.), 2. Liechtensteinisches Wirtschaftsinformatik-Symposium an der FH Liechtenstein. B. G. Teubner Verlag, Stuttgart etc. (2000), S. 333-347

[5] Ortner, E.: Wissensmanagement, Rekonstruktion des Anwendungswissens. (Informatik-Spektrum 23), Heidelberg (2000) 2, S. 100-108

[6] SCHUFA HOLDING AG: Annual Report 2003. Wiesbaden (2004)

[7] SCHUFA HOLDING AG: 75-Jahre SCHUFA. Wiesbaden (2002)

[8] Steinbauer, D.: Kreditvergabe mit der SCHUFA. (DSWR, 5/2004), München (2004), S. 119-121

Data Refinement in a Market Research Applications' Data Production Process

Thomas Ruf, Thomas Kirsche

GfK Marketing Services, Germany
{thomas.ruf, thomas.kirsche}@gfk.de

Abstract. In this contribution, we will show how empirically collected field data for a market research application are refined in a stepwise manner and enriched into end-user market reports and charts. The collected data are treated by selections, transformations, enrichments, and aggregations to finally derive new market knowledge from the raw data material. Besides data-oriented aspects, process- and organization-related aspects have to be considered as well to ensure the required product quality for GfK Marketing Services' customers, which have known GfK for decades as a top-10 player in the international market research area. Based on an ongoing example from the panel-based Retail & Technology application domain, we will show how decentrally collected and pre-processed data are transformed into integrated, global market knowledge in a network of world-wide companies.

1 Introduction

The GfK Group, ranked fifth among market research companies worldwide, actively participates in the following five fields of business: Consumer Tracking, Health Care, Retail & Technology, Media, and Ad Hoc Research. In the fiscal year of 2003, the GfK Group has achieved a turnover of 595 million Euro (previous year: 559 million Euro). Apart from 15 branches in Germany, more than 120 enterprises and shares in 57 nations belong to the GfK Group worldwide. Approximately 1,500 of currently close to 5,500 employees are working in Germany.

In the field of Retail & Technology, the GfK Group regularly provides their clients from trade and industry with information services that are gained on the basis of continuous surveys and analyses of profits of technical consumer products in retail trade in 48 countries worldwide. In the fiscal year of 2003, this line of business generated turnover of 166.7 million Euro. The field of Retail & Technology is represented by GfK Marketing Services (GfK MS).

The processing of data through Retail & Technology from the industry to market reports is a process far from consisting of simple mathematical operations. Even though operations such as additions and average calculations are executed, the value added to

T. Härder and W. Lehner (Eds.): Data Management (Wedekind Festschrift), LNCS 3551, pp. 293-314, 2005.

the end-product lies in the refinement process, which is implemented as a business process with system support. Similar to an engineer, who applies and varies certain procedures for the construction of a component, GfK employees apply acknowledged and independently developed techniques to create reports, which actually reflect market events, from the data material. Artifacts from the random sampling as well as transfer and processing errors have to be identified and eliminated.

Concerning the software level, the refinement process is accompanied by a data production system that has been developed by GfK Marketing Services themselves. The data production system is a "data pump", which forwards data from one processing step to the next. Contrary to production systems for consumer goods, in which individual components are combined to assembly groups and, eventually, to the final product, the data change morphologically due to the processing. The information content can be increased and the entropy decreased respectively by either eliminating interferences or bundling data.

In this chapter, major steps of the refinement process will be explained, always with regard to their interplay with the data production system. In order to do so, a general overview of the initial situation of periodic market research and the data production system will be provided in the next section. In the subsequent sections, it will be shown how the enrichment takes place in the master data system, the data acquisition system, the analysis system, and the reporting system. An outlook will conclude this paper.

2 Data Production at GfK Marketing Services

To get an understanding of the products of the field of Retail & Technology, the first thing to be explained in this section is the basis on which to work. Following this, there will be a short overview of the whole data production system.

2.1 Initial Scenario for the GfK Products

To discuss the business process, a hypothetical example shall be used: a potential customer enters a local Media-Markt branch that is located on the outskirts. This Media-Markt branch is an outlet of the distribution channel of technical supermarkets. This channel of distribution is supported with certain advertising programs for which an advertising agency is responsible. Furthermore, the branch is characterized by annual profits, sales area, available parking areas, and, of course, its geographical location. The customer is interested in a special model of a cell phone of which he or she knows properties such as weight, standby time, Bluetooth connection options, and many more. However, the customer considers the price too high. Therefore, he or she approaches a retail dealer nearby, who cannot offer the same cell phone alone though, but who would sell it together with a 24-month contract and a camera. Eventually, the customer purchases the phone, in a bundle with contract, camera, and an additional battery, which enabled him to bargain another certain discount.

To represent the market, GfK Marketing Services use the perspective of the consumer. The decisive fact, therefore, is what a consumer has bought in what quantity and at what price. However, permanent surveying among a statistically sufficient group of consumers would be too arduous due to the low re-buying rates of technical consumer goods and, thus, it would be too expensive. Instead, basic information such as quantities and profits, as well as additional inventory parameters from the industry, are reported to the GfK. For this, the GfK Group has made respective agreements with the retail industry. Additionally, the characteristics of the branches and items will be recorded. To gain those information, business-side researches are conducted. The properties of the items are either collected by the GfK Group itself or provided by the producers, and complemented with information from publicly accessible information sources (catalogues, Internet).

2.2 Systematics of the GfK MS Product Portfolio

The agreements on data supplies with the industry are usually made under the requirement that the business activity (profits, assortment) of the data provider must not be directly visible from the GfK reports. Rather, it is only acceptable to publish the information in aggregated and/or anonymized form. Nevertheless, it should be possible to create very detailed reports on the sales activity, divided by sales channels or geographical properties. These reports, which can also be created from databases in an interactive and individual way by GfK clients themselves, serve, in the broadest sense, to support business-political decisions. These can be decisions of the producers on distribution measures and weightings; but, similar to Benchmarking processes, they can also provide brand vs. brand suggestions to a product portfolio. GfK clients from the industry use the GfK reports for assortment analyses as well as for decision support on which items to offer.

2.3 Overview of the Data Production System

To be able to connect the supplies from the various numbers of data sources in a meaningful way, but also to enrich the end-product with additional knowledge on the markets, GfK MS used a data production system for more than two decades [1]. This data production system was regularly updated and extended. A few years ago, the system was transferred to a completely new platform and adjusted to the needs of the globally acting clients. Since then, the system has been called StarTrack (System to Analyze and Report on Tracking Data) and is shown with its main modules in Fig. 1.

StarTrack has four main modules: IDAS, Preprocessing, Data Warehouse, and Master Data Management; they cover the major processing steps during the production process: Data Input & Identification, Production & Analysis, as well as Reporting & Delivery. The IDAS module (International Data Acquisition System) processes thousands of different data sources every week and transforms the data provided by the industry, which differ in form and contents, into a consistent analysis base. Here, items

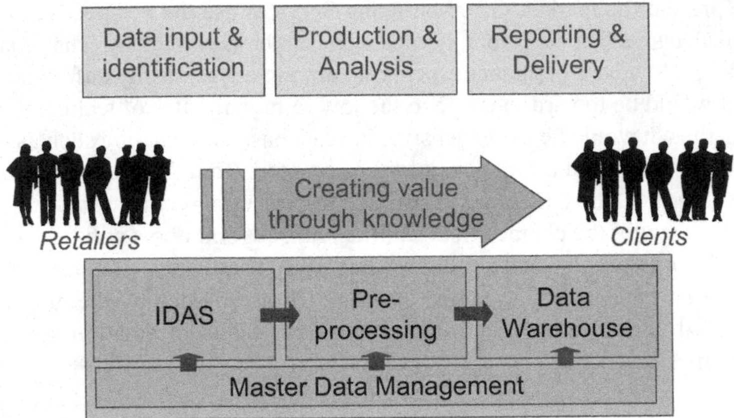

Fig. 1 StarTrack Main Tasks and Modules

and industry branches are uniquely described; this is the result of a procedure called *Identification*, which means assigning industry data to GfK item master data. During this procedure, assignments already in place will be preserved, and only new or outdated assignments will be edited every week. IDAS implements the first part of the quality control based on the data supplies, too.

The Preprocessing module allows to establish a retailer-overlapping market view by applying an extrapolation that has been structurally defined earlier. Whether or not this extrapolation can be used as specified depends on the data actually supplied and on the continued validity of the assumptions made. During the Preprocessing step, the second part of the quality control is executed; eventually, it ensures the market suitability of the processed data.

In the Data Warehouse, not only current data are represented, but especially past values are stored as well. Due to this, it is possible to systematically detect and display both detailed segmentations of the market within a certain period and market shifts over the course of time. Apart from its interactive analysis options, the Data Warehouse is also used as the basis for the creation and delivery of client reports with individual contents and of different formats. These formats range from paper printings and simple report browsers to complex Desktop Data Marts, from which clients can create reports tailored to their individual needs with the help of specific GfK tools.

The foundation for all StarTrack modules is the so-called Master Data Management System. It contains the technical properties of the items sold, the characteristics of the industry branches, and all information on clients and client subscriptions.

Recently, the StarTrack system has been extended with means to monitor and control the production workflow [10, 9]. Unlike the production of cosumer goods, data production exhibits characteristics that require an means beyond workflow management and project management [3].

3 Data Refinement in the Master Data System

The master data system of StarTrack forms a consistent reference point for all other components of StarTrack. Consistency is important, because all systems shall work with a single "truth", and by referencing the same master data, data can be exchanged without conversions. Among the master data are all describing information that is necessary for the interpretation of the periodically incoming transaction data. The master data system, known as MDM (Master Data Management) System, basically comprises information on items (what has been sold), on outlets (where has it been sold), and on customers (who gets what deliverable). From the data modeling perspective, the master data are used for building the dimensions of the Star schema of the DWH, while the transaction data are used to fill the fact table. The presentation in this section focuses on the item base; however, many design properties can be found again in both outlet and customer section of MDM.

3.1 The Concept of Items

Items, sometimes also called products or models, are goods that are offered and purchased by participants in the market. Usually, these goods have certain identifying characteristics. Apart from the actual brand and model description, e.g., Siemens S55 for a certain cell phone, or Humax PVR8000 for a Set Top Box, these can also be keys. A key system commonly used throughout Europe is the EAN code, which is usually represented by a bar code on product packaging. Unfortunately, the same product can appear with different EAN codes in the market, or an EAN code can be reused for different products. The EAN code, as well as its non-European equivalents UPC code and JAN code, are thus not sufficient for the definition of an item.

Therefore, GfK Marketing Services use a concept of items that is based on the sales market. A product from different series with different EAN codes is listed as one item, if the differences are not considerably decisive for a purchase; an example would be an altered production technology.

The item master system MDM groups millions of items in about 250 product groups, which in turn are assigned to product group categories and product group sectors. Every item is described by its brand, the name of the model, and a number of up to 100 properties or function properties—so-called features—respectively. Some examples are shown in Tab. 1.

All products within the same product group are classified by the same features. However, the different nature and functionality of non-food items and product groups require a large variance in the description of features of these products.

3.2 Multi-step and Combined Concepts of Items

Occasionally, the industry attempts to group several products in one offer. For example, mobile phones are often bundled together with contracts and digital cameras. The customer might indeed include this bundle in his decision-making; thus, it has to be recorded differently if a certain mobile phone has been purchased alone or in a bundle. In the master data system, bundles are, therefore, managed both as individual items for sale and in connection with their respective items. Except for their bundle description, bundles do not have any features. The descriptions can be found at the level of the items belonging to the bundle.

Tab. 1 Product Groups and Features (examples)

Product Group Sectors	Product Groups (Selection)	Examples for Features and Their Feature Value
Large Appliances, Small Kitchen Appliances, Jewellery, Furniture	Washing Machines, Vacuum Cleaners, Shavers, Watches, Kitchen Furniture	Water Consumption (in litres), Cable Rewind (with, without), Dust Bags (with, without), etc.
Consumer Electronics	TV Sets, VCRs, Car Radios, DVD Players	Screen Size (in inches), Sound System (Stereo, Mono), TV Norm (NTSC, PAL, SECAM, PAL/SECAM multi), Remote (with/without), Number of Video Heads (2,4,5)
IT/Telecom	Cellular Phones, PCs, Printers, Software	Band (Single-, Dual- or Tri-band), Mounting Form (Mini Tower, Tower, 19", Barebone), Pages per Minute, Application Field (learning game, entertainment, home office)

Apart from the option of grouping items, there is also the possibility of detailing. This option is used in all those cases in which the purchase decision shall not (yet) be documented in detail, but where the detail is necessary for the correct assignment. Among others, typical examples in this regard are models that are offered in different colors, patterns, or finishes. Certainly, it might play a role for the purchasers of a mobile phone whether the cover is sunset-orange, ice-blue, or night-black, but the segmentation of the market by cover colors is currently not desired or necessary. Therefore, the mobile phone is listed as an item, and the color variants are listed as item details.

To be able to handle another specialty of producers, the master data system provides an additional item concept, the so-called product lines. Similar to items, product lines have features and represent the properties of a certain product family. All members of the product family have certain common properties, e.g., Siemens mobile phones S series. In other features, the items can still differ from one another. The assignment of an item to a product line only enforces that the assignments for the features of the product line are the same. From a semantic data modeling perspective, the relationship between items and product lines is an "is-a" relationship, whereas the one between bundles and items is a "has" relationship.

Ultimately, errors during maintenance processes of the item master data cannot be excluded; either erroneous information have been reported, or errors have been committed during the input process. MDM provides ordered options for handling and eliminating such classification errors. The key to this is the storing of item versions, i.e., modifications of an item never overwrite existing data but, instead, they only create a new version of the item. For example, if an item has been detected that either does not exist at all or not in the way described, it is not only possible to invalidate the respective item but it can also be connected to a successor item. This successor relation expresses that existing transaction data of the old item have to be adopted for the successor item. By doing so, the market volumes in the reports will be preserved.

3.3 Product Group Schema and Schema Evolution

At first sight, it might appear surprising that the information for a product are subjected to a continuous modification process. A product has certain properties, and these information should be stable. However, because not all properties are recorded from the beginning—and neither is every detail—the need for a continuous modification of the item master information arises. This also applies to the schema of the product groups. For example, 15 years ago, it was important to state for a stereo whether it has a noise reduction system or not. Nowadays, the different kinds of audio systems (Dolby B/C, Dolby HX pro, Dolby AC3) are the basis for independent market segments of this product category.

As a consequence, with regard to the data model of the MDM, the modification process has to be implemented at the application side. To do so, the set of features belonging to a product group is recorded as meta-data. For every relevant, released modification, these meta-data are used to re-create product group relations according to the now desired feature list. The structure of the product group relations is intuitive—every feature is represented by an attribute, and every item is represented by a tuple (see Fig. 2). The meta-relations mentioned represent the relation between product groups and features, and the feature properties are stored in additional meta-relations.

In general, features of product groups differ from one another, because, for example, refrigerators have different properties than impact drilling machines. Single features, however, can be used in several product groups which are, in most cases, related. For example, a feature called "Image Format" (4:3/16:9) can be found for TV sets, cam-

Product Group Relations					Meta-Relation (Features)		
ID	Feature 1	Feature 2	…	Feature n	PG	Feature	Meaning
Item 1	65	…			A	1	Water Con-sumption
Item 2	27	….			B	1	Screen Size
….					A	2	…

Fig. 2 Product Group Relations and Meta-Relation

corders, DVD players, and other product groups. The MDM system accounts for this multi-usability by storing these features in an identical way for the related product groups. Thus, it is possible in the reporting systems, too, to create a connection between the markets that spans several product groups.

The MDM system is probably one of the most comprehensive international item master databases for consumer products worldwide. Apart from the GfK Group, we do not know of any other institution with a similarly comprehensive and up-to-date information system for the properties of consumer products decisive for a purchase. The value of these information is so unique that they are distributed as an independent product under the name Encodex (www.encodex.com).

4 Data Refinement in the Data Acquisition System

The basis for the products of the field of Retail & Technology of the GfK Group is information from the retail industry. Traditionally, this information has been collected through field work. However, that caused disadvantages in the degree of detailing and caused higher costs in case of frequent surveys. Therefore, several thousand retail companies worldwide report important information on the sale of individual products—especially quantities, prices, and stocks—in a direct, electronic way. The reported data, so-called tracking data in raw format, are considerably different in

- scope (selected assortment or extraction of the relevant section by MS)
- segment level (branch-specific representation or aggregation on the level of a trade center)
- granularity (representation of the sales of multi-packs and sets or specification of components or declaration of the purchase confectioning)
- representation (comprehensive, unique key system or use of retailer-internal abbreviations)

- format (output from standardized merchandise information systems or individual solution)
- quality (identifiability, e.g., by using over-arching classification systems such as the EAN code)

Often, commercial enterprises can be convinced of providing data for market research only after intense negotiations. The options for normalizing tracking data are rather limited concerning the differences on the part of the industry mentioned above.

The task of the data acquisition system IDAS (International Data Acquisition System) is to map the reality of the industry by consistent criteria and structures at a central place. Basically, the information refer to which items have been sold or purchased when and where. As facts, the sale and purchase quantities, as well as the price, are at the center. This information forms the basis for the analysis of the data according to market-relevant criteria in the Data Warehouse. As a preparatory step for the evaluation, the data acquisition system transforms the data from a delivery-connected composition (one outlet, many product groups) into a product-group-oriented composition (one product group, many outlets), too. While doing so, a temporal grouping of delivery periods to reporting periods takes place as well.

The business processes in the GfK MS, especially those of the data acquisition system, have been implemented on a system-technical level years before the Data Warehouse technology gained in importance. If one compares the Data Warehouse terminology currently in use with the processes in the GfK, the data acquisition field would be called Data Cleansing Process, which is aided by ETL (extraction, transformation, loading) technologies. In the following sections, it will become clear that, beyond this, the identification process is central; however, it cannot be found like this in common Data Warehouses.

4.1 Continuous Data Acquisition Process

The starting point for the data acquisition system IDAS is an almost continuous data flow of information on sales provided by the industry. Nowadays, almost 5,000 different data sources are processed with the help of IDAS, most of which are reported weekly, but sometimes, on a monthly, daily, or irregular basis, too. Because the evaluations shall cover certain defined periods of time (usually weekly or monthly), the provision of the data in a consistent reporting base is necessary, independently from all specifics of the data sources. The reporting base is created in a snapshot-like manner. The data acquisition system should, therefore, provide the best available data stock respectively in a preferably continuous manner. Hence, the data are continuously being replenished.

In Fig. 3, the main components of IDAS are represented. On the one hand, they are divided into the fields of extraction, transformation and quality control. On the other hand, components for the identification of unknown keys, the product group implementation and the elimination of other delivery characteristics can be found. The two subparts are called IDAS Local and IDAS Central, for the former is used locally in the GfK branches throughout the world, and the latter is used in the company headquarters.

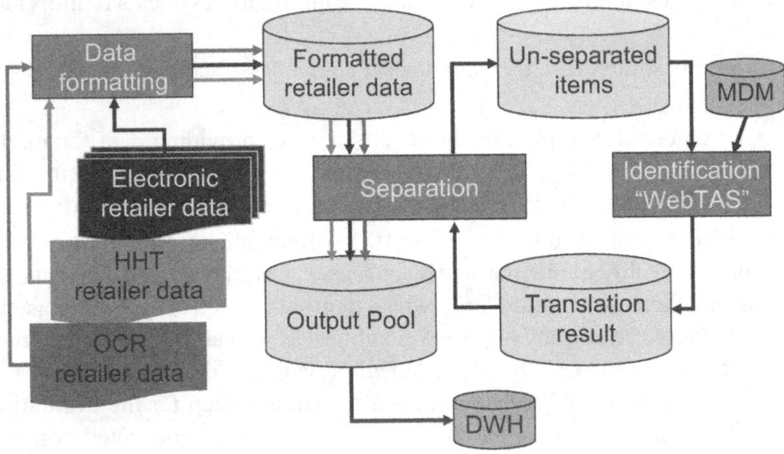

Fig. 3 Complete IDAS Architecture

The main task of the IDAS Local components is to reduce incoming data to the required amount in an effective way. To do so, the data are accepted in almost any electronic format as well as in the form of field work data—acquired as optical character recognition (OCR) data or via handheld terminals (HHT). After various refinement steps (data formatting, separation), these data are made available to IDAS Central. On the one hand, IDAS Central accepts the data provided and aggregates them in the so-called "IDAS Export" into the Data Warehouse downstream. On the other hand, IDAS Central, with its item identification system WebTAS, enables the components of IDAS Local to successively deliver the previously unknown data.

All modules of IDAS Central are controlled by a job execution system, which manages the high number of reports coming in from various countries, starts the respective processing modules, and makes sure that the correct results are forwarded to the respective module. Thereby, the job execution system has been kept in such a general way, that it is used by other components of StarTrack.

An information system reflects the degree of filling of the IDAS output pool. Various views permit grouping by product groups, deliveries, and dates. Thereby, statements are given not only on available data but also on data not yet identified or even on cancelled deliveries. Thus, it is possible to choose an optimal point in time for beginning the analysis. Therefore, the management can be based on the final product, i.e., the client reports.

4.2 Quality Control During the Data Acquisition Process

Many of the sales data, which GfK Marketing Services receive from the industry, are not very qualified for the needs of the panel business. The data acquisition system conducts this qualification in several steps, which are at first rather raw and then become finer. The guideline is: As many data details as necessary, but as few as possible, because with higher processing volume, the costs will rise in all subsequent business processes. Therefore, the rule is that redundant data should be separated from the required data in an early and effective way. At the highest possible aggregation level, IDAS Local provides required data only. Data that are not needed will be ignored, and questionable, unknown data will be qualified in a process step called *Identification*. Only after the identification, it will be known what kind of item is dealt with, e.g., a TV set or an alarm clock radio. It goes without saying that only after the identification of the items such issues as the prices supplied can be checked for their plausibility.

Quality control for data flows faces the permanent dilemma that, on the one hand, an early control should be aspired because possible errors can still be eliminated without delays for the whole process. On the other hand, the quality control shall take place as late as possible, because the control will be the more qualitative the more comparison data are available. For example, price shifts can hardly be evaluated based on the report from one outlet only. However, if many outlets report similar shifts, a control and acceptance is indeed possible. In addition, as has been indicated above, the item information in the data production process are only available to GfK after the identification process.

Therefore, a quality check takes place during the data acquisition process, that gets along without an identification of the data and that draws its comparison values from the past. In this regard, a data structuring that can be found in many data sources is helpful: The items are assigned to product groups which are different from those used by GfK, though. Therefore, they are called foreign product groups in the GfK. Then, for every data provision and every foreign (or retailer) product group, the number of data records, the total of sales, and the profits will be compared with past data. While this kind of control is still relatively self-evident, experience has shown that data problems are often caused by reorganization measures, e.g., in the merchandise information systems of the retailers. To account for that, the keys (item number or the like) used by the data source will be saved together with the complementary item descriptions (model descriptions or the like). For every data delivery, it will be checked whether or not key and complementary item description are still linked in the data delivery. If this is not the case, the item number might have been used for another item. This case is very frequent with EAN codes, the use of which has to be paid for by the producers, which then again often motivates them to reuse old, outdated EAN codes after a certain waiting period.

Because EAN codes are keys that are used by different data sources, it is worth comparing the complementary item descriptions from different data sources, too. They should describe the same item. If this is not the case for a certain data source, it is most likely that this data source is using an incorrect EAN code.

Unfortunately, erroneously positive runaways regularly appear on the agenda. If a foreign product group is split in two, each individual item with its facts can still be correct, even though the volumes of the previous foreign product group are cut in half now.

4.3 Identification

Apart from the quality controls in IDAS Local, the data are refined by the so-called separation module. For this, the separation module uses a unique key of the item. If the item's key is known from previous data provisions, the separation module can decide whether the data are needed or not. If the key of an item, e.g., of a newly delivered one, is not yet available, the separation module takes this item and hands it over to IDAS Central only once, even if it is mentioned in many outlets.

With the help of the identification tool WebTAS (see Fig. 4) in IDAS Central, the key of an item is defined and, provided the item is needed, an assignment to an item of the Non-Food item base is created. The assignment rules are returned to IDAS Local, and the separation module is able, in a second attempt, to correctly transport the tracking data for the item in all outlets to the output interface of IDAS Local, called IDAS (local) Output Pool. From there, the data will be transferred to IDAS Central—either in time-controlled or need-controlled manner—for further processing.

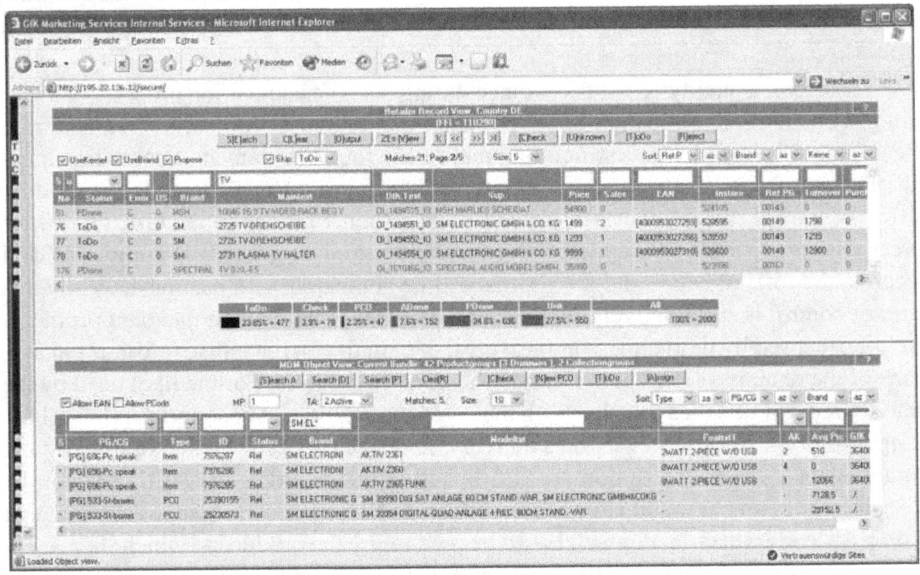

Fig. 4 Central Screen View of WebTAS

In the central screen view of WebTAS (see Fig. 4), the tracking data of the retailer are shown in the upper half of the screen. In the lower half of it, the items of the item base from MDM are searched and displayed. The main action in WebTAS for every (unknown) retailer item is the detection of the suitable item from the GfK item base and, thus, its assignment for processing purposes. WebTAS permits the sorting and selection of the retailer items by various criteria to achieve maximum processing speed. For example, if a retailer delivers three products of different colors as three data records, the sorting process will not only display the three unknown products in a spatially close position for a better assignment decision, but all three records can be assigned with a single mouse click, too. In WebTAS, items that cannot be finally assigned or cancelled immediately can be cached with the help of the PCO (partly classified object) function. Now, the sorting function can be used to clear the most important (because sold most often) items with priority.

Depending on the quality of the retailer data and the demanded item assignments, it is indeed possible for a single person to conduct several hundreds of assignments per minute(!). A good help here is the suggestion system integrated in WebTAS. For every unknown item, a short and, thus, manageable list of possible assignments is created based on text comparisons under consideration of retailer and product group properties. In the ideal case, the people do not have to search the item base themselves, but they can select a suggestion. Depending on the quality of the retailer data and the product group properties, the suggestion system already achieves impressive hit quotas and puts the correct assignment at the first rank of the suggestion list. A fully automatic assignment appears to be actually implementable in certain situations, but currently it is not in use yet.

Another advantage of WebTAS is the option of simultaneous processing of items by several people, according to analysis-oriented priorities. Additionally, the automatic determination of a possible product group for every unknown item, that results from the knowledge of similar, already existing assignments, is helpful. With it, those retailer data records can be specifically processed for which an analysis is pending next.

Apart from pure transaction data, the data acquisition system also provides information on the quality, availability, and completion of the transaction data. Based on these meta-data, the decision on when a meaningful start—and with which part of the analysis—is possible will be made. The processes in the analysis system will be described in the next section.

5 Data Refinement in the Analysis System

The central task of the so-called analysis system in the production process of the GfK Marketing Services is to create the market suitability of the input data provided by the industry. Apart from statistics-based procedures, such as the extrapolation definition for the description of a market model, here, checking and correction steps are prevalent; they will help detect and clear insufficiencies in the provided transaction data. Ultimately, the important goal is to bring the reality of the data deliveries in accordance with the idealized market model of the extrapolation to be able to derive plausible statements on the market activity for clients.

5.1 Overview of the Evaluation Process

The evaluation process, also called preprocessing, is best visible when the processing steps belonging to it are presented in a process and data flow diagram. (cf. Fig. 5):

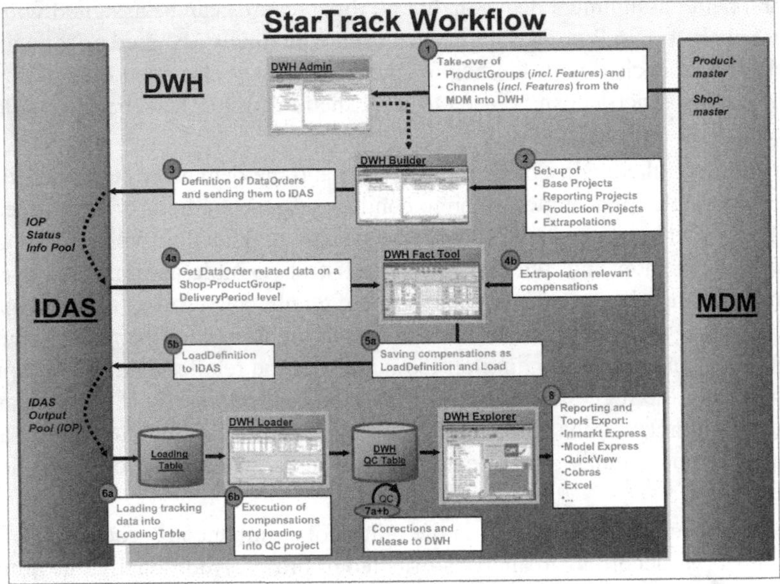

Fig. 5 Overview of Preprocessing

Preprocessing comprises the following steps:

- definition of the underlying data model in the DWH Administrator
- definition of an extrapolation as debit requirement in the DWH Builder
- definition of a DataOrder in the DWH Builder
- processing of the DataOrder in IDAS
- loading the status information from IIS (IDAS Information System) to the DWH FactTool by opening a LoadDefinition in the FactTool
- quality control of the retailer data and, if necessary, correction by means of the DWH FactTool
- saving the extrapolation-relevant compensations in the open LoadDefinition
- comparison of the data of a DataOrder existing in the DWH FactTool with the current IIS status information (already before loading the actual transaction data)
- execution of the LoadDefinition (from within the FactTool), i.e., loading the model-based data from the IOP (IDAS Output Pool) to the DWH
- quality control with fine corrections in the QC project (DWH Explorer) and release to the DWH reporting
- reporting in the DWH Explorer

Whilst the first two steps are only executed once, all subsequent steps have to be performed repetitively reporting period by reporting period.

In the following, the central components of this process—the extrapolation definition, the DWH FactTool and the quality control in the DWH QC—will be described in more detail.

5.2 Extrapolation Definition in the DWH Builder

A first step of the analysis process is the definition of a market model. It has to be defined which outlets in the market shall be included in the survey and with which extrapolation factors they shall be used to also represent the outlets that are not included in the sample. To do so, a disproportional sampling procedure [4], that assigns individual outlets to homogeneous classes under consideration of channel affiliation and profit importance, is used to define a system of extrapolation cells, in which the extrapolation factors of the outlets are either equally distributed to the cell outlets or individually specified for each cell outlet (see Fig. 6).

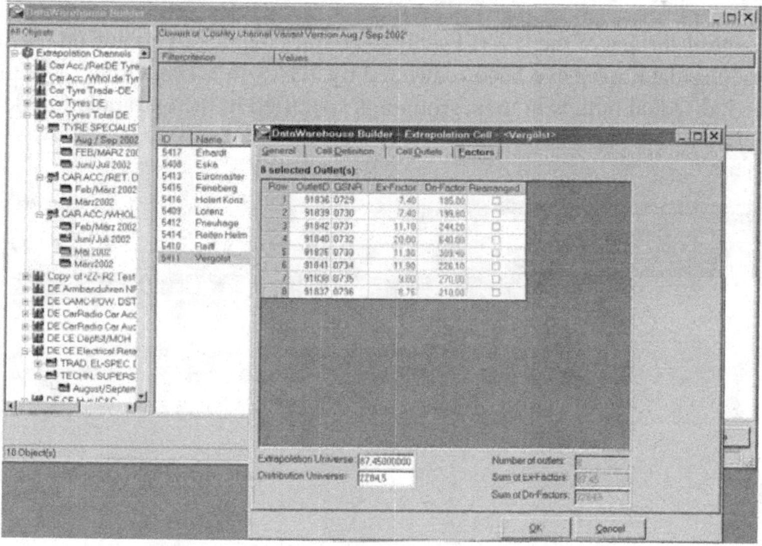

Fig. 6 Definition of Extrapolation Cells

According to the extrapolation model, the transaction data of the cell outlets will then be periodically requested from the data acquisition system IDAS and forwarded to further processing steps.

5.3 Compensation of Delivery Outages in the DWH FactTool

The DWH FactTool is part of the interface between IDAS and the Data Warehouse. As a part of the preprocessing, the DWH FactTool can be used to extrapolate retailer data in such a way that they can be loaded as basis for further extrapolations to DWH base projects. The main task of the DWH FactTool is to balance insufficiencies in the data deliveries of the industry in order to have a continuous, market-related time series of transaction data, from which knowledge on market constellations and market developments can be derived. Typical tasks taking place in the DWH FactTool are:

- outlets with missing data are compensated with data from the preceding period of the same outlet
- outlets with missing data are filled with data from similar outlets of the current period
- outlets with incomplete data are weighted.

Similar characteristics apply to product groups within one outlet and to delivery periods within product groups of an outlet. It becomes clear that a hierarchical descent on the analysis and compensation level is possible (correction of complete outlet / product group within an outlet / delivery period within a product group of an outlet) to allow for a reaction to delivery outages that is ideally compact and efficient (complete outlet) but, if necessary, can also be of very fine granularity (single delivery period within a product group of an outlet).

The central surface of the DWH FactTool enables a quick overview on the status of the transaction data that have been requested by IDAS in a DataOrder. The top level shows the individual outlets in their groupings specified in the extrapolation definition (see Fig. 7).

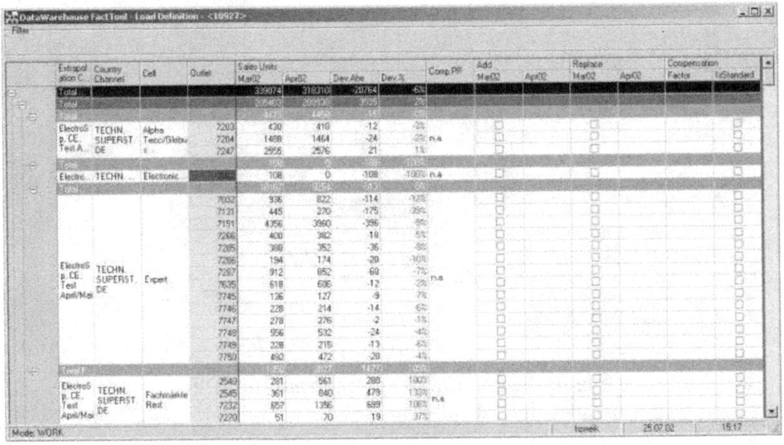

Fig. 7 Main View in the DWH FactTool

The colorings used in the display of the DWH FactTool give a quick overview on the quality of the transaction data being available in IDAS for the selected DataOrder. Green outlets fully meet the requirements, yellow outlets have provided data but only in insufficient quality, and red outlets are marked as a delivery outage in one or more delivery periods. For yellow and red outlets, the DWH FactTool can be used to create a rule for how to handle the insufficient or missing data in the subsequent production process (e.g., replacement of a missing data delivery with the data from the previous period of the same outlet or with a similar outlet in the current period). The decision on which kind of compensation is most suitable for a specific delivery problem is at the discretion of experienced market researchers and cannot be automated according to current assessment.

5.4 Quality Control in the DWH QC

Even though compensations of delivery outages can already be applied in the DWH FactTool, it is still necessary in many cases to let the data, either supplied from the field or created by compensations, undergo a detailed check and, if necessary, a correction, because the consistency of the data quality of the business panel can otherwise not be guaranteed for such a high number of external data sources. Here, too, the system can only provide checking routines and, if needed, correction suggestions; the final decision on whether or not—and if applicable, in what way—the delivered transaction data will be manipulated, can again only be made by market experts with comprehensive, long-time knowledge of the market.

The quality control of the transaction data in the DWH QC (Quality Control) takes place within the context of the reporting system of GfK Marketing Services, the DWH Explorer. The advantage of this is that the full functionality and flexibility of the reporting system can be used for the creation of checking reports. In section 6, this will be explained further. In the following, the specific checking and correction options of the DWH QC will be discussed in more detail.

The DWH QC comprises the following specific quality check and control options:

- price check and correction
- check for runaways and additional set checks (based on constant mass, too) and corrections
- check of alteration rates
- modification of sales, purchases, and stocks
- weightings based on items or aggregates (per factor and per target value input)
- deletion and creation of items (e.g., for influencing the distribution)
- copying and moving transaction data.

5.4.1 Price Check and Correction

In the price-check section of the QC in the DWH Explorer, the parameters for the price check are set, the price check is started, and the results of the automatic price check and price correction are visualized to the user to either approve or edit the suggestions provided by the system. The price check consists of three steps:

- detection of a reference price per item and channel
- checking the prices against the reference price
- price correction, if necessary.

The detection of the reference price takes place according to certain parameters to be defined by the user, e.g., the minimal number of prices found. The reference price detection is based on the current period and includes previous periods for reference price definition only if the entries found in the current period are not sufficient. If the previous periods are not sufficient either, an external price (master data reference price) will be included. If necessary, a sub-product group price will be created to be used as basis for checking, too; the sub-product groups would have to be defined by the user.

The price check is oriented at certain ranges upwards and downwards around the reference price to find out whether or not a price can be accepted. Additionally, it has to be defined if the reference price itself, the lower or upper bound, or the lowest or highest price found within the defined ranges around the reference price shall be used for a price replacement.

The result of the automated price checking routine is a correction catalogue, in which the user is provided with the prices heavily diverging from the detected reference price, along with suggestions for their correction. The user can accept the correction suggestions, enter a manual correction price, or leave the delivered price unchanged.

5.4.2 Further Fact Corrections

With the help of the DWH QC, a user can define correction factors or target values for individual transaction data arrays on an aggregated basis. The necessity of a correction is decided upon by the user based on checking reports, in which, for example, the divergence (in percentage) of the market volumes of certain brands in individual market segments can be represented.

When executing fact corrections, it has to be ensured in the system that the inner consistency of the data material is not violated. An example for this is the relation between initial and final stocks as well as between purchases and sales:

```
final stock = initial stock + purchases - sales,
```

with the additional requirement that the initial stock of the current period has to be equal to the final stock of the preceding period. For example, if the sales quantity is increased, an adjustment over the stock or sales has to be made to obey the formula above. For this purpose, the system offers various settings (see Fig. 8).

With the options of the DWH QC, an experienced market researcher can execute manipulations of the transaction data to eliminate obvious quality problems in the delivered transaction data. If the market suitability of the data can be ensured in this way, they can subsequently be released as a new reporting period into the DWH Reporting.

6 Data Refinement in the Reporting System

In this section, the Data Warehouse Explorer will be introduced as the central reporting instrument of GfK Marketing Services. For that, the analytical options of the system will be presented from an application perspective.

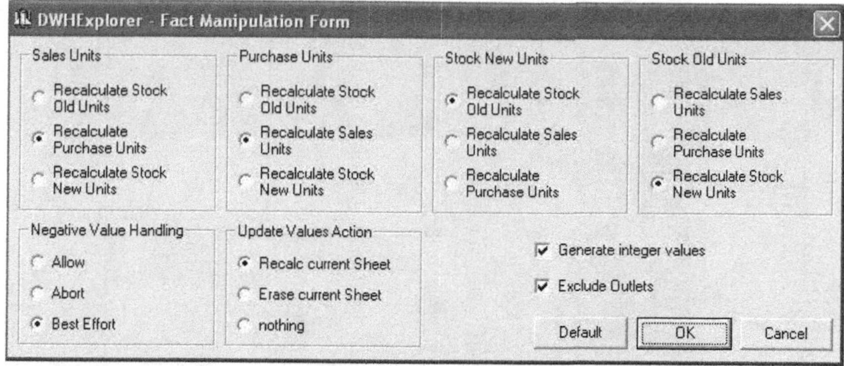

Fig. 8 Fact Manipulation Form in the DWH QC

The Data Warehouse systems commonly used nowadays are marked by some serious limitations with regard to their use for panel data analyses. For example, in basically all systems, it is taken for granted that classification hierarchies have a global validity in the respective dimension [2]. For the application field of panel data research, this would mean that the technical product features, which shall be used especially for fine market segmentations, would have to be modeled globally.

In more specific terms, this would mean that, for example, the classification feature "rotation speed" would have to be reserved for color TV sets the same way as for washing machines. Of course, that is absurd. The other way round, the question about the screen size of a washing machine could hardly be answered either. This creates the need for a modeling that allows for the declaration of product features depending on the current analysis status in a context-oriented way. The important thing, here, is that in those cases in which a feature is actually spanning several product groups—for example, the brand—a systematic representation of the circumstances takes place.

Another problem with the Data Warehouse systems currently in use is the "all-or-nothing" semantics for drill operations. Many systems support drill operations of various kinds: drill-down, drill-up, drill-across, etc. [7]. However, they provide the refinement only for either one initial element of a reporting level or for all elements together. In the product world of GfK, this way of proceeding would either lead to a flood of unconnected partial reports or to unnecessarily extensive global reports.

A better solution would be a system which can be used, for example, to segment TV sets with low screen diagonals further depending on whether they are sold with or without remote control, while this criterion would not be selective for big TV sets, for which, for example, the differentiation should be based on more meaningful features, such as 100-Hertz technology or 16:9 picture format. By doing so, specific knowledge can be gathered from the abundance of available data.

The limitations mentioned above as well as further ones in current Data Warehouse systems, such as the insufficient semantics of the calculation of Totals and Others, led to the GfK Marketing Services' development of their own Data Warehouse system [8]. Apart from the solution of the problems described, this system is marked by a very intuitive user interaction similar to Windows. In this system, the user specifies the desired

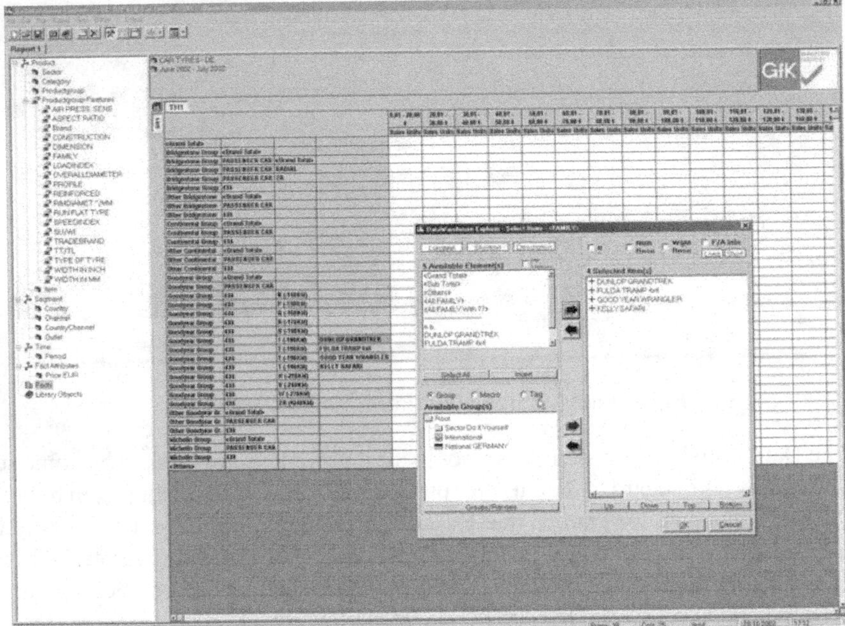

a) Definition View in the DWH Explorer

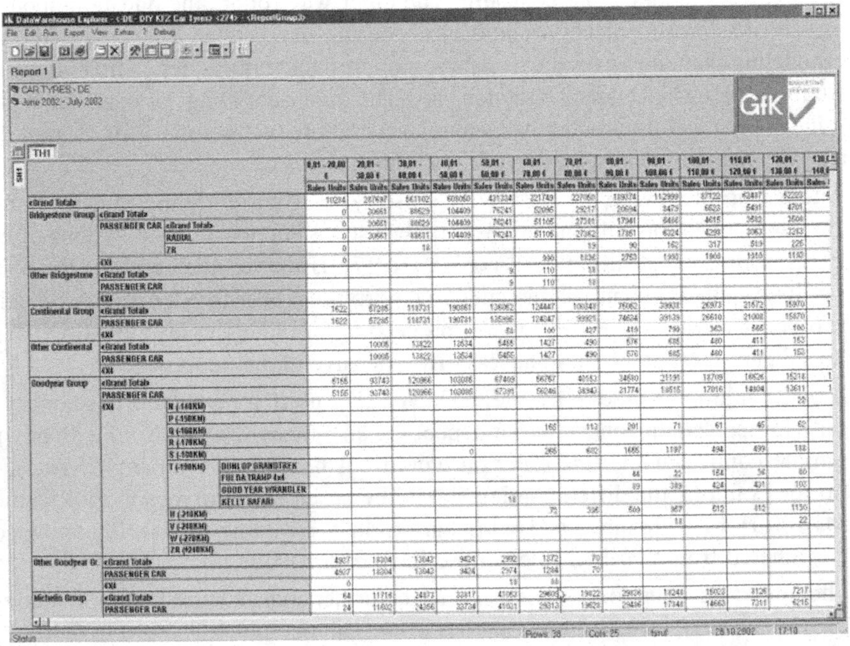

b) Execution View in the DWH Explorer

Fig. 9 Definition and Execution Views in the DWH Explorer

report structure by drag&drop operations. While this happens, the system immediately displays every step in the resulting report structure and updates the context for subsequent specification steps (What You See Is What You Get). This means, the system provides the user with further meaningful analysis options at all times—and only with these [6]. In Fig. 9a, the user interface of the DWH Explorer is shown the way it would look like for a typical market research report during the interactive report specification. Fig. 9b shows the respective market research report in the result view.

On an analytical level, the comprehensive application-specific metrics libraries, for example, those for numerical and weighted distribution parameters, and a context-sensitive hitlist generation have to be emphasized in connection with the Data Warehouse system of GfK Marketing Services. The latter allows to generate item-level, ranked hitlists according to the filter parameters of any data cell—selectable via mouse click—of an initial report, and to continue processing the items or brands constituting the initial cell as an independent report. For example, if a strong growth of the market share for 100-Hertz color TV sets with 16:9 format is detected in a period comparison, this function can be used to execute an immediate detail analysis to find out which individual models or brands have especially contributed to this development. In a subsequent analysis step, it can be examined, for example, whether the strongest brand found shows a similar growth in adjacent product groups and whether, thus, rather a commonly higher brand value appraisal instead of a preference for this specific TV-set segment can be detected.

7 Summary and Outlook

In the paper at hand, the data production process in a market research company was used to explain process-oriented, "engineer-like" Knowledge Discovery for empirically gathered mass data. This perspective on the term Knowledge Discovery is certainly not consistent with the one to be found in the scientific literature [5]; however, it shares several central similarities with it. In both cases, the important aspect, after all, is to generate knowledge at the schema level from data constellations at the object level. Whether this discovered knowledge will then become manifest in a database schema or in the practical knowledge of an experienced employee is only secondary from this perspective. The "classic" Knowledge Discovery, too, is eventually dependent on plausibility and relevance checks of the discovered knowledge by human users. Right from the start, the suggested process-oriented extension of the term incorporates this human decision-making process into the total approach and, thus, reduces the role of the computer to an identification and suggestion system. Overall, this role distribution in practice leads to a robust knowledge base, that is continuously improving, and that could turn out to be the decisive competitive advantage when facing other participants in the market who "only" use machine-supported approaches.

References

[1] Albrecht, J., Lehner, W., Teschke, M., Kirsche, T.: Building a Real Data Warehouse for Market Research. In: Hameurlain, A., Tjoa, A. M.(Eds.): Proceedings 8th International Conference on Database and Expert Systems Applications (DEXA '97, Toulouse, France, September 1-5, 1997), Lecture Notes in Computer Science 1308, Springer, 1997, p. 651-656

[2] Bauer, A., Günzel, H.(Hrsg.): Data Warehouse Systeme. 2nd edition, dpunkt.verlag, 2004

[3] Bussler, C.: Workflow Instance Scheduling with Project Management Tools. In: Quirchmayr, G., Schweighofer, E., Bench-Capon, T. J. M. (Eds.): Proceedings 9th International Conference on Database and Expert Systems Applications (DEXA '98, Vienna, Austria, August 24-28, 1998), Lecture Notes in Computer Science 1460, Springer, 1998, p. 753-758

[4] Cochran, W.G.: Sampling Techniques, New York et al.: John Wiley & Sons 1977

[5] Ester, M., Sander, J.: Knowledge Discovery in Databases. Springer, 2000

[6] Görlich, J., Reinfels, I., Ruf, T.: Dealing with complex reports in OLAP applications. In: Mohania, M. K., Tjoa, A. M. (Eds.): Proceedings First International Conference on Data Warehousing and Knowledge Discovery (DAWAK'99, Florence, Italy, Aug. 30-Sep. 01, 1999), Lecture Notes in Computer Science 1676, Springer, 1999, p. 41-54

[7] Kimball, R.: The Data Warehouse Toolkit. New York et al.: John Wiley & Sons, 1996

[8] Ruf, T.: Das GfK Marketing Services Data Warehouse: Operational Decision Support für die Paneldatenanalyse. In: Proceedings 22. Europäische Congressmesse für technische Kommunikation (ONLINE '99, Düsseldorf, Germany, Feb. 1.-4, 1999), p. C834.01-C834.06

[9] Schanzenberger, A. ; Lawrence, D.R.: Automated Supervision of Data Production - Managing the Creation of Statistical Reports on Periodic Data. In: Meersman, R., Tari, Z. (Eds.): On the Move to Meaningful Internet Systems 2004: CoopIS, DOA, and ODBASE; Proceedings OTM Confederated International Conferences CoopIS, DOA, and ODBASE (CoopIS 2004, Larnaca, Cyprus, Oct. 25-29, 2004), Lecture Notes in Computer Science 3290, Springer, 2004., p. 194-208

[10] Schanzenberger, A., Tully, C., Lawrence, D.R.: Überwachung von Aggregationszuständen in verteilten komponentenbasierten Datenproduktionssystemen. In: Weikum, G., Schöning, H., Rahm, E. (Eds.): Proceedings 10th BTW-Konferenz Datenbanksysteme für Business, Web und Technologie (BTW 2003, Leipzig, Germany, Feb. 26-28, 2003), Lecture Notes in Informatics P-26, Bonner Köllen Verlag, 2003, p. 544 -558

Information Management in Distributed Healthcare Networks

Richard Lenz

University of Marburg
lenzr@mailer.uni-marburg.de

Abstract. Providing healthcare increasingly changes from isolated treatment episodes towards a continuous treatment process involving multiple healthcare professionals and various institutions. Information management plays a crucial role in this interdisciplinary process. By using information technology (IT) different goals are in the focus: To decrease overall costs for healthcare, to improve healthcare quality, and to consolidate patient-related information from different sources.

Consolidation of patient data is ultimately aimed at a lifetime patient record which serves as the basis for healthcare processes involving multiple healthcare professionals and different institutions. To enable seamless integration of various kinds of IT applications into a healthcare network, a commonly accepted framework is needed. Powerful standards and middleware technology are already at hand to develop a technical and syntactical infrastructure for such a framework. Yet, semantic heterogeneity is a limiting factor for system interoperability. Existing standards do support semantic interoperability of healthcare IT systems to some degree, but standards alone are not sufficient to support an evidence-based cooperative patient treatment process across organizational borders.

Medicine is a rapidly evolving scientific domain, and medical experts are developing and consenting new guidelines as new evidence occurs. Unfortunately, there is a gap between guideline development and guideline usage at the point of care. Medical treatment today is still characterized by a large diversity of different opinions and treatment plans. Medical pathways and reminder systems are an attempt to reduce the diversity in medical treatment and to bring evidence to the point of care. Developing such pathways, however, is primarily a process of achieving consensus between the participating healthcare professionals. IT support for pathways thus requires a responsive IT infrastructure enabling a demand-driven system evolution.

This article describes modern approaches for "integrated care" as well as the major challenges that are yet to be solved to adequately support distributed healthcare networks with IT services.

T. Härder and W. Lehner (Eds.): Data Management (Wedekind Festschrift), LNCS 3551, pp. 315-334, 2005.

1 Introduction

Healthcare heavily depends on both information and knowledge. Thus, information management plays an important role in the patient treatment process. Numerous studies have demonstrated positive effects of the use of IT in healthcare. In particular, the preventability of adverse events in medicine has been in the focus of recent studies. Adverse events are defined as unintended injuries caused by medical management rather than the disease process [62]. It turned out that insufficient communication and missing information are among the major factors contributing to adverse events in medicine (cf. [9, 12, 13, 32, 64, 65]). IT has the potential to reduce the rate of adverse events by selectively providing accurate and timely information at the point of care (cf. [39]). Yet, there is a discrepancy between the potential and the actual usage of IT in healthcare. A recent IOM report even states that there is an "absence of real progress towards applying advances in information technology to improve administrative and clinical processes" [15]. To understand this discrepancy, both the potential of IT and the challenges to be solved should be seen.

One major challenge is certainly the increasingly distributed nature of the healthcare process. Healthcare changes from isolated treatment episodes towards a continuous treatment process involving multiple healthcare professionals and various institutions. This change imposes new demanding requirements for IT support. System integration and inter-institutional support of healthcare processes are needed [8]. Advanced concepts for data security must provide a solid basis for IT services.

IT support starts with electronic transmission of prescriptions, discharge letters and reports. Gathering such information is ultimately aimed at a lifetime patient record or "Electronic Health Record" (EHR), which is independent from specific healthcare facilities. The vision of a cooperative patient treatment process based on such a unified EHR involves the seamless integration of medical guidelines, pathways, telemedicine applications, and medical trials. The patient is expected to receive more and more responsibility and competence as she is provided with information from her patient record, and as she governs the use of her own healthcare data (patient empowerment).

One of the most frequently cited works in the context of healthcare telematics perspectives in Germany is a study by Roland Berger from 1997 [7]. It illustrates the vision of integrated care by exemplarily describing a hypothetical patient encounter:

"... The patient is called into the physicians consulting room. In agreement with the patient the physician views her EHR at his terminal. The EHR contains all previously collected reports from other physicians and other institutions. An automatic summary and evaluation of previous results is provided. Current literature on the patient's problem and available guidelines are offered and can be accessed online. In addition, new medications and available services related to the patient's case are selectively provided. The physicians system has been individually configured to ensure that he is only provided with relevant information he really wants to see. Based on the information contained in the EHR, the physician receives hints for suitable anamnesis questions. In any case, the physician can obtain additional information concerning differential diagnoses. By integrating different sources of information and knowledge from a world-wide healthcare network the EHR provides more information than originally collected. This information is provided in the form and language preferred by the individual physician. ..."

In this vision, the EHR not only plays the central role as the source of information, it is also the basis for providing medical knowledge in the current context of the treatment process. However, the vision leaves open where information and knowledge come from and how they are linked together in a meaningful way. Stead et al. state that the computerized patient record (CPR), which can be seen as a predecessor of the EHR, should be a byproduct of care processes rather than a direct task. Consequently, the use of IT applications should be an integral part of the patient treatment process. IT applications should guide data acquisition in a way that data are placed in a meaningful context from the beginning, so that they are ready for reuse in different contexts without the need to manually index or transform the data. Reuse of data comes in different forms:

1. Direct access by healthcare professionals to data stored in the EHR
2. Aggregation of data from the EHR for different kinds of analytical purposes
3. Automated interpretation of data stored in the EHR by IT applications to provide different kinds of functionality for decision support.

In order to support these requirements within the context of a distributed healthcare process, far reaching standards for systems integration are needed. Moreover, as medicine is a rapidly evolving domain, concepts for system evolution are needed. In this paper, requirements for system integration and current solution approaches are described and open questions and challenges are identified.

The remainder of this chapter is organized as follows. In the next section, general integration requirements are summarized and available standards and integration initiatives in healthcare are categorized accordingly. Effective decision support in a distributed healthcare process requires more than standardized ontologies and terminologies. So, the following section describes approaches for decision support in healthcare. Finally, current efforts for building up infrastructures for healthcare are described.

2 Integrating Health Information Systems

Integrating autonomous software components is a difficult task, as individual applications usually are not designed to cooperate. In particular, applications are often based on differing conceptualizations of the application domain, which are not necessarily compatible. Today powerful integration tools (e.g., different kinds of message-oriented middleware [1]) are available to overcome technical and syntactical heterogeneity of autonomous system components. Yet, semantic heterogeneity remains as a major barrier to seamless integration of autonomously developed software components. Semantic heterogeneity occurs when there is a disagreement about the meaning, interpretation, or intended use of the same or related data [54]. It occurs in different contexts, like database schema integration, ontology mapping, or integration of different terminologies.

The underlying problems are more or less the same, though they are often complex and still poorly understood.

Stonebraker characterizes disparate systems as "islands of information" and points out two major factors which aggravate systems integration [57]:

1. Each island (i.e., application) will have its own meaning of enterprise objects.
2. Each island will have data that overlaps data in other islands. This partial redundancy generates a serious data integrity problem.

Based on this statement, data integration can be reduced to a mapping problem (how to map different conceptualizations in a semantically correct way) and a synchronization problem (how to ensure mutual consistency of redundant data which are stored in different databases under the control of autonomous applications). The mapping problem is essentially related to the schema integration problem of database systems, which has been extensively discussed in the database literature in recent years (e.g., [11, 16, 19, 48]). A frequently cited classification of problems related to semantic data integration is an article from Kim and Seo [31]. They distinguish between data conflicts and schema conflicts, which corresponds to a distinction between type level and instance level conflicts. Schema conflicts are further divided into naming conflicts, structural conflicts and integrity conflicts. Data conflicts may arise due to differing data representations, missing or contradicting database contents. Approaches for data integration are classified in [48] and in [4]. A major perception in data integration research has been that schema integration cannot be automated in general. In [4] it is stated: „*The general problem of schema integration is undecidable*". Heiler explicitly refers to the problem of *semantic* integration: „*Understanding data and software can never be fully automated*" [27]. As a consequence, the process of schema integration always needs a human integrator for semantic decisions. Colomb even goes a step further by stating that there are cases where no consistent interpretation of heterogeneous sources is possible ("*fundamental semantic heterogeneity*"). Resolving fundamental semantic heterogeneity necessarily results in compromising design autonomy. Typically, systems have to be modified to resolve fundamental semantic heterogeneity.

2.1 Aspects of Integration

So far, integration of disparate systems has only been viewed under a data integration perspective. The reason for this is that data integration is considered to be the most important precondition for further integration. Data integration is the backbone and starting point of each successful integration project, because any process control always requires a meaningful exchange of data, too [2]. Yet, distinguishing further integration aspects is helpful to categorize different integration approaches and standards in healthcare [36]:

- *Data integration:* The goal of data integration is to create a unique semantic reference for commonly used data and to ensure data consistency. To create such a semantic reference different facets of data semantics have to be considered. In this article, three facets are roughly distinguished:

1. The *instance level*, referring to the semantics of individual data objects, which corresponds to the meaning of entries in a database.
2. The *type level*, designating the semantic classification of data objects, which roughly corresponds to the database schema.
3. The *context,* which refers to the semantic relationships that associate an object with other objects.

To illustrate the difference of these aspects we may consider a concept "diagnosis" at the type level, and a particular instance, say "Encephalitis", and the context of this instance which is determined by the patient, the physician who made the diagnosis, and other objects that contribute to a particular statement (information).

The most important means to ease data integration are common standardized domain-specific ontologies and terminologies, which serve as a semantic reference for system programmers and users (cf. [35]). Today, such standards can be built on the basis of well accepted syntactical frameworks such as XML and RDF, which can be used to refer to common name spaces with defined semantics. Even existing standards in healthcare are already being transformed into these formats to improve syntactical compatibility with commonly accepted data processing formats.

- *Functional integration* refers to the meaningful cooperation of functions of different software components. Uncontrolled data redundancy is often the result of an insufficient functional integration of disparate systems. Autonomously developed systems often overlap in their functionality, partly providing the same or only slightly differing functionality. This aggravates integration even if the systems are already based on common ontologies. To avoid these difficulties, common frameworks are required which serve as a reference for programmers to create compatible software components. Examples for such domain specific application frameworks are given in [20]. Requirements for an application framework directed towards open systems in the healthcare domain are described in [33]. In general, such a framework must provide clear specifications of interfaces and interaction protocols which are needed for embedding a software component into a system of cooperating components.
  So far, the term "functional integration" has been used to depict a property of a distributed system comprising multiple interacting components. It should be mentioned, though, that the terms "data integration" and "functional integration" are also often used to designate complementary *ways of integrating* pre-existing heterogeneous systems. Thereby, functional integration concentrates on application logic rather than data management. This approach typically causes a much higher integration effort, because semantic mapping of data is only done indirectly by using data appropriately to parameterize function calls [57]. In many cases, data can only be accessed via predefined functions provided by a more or less closed application system. A direct database access is often prohibited to preserve data consistency, because integrity constraints are not controlled at the database level but within the applications [26]. In these cases, functional integration is the only way to integrate heterogeneous application systems.

- *Desktop Integration* or *presentation integration* refers to the user interface of a distributed system. Desktop integration is aimed at user transparency, meaning that the user would not know what application was being used or what database was being queried [46]. This requires more than a unified layout and uniform interaction mechanisms. Examples for functions needed to achieve desktop integration are "single sign on" and "desktop synchronization". Desktop synchronization is needed when a user has multiple windows to different applications on his or her desktop that share a common context. Synchronization is required when the context is changed in one of the interlinked applications. As an example, a clinical user might have several windows on the desktop that show data of the same patient stemming from different applications; changing the current patient in one application must be synchronized with the other applications. The architecture of a distributed system must adhere to certain requirements, such as a central context manager, in order to enable desktop synchronization. Moreover, the applications to be synchronized must agree on the semantics of context data and on a common coordination protocol for context synchronization.

- *Process integration.* Each of the previously introduced integration aspects refers to a different layer of distributed systems: data management, application logic, and presentation. Process integration is complementary to these purely system-related aspects, as it refers to the alignment of IT and business process needs. Thus, process integration can be viewed as the superior integration goal (cf. [37, 58]). Process integration has to be viewed as an integration aspect of its own right, because information systems are socio-technical systems comprising human actors as the major contributors to information processing. A technically perfectly integrated system might be useless within a concrete organization if it does not fulfil the user's requirements.

Data integration, functional integration, and desktop integration can be summarized under the term "application integration". Adherence to standards is of critical importance to ease application integration. In the next section, approaches to application integration in healthcare are categorized according to their contribution to the different system integration aspects.

2.2 Standards for Semantic Integration in Healthcare

The architecture of typical hospital information systems is characterized by many different departmental systems, which are usually optimized for the support of different medical disciplines (e.g., radiology, cardiology, or pathology). The need to consolidate the data produced by these ancillary systems to a global patient-centred view and to support the cross-departmental processes has motivated the development of standards for data interchange in healthcare. These standards also play an important role when not only cross-departmental but also cross-organizational healthcare processes are to be supported. The most important standards used in commercial healthcare software are briefly characterized subsequently.

- **HL7**
  HL7 is the leading standard for systems integration in healthcare. The name "Health Level 7" refers to the application layer in the OSI reference model [59]. HL7 is a

message-based standard for the exchange of data among hospital computer applications. The standard defines which data items are to be interchanged when certain clinical trigger events occur (admission, discharge, or transfer of a patient are examples for such events). Since version 2.3 (1997), the standard covers trigger events for patient administration, patient accounting, order entry, medical information management, clinical observation data, patient and resource scheduling, and others. The standard is continuously extended and newly arising topics, such as the integration of genomic data in Electronic Health Records, are handled in special interest groups (SIGs).

Today's commercially available healthcare software usually implements a relatively small portion of HL7 only, covering those communication patterns that are typically requested as essential basis for interconnecting disparate applications. As HL7 does not comprise an architectural framework for health information systems, it does not tackle questions of functional integration of different software components within a healthcare network. The core of the standard is concerned with data semantics, primarily at the type level. Yet, to a limited degree HL7 also contains tables that define the allowable values for certain data elements. In addition, HL7 supports the use of external coding schemes such as LOINC or SNOMED within HL7 messages. The HL7 Vocabulary Technical Committee (TC) was organized to select and maintain the vocabulary used in HL7 messages. The goal is to make implementations of the version 3 HL7 standard more plug-and-play compatible. To make the vocabulary readily accessible to the public, HL7 is collaborating with the U.S. National Library of Medicine (NLM) to include HL7 vocabulary in the Unified Medical Language System (UMLS) Metathesaurus [28].

With version 3.0 the standard has moved to an object-oriented basis. Core of version 3.0 is the HL7 Reference Information Model (*RIM*), which is intended to serve as a reference for consistent generation of new HL7 messages. Though it was originally intended as a comprehensive data model, it is primarily used as a generic schema which allows classifying medical concepts into generally applicable categories.

The Clinical Document Architecture (*CDA*) is an emerging standard on the basis of HL7 and the RIM intended for interchange of medical contents. CDA is an XML-based standard for clinical documents. A clinical document is the unit of data transmission which also serves as a unit of authentication. The standard contains three different levels of abstraction. Level one comprises annotation of the general context in which a document was created as well as generic type level annotations for document contents. The levels two and three are intended to add more detailed annotations.

The „Clinical Context Object Working group“ of the HL7 group gave the name for the standard CCOW, a standard for desktop integration in the healthcare domain [53]. On the basis of HL7, the standard specifies context data that are to be synchronized as well as synchronization protocols.

- **DICOM**

  DICOM („Digital Imaging and Communications in Medicine“) [10] is a well established standard for communicating medical image data. It is structured as a nine part document to accomodate evolution of the standard. DICOM supports data integration on a type level, as it comprises an object-oriented data model. To some degree it also contributes to functional integration, as it introduces service classes to specify well defined operations across the network. Recently DICOM has significantly extended its scope towards clinical contents by introducing DICOM SR (structured reporting).

- **IHE**
  Despite well accepted standards for data integration like HL7 and DICOM, healthcare applications are still far from plug-and-play compatibility. One reason for this is that the existing standards do not address functional integration issues sufficiently. The IHE initiative ("Integrating the Healthcare Enterprise") [61] does not develop new standards for data interchange but specifies integration profiles on the basis of HL7 and DICOM. Thereby, actors and transactions are defined independently from any specific software product. An integration profile specifies how different actors interact via IHE transactions in order to perform a special task. These integration profiles serve as a semantic reference for application programmers, so that they can built software products that can be functionally integrated into an IHE-conformant application framework.

The standards and integration approaches mentioned so far are primarily focused on standard ontologies for type level data integration. Few approaches are aimed at functional integration. Among these is the IHE initiative, which is still primarily focused on image communication involvig software components like RIS (Radiology Information System) and PACS (Picture Archiving and Communication System) as well as medical imaging devices. To achieve data compatibility at the data instance level, additional standards for coding are required:

- **ICD / ICPM**
  The International Classification of Diseases (ICD) and the International Classification of Procedures in Medicine (ICPM) are well accepted standards which are mostly used for accounting purposes. For medical decision making, however, a significantly more detailed documentation is required.

- **LOINC**
  Logical Observation Identifiers Names and Codes (LOINC) is a standard for coding of laboratory observations developed in 1994 and continuously extended since then.

- **MeSH**
  The Medical Subject Headings (MeSH) are the thesaurus which is used to index the Medline databases. The MeSH also comprises a dictionary with definitions of MeSH terms, and it is continuously updated with new terms.

- **SNOMED CT**
  The Systematized Nomenclature in Medicine (SNOMED) is a multiaxial classification system for medical concepts. The number of SNOMED dimensions has significantly increased over time. While in [66] 7 dimensions were distinguished, the current version of SNOMED CT (Clinical Terms) already comprises 18 hierarchically organized dimensions. By combining terms of different dimensions, a large number of medical concepts can be described in a standardized way.

- **UMLS**
  The Unified Medical Language System (UMLS) is a metathesaurus for healthcare terminologies, covering multiple relationships between various source vocabularies, such as ICD, LOINC, and SNOMED CT. Today the UMLS covers more than 100 source vocabularies in more than 15 languages.
- **GALEN**
  The GALEN project is aimed at a language independent coding system based on a compositional and generative formal approach for modeling concepts [49, 50]. GALEN tries to avoid the combinatorial explosion of terms in enumerative systems (such as ICD or LOINC) as well as the generation of nonsensical terms in partially compositional systems (such as SNOMED CT).

The list of standards mentioned here is far from complete, but it contains the most important standards which are used in today's healthcare software. The contribution of existing standards to systems integration is roughly indicated in Tab. 1.

Tab. 1 Contribution of Healthcare Standards to Semantic Integration

	Data integration			Functional integration	Presentation integration
	Instance level	Type level	Context		
Standards and approaches for systems integration					
HL7	HL7 vocabulary (limited domain coverage)	RIM: Generic data model CDA: Framework for clinical contents		-	CCOW: Desktop synchroniz.
DICOM	-	DICOM object model		DICOM Services	-
IHE	-	-	-	Integration profiles (limited domain coverage)	-
Terminology, classification					
ICD/ICPM	Diagnoses and procedures	-	-	-	-
LOINC	Laboratory results	-	-	-	-
MeSH	Terms used for indexing medical literature		-	-	-
UMLS	Metathesaurus for medical terminologies / semantic network		-	-	-
SNOMED	Multiaxial nomenclature for medical concepts		-	-	-
GALEN	Terminology for medical concepts based on a formal reference model for knowledge representation		-	-	-

Tab. 1 shows that there are numerous standards for medical terminology. Yet, despite of many attempts, a unique and comprehensive ontology of the medical domain is not within sight. The various examples also show that medical terminologies continuously evolve over time, and that there is no stable reference for system programmers. Thus, semantic integration of heterogeneous systems in healthcare will have to deal with volatile medical concepts.

In order to be able to build integrated systems capable of adapting to new requirements that arise from an evolving application domain, it is necessary to start with frameworks that are usable as a stable basis for further system evolution. Thereby, different levels of integration can be distinguished.

2.3 Incrementally Improving Integration

The first step and the most basic requirement for establishing an electronic health record is a unique patient identification. Today, this is still one of the major obstacles to automatically consolidating patient-related information from different sources. A less optimistic prognosis from Haux et al. contains the hypothesis that the Health Record will still not be reality by the year 2013 and that more than 90 % of all patient-related data will still be stored in institution-specific databases or regional healthcare networks with proprietary patient identification systems [24].

Healthcare organizations typically use a computer-based Master Patient Index (MPI) to store patient identification information, e.g., basic demographic data collected during the patient registration process. Once the patient is successfully identified, he or she is associated to a unique patient identifier. In a distributed scenario with multiple feeder systems, an MPI is an essential central service that maps such patient identifiers from different systems. With the help of an MPI arbitrary patient-related files can be linked together under a common patient identification. This, however, is not sufficient to build an electronic health record that is capable of supporting the healthcare process in a seamless way. Reuse of data in computer applications requires semantic compatibility of document contents. Thus, further steps are required to achieve comparable contents.

An approach for incrementally improving semantic compatibility of patient data can be supported by multi-layered ontologies such as the leveled approach of the CDA, formerly known as PRA (Patient Record Architecture). The scope of the CDA is the standardization of clinical documents for exchange. The XML-based leveled approach supports incremental improvement of semantic compatibility in several ways: Level one already contains sufficient information to consolidate documents under a common context. Thus, a basic health record can be established before detailed annotation is available. CDA documents are human readable, and can be displayed with appropriate XSLT stylesheets regardless of the degree of semantic annotation. As the detail of standardized semantic annotations increases, new applications can make use of the contents of CDA documents, e.g., for decision support purposes.

To understand how an electronic health record can support the patient treatment process, it is necessary to take a closer look at medical practice and the structure of medical records.

3 Embedding Decision Support into the Healthcare Process

The healthcare process is often called a diagnostic-therapeutic cycle comprising observation, reasoning, and action. Each pass of this cycle is aimed at decreasing the uncertainty about the patient's disease or the actual state of the disease process [60]. Thus, the observation stage always starts with the patient history (if it is available) and proceeds with diagnostic procedures which are selected based on available information. It is the job of an EHR to assist healthcare personnel in making informed decisions. Consequently, the system should present relevant information at the time of data acquisition and at the time of order entry. Thereby, an important question to be answered is how to determine what is relevant.

3.1 The EHR as a Tool for Decision Support

A patient record is commonly defined as the repository of information about a single patient, generated by healthcare professionals as a direct result of interaction with a patient [18]. To provide a coherent picture of a patient's current situation and to avoid unnecessary examinations, it is important to provide a comprehensive overview of available information. However, it is useless to only offer large collections of documents and files that contain detailed information but no summary of the most relevant issues. Therefore, it is of paramount importance to appropriately organize an electronic patient record for easy access by a physician. An appropriate organization of the health record should be adapted to the way clinicians use the record, i.e., the functions the record has to fulfill efficiently. Basically, these functions are data collection, problem definition, systematic planning, and follow-up documentation as a basis for continuity of care.

This model of clinical thinking dates back to 1956, when Lawrence Weed began developing the problem-oriented medical record (POMR) [63] based on problem lists containing a patient's active and inactive problems. The fundamental principle of the POMR is the idea of problem-related progress notes that summarize the current status of a problem's treatment according to the so-called "SOAP"-principle: Subjective (the patient's own observations as reported in the anamnesis), Objective (the physician's observations and results of diagnostic treatment), Assessment (the physician's understanding of the problem), and Plan (goals, actions, advice, etc.). The POMR and SOAP progress notes are well accepted in the scientific community. Yet, many commercially available systems still fail to follow its simple rules. Instead, electronic patient records for hospital information systems are usually organized according to the departmental organization of the hospital. In addition, patient records in hospitals are often organized according to accounting requirements, which also might hinder continuity of care. For a lifetime EHR intended to serve as the information basis in a distributed healthcare network, an organization according to the POMR appears to be more appropriate, as it explicitly issues follow-up documentation and easy access to relevant information, which is particularly important when multiple healthcare providers are involved in a patient's treatment.

Decision support that goes beyond the structure of the EHR requires some kind of automatic interpretation of medical data. This requires medical knowledge to be formally represented.

3.2 Bringing Medical Knowledge to the Point of Care

Supporting the healthcare process by bringing medical knowledge to the point of care is closely related to developing and implementing medical practice guidelines. The MeSH dictionary defines medical practice guidelines as "work consisting of a set of directions or principles to assist the healthcare practitioner with patient care decisions about appropriate diagnostic, therapeutic, or other clinical procedures for specific clinical circumstances". Guidelines are aimed at an evidence-based and economically reasonable medical treatment process, and at improving outcomes and decreasing the undesired variation of healthcare quality [23]. Developing guidelines is essentially a consensus process among medical experts. Yet, there is a gap between the information contained in published clinical practice guidelines and the knowledge and information that are necessary to implement them [23, 56]. Methods for closing this gap by using information technology have been in the focus of medical informatics research for decades (e.g., [3, 38, 56]).

Medical pathways can be used as a basis for implementing guidelines [52] and sometimes they are confused with guidelines. In contrast to guidelines, though, pathways are related to a concrete setting and include a time component: Pathways are planned process patterns that are aimed at improving process quality and resource usage. Pathways are not *standardized* generic processes like those described within the IHE integration profiles. Pathways need a consensus process. This consensus, however, is to be achieved among the process participants within a concrete setting. Pathways can be used as a platform to implement guidelines, e.g., by routinely collecting the information required by a guideline. Selecting a guideline for implementation also requires an agreement of healthcare professionals and patients, because there are different kinds of guidelines with different origins and goals, and sometimes even conflicting recommendations. Likewise, to improve a patient treatment process across organizational borders, consensus on common practices is required in the first place. Once this consensus is achieved, the next question is how to implement it in practice. To be effective, a guideline must be easily accessible. Ideally, it should be embedded into the clinical work practice, and the physician should not need to explicitly look it up. Otherwise, there is always a risk of overlooking important information while the patient is in the office. Previous work has primarily demonstrated a positive influence of computer-generated alerts and reminders [55], which can be integrated into clinical work practice. Recent research indicates that this is exactly the major difficulty with implementing more complex multi-step guidelines: How to integrate them into the clinical workflow [38].

Medical pathways are one attempt to establish a *platform* for implementation of complex guidelines. Thereby, predefined checklists that ask the right questions in the right context, predefined order sets, and well-placed reminders are some of the techniques that can be used to improve process quality and reduce the required documentation overhead. In any case, all these techniques require the computer to be able to make use of the patient's clinical data. The first obstacle to achieving this is to represent guidelines in a computer-interpretable form, i.e., translating narrative guidelines into equivalent ones that use coded data. This process is cumbersome and also bares the risk of distorting the intent of the original guideline. To overcome such problems numerous models have been developed to formally represent medical guidelines and medical knowledge (e.g., Arden Syntax [30], GLIF [42, 44], PROforma [22], EON [41], etc.). Recent surveys have compared these different approaches [17, 45]. One of the central goals of these approaches is to define standard representation formats for medical knowledge in order to be able to share guidelines among different information systems in different organizations. In practice, however, it turned out that the main obstacle to be solved here is—once again—an integration problem: The data definitions in predefined formal guidelines may not map to the data available in an existing electronic health record system [47]. Typically, operational systems have to be modified and extended in order to acquire the necessary information needed for guideline implementation. Few guidelines have been successfully implemented into real clinical settings by using these systems and predefined formally specified guidelines. Recent research has recognized these difficulties and focuses on process models for transforming text-based guidelines into clinical practice (e.g., [56]). Standard formats for guideline representation do have their place in guideline implementation, but the integration problems to be solved are a matter of semantics rather than format.

Guideline implementation requires a high level of data integration, because computerized reminders typically refer to both type level and instance level semantics, and more complex guidelines also need to refer to a formally established context comprising status information. The challenge to be solved for distributed healthcare networks is to establish a sufficient degree of integration as a basis for guideline implementation, and to find practical solutions to cope with the continuous evolution of the healthcare domain.

In the next section, requirements for responsive IT infrastructures are outlined and some of the most promising approaches supporting system evolution in healthcare are briefly introduced. Lessons learned from these approaches in clinical settings are likely to influence the development of IT architectures for emerging healthcare networks.

4 Evolutionary Information Systems in Healthcare

Because the development of medical pathways and the implementation of guidelines is primarily viewed as a consensus process among healthcare professionals in a concrete setting, the functional evolution of information systems should be a demand-driven process under the control of healthcare professionals. Standards for systems integration have already been listed and categorized. Process integration, though, is not adressed by standards, but by appropriate models for demand-driven software development (e.g., [34]). Desiderata for such a demand-driven process are:

- *Rapid application development*
  To be able to flexibly react to newly arising demands, tools and techniques for rapid application development (RAD) are desirable. To reuse existing data and services and to achieve integrated applications, such tools should be build upon a standard IT infrastructure for healthcare networks.

- *Robust and stable integrated domain-specific IT infrastructure*
  An IT infrastructure for a healthcare network should provide a robust and stable basis for application development. Thus, the framework should be based on generic domain models instead of comprehensive but volatile domain models.

- *Separation of domain concepts and system implementation*
  To cope with domain evolution, modeling of domain concepts should be separated from IT system implementation. IT systems should be implemented by IT experts and medical knowledge should be modeled and maintained by domain experts. Yet, separating the modeling of medical knowledge from implementing an IT infrastructure is not easy, because algorithms (such as reminder systems) typically refer to medical knowledge to fulfill their task.

- *Multi-level software engineering approach*
  To bring application development as close to the end user as possible, a multi-layered software engineering approach is proposed. An idealized abstract model for such a multi-level approach for software engineering is shown in Fig. 1.

Layered approaches have proven to be a successful technique for separating concerns. In different traditional areas of computer science such as operating systems, database systems [25], and communication systems [59] layered approaches have been successfully used to reduce system complexity. Transferring this principle to the development of information systems in complex application domains in order to achieve both flexibility and robustness seems to be self-evident. The rationale in this particular context is to allow application developers and end users to build well integrated healthcare applications without the need to do low level encoding [8]. Appropriate tool support is needed at each level of abstraction to effectively make use of the lower system layers.

A layered approach, as sketched above, fosters a system evolution process that follows the principle of "deferred systems design" [43], which is particularly suitable for evolving application domains. Some important techniques and tools directed towards such multi-layered approaches are briefly introduced.

4.1 Terminology Servers

Controlled vocabularies can significantly contribute to a successful guideline implementation. Thus, standard vocabularies and terminology servers supporting their use in healthcare IT applications are highly desirable. A terminology server can help to separate terminological control from application development. A successful proprietary example of such a terminology server is the Medical Entities Dictionary (MED) from Columbia Presbyterian Medical Center [14, 21]. The MED comprises more than 70000

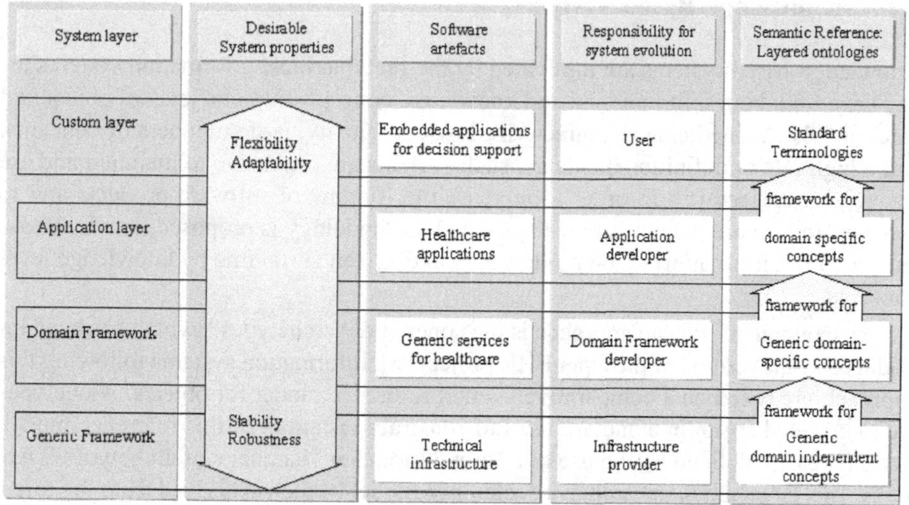

Fig. 1 A Layered Approach for System Evolution

concepts and is continuously being extended (about 6000 entries per year). It is based on comprehensive external thesauri (such as the UMLS) and integrates standard classifications such as ICD and LOINC [51].

Basically, the MED is a semantic network incorporating a classification hierarchy. This classification is based on an acyclic directed graph. At least one path connects each node in this graph representing a medical concept with the root node representing the concept "Medical Entity". In addition to this hierarchy arbitrary concepts can be interconnected via "semantic links". A concept editor is used to maintain and extend the contents of the MED. User interfaces for presentation, navigation, and programming interfaces used within new applications are essential parts of the terminology server.

By the use of such a terminology server the task of semantic integration can be addressed. Thereby a two level software engineering approach is assumed: Existing applications and COTS ("Commercial Off-the-Shelf") components are connected to the MED by mapping the proprietary concepts of these systems to MED concepts. If necessary, the MED is extended appropriately. In essence, this mapping process is a typical data integration process which cannot be automated and in some cases even requires the modification of a software component. However, an additional software layer of new applications can benefit from the MED, because new applications can use the MED to refer to medical data via generic concepts. Thus, these applications do not need to be modified when the conceptualization of some ancillary system is changed.

The MED is just one example of a successful proprietary terminology server. Most hospitals in Germany use controlled terminologies only for consistent encoding of diagnoses and procedures (ICD/ICPM). However, more comprehensive terminology servers based on available terminology standards are increasingly being offered commercially [29].

4.2 Knowledge-Based Systems

Knowledge-based systems are motivated by the fact that most information systems today have built both informational and knowledge concepts into one level of object and data models. As medicine is characterized by complexity, large numbers of concepts, and a high rate of definitional change, such systems are expensive to maintain and are frequently replaced [5]. In order to increase the lifetime of software products and to make systems more maintainable, a two-level methodology is proposed, in which systems are built from information models only and driven at runtime by knowledge level concepts.

An example of such an approach is the concept of "archetypes", which has been introduced in the context of the OpenEHR project [6]. Information systems following this approach are based on a comparatively small reference model for objects. Archetypes are interpreted at runtime and are used to constrain instances of this reference model. Archetypes are defined by the use of a formal model or "language of archetypes". Actually, this language is an "archetype reference model" which is derived from the reference model of the information system under concern—any given archetype is an instance of this model. The advantage of the archetype concept is that medical knowledge can be modeled by medical experts instead of computer scientists and added to a running system without the need for schema modifications.

Another example for a rigorous knowledge-based approach is the EON system for guideline implementation. EON strictly separates the knowledge that a decision support system contains and the problem-solving procedures that operate on that knowledge [40]. Unlike traditional stand alone decision support systems that require physicians to explicitly enter data before recommendations are given, EON is intended to be embedded into some healthcare information system. The motivation for this is to learn from the success of simple reminder systems that are able to instantly respond to changes in the clinical situation, e.g., as soon as the data is entered into the computer. Thus, EON addresses both separation of concerns and embedding decision support into clinical work practice.

Today, approaches like EON and archetypes are still rarely used in practice, but the underlying ideas address some of the core problems of systems integration which need to be solved when IT-enabled cross organizational evidence-based medicine should become reality.

5 Infrastructure for Healthcare Networks

Current efforts in many countries are aimed at establishing the necessary infrastructures for healthcare networks. Yet, the vision sketched in this article is still in its early stages. Along with legal and organizational questions, the highest priority is typically attributed to security and integration issues. To enable rapid progress, integration is typically tackled by focusing on HL7 and particularly CDA, whereas the question of patient identification and some kind of MPI functionality is the necessary first step to consolidate patient data from different sources.

Basic infrastructures are being built in different countries. Smart cards for both patients and healthcare professionals are increasingly used for authentication purposes. In Germany, basic demographic information is already stored on obligatory patient insurance cards. Current initiatives are intended to significantly broaden the scope of patient cards. In the first instance, the new patient card is primarily intended to serve as a medium for electronic prescriptions. Yet, it is already designed to carry both administrative data (e.g., patient demographics, physician and insurance information) and clinical data (such as problem list, discharge letter, emergency record, etc.). The most important contribution is a unique personal identification number stored on the card, which is a big step towards a consolidation of patient data from disparate institutions. In principle, this identification is sufficient to enable access to patient-related data stored in some (possibly virtual) EHR, provided that an appropriate security infrastructure is in place. Storing additional *structured* data on the patient card will lead to a schema-matching problem with existing healthcare information systems. Thus, to achieve a usable instrument within a reasonable time, which still can be used for varying purposes and even newly arising purposes, the standardization of patient card contents should be limited to essential data items and generic fields. The core functionality of the patient card should be to provide access to an evolving healthcare network. The final architecture of this network cannot be predicted and will result from domain-specific demands.

There is still a long way to go until these first steps will lead to an architecture for a distributed lifetime patient record. A leveled approach as presented in this article could help to rapidly start with a workable solution and incrementally improve the quality of healthcare on this basis.

References

[1] Alonso G, Casati F, Kuno H, Machiraju V. Web Services—Concepts, Architectures and Applications. Berlin: Springer, 2003.

[2] Bange C. Von ETL zur Datenintegration . IT Fokus 2004; 3(4): 12-16.

[3] Bates DW, Kuperman GJ, Wang S, Gandhi T, Kittler A, Volk L, et al. Ten commandments for effective clinical decision support: making the practice of evidence-based medicine a reality. J Am Med Inform Assoc 2003; 10(6): 523-530.

[4] Batini C, Lenzerini M, Navathe SB. A Comparative Analysis of Methodologies for Database Schema Integration. ACM Computing Surveys 1986; 18(4): 323-364.

[5] Beale T. Archetypes: Constraint-based Domain Models for Future-proof Information Systems. In: OOPSLA 2002 workshop on behavioural semantics: 2002

[6] Beale T. Archetypes and the EHR. Stud Health Technol Inform 2003; 96: 238-244.

[7] Berger R. Telematik im Gesundheitswesen – Perspektiven der Telemedizin in Deutschland. München: Bundesministerium für Bildung, Wissenschaft, Forschung und Technologie und Bundesministerium für Gesundheit, 1997.

[8] Beyer M, Kuhn KA, Meiler C, Jablonski S, Lenz R. Towards a flexible, process-oriented IT architecture for an integrated healthcare network. In: Proceedings of the 2004 ACM Symposium on Applied Computing (SAC), ACM, 2004: 264-271.

[9] Bhasale AL, Miller GC, Reid SE, Britt HC. Analysing potential harm in Australian general practice: an incident-monitoring study. Med J Aust 1998; 169(2): 73-76.

[10] Bidgood WD, Horii SC, Prior FW, Van Syckle DE. Understanding and Using DICOM, the Data Interchange Standard for Biomedical Imaging. Journal of the American Medical Informatics Association 1997; 4(3): 199-212.

[11] Bouguettaya A, Benatallah B, Elmagarmid A. Interconnecting Heterogeneous Information Systems. Boston: Kluwer Academic Publishers, 1998.

[12] Brennan TA, Leape LL. Adverse events, negligence in hospitalized patients: results from the Harvard Medical Practice Study. Perspect Healthc Risk Manage 1991; 11(2): 2-8.

[13] Brennan TA, Leape LL, Laird NM, Hebert L, Localio AR, Lawthers AG, et al. Incidence of adverse events and negligence in hospitalized patients. Results of the Harvard Medical Practice Study I. N Engl J Med 1991; 324(6): 370-376.

[14] Cimino JJ. From data to knowledge through concept-oriented terminologies: experience with the Medical Entities Dictionary. J Am Med Inform Assoc 2000; 7(3): 288-297.

[15] Committee on Quality of Health Care in America IoM. Crossing the Quality Chasm: A New Health System for the 21st Century. IOM, 2001.

[16] Conrad S. Schemaintegration – Integrationskonflikte, Lösungsansätze, aktuelle Herausforderungen. Informatik – Forschung und Entwicklung 2002; 17(3): 101-111.

[17] de Clercq PA, Blom JA, Korsten HH, Hasman A. Approaches for creating computer-interpretable guidelines that facilitate decision support. Artif Intell Med 2004; 31(1): 1-27.

[18] Dick RS, Steen EB. The Computer-Based Patient Record: An Essential Technology for Health Care. 2nd ed. Washington DC: National Academy Press, 1997.

[19] Elmagarmid, A., Rusinkiewicz, M., and Sheth, A. eds. Management of Heterogeneous and Autonomous Database Systems. San Francisco, CA: Morgan Kaufmann Publishers, 1999.

[20] Fayad M, Johnson R. Domain-specific application frameworks frameworks experience by industry. New York: John Wiley, 2000.

[21] Forman BH, Cimino JJ, Johnson SB, Sengupta S, Sideli R, Clayton P. Applying a controlled medical terminology to a distributed, production clinical information system. In: Proc.Annu.Symp.Comput.Appl.Med.Care; 1995: 421-425.

[22] Fox J, Johns N, Rahmanzadeh A. Disseminating medical knowledge: the PROforma approach. Artif Intell Med 1998; 14(1-2): 157-181.

[23] Gross PA, Greenfield S, Cretin S, Ferguson J, Grimshaw J, Grol R, et al. Optimal methods for guideline implementation: conclusions from Leeds Castle meeting. Med Care 2001; 39(8 Suppl 2): II85-II92.

[24] Haux R, Ammenwerth E, Herzog W, Knaup P. Gesundheitsversorgung in der Informationsgesellschaft – eine Prognose für das Jahr 2013. Informatik – Biometrie und Epidemiologie in Medizin und Biologie 2004; 35(3): 138-163.

[25] Härder T. Realisierung von operationalen Schnittstellen. In: Lockemann PC, Schmidt JW, editors. Datenbank-Handbuch. Berlin: Springer-Verlag, 1987.

[26] Härder T, Hergula K. Ankopplung heterogener Anwendungssysteme an Föderierte Datenbanksysteme durch Funktionsintegration. Informatik – Forschung und Entwicklung 2002; 17(3): 135-148.

[27] Heiler S. Semantic Interoperability. ACM Computing Surveys 1995; 27(2): 271-273.

[28] Huff SM, Bidgood WD, Jr., Cimino JJ, Hammond WE. A proposal for incorporating Health level seven (HL7) vocabulary in the UMLS Metathesaurus. In: Proc.Amia.Symp.; 1998: 800-804.

[29] ID GmbH. ID MACS – Das semantische Netz. 2004. Berlin, ID – Gesellschaft für Information und Dokumentation im Gesundheitswesen mbH. http://www.id-berlin.de/deu/_2produkte/macs.php

[30] Jenders RA, Hripcsak G, Sideli RV, DuMouchel W, Zhang H, Cimino JJ et al. Medical decision support: experience with implementing the Arden Syntax at the Columbia-Presbyterian Medical Center. In: Proc.Annu.Symp.Comput.Appl.Med.Care; 1995: 169-173.

[31] Kim W, Seo J. Classifying Schematic and Data Heterogeneity in Multidatabase Systems. IEEE Computer 1991; 24(12): 12-18.

[32] Kohn LT, Corrigan JM, Donaldson MS. To Err Is Human. Building a Safer Health System. Washington D.C.: National Academy Press, 2000.

[33] Lenz R, Huff S, Geissbühler A. Report of conference track 2: pathways to open architectures. Int J Med Inf 2003; 69(2-3): 297-299.

[34] Lenz R, Kuhn K.A. Towards a Continuous Evolution and Adaptation of Information Systems in Healthcare. Int J Med Inf 2004; 73(1): 75-89.

[35] Lenz R, Kuhn KA. Intranet meets hospital information systems: the solution to the integration problem? Methods Inf Med 2001; 40(2): 99-105.

[36] Lenz R, Kuhn KA. Zur Architektur und Evolution von Krankenhausinformationssystemen. In: Dittrich K, König W, Oberweis A, Rannenberg K., Wahlster W, (eds.): Informatik 2003 – Innovative Informatikanwendungen, Beiträge der 33.Jahrestagung der Gesellschaft für Informatik e.V.(GI);2: Lecture Notes in Informatics (LNI), 2003: 435-444.

[37] Luftman JN, Papp R, Brier T. Enablers and Inhibitors of Business-IT Alignment. Communications of the Association for Information Systems 1999; 1(11).

[38] Maviglia SM, Zielstorff RD, Paterno M, Teich JM, Bates DW, Kuperman GJ. Automating complex guidelines for chronic disease: lessons learned. J Am Med Inform Assoc 2003; 10(2): 154-165.

[39] McDonald CJ, Hui SL, Smith DM, Tierney WM, Cohen SJ, Weinberger M, et al. Reminders to physicians from an introspective computer medical record. A two-year randomized trial. Ann Intern Med 1984; 100(1): 130-138.

[40] Musen M, Shahar Y, Shortliffe EH. Clinical decision support systems. In: Shortliffe EH, Perreault LE, Wiederhold G, Fagan LM, editors. New York: Springer, 2000: 573-609.

[41] Musen MA. Domain ontologies in software engineering: use of Protege with the EON architecture. Methods Inf Med 1998; 37(4-5): 540-550.

[42] Ohno-Machado L, Gennari JH, Murphy SN, Jain NL, Tu SW, Oliver DE, et al. The guideline interchange format: a model for representing guidelines. J Am Med Inform Assoc 1998; 5(4): 357-372.

[43] Patel N. Adaptive Evolutionary Information Systems. London: Idea Group Publishing, 2003.

[44] Peleg M, Boxwala AA, Ogunyemi O, Zeng Q, Tu S, Lacson R, et al. GLIF3: the evolution of a guideline representation format. Proc Amia Symp 2000; 645-649.

[45] Peleg M, Tu S, Bury J, Ciccarese P, Fox J, Greenes RA, et al. Comparing computer-interpretable guideline models: a case-study approach. J Am Med Inform Assoc 2003; 10(1): 52-68.

[46] Pille BT, Antczak RK. Application Integration. In: Ball MJ, Douglas JV, editors. Performance Improvement Through Information Management. New York: Springer, 1999: 144-152.

[47] Pryor TA, Hripcsak G. Sharing MLM's: an experiment between Columbia-Presbyterian and LDS Hospital. In: Proc.Annu.Symp.Comput.Appl.Med Care; 1993: 399-403.

[48] Rahm E, Bernstein PA. A survey of approaches to automatic schema matching. The VLDB Journal 2001; 10(4): 334-350.

[49] Rector AL, Nowlan WA. The GALEN project. Comput Methods Programs Biomed 1994; 45(1-2): 75-78.

[50] Rector AL, Nowlan WA, Glowinski A. Goals for concept representation in the GALEN project. In: Proc.Annu.Symp.Comput.Appl.Med.Care; 1993: 414-418.

[51] Rocha RA, Huff SM. Coupling vocabularies and data structures: lessons from LOINC. In: Proc.AMIA.Annu.Fall.Symp.; 1996: 90-94.

[52] Schriefer J. The synergy of pathways and algorithms: two tools work better than one. Jt Comm J Qual Improv 1994; 20(9): 485-499.

[53] Seliger, R. Overview of HL7's CCOW Standard. 2001. Health Level Seven, Inc. http://www.hl7.org/library/committees/sigvi/ccow_overview_2001.doc

[54] Sheth A, Larsen J. Federated Database Systems for Managing Distributed, Heterogeneous, and Autonomous Databases. ACM Computing Surveys 1990; 22(3): 183-235.

[55] Shiffman RN, Liaw Y, Brandt CA, Corb GJ. Computer-based guideline implementation systems: a systematic review of functionality and effectiveness. J Am Med Inform Assoc 1999; 6(2): 104-114.

[56] Shiffman RN, Michel G, Essaihi A, Thornquist E. Bridging the guideline implementation gap: a systematic, document-centered approach to guideline implementation. J Am Med Inform Assoc 2004; 11(5): 418-426.

[57] Stonebraker M. Integrating islands of information. EAI Journal 1999;(September/October): 1-5.

[58] Tan FB, Gallupe RB. A framework for research into business-IT alignment: a cognitive emphasis. In: Kangas K, editor. Business strategies for information technology management. Hershey, PA, USA: Idea Group Publishing, 2003: 50-73.

[59] Tanenbaum AS. Computer networks. 2nd ed. Englewood Cliffs, N.J: Prentice-Hall, 1988.

[60] van Bemmel, J. H. and Musen, M. A. eds. Handbook of Medical Informatics. Heidelberg: Springer, 1997.

[61] Vegoda P. Introducing the IHE (Integrating the Healthcare Enterprise) concept. J Healthc Inf Manag 2002; 16(1): 22-24.

[62] Vincent C, Neale G, Woloshynowych M. Adverse events in British hospitals: preliminary retrospective record review. BMJ 2001; 322(7285): 517-519.

[63] Weed LL. Medical records that guide and teach. The New England Journal of Medicine 1968; 278(12): 652-657.

[64] Wilson RM, Harrison BT, Gibberd RW, Hamilton JD. An analysis of thc causes of adverse events from the Quality in Australian Health Care Study. Med J Aust 1999; 170(9): 411-415.

[65] Wilson RM, Runciman WB, Gibberd RW, Harrison BT, Newby L, Hamilton JD. The Quality in Australian Health Care Study. Med J Aust 1995; 163(9): 458-471.

[66] Wingert F. SNOMED-Manual. Berlin: Springer-Verlag, 1984.

Data Managment for Engineering Applications

Hans-Peter Steiert

DaimlerChrysler Research, Ulm, Germany
hans-peter.steiert@daimlerchrysler.com

Abstract. Current database technology has proven to fulfill the requirements of business applications, i.e., processing a high number of short transactions on more or less simple-structured data. Unfortunately, the requirements of engineering applications are quite different. A car's bill of material, for example, is a deep tree with many branches at every level. Data objects become even more complex if we consider the engineered design objects themselves, as for example a gear box with its parts and how they are related to each other. Supporting complex data objects has many implications for the underlying data management system. It needs to be reflected at nearly any layer, from the API down to the storage system. Besides complex objects, the way design objects are processed in engineering applications differs from business applications. Because engineering is an explorative task, the concept of short transactions does not fit here. Working with design objects is a task of days, which leads to a different programming model for engineering applications. In addition, the data management system needs to support versioning of objects and configuration management. Furthermore, engineering is done in a collaborative team. Hence, sharing of design objects in a team is necessary while, at the same time, their collaborative work has to be synchronized. All those special requirements have to be considered in data management systems for engineering applications. In this contribution, the special requirements, as sketched above, are characterized. Also the approaches developed to cope with these requirements will be described.

1 Introduction

Business applications have been always the main focus of data management systems. Hence, current data management technology is able to serve most of the demands of this domain very well. Other domains with differing requirements have to cope with less support, for example, the engineering domain. Although engineering databases have been well researched [2, 10, 18, 23], support for engineering applications in current database or middleware technology is still marginal. Therefore, existing technology still requires adoption to the needs of the engineering applications.

T. Härder and W. Lehner (Eds.): Data Management (Wedekind Festschrift), LNCS 3551, pp. 335-356, 2005.

The most demanding challenge today is not data management itself but to support a seamless flow of data through all tools used in the product creation process, i.e., construction tasks as well as production-related activities. Of course, this has a lot of different aspects and discussing all of them is beyond the scope of this paper. Therefore, we will focus on a selection of topics which are of special interest because of new trends:

- Building up an IT infrastructure never starts at the open field. Instead it is always the result of an evolutionary process. This is the first reason, why the IT landscape of any larger company will always be heterogeneous. The second reason for heterogeneity is that engineering processes need to be supported by many highly specialized engineering applications. Therefore, the all-in-one engineering tool is more utopia than reality. Each of these tools is optimized for a given task and so are the data structures: CAD applications may work with data structures that support free-form surfaces. Tools for crash simulation require, for example, finite-element meshes. The bill of material may be implemented as a graph with simple-structured nodes which contain links to large chunks of external information. The challenge for data management is to support each tools with its appropriate data format, ensure the seamless flow between tools and enable an integrated view upon all relevant data, if required. In section 2 we will discuss the utilization of current integration technology within engineering processes.
- Another important aspect in engineering processes is agility. Because such processes cover long running activities, there is always a need to adapt to new requirements. On the other hand, application integration creates dependencies between applications and those are an inherent risk for agility, because changes within one application or within the process need to consider all dependent applications. That is why we need to take countermeasures to ensure that changes can still be applied. In section 3 we will describe an approach for development and maintenance of integration solutions which does reflect this need.
- Engineering processes involve many parties inside and outside a company. Especially, integration of suppliers has become more and more important during the last years. This results in a need to manage the flow of engineering data in the product creation process as it leaves the company and comes back again. In such a scenario, the task of providing the required data in the right format at the right time is a demanding challenge. In section 4 we will describe first steps done towards managed cross-company data flows.

In the next paragraphs, we will discuss these three challenges of engineering data management.

2 Applying Integration Technology in Engineering Domains

Application integration is a crucial point in order to support faster engineering processes. The advantages of application integration have already been discussed [11, 22]. Sev-

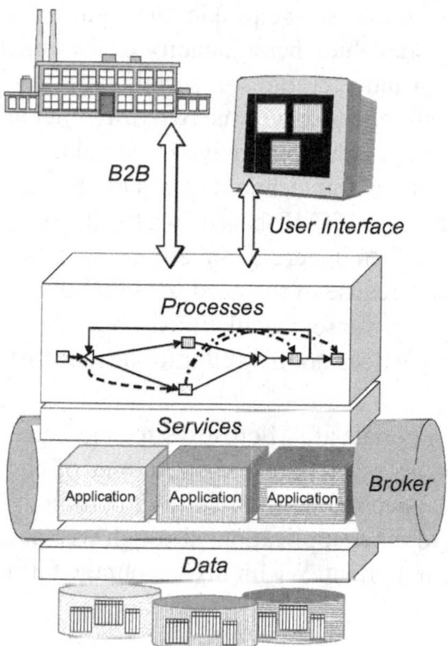

Fig. 1 Layers of Integration

eral integration technologies (and related products) do address the problem of application integration. As often, it is helpful to discuss applications integration in layers, from the data management layer at the bottom to the graphical user interface layer at the top. For each of these layers, integration technology has been developed in order to cope with the particular challenges. And because each layer has its own demands, the answers have been quite different. Fig. 1 shows an abstract representation of a layered integration architecture.

The overall goal of application integration is to cope with distribution, heterogeneity, and autonomy [28]. Distribution means that data and operations are spread over several data stores and application systems. Heterogeneity refers to the semantics of data and operations, the syntax of data formats and signatures, and the technologies used. Autonomy is related to the fact that each application has been developed and is maintained on its own. Through application integration autonomy is reduced, usually.

In Fig. 1, we also show B2B integration but, because this will be our topic in section 4, we skip it here and start with integration at the front end.

2.1 Integration at the User Interface Level

From the end-user's perspective, integration has been successful, if the user is not able to differentiate the sources of data and functionality it accesses from the user interface. In the area of web applications, so-called portals have been successfully applied in providing user-interface-level integration, i.e., providing integrated access to data and applications through one common user interface.

Although portal technology is very helpful in the engineering domain [1], too, it has several limitations. First, portals hide heterogeneity of user interfaces but are not able to hide heterogeneity of data and operations. If serial numbers stem from different systems with distinct formats, the end user will see two different numbers, even if the same part is displayed at the screen. Such effects have to be hidden at lower levels of the integration architecture. Second, portal technology has its strength in integrating web applications, i.e., applications with HTML-based front end. Unfortunately, web applications do not fit very well in the engineering domain. Many tasks require highly specialized rich client applications because of the need for presenting complex CAD data and high demands on computing power for calculations. Third, the engineer's work is highly creative and interactive which does not fit well into the mask-oriented user guidance of web applications.

An alternative to using portals are Microsoft's technologies, e.g., Object Link Embedding (OLE), for giving access to data and operations of one desktop application to another. Unfortunately, no open standards are known for this. With Microsoft enabling its office tools for access to other applications through web services, this kind of integration may become more important. We highly encourage further research in this field.

2.2 Integration at the Engineering Process Level

Some of the drawbacks of today's integration technology at the user interface can be reduced through process-level integration. The idea is to provide suitable data formats to the engineering application as part of a workflow (Fig. 2). Preceding steps in the workflow fetch data from the data sources and apply transformations so that the engineering application receives the data to work with in an integrated and homogenized format. After the engineering task has been fulfilled, the result is distributed to the data sources and transformed back into their proprietary formats. This works fine for the large and complex data chunks which are typical for engineering data. One further advantage is that usually no changes need to be done to the participating applications, i.e., a high degree of autonomy is preserved. Unfortunately, it does not fit well for fine-grained data and short operations because of the overhead generated by the workflow control mechanism. Another drawback is that the workflows need to be preplanned which is not very common in engineering, as we have discussed before.

2.3 Integration at the Engineering Service Level

Support for access to fine-grained data and short operations (today often called "services") provided by application systems is the task of levels below processes. We call it service-level integration. The idea behind this is to provide an integrated view to several data sources and service providers (base services) through an application programming interface (API) which consists of a collection of services. From a client's point of view the API seems to give access to one application system , because all aspects of heterogeneity are hidden behind the API in the services implementation. The services do hide

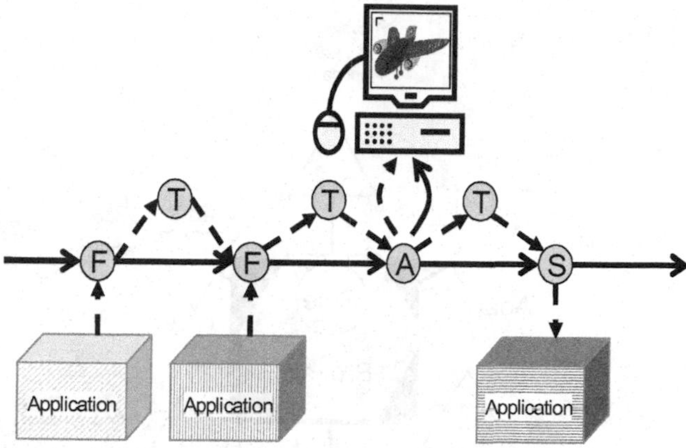

Fig. 2 Process-level Integration

both, the underlying implementation technology as well as the communication protocols used to access the base services. Further, the API provides an integrated view upon the base services, because it integrates the data from several base services to one common object model. In addition, the API may provide value-added services.

This approach is well supported by a set of emerging technologies in the area of J2EE (Java 2 Enterprise Edition) [33] and Web services [35]. Service aggregation is supported by BPEL (Business Process Execution Language) [13] which becomes available in the next generation of J2EE servers [14]. Access to applications is supported through the J2EE Connector Architecture (J2A) standard [34], message-driven beans [33] and support for calling Web services. Using XML [36] has become the standard way for technology-independent representation of data and XSLT [8] is widely used for data transformation. If it comes to signatures, WSDL [7] is used to describe services in an technology-independent way.

Integration at the service layer is well suited if online access to the base services is required. Unfortunately, the efforts for integration are high because of the need for a federated data model of the underlying data sources. Also, overall performance highly depends on choosing the granule of data and operations well. Additionally, existing applications need to be adapted if access to the integration layer is required.

2.4 Integration Through Message Brokers

There exists a second approach which does access the base services provided by application systems. The idea of message-broker-based integration is to recognize events in the application systems which are relevant to others. This task is performed by an adapter which connects the application system to the message broker [15]. If the adapter has recognized an event, it fetches the related data from the application. Afterwards the message broker receives a message from the adapter. Because of routing rules the message broker knows for which applications this event is relevant. It forwards the message

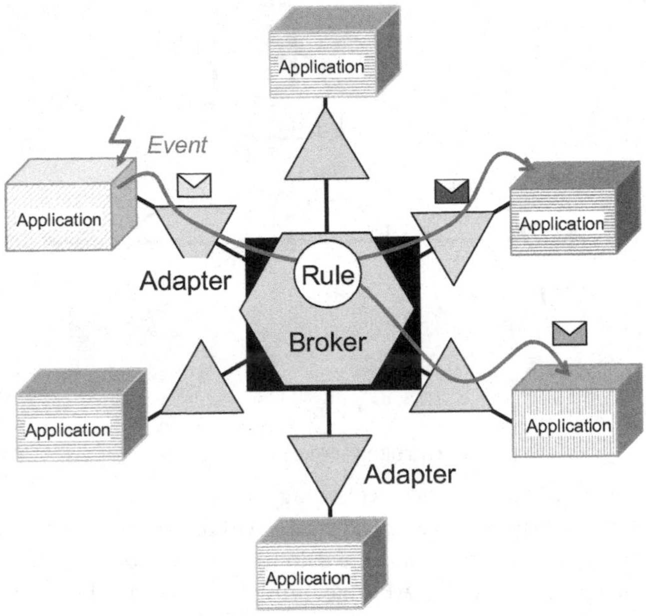

Fig. 3 Broker-based Integration

to the adapters of those systems. If data transformations are required, those are performed by the broker (Fig. 3).

Message brokering is usually not used in engineering so far for several reasons. First, no adapters are available for the engineer's desktop applications so that the usage is limited to backend applications. Second, data exchange between backend applications usually does mean to transmit large chunks of data, e.g., a CAD file from a PDM system to another. Current broker technology has been developed for business applications with a high number of small data items and it is not able to handle large data items well.

2.5 Integration at the Database Management Layer

Database layer integration has been researched very well. Database replication, data warehousing, federated databases, distributed databases, and many other approaches have been developed in this area. Some of them have been successfully applied in engineering domains.

For example, data warehousing becomes important as a base technology for building business intelligence solutions in order to support project management [12]. Even if the amount of data is low, compared with similar applications in the business domain, there are quite a few challenges. For example, we have to cope with much more heterogeneity, because a lot of (semi-structured) data is stored in office applications on the desktop and not in backend systems.

Also, concepts from federated databases have been applied [32]. Unfortunately, most databases are hidden within the application systems. Therefore, integration at the database layer is mostly not possible because of a lack of information about the semantics of the database schema. Nevertheless, many concepts from federated databases have been successfully used for integration at the service layer.

3 Enabling Agility in the Presence of Integration

Unfortunately, the risks of application integration are often neglected. Because integration means to create dependencies between applications this may reduce the ability of an IT infrastructure to adapt to changes, i.e., its agility. Dependencies are bad, because they increase complexity which leads to increased efforts and a higher probability of making mistakes.

For example, if changes need to be applied to one application all other dependent applications have to be checked whether or not they are affected by the change. Without counter measures the result of integration may be one big integrated system of interconnected applications where no changes can be done any more because no one knows what will happen. This is especially worse in engineering, because the number of systems is even higher than in the business domain. Further, engineering processes are less strict. Therefore, frequent changes are typical and the ability to adapt also the IT is crucial. Why is agility so hard to ensure? There are three main reasons:

- No consistent view on all current application systems.
- Heterogeneity of all artefacts, technical and non-technical.
- Distribution of application systems and organizations.

The first point results from the fact that it seems nearly impossible to ensure consistency of documentation and running systems. Because usually informal methods are used, documentation does not provide a detailed view on the system even in the beginning. Things become worse during the system's lifetime when changes are made in order to react spontaneous to new business demands or to fix problems. Typically, documentation falls behind the real environment fast. But without a consistent view upon the application systems we can not really understand the effects of changes.

The second point does not only cover heterogeneity of the application systems themselves. It is also related to all other artefacts as metadata, integration toolsets, documentation templates, development processes and so on. This is because every consulting firm brings in its own development process and documentation guidelines into the project. Further, there is no "one tool fits it all" way of integration. If multiple integration technologies are applied in a project, e.g., a portal and an integration service, then each of those has its own tools and metadata standards. Therefore, we have to look in many different information sources in order to gain a snapshot of what is currently running.

The third point does also cover more than just the technical stuff. From the technical perspective it is difficult enough to ensure that all changes have been applied consistent in a distributed system. But there is also an organizational aspect: Application integration means to bring together applications owned, managed and maintained by different departments. Hence, no single source of information exists. Even simple maintaining tasks require workshops with many people from different organizational units. Experience shows that it is even more difficulty to ensure that humans talk about the same than it is for computers.

If we want to cope with those challenges we have to ensure that there is one central documentation source which does reflect the current state of the whole integrated system. A development and maintenance process with appropriate tool support has to ensure that the documentation becomes consistent in the beginning and stays consistent during the whole life-cycle. The approach has to fit in current development methods and needs to be practicable with multiple integration toolsets. Four scenarios need to be supported (Fig. 4):

- Central, uniform and automated documentation.
- Developing a new integrated system.
- Updating and maintaining an existing integrated system.
- Migrating an integrated system to new technology.

The key idea behind supporting the first point is to take advantage of the most current information available, which resides in the metadata stores of development tools and integration toolsets. It describes the current productive environment. This information needs to be automatically imported into a central documentation repository (which means integration of metadata of heterogeneous sources!). Further, information should be collected where it is created. Because development tools, administration tools and documentation tools usually provide the ability to add comments, this feature has to be used extensively. All those comments have to be collected, needs to be related to the metadata and stored in the repository. In order to be able to cover also the information created by humans as documents those have to follow strict documentation standards. So the documents can be analyzed automatically and the content can be stored in the repository together with the other data. The advantage of this approach is that it becomes much easier to hold reality and documentation consistent. Because everything is stored in a central repository and related to each other it becomes possible to check consistency, completeness, and correctness with respect to guidelines. The central repository helps to get a current view on the system and to avoid heterogeneity of non-technical artefacts.

The second point is about creating a new system from scratch. An appropriate development process has to ensure that the repository is filled with meaningful information. In order to support development well, we need

- an appropriate iterative development process which starts with an abstract plan and leads to a solution in a sequence of refinement steps,
- formalized intermediate results which can be stored within the repository,

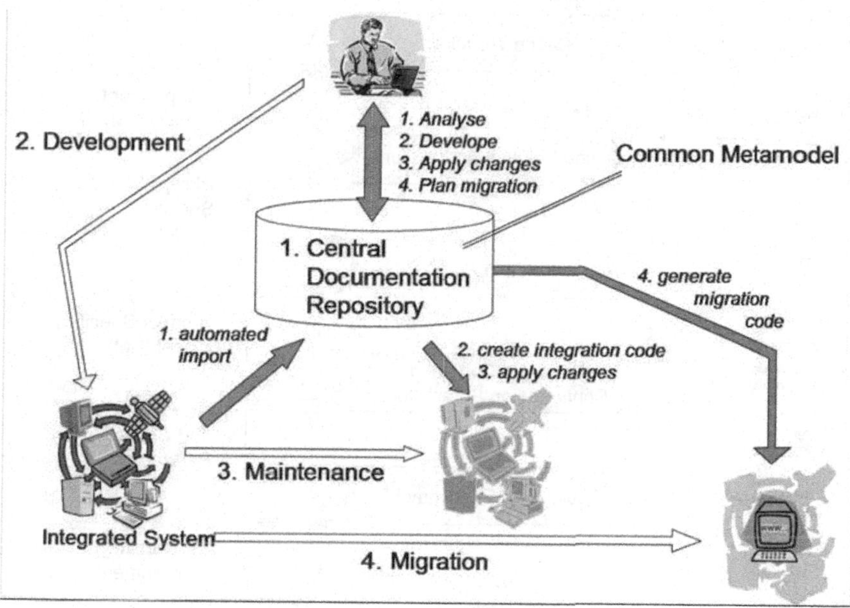

Fig. 4 Repository-based Approach

- support for an overall view on the results of each level of refinement,
- support for navigation from the more abstract level to the more concrete level and vice versa,
- refinement relationships in the repository have a well defined meaning and enable tools to check whether or not a refinement is valid w.r.t. to the level above, and
- tools to (semi-)automatically generate a integration solution from the lowest level of refinement.

The third point, maintenance, has to be supported in both directions. In a top down approach, changes may be applied in the same way as described for development. We start at the abstract level and iteratively refine the artifacts until code generation can occur. Because experience shows that often changes need to be applied fast, we also have to support a bottom-up approach. Those changes need to be propagated from the lowest level up to the highest level of abstraction. This has to happen automatically as far as possible. If propagation is not possible the repository must at least identify whether or not the changes are in conflict with the specifications made at the level above.

Last but not least, the biggest step will be support for migration to a new product, i.e., integration toolset. So far, this means a re-implementation of the whole integrated system. With a central repository storing all the information collected from the metadata and all artifacts from the development process it will be much easier. Through appropriate input filters and code generators for the new product the content of the repository may serve as an 'exchange format'.

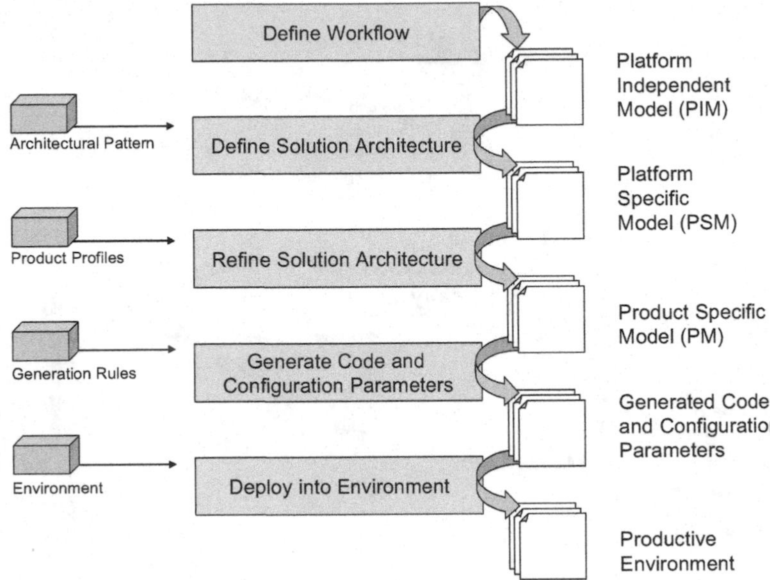

Fig. 5 Model-driven Integration Process

On the first glance all this seems to be more a wish than a reachable goal. But in real products some vendors have done the first step towards this approach [31]. Unfortunately this does not fit well in large enterprises, because a vendor-specific approach is always related only to one integration toolset. In the next paragraph we will sketch how this wish may become reality through model-based application integration even for multiple products.

3.1 Model-Based Management of Integrated Systems

The approach presented here is related to the OMG's (Object Management Group) proposal for model-based software development: Model-Driven Architecture (MDA) [21]. It has been developed at the University of Stuttgart in cooperation with DaimlerChrysler Research and Technology and is named RADES (Reference Architecture for the Documentation and Support of EAI Solutions) [9].

In MDA a software system is developed in three major phases. First, a conceptual model of the system to be developed is created. This model describes the system as precise as possible but does not contain any information related to the technology used for implementation. It is called the platform independent model (PIM). In the second step this model is refined by adding implementation specific details. If more than one target platform has to be supported multiple of those platform-specific models (PSM) may be created. The term platform is used for the set of technologies used for implementation. One key idea behind this refinement step is to enable semi-automatic transformations

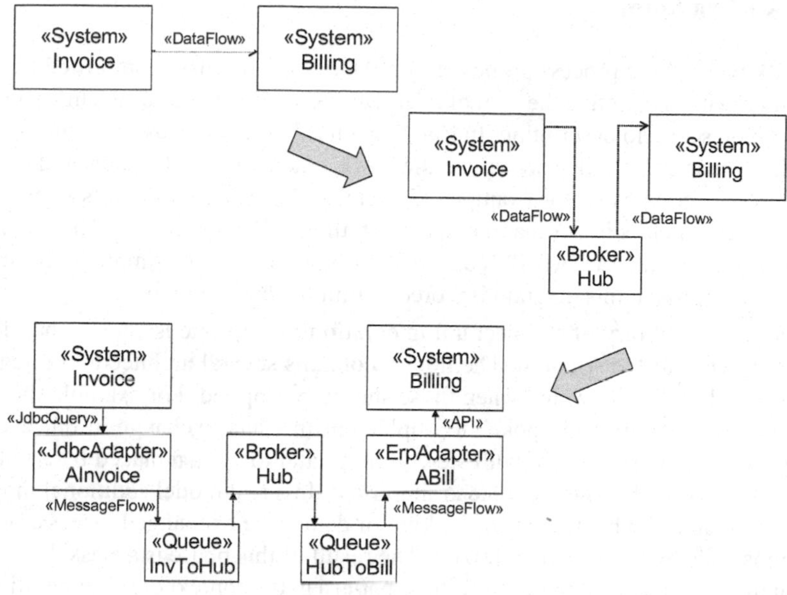

Fig. 6 Example

from PSM to PIM. In last step generators create code and deployment information from the PSM. Within MDA all activities are related to one model of the system, which is typically expressed using the language elements of UML [25, 26].

This three step approach is to simplistic for real integration projects. Therefore, the RADES approach introduces two additional phases. In RADES the PSM is still product independent and does only describe the overall architecture. It is more precise than the PIM, because, because it does describe the architectural integration pattern to be used for the implementation. But it does not contain any product specific details. Hence, an additional step is needed to refine the model and add such details. This split is required in order to reflect that multiple products can be used to implement the same architectural integration pattern. Especially, it is needed in order to support the migration scenario.

Another limitation of MDA is that it does not cover the deployment step. In our case this is necessary in order to support the maintenance scenario. In order to be able to use the generated code in several physical environments, it can not include information about physical layout, as for example IP addresses. Hence, RADES introduced a deployment step in which logical names are replaces by physical ones and the result is deployed to physical machines.

All artefacts created within the RADES process are described using the same modelling language, i.e., UML, except for the last two. Those are source code and configuration parameters which are specific to the used products. Even if possible, it does not make sense to use UML for this, in our point of view. Nevertheless, all artefacts including source code and parameters are managed by the repository.

3.2 An Example

Let's walk through the process proposed by RADES and discuss a simplified example: The first activity is to define the goal of an integration project and results in a workflow or integration scenario description. In Fig. 5, we used an UML class diagram for modelling the scenario. Note that we utilize the UML extension mechanisms and have defined some stereotypes as for example “System”. Those will help tools to recognize which semantic a class in our diagram has w.r.t. the RADES approach. There exists already a “UML Profile for EAI” [27] but we did not use it here for simplicity reasons. In the RADES approach this diagram is stored within the central repository.

Next, from a library of architectural integration pattern one is chosen that does fit best to the needs of the scenario. The library contains several architectural integration patterns and describes how and when those should be applied. For example the developer may choose “Hub-and-Spoke” to implement the data exchange in our example. This means that the simple arc with stereotype “DataFlow” is replaced by a hub-and-spoke pattern. Note that this example is simplified. In a real model additional model elements are required which describe the kind of data to be exchanged, necessary transformations done by the broker and so on. The result of this phase is a class diagram describing the participants of this architectural pattern in the context of the integration scenario. This is the platform specific model and it is stored in the repository which does also track transformations that have been applied. We will need this information later if we discuss the bottom-up approach. RADES will take advantage of several approaches for transforming UML diagrams automatically [29].

Now a product is chosen for implementing this pattern. For each architectural pattern the repository manages implementation patterns on the base of commercial products. The platform specific model is refined by applying an implementation pattern to the hub-and-spoke architecture. In our example each communication link between an application systems and the broker is replaced by an adapter with communication links to the application system and to the broker. Because the properties of the application system are also stored within the repository development tools can check whether or not the adapter is well suited for the application system. In our case the adapter communicates with the application system through a JDBC connection and with the broker through a messaging system. Therefore, message queues are also added to the model. The result is a product specific model (PM).

The PM contains all information necessary to create install scripts, configuration scripts, queue definitions, adapter configuration files and so on. The user still has to provide logical names for the instances of each model element to the generator. Hence, the result is still environment independent, e.g., it does not contain physical IP addresses but logical names. If the resulting package is deployed to a concrete environment, then the deployment tool replaces logical names by physical ones. Appropriate information about the environment and the mapping has to be provided by the developer/deployer. Of cause all this information is also managed by the repository.

So far we did describe the top down process. Because of the layers of abstraction the RADES approach is also well suited to support a bottom-up approach. This is required in order to support the maintenance scenario. Assume, a queue name is changed by an administrator. Utilizing the information about the environment and the PM a check utility may detect that a queue mentioned in the repository does not longer exist and triggers an administrator to update the model. After the information about the physical implementation has been updated, the tool can also check if the change made by the administrator is still consistent with the model at the higher level. For example, renaming a queue will only affect the lowest level because the logical name is still valid. But using two queues between adapter and broker will require changes up to the product specific model.

4 Data Flow in Engineering Processes

As engineering becomes more and more complex not all tasks are done within the enterprise itself. The special know how of external firms is exploited, too. This results in engineering processes which are partly executed by partners. Managing such processes means to cope with the interdependencies between internal and external engineering processes and the data flow in between. Typically this is what workflow management systems have been developed for.

Traditionally, workflow management systems were intended to be used for automating business processes within the same company. Compared to business processes, engineering processes are different in many aspects. First of all, engineering processes are long running tasks. Constructing a car lasts for many years and the next model of a large airliner is the result of a decade of engineering and production planning. Second, engineering processes have to cope with uncertainty because of their mixture of creative work, collaborative tasks and repeating activities. This results in more complex processes with many alternative paths and sections that can not be planed in advanced [3]. Third, engineering data is different from business data. While business applications have to cope with a large number of simple structured data items engineering processes manage large and complex structured data items but the number is comparative small. Several proposals have been made to take advantage of workflow management in the engineering domain [3, 30, 17].

Data management is one of the crucial issues in engineering processes. For example the CONCORD approach [30] is a database-oriented processing model for design applications. It exploits the enhanced data management abilities of the underlying data store VStore [24] which was especially developed for managing complex engineering data. Another example is described in [3]. In this approach the focus is not on managing the control flow between activities. The key idea is to manage data exchange dependencies instead of control flow between engineering activities. The author argues that engineering processes are result driven, which means in the terms of IT that they are data driven.

If it comes to cross-organizational workflows, data management becomes even more challenging. For reasonable cooperation it is essential to share data between the participating groups. As an example, consider engineers constructing a new automotive vehicle. To examine the accuracy of the fittings a kind of digital mock up (DMU) may be performed. This means at a given point of time all participants have to exchange the CAD geometries in order to create a digital version of the whole vehicle. Even in large companies a central data store is difficult to achieve. In the case of cross-organizational cooperation it is in fact impossible.

In the COW project (cross-organizational workflows [19]) first research towards the description of company-spanning processes and support of global flow of control has been performed. Complementary the role of cross-organizational dataflow has been investigated in the COD project [4, 5] at the University of Kaiserslautern in cooperation with DaimlerChrysler Research and Technology. It is described in detail in [6].

4.1 The COD Approach

Company-spanning development processes take already place today and electronic data exchange is also widespread used, so what is the problem?

First, even if collaboration between engineering partners already follows a strict process with agreed deliverables at given points in time, this process is not enacted through workflow technology. Either data flow occurs at given time intervals, e.g., every night, or in an ad-hoc manner. Exchanging data every night results in many unnecessary data exchanges because an engineering task at the provider's side may not have finished a new result and the old one has already been sent. Ad-hoc exchange depends heavily on the competence and reliability of people involved. It is very error-prone and often the exchange has to be done several times before reaching the expected result. Hence, high efforts have to be spent to cope with mistakes made during this process.

Second, today's data exchange is usually point-to-point between two activities in the process. Hence, no global view on the current location of data within the overall process is possible. Where is the data? Who is the owner of the data? Who is allowed to apply changes? Who should be informed about changes? These questions can only be answered with high efforts for investigation. Therefore, many errors occur which need to be avoided.

Third, no standardized procedure and technology is used for data exchange. Each point-to-point exchange is developed with a per-project view and utilizes the technology at hand. This makes maintenance difficult and does not allow sharing experience or even reusing software between two data exchange projects.

For theses reasons, the goal of COD is to make the flow of data between partners transparent, to increase control over data even after it has left the company and to enact data flow through integration with workflow management.

Within the COD approach we meet those challenges by identifying typical data exchange pattern at the logical level. For this purpose four aspects of cross-organizational data exchange and their interdependencies have been studied. The result is a set of implementation-independent dataflow integration pattern. One of the advantages of patterns is that their implementation does not vary too much from one instantiation in an integration project to the next if the underlying integration architecture is the same. This gives a high potential for reuse of code fragments and know-how.

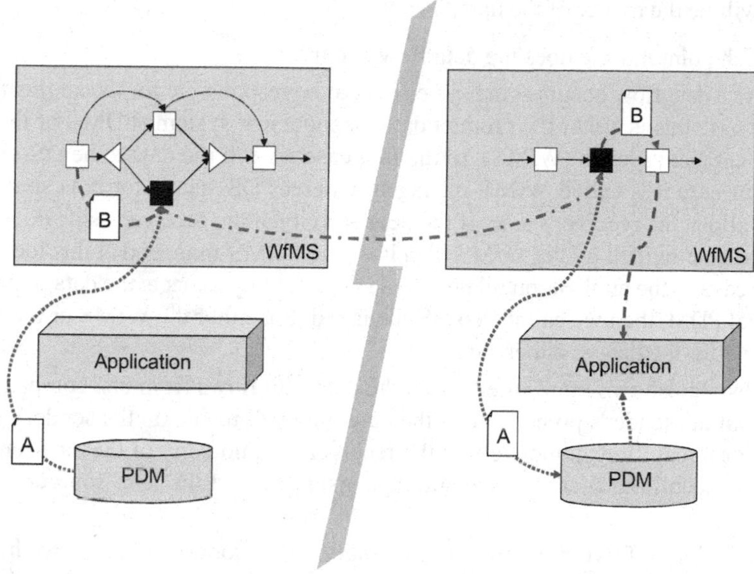

Fig. 7 Cross-organizational Data Flow

Note that one constraint in our research was to use of-the-shelf software wherever applicable. This stems from our goal to support real-world integration projects. For this reason we have examined current enterprise application integration (EAI) technology and how we can take advantage of it.

Before we will introduce the dataflow integration patterns we have to explain our scenario. Afterwards we will discuss the aspects of integration patterns and our integration architecture. We will argue why it is suitable for implementing our patterns.

Fig. 7 shows a cross-organizational data flow. A data flow edge (the dotted-dashed line) connects an activity of the source side's workflow with an activity at the target side's workflow. Note that we assume special activities to be inserted into the local workflow specification. Those represent the interaction of the WfMS with the COD middleware. All other arcs and boxes will be explained later.

4.2 Dataflow Integration Pattern

The idea of patterns is to describe the invariant parts of a solution and how it can be adapted to a given scenario for a particular specification of the variant parts. So, what are the invariant parts in our case?

- Who is responsible for the data at either side?
- What will be the effect of data flow at both sides?

- Who will be the owner of the data?
- At which point in time does the data flow occur?

Before a data flow occurs some system has to be responsible for the application data. In our case this is either the product data management system (PDM), or the workflow management system (WfMS). In the first case we call the data to be DS-managed in the later case it is called WfMS-managed, whereas DS stands for data source. The same is valid at the receiver's side. If the next activity at the receiver's side does expect the data to be provided by the WfMS then it is also WfMS-managed at this location. In the other case, if the application related to the next activity expects the data to be stored in the local PDM, then we call it also DS-managed. So, either the WfMS or the PDM is responsible for the data at either side.

We distinguish two kinds of effect on the data as it flows from one company to the other. From the sender's point of view the data may still reside on the sender's side afterwards or it may flow completely to the receiver, i.e., no copy of the data remains at the sender's side. The first is called source-conserving and the later source-consumptive.

We can think of two possible modes to supply the cooperation data to the target, materialized or referenced. Materialized means that the data is provided physically at the target island for local access direct after the data flow has been performed. Because we have to consider data from the CAx domain to be huge in size, unnecessary physical transfers have to be avoided. Materialized data may be outdated before it is required or may not be required at all. Therefore, the mode referenced transfers only a reference of the data. If data is effectively required this reference is used by the COD middleware to fetch the physical data on demand.

The next aspect is related to the semantics of the data flow. In cross-organizational collaboration there is a difference between the owner of data and the possessor of data. From the engineering processes' point of view the owner is responsible for validity and consistency. If the owner hands the data over this does not necessarily imply the loss of ownership. In fact, it is also possible to be the owner of data even if there is no physical copy accessible to the owner. The possessor always has a physical copy of the data but has only limited rights on it. Tab. 1 shows the possible effects of switching ownership and possession.

Last but not least the receiver may expect an other data format as it is available at the sender's side. Therefore, selecting, filtering and transforming data has to be done. This needs to be considered by the dataflow integration pattern.

Tab. 1 Relationship between Ownership and Possession

	Before		**After**	
	Source	**Target**	**Source**	**Target**
A	O,P	-	O,P	P
B	O,P	-	P	O,P
C	O,P	-	O,P	O,P
D	O,P	-	O	P
E	O,P	-	-	O,P
F	P	O	-	O,P
G	P	O	P	O,P

The aspects introduced above are not orthogonal. For example the possessor always holds a physical copy of the data. Hence, if the source side is intended to be still a possessor after the data flow occurred than the transfer can not be source-consuming. Tab. 2 shows the useful combinations for which integration pattern need to be provided.

Tab. 2 Useful Combinations of the Integration Pattern Invariants

Source-Side Manager	**Supply Mode**	**Effect**	**Target-Side Manager**	**Ownership/ Possession Category**
DS	materialized	Source Conserving	DS	A, B, C, G
	referenced	Source Consumpting	DS	D, E, F
		Source Conserving	WfMS	A, B, C, G
		Source Consumpting	WfMS	D, E, F
WfMS	materialized	Source Conserving	DS	A, B, C, G
		Source Consumpting	DS	D, E, F
		Source Conserving	WfMS	A, B, C, G
		Source Consumpting	WfMS	D, E, F

4.3 A COD Middleware Architecture

During the e-Hype it was usual to start from scratch and build new applications or middleware systems for each use case. Since then, cost cuts have hit most IT departments and reducing costs has become one of the core drivers. That's why so called Service-Oriented Architectures (SOA) [14] are en vogue. The idea is to build new systems through aggregation of services provided by existing ones and to glue those together with flow-oriented orchestration [13]. Services are made accessible through Web Services technologies which are based upon open standards [36, 7] and promise high interoperability. For the same reasons and in order to ensure applicability in practice, one design goal of the COD project was to utilize existing technologies as far as possible. What are the requirements a middleware system supporting the COD approach has to fulfil?

1. In our scenario each data exchange is triggered by a local WfMS through an exchange activity in the local workflow definition. At both sides different workflow products may be in use. Hence, the middleware has to support easy integration with heterogeneous WfMSs.
2. The data to be exchanged may stem from multiple data sources; i.e., the local WfMS or one of the local PDM systems. At the receiver's side the same alternatives exist. Hence, the COD middleware has to be able to work with heterogeneous data sources and application systems.
3. Data exchange between companies is a typical B2B scenario. Beside heterogeneity of applications and data sources the COD middleware has to support several communication mechanisms and data exchange protocols in order to be able to bridge between heterogeneous islands.
4. As data flows between the heterogeneous applications of different companies the data format used on both sides will probably not be the same. Therefore, data transformation has to be applied on the data's way from the source to the target. The data exchange middleware has to support powerful data transformation and filtering mechanisms for this purpose.
5. One reason for using a central middleware for data exchange instead of a per-project solution is to be able to track the flow of data. The COD middleware has to support tracking the data flow. Either this has to be a functionality of the middleware itself or the middleware must enable integration of a special software component for this purpose.
6. Some of the properties of data objects exchanged between companies, as for example ownership of data, will not be supported by off-the-shelf products because those properties are application specific. Managing these properties will require custom software components. The COD middleware has to be able to integrate with such components.

As those requirements show, most of the demands are related to integration of heterogeneous systems, i.e., applications, data stores, WfMS, communication middleware and self-developed components. This is a typical application scenario, message brokers have been developed for [14].

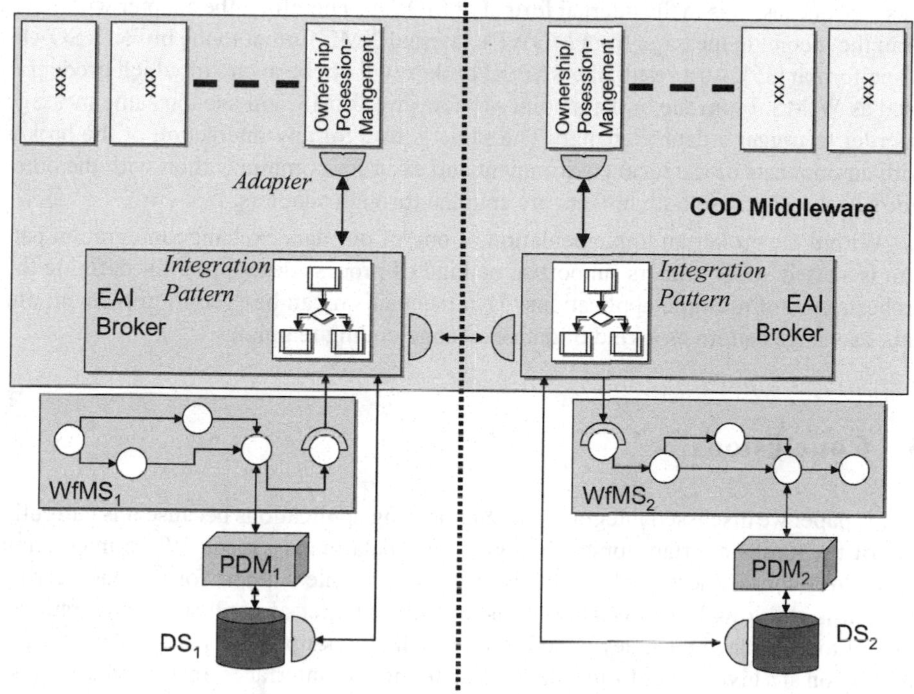

Fig. 8 Cross-organizational Data Flow

In [16] several architectures for using message brokers are discussed. We will describe here the one introduced in [5]. In [6] it is classified as 'distributed approach' because it assumes message brokers at both sides. Note that there is no reason for using the same message broker by both companies. The sender may have IBM's Websphere Business Integration Server [16] in productive use and the receiver may use Microsoft's BizTalk [20], for example. We will now describe the architecture as it is shown in Fig. 7.

The core component is the central message broker. For simplicity reasons we only describe the sender's side because the receiver's side looks exactly the same. The message broker is connected through adapters with the other software components, i.e., the WfMS, local application systems, local PDMSs and custom components for managing ownership or tracking data flow or similar.

The purpose of adapters is to hide the heterogeneity of the systems connected to the broker. Assume we use WebSphere MQ Workflow (MQWF) for workflow enactment. If a dataflow activity is started by MQWF it will put a message into a WebSphere MQ (WMQ) queue. This queue is intended to trigger an application system to perform the activity. In our case this application system will be the message broker, e.g., SAP XI [31] which uses HTTP for internal communication. Hence, the first purpose for the adapter is to receive the message from WMQ and forward it to the broker through an HTTP call. Unfortunately, SAP XI will not be able to understand the meaning of the message because it is in the internal format of MQWF. Therefore, the adapter will transform the incoming message from MQWF's internal XML format to the broker's SOAP-based format [35]. As a result, the SAP XI broker will not be aware of which product is used as WfMS. From the brokers point of view any WfMS will use the same message in order to trigger a data exchange. The same is true for any interaction of the broker with components of the local environment and even for communication with the other side's broker, because both brokers are coupled through adapters, too.

Within the broker an implementation of one of our data exchange integration pattern is started. Most brokers support some kind of process description for defining the orchestration of multiple applications. This mechanism can be used to implement our data exchange pattern as a kind of data exchange coding templates.

5 Conclusions

In this paper we discussed integration of engineering applications because it is currently one of the most important topics in engineering data management. While integration technology for business applications is broadly available support for the engineering domain is still low. Because there exists no "silver bullet of application integration", several toolsets have been developed, each of which does provide mechanisms for the integration at a given layer from databases up to the user interfaces. In section 2, we discussed the pros and cons of those tools in the context of engineering applications. Although all of them can be applied successfully in engineering, too, special demands of this domain are not supported.

In the remainder of the paper, we had a closer look on two topics which are currently under our observation. First, we introduced an approach for developing integrated applications without loosing agility. The RADES approach proposes a model-based top-down development model. Through extensive usage of a central repository many development and maintenance task can be automated which enables faster adoptions to new needs. Second, we presented an approach for managing cross-organizational data flows. The idea was to provide a standard integration architecture for all kinds of data flows between enterprises and a box of so-called integration pattern which provide pre-build solutions to this problem. Note that the idea of integration patterns fits very well into the RADES approach.

Future research has to be done for both approaches in order to make them applicable in real-world integration scenarios in the domain of engineering.

References

[1] Audi: Engineering Portal Audi Quickreferenz. available from https://extranet.audi.de/QuickReferenz_V08.pdf, access 2005-01-05

[2] Bernstein, P. A., Dayal, U.: An Overview of Repository Technology, in Proc. 20th Int. Conf. Very Large Data Bases, 1994, Santiago de Chile, Morgan Kaufmann, pp. 705-713

[3] Beuter, T.: Workflow-Management für Produktentwicklungsprozesse. Der Andere Verlag, Wissenschaftlicher Buchverlag, http://www.der-andere-verlag.de/bookshop/default.html?fachgebiet_rechts-_und_wirtschaftswissenschaften.htm.

[4] Bon, M., Ritter, N., Härder, T.: Sharing Product Data among Heterogeneous Workflow Environments, in Proc. Int. Conf. CAD 2002—Corporate Engineering Research, Dresden, March 2002, pp. 139-149.

[5] Bon, M., Ritter, N., Steiert, H.-P.: Modellierung und Abwicklung von Datenflüssen in unternehmensübergreifenden Prozessen, in: Proc. 10. GI-Fachtagung für Datenbanksysteme in Business, Technologie und Web, Leipzig, March 2003, pp. 433-442.

[6] Bon, M.: Modellierung und Abwicklung von Datenflüssen in unternehmensübergreifenden Geschäftsprozessen, Logos Verlag Berlin, 2004.

[7] Christensen, E., Curbera, F., Meredith, G., Weerawarana, S.: Web Services Description Language (WSDL) 1.1, W3C Note 15 March 2001

[8] Clark, J. (ed.): XSL Transformations (XSLT), Version 1.0. W3C Recommendation 16 November 1999

[9] Dorda, C., Steiert, H.-P., Sellentin, J.: Modellbasierter Ansatz zur Anwendungsintegration. it – Information Technology 46(4): pp. 200-210 (2004).

[10] Encarnaçao, J., Lockemann, P. (eds): Engineering Databases, Connecting Islands of Automation Trough Databases. Springer Verlag, 1990

[11] Häuschen, H.: EAI—Enterprise Application Integration. available from http://www.ifi.unizh.ch/ikm/Vorlesungen/ebusiness/ws04/material/FolienEAI.pdf, access 2005-01-06

[12] Hilliger von Thile, A., Melzer, I.: Smart Files: Combining the Advantages of DBMS and WfMS with the Simplicity and Flexibility of Spreadsheets, in Proc. 11. GI-Fachtagung für Datenbanksysteme in Business, Technologie und Web, Karlsruhe, March 2005.

[13] IBM: Business Process Execution Language for Web Services, Version 1.1. available from ftp://www6.software.ibm.com/software/developer/library/ws-bpel.pdf, BEA Systems, IBM Corporation, Microsoft Corporation, SAP AG, Siebel Systems, 2003

[14] IBM: Patterns: Implementing an SOA Using an Enterprise Service Bus. IBM International Technical Support Organization, July 2004

[15] IBM: Patterns: An EAI Solution using WebSphere Business Integration (V4.1). IBM International Technical Support Organization, July 2003

[16] IBM: WebSphere Business Integration Server, Product Information, available at http://www-306.ibm.com/software/integration/wbiserver/

[17] Jordan, J., Kleinhans, U., Kulendik, O., Porscha, J., Pross, A., Siebert, R.: Transparent and Flexible Cross-Organizational Workflows for Engineering Cooperations in Vehicle Development, in: PDT Europe 2002, Torino, Italy: Quality Marketing Services, Sandhurst, UK, May 7, 2002, pp. 101-108.

[18] Käfer, W.: Geschichts- und Versionierungsmodellierung komplexer Objekte. Dissertation, TU Kaiserslautern, 1992

[19] Kulendik, O., Rothermel, K., Siebert, R.: Cross-organizational Workflow Management: General approaches and their suitability for Engineering Processes, in: Proc. First IFIP Conference on e-Commerce, e-Business, e-Government. Zürich, Schweiz, Oktober 2001.

[20] Microsoft: Microsoft Biztalk Server 2004, Product Information, available at http://www.microsoft.com/biztalk/

[21] Miller, J., Mukerji, J. (eds.): MDA Guide Version 1.0.1., Object Management Group, Document Number: omg/2003-06-01, 2003

[22] Möckel, S.: EAI-Überblick und Basistechnologien des EAI, available from http://ais.informatik.uni-leipzig.de/download/2002s_s_ieb/SilvioMoeckel_EAI.pdf, access 2005-01-06

[23] Nink, U.: Anbindung von Entwurfsdatenbanken an objektorientierte Programmiersprachen. Dissertation, TU Kaiserslautern, Shaker-Verlag, Aachen, 1999

[24] Nink, U., Ritter, N.: Database Application Programming with Versioned Complex Objects, in: Proc. 7. GI-Fachtagung 'Datenbanksysteme in Büro, Technik und Wissenschaft', K.R. Dittrich, A. Geppert (Hrsg.), Informatik aktuell, Ulm, März 1997, Springer-Verlag, pp. 172-191.

[25] OMG: UML 2.0 Infrastructure Specification—OMG Adopted Specification. Object Management Group, Document Number: ptc/03-09-15, 2003

[26] OMG: UML 2.0 Superstructure Specification—OMG Adopted Specification. Object Management Group, Document Number: ptc/03-08-02, 2003

[27] OMG: UMLTM Profile and Interchange Models for Enterprise Application Integration (EAI) Specification—OMG Formal Specification. Object Management Group, Document Number: formal/04-03-26, March 2004

[28] Özsu, M.T., Valduriez, P.: Distributed Data Management: Unsolved Problems and New Issues, in Casavant, T. L., Singhal, M. (eds): Readings in Distributed Computing Systems. IEEE Press, 1994

[29] Peltier, M., Bezivin, J., Guillaume, G.: MTRANS: A general framework, based on XSLT for model transformations, in: Proc. Workshop on Transformations in UML (WTUML'01), Genova, Italy, Apr. 2001.

[30] Ritter, N.: DB-gestützte Kooperationsdienste für technische Entwurfsanwendungen,. DISDBIS 33, Infix-Verlag, 1997.

[31] SAP Help Portal. accessible through http://help.sap.com/.

[32] Sauter, G.: Interoperabilität von Datenbanksystemen bei struktureller Heterogenität – Architektur, Beschreibungs- und Ausführungsmodell zur Unterstützung der Integration und Migration. DISDBIS 47, infix-Verlag, 1998.

[33] Sun Microsystems: Java 2 Platform Enterprise Edition Specification, v1.4. Sun Microsystems, Inc., 2003

[34] Sun Microsystems: J2EE Connector Architecture Specification, Version: 1.5, Release: November 24, 2003. Sun Microsystems, Inc., 2003

[35] W3C: SOAP Version 1.2—W3C Recommendation 24 June 2003. available from http://www.w3.org/2002/ws/, access 2005-01-05

[36] Yergeau, F., Bray, T., Paoli, J., Sperberg-McQueen, C. M., Maler, E. (eds.): Extensible Markup Language (XML) 1.0 (Third Edition). W3C Recommendation 4th February 2004

List of Authors

- **Altinel, Mehmet**
  IBM Almaden Research Center
  650 Harry Road; San Jose, CA 95120-6099; USA
  Phone: +1-408-927-1916
  EMail: maltinel@us.ibm.com
- **Brown, Paul**
  IBM Almaden Research Center
  650 Harry Road; San Jose, CA 95120-6099; USA
  Phone: +1-408-927-1463
  EMail: pbrown1@us.ibm.com
- **Bussler, Christoph**
  National University of Ireland
  Digital Enterprise Research Institute (DERI)
  University Road; Galway; Ireland
  Phone: +353-91-512603
  E-Mail: chris.bussler@deri.org / chbussler@aol.com
- **Doraiswamy, Sangeeta**
  IBM Almaden Research Center
  650 Harry Road; San Jose, CA 95120-6099; USA
  Phone: +1-408-927-1824
  EMail: dsang@us.ibm.com
- **Grossmann, Matthias**
  Universität Stuttgart
  Fakultät Informatik, Elektrotechnik und Informationstechnik
  Universitätsstr. 38; 70569 Stuttgart; Germany
  Phone: +49-711-7816-402
  E-Mail: grossmms@informatik.uni-stuttgart.de
- **Haas, Peter**
  IBM Almaden Research Center
  650 Harry Road; San Jose, CA 95120-6099; USA
  Phone: +1-408-927-1702
  EMail: phaas@us.ibm.com

- **Härder, Theo**
  Technische Universität Kaiserslautern
  Fachgebiet Informatik / Lehrgebiet Informationssysteme
  Arbeitsgruppe Datenbanken und Informationssysteme;
  67653 Kaiserslautern; Germany
  Phone: +49-631-205-4030
  E-Mail: haerder@informatik.uni-kl.de
- **Henrich, Andreas**
  Otto-Friedrich-Universität Bamberg
  Fakultät für Wirtschaftsinformatik und Angewandte Informatik
  Lehrstuhl für Medieninformatik
  96045 Bamberg; Germany
  Phone: +49-951-863-2850
  E-Mail: andreas.henrich@wiai.uni-bamberg.de
- **Hönle, Nicola**
  Universität Stuttgart
  Fakultät Informatik, Elektrotechnik und Informationstechnik
  Universitätsstr. 38; 70569 Stuttgart; Germany
  Phone: +49-711-7816-232
  E-Mail: hoenlena@informatik.uni-stuttgart.de
- **Jablonski, Stefan**
  Friedrich-Alexander-Universität Erlangen-Nürnberg
  Technische Fakultät / Institut für Informatik
  Martensstr. 3; 91058 Erlangen; Germany
  Phone: +49-9131-85-27885
  E-Mail: jablonski@informatik.uni-erlangen.de
- **Kirsche, Thomas**
  GfK Marketing Service GmbH & Co. KG
  Nordwestring 101; 90319 Nürnberg; Germany
  Phone: +49-911-395-2918
  E-Mail: thomas.kirsche@gfk.de
- **Lehner, Wolfgang**
  Technische Universität Dresden
  Fakultät Informatik / Lehrstuhl Datenbanken
  01062 Dresden; Germany
  Phone: +49-351-463-38383
  EMail: lehner@inf.tu-dresden.de
- **Lenz, Richard**
  Philipps-Universität Marburg
  Institut für Medizinische Informatik
  Bunsenstr. 3; 35037 Marburg; Germany
  Phone: +49-6421-28-66298
  EMail: lenzr@mailer.uni-marburg.de

- **Mandl, Stefan**
  Friedrich-Alexander-Universität Erlangen-Nürnberg
  Technische Fakultät / Institut für Informatik
  Am Weichselgarten 9; 91058 Erlangen-Tennenlohe; Germany
  Phone: +49-9131-85-29913
  E-Mail: mandl@informatik.uni-erlangen.de
- **Meyer-Wegener, Klaus**
  Friedrich-Alexander-Universität Erlangen-Nürnberg
  Technische Fakultät / Institut für Informatik
  Martensstr. 3; 91058 Erlangen; Germany
  Phone: +49-9131-85-27892
  EMail: kmw@informatik.uni-erlangen.de
- **Mitschang, Bernhard**
  Universität Stuttgart
  Fakultät Informatik, Elektrotechnik und Informationstechnik
  Universitätsstr. 38; 70569 Stuttgart; Germany
  Phone: +49-711-7816-449
  E-Mail: bernhard.mitschang@informatik.uni-stuttgart.de
- **Mohan, C.**
  IBM Almaden Research Center
  650 Harry Road; San Jose, CA 95120-6099; USA
  Phone: +1-408-927-1733
  EMail: mohan@almaden.ibm.com
- **Myllymaki, Jussi**
  IBM Almaden Research Center
  650 Harry Road; San Jose, CA 95120-6099; USA
  Phone: +1-408-927-1723
  EMail: jussi@us.ibm.com
- **Nicklas, Daniela**
  Universität Stuttgart
  Fakultät Informatik, Elektrotechnik und Informationstechnik
  Universitätsstr. 38; 70569 Stuttgart; Germany
  Phone: +49-711-7816-217
  E-Mail: danickla@informatik.uni-stuttgart.de
- **Ortner, Erich**
  Technische Universität Darmstadt
  Fachgebiet Wirtschaftsinformatik I
  Hochschulstraße 1; 64289 Darmstadt; Germany
  Phone: +49-6151-16-4309
  E-Mail: ortner@winf.tu-darmstadt.de

- **Palmer, Stewart**
  IBM T.J. Watson Research Center
  19 Skyline Drive; Hawthorne, NY 10532; USA
  Phone: +1-914-784-7171
  E-Mail: slp@us.ibm.com
- **Parr, Francis**
  IBM T.J. Watson Research Center
  19 Skyline Drive; Hawthorne, NY 10532; USA
  Phone: +1-914-784-7145
  E-Mail: fnparr@us.ibm.com
- **Peinl, Peter**
  Fachhochschule Fulda
  Fachbereich Angewandte Informatik
  Marquardstraße 35; 36039 Fulda; Germany
  Phone: +49-661-9640-381
  E-Mail: peter.peinl@informatik.fh-fulda.de
- **Pirahesh, Hamid**
  IBM Almaden Research Center
  650 Harry Road; San Jose, CA 95120-6099; USA
  Phone: +1-408-927-1754
  EMail: pirahesh@almaden.ibm.com
- **Reinwald, Berthold**
  IBM Almaden Research Center
  650 Harry Road; San Jose, CA 95120-6099; USA
  Phone: +1-408-927-2208
  EMail: reinwald@almaden.ibm.com
- **Reuter, Andreas**
  European Media Laboratory GmbH
  Schloss-Wolfsbrunnenweg 33; 69118 Heidelberg; Germany
  Phone: +49-6221-533200
  E-Mail: Andreas.Reuter@villa-bosch.de
- **Ruf, Thomas**
  GfK Marketing Service GmbH & Co. KG
  Nordwestring 101; 90319 Nürnberg; Germany
  Phone: +49-911-395-4164
  E-Mail: thomas.ruf@gfk.de
- **Schmidt, Sebastian**
  Friedrich-Alexander-Universität Erlangen-Nürnberg
  Technische Fakultät / Institut für Informatik
  Am Weichselgarten 9; 91058 Erlangen-Tennenlohe; Germany
  Phone: +49-9131-85-29911
  E-Mail: sebastian.schmidt@informatik.uni-erlangen.de

- **Schuster, Hans**
  Consileon Business Consultancy GmbH
  Zähringerstr. 84; 76133 Karlsruhe; Germany
  Phone: +49-721-3546080
  E-Mail: hans.schuster@consileon.de
- **Schwarz, Thomas**
  Universität Stuttgart
  Fakultät Informatik, Elektrotechnik und Informationstechnik
  Universitätsstr. 38; 70569 Stuttgart; Germany
  Phone: +49-711-7816-217
  E-Mail: schwarts@informatik.uni-stuttgart.de
- **Shrinivas, Lakshmikant**
  University of Wisconsin-Madison
  1402 Regent Street #730
  Madison, WI 53711; USA
  Phone: +1-608-628-2871
  E-Mail: lshrinivas@wisc.edu
- **Sismanis, Yannis**
  IBM Almaden Research Center
  650 Harry Road; San Jose, CA 95120-6099; USA
  Phone: +1-408-927-1714
  EMail: syannis@us.ibm.com
- **Steiert, Hans-Peter**
  DaimlerChrysler AG, Research and Technology
  Data and Process Management 096/U800 - RIC/ED
  Postfach 2360; 89013 Ulm; Germany
  Phone: +49-731-505-2846
  E-Mail: hans-peter.steiert@daimlerchrysler.com
- **Steinbauer, Dieter**
  Schufa Holding AG
  Hagenauer Straße 44; 65203 Wiesbaden; Germany
  Phone: +49-611-9278-120
  E-Mail: dieter.steinbauer@schufa.de
- **Störl, Uta**
  Fachhochschule Darmstadt
  Haardtring 100; 64295 Darmstadt; Germany
  Phone: +49-6151-168424
  E-Mail: stoerl@fbi.fh-darmstadt.de
- **Stoyan, Herbert**
  Friedrich-Alexander-Universität Erlangen-Nürnberg
  Technische Fakultät / Institut für Informatik
  Am Weichselgarten 9; 91058 Erlangen-Tennenlohe; Germany
  Phone: +49-9131-85-29906
  E-Mail: hstoyan@informatik.uni-erlangen.de

- **Vogel, Mario**
  Friedrich-Alexander-Universität Erlangen-Nürnberg
  Technische Fakultät / Institut für Informatik
  Am Weichselgarten 9; 91058 Erlangen-Tennenlohe; Germany
  Phone: +49-9131-85-29907
  E-Mail: mario.vogel@informatik.uni-erlangen.de

Children – Grandchildren – Great-Grandchildren ...

Academic Children of Hartmut Wedekind

1. Heinz Kreuzberger: Verfahren zur Lösung ganzzahliger linearer Optimierungsprobleme (1969)
2. Joachim Petzold: Systemanalyse als Instrument zur Einsatzvorbereitung für elektr. Datenverarbeitungsanlagen in Industriebetrieben (1970)
3. Rainer Bastian: Zeitberechnung peripherer Speicher (1972)
4. Bernd Osswald: Die Analyse des Leistungsvermögens einer elektronischen Datenverarbeitungsanlage als Instrument zur Verbesserung der Betriebseigenschaften und der Anlagenauswahl (1972)
5. Hans Clüsserath: Einsatzmöglichkeiten operationsanalytischer Planungstechniken bei einer EDV-Unterstützten Auftragsabwicklung (1972)
6. Olaf Leue: Automatische Stundenplankonstruktion für Schulen mit kursorientiertem Unterricht (1972)
7. Wolfgang Albrecht: Die Konstruktion von Binärzugriffsbäumen (1974)
8. Theo Härder: Das Zugriffszeitverhalten von Relationalen Datenbanksystemen (1975)
9. Ernst-Ludwig Dittmann: Datenunabhängigkeit beim Entwurf von Datenbanksystemen (1977)
10. Waldemar Haag: Dokumentation von Anwendungssystemen aus der Sicht der Benutzer (1981)
11. Erich Ortner: Aspekte einer Konstruktionssprache für den Datenbankentwurf (1982)
12. Werner Eberlein: Architektur Technischer Datenbanken für Integrierte Ingenieursysteme (1983)
13. Dieter Steinbauer: Transaktionen als Grundlage zur Strukturierung und Integritätssicherung in Datenbankanwendungssystemen (1983)
14. Klaus Kratzer: Komponenten der Datenverwaltung in der Büroorganisation (1986)
15. Dieter Schön: Die Einbindung heterogener rechnergestützter Entwicklungssysteme in die Technische Dokumentation (1987)
16. Georg Zörntlein: Flexible Fertigungssysteme: Belegung, Steuerung, Datenorganisation (1987)
17. Clemens Beckstein: Zur Logik der Logikprogrammierung – Ein konstruktiver Ansatz (1988)

18. Stefan Jablonski: Datenverwaltung in Verteilten Systemen – Grundlagen und Lösungskonzepte (1989)
19. Ulf Schreier: Deduktive Datenbanken im Mehrbenutzerbetrieb (1989)
20. Peter Hofmann: Konzepte der Fehlerbehandlung in Flexiblen Fertigungssystemen (1990)
21. Hans-Werner Nau: Die Rekonstruktion von Büroarbeiten als Grundlage für die Büroautomation (1990)
22. Michael Tielemann: Zur Konstruktion technischer Objekte – Ein integrierender Ansatz (1990)
23. Thomas Ruf: Flexible Integration rechnergestützter Produktionssysteme – Grundlagen und Lösungskonzepte (1991)
24. Martin Nagler: Objektorientierter Schemaentwurf – Konzepte und Realisierungen (1992)
25. Berthold Reinwald: Workflow-Management in verteilten Systemen – Entwurf und Betrieb geregelter arbeitsteiliger Anwendungssysteme (1993)
26. Claudia Sommer: MoKon – Ein Ansatz zur wissensbasierten Konfiguration von Variantenerzeugnissen (1993)
27. Thomas Kirsche: Datenbankkonversationen – Unterstützung kooperativer Gruppenarbeit aus datenorientierter Sicht (1994)
28. Horst Lührsen: Die Entwicklung von Datenbanken für das Produktmodell der ISO-Norm STEP (1996)
29. Claus Schottmüller: Mehrparteien-Dateitransfer in kooperativen Anwendungen – Dienst und Protokollarchitektur (1996)
30. Richard Lenz: Adaptive Datenreplikation in verteilten Systemen (1997)
31. Hans Schuster: Architektur verteilter Workflow-Management-Systeme (1997)
32. Wolfgang Lehner: Aggregatverarbeitung in multidimensionalen Datenbanksystemen (1998)
33. Norbert Lotter: System Integration in the Design Process of the Manufacturing Industry based on OMG and ISO Standards (1998)
34. Michael Teschke: Datenkonsistenz in Data-Warehouse-Systemen (1999)
35. Jens Albrecht: Anfrageoptimierung in Data-Warehouse-Systemen auf Grundlage des multidimensionalen Datenmodells (2001)
36. Holger Günzel: Darstellung von Veränderungen im multidimensionalen Datenmodell (2001)
37. Andreas Bauer: Datenallokation und Anfrageoptimierung in verteilten, föderierten Data-Warehouse-Systemen (2002)
38. Wolfgang Hümmer: Vertragsverhandlungen um konfigurierbare Produkte im elektronischen Handel (2004)

Academic Grandchildren Via Härder

1. Andreas Reuter: Fehlerbehandlung in Datenbanksystemen (1981)
2. Wolfgang Effelsberg: Systempufferverwaltung in Datenbanksystemen (1981)
3. Klaus Küspert: Fehlererkennung und Fehlerbehandlung in Speicherungsstrukturen von Datenbanksystemen (1985)
4. Klaus Meyer-Wegener: Transaktionssysteme – eine Untersuchung des Funktionsumfangs, der Realisierungsmöglichkeiten und des Leistungsverhaltens (1986)
5. Peter Peinl: Synchronisation in zentralisierten Datenbanksystemen – Algorithmen, Realisierungsmöglichkeiten und quantitative Bewertung (1986)
6. Bernhard Mitschang: Ein Molekül-Atom-Datenmodell für Non-Standard-Anwendungen – Anwendungsanalyse, Datenmodellentwurf, Implementierung (1988)
7. Erhard Rahm: Synchronisation in Mehrrechner-Datenbanksystemen – Konzepte, Realisierungsformen und quantitative Bewertung (1988)
8. Andrea Sikeler: Implementierungskonzepte für Non-Standard-Datenbanksysteme verdeutlicht am Beispiel des DB-Kernsystems PRIMA (1989)
9. Nelson Mattos: An Approach to Knowledge Base Management – Requirements, Knowledge Representation and Design Issues (1989)
10. Stefan Pappe: Datenbankzugriff in offenen Rechnernetzen (1990)
11. Weixia Yan: Auswertung rekursiver Anfragen in Deduktiven Datenbanksystemen – eine Untersuchung der Strategien, des Leistungsverhaltens und der Realisierungsmöglichkeiten (1991)
12. Christoph Hübel: Ein Verarbeitungsmodell für datenbankgestützte Ingenieuranwendungen in einer arbeitsplatzrechnerorientierten Ablaufumgebung (1992)
13. Wolfgang Käfer: Geschichts- und Versionsmodellierung komplexer Objekte – Anforderungen und Realisierungsmöglichkeiten am Beispiel des NDBS PRIMA (1992)
14. Bernd Sutter: Ansätze zur Integration in technischen Entwurfsanwendungen – angepaßte Modellierungswerkzeuge, durchgängige Entwurfsunterstützung, datenorientierte Integration (1992)
15. Harald Schöning: Anfrageverarbeitung in Komplexobjekt-Datenbanksystemen (1992)
16. Stefan Deßloch: Semantic Integrity in Advanced Database Management Systems (1993)
17. Yangjun Chen: Processing of Recursive Rules in Knowledge-based Systems – Algorithms and Performance Measurements for Handling Recursive Rules and Negation information (1995)
18. Robert Marek: Parallele Anfrageausführung in Shared-Nothing-Datenbanksystemen – Architektur, Leistungsanalyse und -optimierung (1995)

19. Joachim Reinert: Ein Regelsystem zur Integritätssicherung in aktiven relationalen Datenbanksystemen (1996)
20. Joachim Thomas: An Approach to Query Processing in Advanced Database Systems (1996)
21. Axel Herbst: Anwendungsorientiertes DB-Archivieren – Neue Konzepte zur Archivierung von Daten in Datenbanksystemen (1996)
22. Fernando de Ferreira Rezende: Transaction Services for Knowledge Base Management Systems – Modeling Aspects, Architectural Issues and Realization Techniques (1997)
23. Norbert Ritter: DB-gestützte Kooperationsdienste für technische Entwurfsanwendungen (1997)
24. Michael Gesmann: Parallele Anfrageverarbeitung in Komplexobjekt-Datenbanksystemen – Verarbeitungskonzepte, Realisierungsaspekte und Betriebsystemeinbettung (1997)
25. Günter Sauter: Interoperabilität von Datenbanksystemen bei struktureller Heterogenität – Architektur, Beschreibungs- und Ausführungsmodell zur Unterstützung der Integration und Migration (1998)
26. Udo Nink: Anbindung von Entwurfsdatenbanken an objektorientierte Programmiersprachen (1999)
27. Angelo Brayner: Transaction Management in Multidatabase Systems (1999)
28. Nan Zhang: Supporting Semantically Rich Relationships in Extensible Object-Relational Database Management Systems (2000)
29. Henrik Loeser: Einsatz objekt-relationaler Datenbanksysteme für Web-Informationssysteme (2000)
30. Hans-Peter Steiert: Aspekte der generativen Entwicklung von ORDBMS-basierten Datenverwaltungsdiensten (2001)
31. Ulrich Marder: Multimedia-Metacomputing in Web-basierten multimedialen Informationssystemen (2002)
32. Weiping Zhang: Supporting Object-Oriented Software Development by Object-Relational Database Technology – A Performance Study (2002)
33. Klaudia Hergula: Daten- und Funktionsintegration durch Föderierte Datenbanksysteme (2003)
34. Wolfgang Mahnke: Komponentenbasierter Schemaentwurf für objekt-relationale Datenbankverwaltungssysteme (2004)
35. Markus Bon: Modellierung und Abwicklung von Datenflüssen in unternehmensübergreifenden Geschäftsprozessen (2004)
36. Marcus Flehmig: Datenintegration über das Web mit SHARX – Datengetriebene, XML-basierte Datenintegrationskonzepte und Systemarchitekturen in unternehmensweiten Anwendungen (2005)
37. Jernej Kovse: Model-Driven Development of Versioning Systems (2005)

Academic Grandchildren Via Petzold

1. Stefan Albers: Modellbasiertes Prototyping (1995)
2. Susanne Stahlinger: Metamodellierung als Instrument des Methodenvergleichs (1996)

Academic Grandchildren Via Ortner

1. Thomas Hellmuth: Terminologiemanagement (1997)
2. Bruno Schienmann: Objektorientierter Fachentwurf (1997)
3. Bernd Britzelmaier: Informationsverarbeitungs-Controlling: ein datenorientierter Ansatz (1998)
4. Frank Lehmann: Fachlicher Entwurf von Workflow-Management-Anwendungen (1998)
5. Peter Schieber: Business Reengineering und strategische Informationsplanung (1998)

Academic Grandchildren Via Jablonski

1. Christoph Bussler: Organisationsverwaltung in Workflow-Management-Systemen (1997)
2. Karin Stein: Integration von Anwendungsprozessmodellierung und Workflow-Management (1998)
3. Petra Heinl: Entwicklung und Einsatz eines Qualitätsmodells für Workflow-Management-Anwendungen (1999)
4. Jens Neeb: Administration von Workflow-Management-Lösungen (2001)
5. Joachim Klausner: Planen und intelligentes Workflow-Management (2001)
6. Rolf Schamburger: Integrierte Betrachtung von Anwendungen und Systemen zur verteilten Workflowbearbeitung (2001)
7. Stefan Horn: Die schemabasierte Modellierung und Steuerung von Projektvorgängen (2003)
8. Luo Xiao: Information Extraction in Practical Applications Systems and Techniques (2003)
9. Michael Schlundt: Historienverwaltung in Workflow-Management-Systemen (2004)
10. Christian Meiler: Modellierung, Planung und Ausführung Klinischer Pfade (2005)

Academic Grandchildren Via Beckstein

1. Klaus Meier: Neuronale Netze zur Steuerung von einbeinigen Bewegungssystemen (1999)
2. Joachim Klausner: Planen und intelligentes Workflow-Management (2001)

Academic Grandchildren Via Lehner

1. Lutz Schlesinger: Qualitätsgetriebene Konstruktion globaler Sichten in Grid-organisierten Datenbanksystemen (2004)

Academic Great-Grandchildren Via Härder – Reuter

1. Bernd Walter: Betriebssystemkonzepte für fortgeschrittene Informationssysteme (Habilitation, 1985)
2. Cai Jian: Pufferverwaltung in verteilten Datenbanksystemen (1987)
3. Christos Garidis: Clustering-Konzepte für optimalen Zugriff auf große und datenbankresidente Wissensbasen (1990)
4. Norbert Duppel: Optimierung komplexer Datenbankanfragen auf einen Multiprozessorsystem am Beispiel einer Parallelen Deduktiven Datenbank (1991)
5. Shiqi Han: Testen in Verteilten Systemen (1991)
6. Christina Liebelt: Unterstützung des Entwurfs konsistenzerhaltender Datenbankanwendungen (1991)
7. Gerhard Schiele: Kontrollstrukturen zur Ablaufsteuerung massiv paralleler Datenbankanwendungen in Multiprozessorsystemen (1991)
8. Hansjörg Zeller: Adaptive Hash-Join-Algorithmen (1991)
9. Jörg Röhrle: Ein regelbasierter Testgenerator für das Rapid-Prototyping von Datenbankanwendungen (1994)
10. Andreas Winckler: Kontext-sensitive Lastbalancierung (1994)
11. Wolfgang Becker: Dynamische adaptive Lastbalancierung für große, heterogen konkurrierende Anwendungen (1995)
12. Roger Günthör: Ein Basisdienst für die zuverlässige Abwicklung langdauernder Aktivitäten (1996)
13. Helmut Wächter: Zuverlässige Abwicklung langlebiger und verteilter Anwendungen auf Datenbanken (1996)
14. Bernhard Wörner: Implizite Darstellung von Parallelität auf der Ebene des Programmiermodells (1996)
15. Ursula Thalheimer: Bearbeitungstransaktionen – Ein Konzept zur Integration physischer Operationen in das Transaktionsmodell (1997)
16. Rainer Pollak: Auswirkungen verschiedener Informationsebenen auf die Effizienz der dynamischen Lastbalancierung (1999)
17. Leonore Zink: Einbettung von Interpolationsfunktionen in die Datenbanksprache SQL – Datenbankunterstützung für die Umweltforschung (2000)
18. Kerstin Schneider: The Reliable Execution of Workflows – Compensation-based Failure and Exception Handling Mechanisms (2003)

Academic 2nd Great-Grandchildren Via Härder – Reuter – Walter

1.. Günter Karjoth: Prozeßalgebra und Temporale Logik – angewandt zur Spezifikation und Analyse von komplexen Protokollen (1987)
2. Thomas Ludwig: Database Support for Knowledge-Based Systems (1992)
3. Erich Gehlen: Optimierung der Anfrageauswertung in einem Deduktiven Datenbanksystem (1992)
4. Albert Maier: Einbettung von Konzepthierarchien in ein deduktives Datenbanksystem (1992)
5. Michael Ley: Ein Datenbankkern zur Speicherung variabel strukturierter Feature-Terme (1993)
6. Thomas Benzschawel: Implementierung einer effizienten Anfrageauswertung für ein deduktives Datenbanksystem (1995)
7. Dirk Rüttgers: Anfrageoptimierung durch abstrakte Interpretation für ein deduktives Datenbanksystem (1997)
8. Gerd Hoff: Ein Verfahren zur thematisch spezialisierten Suche im Web und seine Realisierung im Prototypen HomePageSearch (2002)

Academic Great-Grandchildren Via Härder – Meyer-Wegener

1. Walter Krasser: Leistungsbewertung von Transaktionssystemen mit analytischen Methoden unter besonderer Berücksichtigung des Synchronisationsmechanismus in der Datenbank (1992)
2. Kai Bruns: Die Konfigurierung modular aufgebauter Datenbankbetriebssysteme (1994)
3. Rolf Käckenhoff: Datenmodellierung in Multimedia-Systemen: multimediale und symbolische Datenobjekte mit ihren Beziehungen (1995)
4. Tilo Hegel: Ein formal spezifiziertes objektorientiertes Datenmodell mit Anfragesprache und algebraischer Optimierung (1995)
5. Christoph Baumgarten: Probabilistic Information Retrieval in a Distributed Heterogeneous Environment (1999)
6. Wolfgang Schulze: Ein Workflow-Management-Dienst für ein verteiltes Objektverwaltungssystem (1999)
7. Markus Böhm: Systematische Konstruktion von Workflow-Typen für Workflow-Management-Anwendungen (1999)
8. Henrike Berthold: A Federal Multimedia Database System (2002)

Academic Great-Grandchildren Via Härder – Effelsberg

1. Udo Bär: OSI-Konformitätstests - Validierung und qualitative Bewertung (1993)
2. Erwin Mayer: Multicast-Synchronisationsprotokolle für kooperative Anwendungen (1993)

3. Bernd Hofmann: Generierung effizienter Protokollimplementierungen aus ESTELLE-Spezifikationen (1993)
4. Bernd Lamparter: XMovie: Digitale Filmübertragung in Rechnernetzen (1994)
5. Thomas Meyer-Boudnik: Interaktive Multimedia-Präsentationen in offenen Systemen – Entwurf und Implementierung einer Laufzeitumgebung zur Evaluation und Verbesserung des zukünftigen Standards MHEG (1994)
6. Ralf Keller: Anwendungsprotokolle für Verteilte Multimedia-Systeme (1996)
7. Stefan Fischer: Formale Spezifikation und Implementierung von Hochleistungsprotokollen (1996)
8. Stephan Fischer: Indikatorenkombination zur Inhaltsanalyse digitaler Filme (1997)
9. Wieland Holfelder: Aufzeichnung und Wiedergabe von Internet-Videokonferenzen (1998)
10. Rainer Lienhart: Verfahren zum Vergleich von Videosequenzen und deren Anwendungen (VisualGREP: Query by Video Sequence and its Applications) (1998)
11. Silvia Pfeiffer: Information Retrieval aus digitalisierten Audiospuren von Filmen (1999)
12. Werner Geyer: Das Digital Lecture Board – Konzeption, Design und Entwicklung eines Whiteboards für synchrones Teleteaching (1999)
13. Martin Mauve: Distributed Interactive Media (2000)
14. Rüdiger Weis: Cryptographic Protocols and Algorithms for Distributed Multimedia Systems (2000)
15. Christoph Kuhmünch: Videoskalierung und Integration interaktiver Elemente in Teleteaching-Szenarien (2001
16. Volker Hilt: Netzwerkbasierte Aufzeichnung und Wiedergabe interaktiver Medienströme (2001)
17. Claudia Schremmer: Multimedia Applications of the Wavelet Transform (2002)
18. Gerald Kühne: Motion-based Segmentation and Classification of Video Objects (2002)
19. Jörg Widmer: Equation-Based Congestion Control for Unicast and Multicast Data Streams (2003)
20. Robert Denda: Fairness in Computer Networks (2004)
21. Thomas Haenselmann: Signalanalyse-Verfahren zur Segmentierung von Multimediadaten (2004)
22. Jürgen Vogel: Consistency Algorithms and Protocols for Distributed Interactive Applications (2004)

Academic Great-Grandchildren Via Härder – Mitschang

1. Harald Kosch: Exploiting Serialized Bushy Trees for Parallel Relational Query Optimization (1997)
2. Michael Jaedicke: New Concepts for Parallel Object-Relational Query Processing (1999)
3. Jürgen Sellentin: Konzepte und Techniken der Datenversorgung für komponentenbasierte Informationssysteme (1999)
4. Friedemann Schwenkreis: Korrektheit und deren Durchsetzung im Umfeld langdauernder Abläufe (2001)
5. Simonas Saltenis: Indexing Techniques for Continuously Evolving Phenomena (2001)
6. Aiko Frank: Das ASCEND-Modell zur Unterstützung kooperativer Prozesse (2002)
7. Holger Schwarz: Integration von Data Mining und Online Analytical Processing: Eine Analyse von Datenschemata, Systemarchitekturen und Optimierungsstrategien (2002)
8. Ralf Rantzau: Query Processing Concepts and Techniques to Support Business Intelligence Applications (2004)
9. Marcello Mariucci: Design and Implementation of a Model-Driven Earth Observation Integration Framework (2004)

Academic Great-Grandchildren Via Härder – Küspert

1. Uta Störl: Backup und Recovery in Datenbanksystemen: Verfahren, Klassifikation, Implementierung und Bewertung (1999)
2. Ralf Schaarschmidt: Konzept und Sprache für die Archivierung in Datenbanksystemen (1999)
3. Frank Hüsemann: Datenbankmigration – Methodik und Software-Unterstützung (2002)

Academic Great-Grandchildren Via Härder – Rahm

1. Robert Müller: Event-oriented Dynamic Adaptation of Workflows: Model, Architecture and Implementation (2002)
2. Sergej Melnikj: Generic Model Management (2004)

Academic 2nd Great-Grandchildren Via Härder – Effelsberg – Fischer

1. Ulrich Walther: Service Support for Virtual Groups in Mobile Environments (2003)
2. Horst Hellbrück: Analytische und simulationsbasierte Verfahren zur Konnektivitätsbestimmung und -verbesserung in Ad-hoc-Netzen (2004)

Lecture Notes in Computer Science

For information about Vols. 1–3459

please contact your bookseller or Springer

Vol. 3569: F. Bacchus, T. Walsh (Eds.), Theory and Applications of Satisfiability Testing. XII, 492 pages. 2005.

Vol. 3562: J. Mira, J.R. Álvarez (Eds.), Artificial Intelligence and Knowledge Engineering Applications: A Bioinspired Approach, Part II. XXIV, 636 pages. 2005.

Vol. 3561: J. Mira, J.R. Álvarez (Eds.), Mechanisms, Symbols, and Models Underlying Cognition, Part I. XXIV, 532 pages. 2005.

Vol. 3560: V.K. Prasanna, S. Iyengar, P. Spirakis, M. Welsh (Eds.), Distributed Computing in Sensor Systems. XV, 423 pages. 2005.

Vol. 3559: P. Auer, R. Meir (Eds.), Learning Theory. XI, 692 pages. 2005. (Subseries LNAI).

Vol. 3556: H. Baumeister, M. Marchesi, M. Holcombe (Eds.), Extreme Programming and Agile Processes in Software Engineering. XIV, 332 pages. 2005.

Vol. 3555: T. Vardanega, A. Wellings (Eds.), Reliable Software Technology – Ada-Europe 2005. XV, 273 pages. 2005.

Vol. 3552: H. de Meer, N. Bhatti (Eds.), Quality of Service – IWQoS 2005. XV, 400 pages. 2005.

Vol. 3551: T. Härder, W. Lehner (Eds.), Data Management in a Connected World. XIX, 371 pages. 2005.

Vol. 3548: K. Julisch, C. Kruegel (Eds.), Intrusion and Malware Detection and Vulnerability Assessment. X, 241 pages. 2005.

Vol. 3547: F. Bomarius, S. Komi-Sirviö (Eds.), Product Focused Software Process Improvement. XIII, 588 pages. 2005.

Vol. 3543: L. Kutvonen, N. Alonistioti (Eds.), Distributed Applications and Interoperable Systems. XI, 235 pages. 2005.

Vol. 3541: N.C. Oza, R. Polikar, J. Kittler, F. Roli (Eds.), Multiple Classifier Systems. XII, 430 pages. 2005.

Vol. 3540: H. Kalviainen, J. Parkkinen, A. Kaarna (Eds.), Image Analysis. XXII, 1270 pages. 2005.

Vol. 3537: A. Apostolico, M. Crochemore, K. Park (Eds.), Combinatorial Pattern Matching. XI, 444 pages. 2005.

Vol. 3536: G. Ciardo, P. Darondeau (Eds.), Applications and Theory of Petri Nets 2005. XI, 470 pages. 2005.

Vol. 3535: M. Steffen, G. Zavattaro (Eds.), Formal Methods for Open Object-Based Distributed Systems. X, 323 pages. 2005.

Vol. 3533: M. Ali, F. Esposito (Eds.), Innovations in Applied Artificial Intelligence. XX, 858 pages. 2005. (Subseries LNAI).

Vol. 3532: A. Gómez-Pérez, J. Euzenat (Eds.), The Semantic Web: Research and Applications. XV, 728 pages. 2005.

Vol. 3531: J. Ioannidis, A. Keromytis, M. Yung (Eds.), Applied Cryptography and Network Security. XI, 530 pages. 2005.

Vol. 3530: A. Prinz, R. Reed, J. Reed (Eds.), SDL 2005: Model Driven Systems Design. XI, 361 pages. 2005.

Vol. 3528: P.S. Szczepaniak, J. Kacprzyk, A. Niewiadomski (Eds.), Advances in Web Intelligence. XVII, 513 pages. 2005. (Subseries LNAI).

Vol. 3527: R. Morrison, F. Oquendo (Eds.), Software Architecture. XII, 263 pages. 2005.

Vol. 3526: S.B. Cooper, B. Löwe, L. Torenvliet (Eds.), New Computational Paradigms. XVII, 574 pages. 2005.

Vol. 3525: A.E. Abdallah, C.B. Jones, J.W. Sanders (Eds.), Communicating Sequential Processes. XIV, 321 pages. 2005.

Vol. 3524: R. Barták, M. Milano (Eds.), Integration of AI and OR Techniques in Constraint Programming for Combinatorial Optimization Problems. XI, 320 pages. 2005.

Vol. 3523: J.S. Marques, N.P. de la Blanca, P. Pina (Eds.), Pattern Recognition and Image Analysis, Part II. XXVI, 733 pages. 2005.

Vol. 3522: J.S. Marques, N.P. de la Blanca, P. Pina (Eds.), Pattern Recognition and Image Analysis, Part I. XXVI, 703 pages. 2005.

Vol. 3521: N. Megiddo, Y. Xu, B. Zhu (Eds.), Algorithmic Applications in Management. XIII, 484 pages. 2005.

Vol. 3520: O. Pastor, J. Falcão e Cunha (Eds.), Advanced Information Systems Engineering. XVI, 584 pages. 2005.

Vol. 3519: H. Li, P. J. Olver, G. Sommer (Eds.), Computer Algebra and Geometric Algebra with Applications. IX, 449 pages. 2005.

Vol. 3518: T.B. Ho, D. Cheung, H. Li (Eds.), Advances in Knowledge Discovery and Data Mining. XXI, 864 pages. 2005. (Subseries LNAI).

Vol. 3517: H.S. Baird, D.P. Lopresti (Eds.), Human Interactive Proofs. IX, 143 pages. 2005.

Vol. 3516: V.S. Sunderam, G.D.v. Albada, P.M.A. Sloot, J.J. Dongarra (Eds.), Computational Science – ICCS 2005, Part III. LXIII, 1143 pages. 2005.

Vol. 3515: V.S. Sunderam, G.D.v. Albada, P.M.A. Sloot, J.J. Dongarra (Eds.), Computational Science – ICCS 2005, Part II. LXIII, 1101 pages. 2005.

Vol. 3514: V.S. Sunderam, G.D.v. Albada, P.M.A. Sloot, J.J. Dongarra (Eds.), Computational Science – ICCS 2005, Part I. LXIII, 1089 pages. 2005.

Vol. 3513: A. Montoyo, R. Muñoz, E. Métais (Eds.), Natural Language Processing and Information Systems. XII, 408 pages. 2005.